TAX LAW IN TIMES OF CRISIS AND RECOVERY

This book examines the relationship between tax law and crisis. In times of environmental, financial, and public health breakdown, policymakers look to tax for solutions. Yet these crises also constrain the ways in which tax liabilities can be imposed and administered, and limit the revenues that can be collected. What should governments do in these circumstances and what are the wider consequences for states, societies, and institutions such as the EU?

The book shows how crises place strain on the basic functions of tax, including revenue-raising, institution-building, regulation, redistribution, and the structuring of society. These strains bear more heavily on some sections of business and society than others. This makes the tax consequences of crisis unpredictable. It also means that the best choice of legal response is not merely a technical matter. Instead, it engages deeper attitudes towards crisis relief, change, social values, and democratic control.

These issues are highlighted by COVID-19 but are of utmost lasting importance. The book takes a comprehensive approach and looks in more depth at the systemic roles that crises play in contemporary tax systems. It features an impressive cast of leading researchers across multiple jurisdictions and is essential for policymakers and scholars alike.

Tax Law in Times of Crisis and Recovery

Edited by
Dominic de Cogan
Alexis Brassey
and
Peter Harris

•HART•
OXFORD • LONDON • NEW YORK • NEW DELHI • SYDNEY

HART PUBLISHING

Bloomsbury Publishing Plc

Kemp House, Chawley Park, Cumnor Hill, Oxford, OX2 9PH, UK

1385 Broadway, New York, NY 10018, USA

29 Earlsfort Terrace, Dublin 2, Ireland

First published in Great Britain 2023

A catalogue record for this book is available from the British Library.

A catalogue record for this book is available from the Library of Congress.

ISBN: HB: 978-1-50995-803-0
ePDF: 978-1-50995-805-4
ePub: 978-1-50995-804-7

Typeset by Compuscript Ltd, Shannon

Tax Law in Times of Crisis and Recovery

Edited by
Dominic de Cogan
Alexis Brassey
and
Peter Harris

•HART•
OXFORD • LONDON • NEW YORK • NEW DELHI • SYDNEY

HART PUBLISHING

Bloomsbury Publishing Plc

Kemp House, Chawley Park, Cumnor Hill, Oxford, OX2 9PH, UK

1385 Broadway, New York, NY 10018, USA

29 Earlsfort Terrace, Dublin 2, Ireland

First published in Great Britain 2023

A catalogue record for this book is available from the British Library.

A catalogue record for this book is available from the Library of Congress.

ISBN: HB: 978-1-50995-803-0
ePDF: 978-1-50995-805-4
ePub: 978-1-50995-804-7

Typeset by Compuscript Ltd, Shannon

TABLE OF CONTENTS

CONTRIBUTORS

Alexis Brassey is an Affiliated Lecturer at the University of Cambridge, Faculty of Law and Visiting Fellow of the Centre for Tax Law at the University of Cambridge. He is also the course convenor for the Tax Law and Policy course, as well as researching in tax and constitutional law and political philosophy. Previously, Alexis was the Managing Partner of Cavendish Legal Group after working in senior management at a number of investment banks including BZW, Lehman Brothers, Citibank, Sakura Bank and Sumitomo Mitsui Banking Corporation. He is currently non-executive Chairman of Cranborne Technology.

Dominic de Cogan is Associate Professor, Academic Secretary and Assistant Director of the Centre for Tax Law at the Faculty of Law, University of Cambridge.

Wei Cui is a Professor of Law at the University of British Columbia. His research and writing span a wide range of topics in tax law and policy, including international taxation, tax administration and compliance, tax and development, the value added tax and tax and spending policies targeted at the labour market. He is the author of *The Administrative Foundation of China's Fiscal State* (2022) and a co-author of *Value Added Tax: A Comparative Approach* (2015), both published by Cambridge University Press.

Hanna Filipczyk is judge at the Provincial Administrative Court in Warsaw and researcher at the University of Białystok (Poland). She is doctor habilitatus in law, and has written almost 100 publications on a range of topics in tax law and theory of law, including four books.

Bastiaan van Ganzen is a Lecturer and PhD candidate at the Institute of Tax Law and Economics of Leiden University, the Netherlands.

Carlo Garbarino holds a combined programme PhD (Law) degree at University of Genoa, Italy, is Visiting Scholar at Yale Law School, 1987–89 under a Rotary Foundation Scholarship and holds an LLM at University of Michigan Law School, 1986. He is Professor of Law, Bocconi University Milan where he is the Director of Osservatorio Fiscale; Senior Emily Noel Fellow, NYU Law School, 2016–17; Hauser Global Visiting Faculty, NYU Law School, 2013–14 and 2019–20. He has been Grotius Research Scholar, University of Michigan, Senior Fellow of the Melbourne Law School, and Visiting Professor at the University of Michigan Law School, Levin College of Law of the University of Florida, Faculdade de Direito Universidade de São Paulo, Sorbonne Université. He teaches regularly at the Master of tax law, Wirtschaftsuniversität Wien.

Dr Stefanie Geringer is a post-doc researcher in the department of tax law at the University of Vienna and a tax adviser at BDO Austria. Her current research is focused on procedural autonomy in EU VAT, VAT in times of crisis, digitalisation of tax administration and environment-related measures in tax policy.

Pablo Hernández González-Barreda is Lecturer of Tax Law at Universidad Pontificia Comillas of Madrid (on leave to the government of Spain). He has been visiting professor or academic in several universities such as Harvard, Oxford, Vienna, Externado de Colombia or Beijing of Business and Economics. He has codirected four treatises, written two books and several articles and chapters on international and European tax law, taxation of the financial sector and tax policy. He is the author of *Beneficial Ownership in Tax Law and Tax Treaties* published by Hart.

Dr Francesco Emanuele Grisostolo is a Researcher in Comparative Public Law at the University of Udine. In March 2019, he obtained his PhD in Juridical Sciences with distinction from the University of Udine and he is *Doctor en Dret i Ciència Política* at the University of Barcelona (double title). He published a book about Fiscal Autonomy of the Regions in Italy and Spain and in August 2021 he obtained a National Academic Qualification as Associate Professor in Comparative Law. From January 2019, he is also a legal counsellor at the Italian tax bar.

Ashrita Prasad Kotha is a doctoral candidate at WU, Vienna. Ashrita has been an Assistant Professor at Jindal Global Law School, India where she taught tax law. She has delivered guest lectures on tax law at various Indian universities. She has received scholarships for research stays at Max Planck Institute for Tax Law and Public Finance and University of New South Wales. Her doctoral work analyses earmarked taxes from the lens of tax treaty, EU law and tax policy.

Yvette Lind is a Professor of Law at the Department of Law and Governance and a Member of the Business History Centre at BI Norwegian Business School. Lind has a Juris Doctor (Jur.dr.) from Umeå University, Sweden.

Artemis Loucaidou is a lawyer in Cyprus and she works as a Senior Tax Associate in the private sector. She is a graduate of the Oxford University MSc in Taxation programme, for which she received the Tax Executive Institute Prize for the best overall performance. She holds an LLB in Law from the University of Durham and she is a Research Fellow of the Working Party on Tax and Legal Matters.

Laura Panadès-Estruch is Master of Laws in International Finance Course Leader and Lecturer at the Truman Bodden Law School of the Cayman Islands, in partnership with the University of Liverpool, and PhD candidate in Law at the University of Cambridge in the UK. She is a member of the Cayman Islands Public Procurement Committee, reviewing government contracts with values exceeding CI$250,000 (USD300,000) and non-competitive awards.

Katerina Pantazatou is an associate professor in tax law at the University of Luxembourg and the co-director of the LLM in European and International Tax Law at the same University. She has visited the Institute for Austrian and International Taxation in

Vienna as an Ernst Mach scholar and she has been a visiting researcher at Harvard University, under a grant from the Institut Luxembourgeois des Administrateurs and the FNR.

Natalia Pushkareva is a PhD Candidate in Global Studies at University of Urbino, Italy, and a Regional Programme Specialist at UNDP Istanbul Regional Hub, Türkiye. She has degrees in Law and Finance from Lomonosov Moscow State University and University of Oxford, and has been working on tax policy issues for a number of years as a tax policy professional and a researcher.

Amedeo Rizzo is a DPhil in Law at the University of Oxford and a Transatlantic Technology Forum Fellow at the University of Stanford and the University of Vienna. He works as Academic Fellow of Taxation at Bocconi University and SDA Fellow of Tax and Accounting at SDA Bocconi School of Management, where he coordinates the Accounting & Tax Policy Observatory and the Transfer Pricing Forum. He is a Research Fellow of the Working Party on Tax & Legal Matters.

Dr Luisa Scarcella is the Global Policy Lead on Taxation and Trade at the International Chamber of Commerce. She is also research fellow at the DigiTax Centre of the University of Antwerp where she has previously worked as postdoctoral researcher. In October 2020, she obtained her PhD in tax law with distinction from the University of Graz where she has also worked since 2016 as research and teaching assistant. In the past, she worked as researcher for the International Fiscal Association (IFA), the Cambridge Centre for Alternative Finance and she was a visiting scholar at KU Leuven University (2019) and at Sorbonne University (2022).

Erika Scuderi is a Teaching and Research Associate at the Institute for Austrian and International Tax Law, Doctoral candidate at WU – Vienna University of Economics and Business, and Visiting Researcher at Harvard Law School. She holds a Master's Degree in Law and a Postgraduate Master's Degree in Taxation (Bocconi). Prior to joining the Institute, she was a tax associate at the Chiomenti Law Firm in Milan, Italy.

Suranjali Tandon is Assistant Professor at National Institute of Public Finance and Policy, India. She has worked on several projects concerning key policy issues for the Department of Revenue and Department of Economic Affairs, India. She currently leads the institute's work on international taxation. She received a PhD in economics from Jawaharlal Nehru University, India.

Henk Vording is Professor of Tax Law, Leiden University.

Richard Walters is a Lecturer of Law at Queen Mary University of London where he teaches Revenue Law. For many years, he worked at the Inland Revenue (later HMRC) Solicitor's Office, latterly as Assistant Solicitor (Deputy Director) responsible for capital taxes. He was involved in many court cases as well as policy issues around tax legislation.

Yige Zu is Assistant Professor in Tax Law at Durham Law School, Durham University.

1

Introduction

DOMINIC DE COGAN AND ALEXIS BRASSEY

I. Overview

This book is about the interaction of tax law and crises. At first sight this may seem a straightforward or even trivial matter. Crises happen and tax policy might help. Yet even the most cursory further examination suggests a much more complex picture. Tax systems operate in a social and economic context. Crises place intense pressure on societies and economies and hence change the context in which taxes operate. This can have both direct and indirect consequences for tax systems. In direct terms, crises often depress tax revenues whilst increasing the need for public funds, thus creating or exacerbating fiscal deficits. In indirect terms, crises can have uneven consequences for different demographics and sectors of the economy, disadvantaging some, leaving some relatively untouched and advantaging others. Crises can also exacerbate existing social problems, making the need for solutions to those problems even more pressing. All of this changes the profile of actors and activities subject to tax, with potential knock-on consequences for the revenue, distribution, behavioural and other implications of existing tax rules. In many instances these pressures are likely to be temporary, but in some circumstances they can contribute to 'critical junctures' and trigger more fundamental changes to tax law, states and societies.

These fundamental changes may initially appear temporary in nature. After all, during times of crisis, populations often look to government to solve extraordinary and temporary problems. For example, government responses to wartime conditions have typically extended well beyond the tax system and have involved such draconian measures as conscription and expropriation. Although these types of policy are often reversed after the cessation of hostilities, wartime tax measures can be extraordinarily persistent. The UK income tax itself was introduced in the last years of the eighteenth century and was presented as a temporary measure to pay for the French Revolutionary and Napoleonic Wars, and though it was repealed in 1816, it was reintroduced in 1842 and has been in place ever since.[1] Similarly, the modern UK General Anti-Abuse Rule (GAAR) has echoes in earlier similar provisions in the Munitions Levy and Excess Profits

[1] Walters, ch 3.

Duty of 1915 and the Excess Profits Tax of 1939.[2] In short, crises present challenges for governments in adapting tax systems to rapidly changing conditions but also opportunities for reform.

The ways in which crises affect tax systems are as various as the people, businesses and activities taxed, which is to say that they are almost impossible to categorise neatly. However, a convenient scheme that captures almost all of the phenomena discussed within this book is the division of the functions of tax into revenue-raising, regulation and redistribution. Hence, the raising of revenues during crises and the associated risks and opportunities for states forms the basis of the first part of this book, with the second part looking at similar matters in relation to the EU and other supranational institutions. The third part looks at the regulatory role of taxation with particular reference to the climate crisis, whilst the final and fourth part examines the implications of crises for tax justice, the distribution of resources and the social impact of taxation more generally.

II. Literature Review

The existing literature on tax law and crisis is extremely fragmented. As such, we are not aware of any existing publication that covers the same ground as the present volume despite the high importance of the topic. Nevertheless, this volume is rooted firmly in existing literature. In order to explore this literature, it is convenient to follow the basic structure outlined above, starting with 'revenues and the tax state' and then moving to 'revenues and institution building above the state', 'environment and regulation' and finally 'justice, distribution and society'.

A. Revenues and the Tax State

There are relatively extensive literatures on the relationship between crises, state-building and state preservation. Much of this scholarship is historical in nature, partly because of the value of hindsight and archival material, and partly because scholarship on present-day tax systems often emphasises the importance of internationally coordinated responses and correspondingly downplays discussion of the tax state at national level. There is, in any case, a wealth of material on the systemic effects of historical crises on the development of tax and constitutional systems, including wars, epidemics, leadership disputes, ethnic tensions, financial crashes, poor infrastructure, corruption, administrative difficulties and long-term shortfalls in revenues.[3] These matters are widely disputed by historians and fiscal sociologists but also attract some high-quality

[2] Tandon, ch 4; P Harris, 'The Profits Tax GAAR: An Aid in the "Hopeless" Defence Against the Dark Arts' in P Harris and D de Cogan (eds), *Studies in the History of Tax Law Volume 8* (Oxford, Hart Publishing, 2017).

[3] There is an outstanding review of this literature in the first few pages of A Likhovski, *Tax Law and Social Norms in Mandatory Palestine and Israel* (Cambridge, Cambridge University Press, 2019); see also IW Martin, AK Mehrotra and M Prasad, 'The Thunder of History: The Origins and Development of the New Fiscal Sociology' in IW Martin, AK Mehrotra and M Prasad (eds) *The New Fiscal Sociology: Taxation in Historical and Comparative Perspective* (Cambridge, Cambridge University Press, 2009).

legal commentary. To the extent that some of these challenges are still being experienced in at least some less-wealthy states, they are also discussed in the tax and development literature, which again includes important contributions by lawyers.[4]

There is less commentary to be found on the domestic implications of contemporary crises for developed states, though there is some interesting discussion in the predominantly economics-based volume, *Taxation and the Financial Crisis*.[5] The intense pressure exerted on the public finances by COVID-19 and the relatively national scale of some of the fiscal implications (eg, assisting high-street newsagents forced to close under health regulations, as opposed to bailing out RBS and Lloyds Bank) has increased the level of attention paid to domestic tax policy though this emerging literature is still relatively disparate.

B. Revenues and Institution Building above the State

The dearth of literature on contemporary crises and the tax state is partly explained by the heavy emphasis which policymakers and scholars have placed on internationally coordinated responses to crises. Indeed, the OECD's long-running Base Erosion and Profits Shifting (BEPS) project can itself be seen partly as a response to the pressures created by the 2007–08 financial crash. The BEPS project aside, much of the most interesting recent writing has been on the challenges faced by the EU in responding to the heavy debt burdens of many Member States, in ways that are permitted under the Treaties and which support the aims of the Union.[6] On the tax side, a great deal of attention has been paid to the possibility that the EU could raise more of its own revenues rather than being dependent on payments from Member States.[7] This in turn raises fascinating questions about whether increasing the EU's own revenues would help to transform the organisation into something more like conventional statehood.[8]

Churchill remarked that one ought never to let a good crisis go to waste. He made this comment after World War II whist working with other nations to form the UN. In a similar vein Alesina, Ardagna and Trebbi's empirical work suggests that structural reforms of large and increasing budget deficit stabilisation often take place during times of crisis. Their paper 'Who Adjusts and When? The Political Economy of Reforms'[9] argues that the constraints that apply to the executive during normal times are often

[4] An excellent example is Y Brauner and M Stewart, *Tax, Law and Development* (Cheltenham, Edward Elgar, 2013).

[5] JS Alworth and G Arachi, *Taxation and the Financial Crisis* (Oxford, Oxford University Press, 2012).

[6] See eg A Estella, 'The "Muting" of the Stability and Growth Pact' (2021) 23 *Cambridge Yearbook of European Legal Studies* 73–90; C Kamps and N Leiner-Killinger, 'Taking stock of the functioning of the EU fiscal rules and options for reform' (ECB Occasional Paper Series no 232, 2019); F De Angelis and F Mollet, 'Rethinking EU economic governance: The Stability and Growth Pact' (European Policy Centre, 2021).

[7] Grisostelo and Scarcella, ch 10.

[8] There is a significant and growing literature on these interactions between crisis, the EU, taxation and state-building, examples of which include D Weber and O Marres (eds), *Taxing the Financial Sector: Financial Taxes, Bank Levies and More* (Amsterdam, IBFD, 2012) and J Schmidt, C Esplugues Mota and R Arenas Garcia (eds), *EU Law after the Financial Crisis* (Cambridge, Intersentia, 2016).

[9] A Alesina, S Ardagna and F Trebbi, 'Who Adjusts and When? The Political Economy of Reforms' (2006) 53 *IMF Staff Papers* 1–29.

suspended permitting more dramatic action. The EU's response to COVID-19 might be seen as an example of this phenomenon, in view of the issuance of pan-EU bonds during the pandemic despite decades of objections to this type of instrument.

C. Environment and Regulation

There is nothing new about the use of tax for regulatory purposes, but the possibility that tax law may either exacerbate or alleviate wider challenges has become much more prominent in consequence of recent crises. Many of the volumes already mentioned consider whether tax should be seen as a cause of crisis, a potential solution or both. One of the most thorough attempts to address systemic questions, though it contains limited coverage of tax, is the recent volume by Yair Listokin, *Law and Macroeconomics: Legal Remedies to Recessions*.[10] The author advocates a prominent role for legal mechanisms in response to the challenges associated with economic cycles, alongside more conventional applications of fiscal and monetary policy, and as such helps to situate tax law within a wider context.

Perhaps the most prominent of all contemporary debates on tax law and regulation relates to the role of tax in alleviating environmental crisis, and in particular the idea that tax can help to shift some of the costs of pollution from the community back onto the polluters. This in turn should incentivise the polluters to reduce their own costs by finding more environmentally sensitive ways of achieving their objectives, hence reducing the level of pollution to more acceptable levels. Although these are fundamentally economists' ideas, there is a sophisticated body of legal literature relating to the implementation of environmental taxes. In particular, the Environmental Tax Policy Institute in Vermont Law School has curated a number of volumes in the *Critical Issues in Environmental Taxation* series. Another notable example is John Snape and Jeremy Souza's *Environmental Taxation Law*.[11]

D. Justice, Distribution and Society

A great deal of literature since the financial crisis has dealt with the distributional consequences of tax rules and their role in shaping society. Much of this literature is written from a politically progressive and jurisprudentially critical perspective. A reasonably representative example of this is Attiya Waris and Jeremy Leaman's *Tax Justice and the Political Economy of Global Capitalism*.[12] However, it is fair to say that the social implications of crisis and the potential significance of tax are now attracting attention from across the political spectrum as well as from various international organisations.

[10] Y Listokin, *Law and Macroeconomics: Legal Remedies to Recessions* (Cambridge MA, Harvard UP, 2019).

[11] J Snape and J de Souza, *Environmental Taxation Law: Policy, Contexts and Practice* (Abingdon, Ashgate, 2006, reprinted by Routledge in 2020).

[12] A Waris and J Leaman (eds), *Tax Justice and the Political Economy of Global Capitalism, 1945 to the Present* (New York, Berghahn, 2013).

It is widely recognised, for example, that the way in which tax law responds to the COVID-19 pandemic is likely to influence social structure and the distribution of income and wealth for years to come. This, once again, reflects the point made throughout this volume about the non-linear implications of crisis for tax systems. If a crisis affects some demographics or business sectors more than others, as most crises do, this makes distributional questions unavoidable.

A different set of distributional questions is raised by the introduction of austerity by governments in response to post-crisis expansion of fiscal expenditure. The policy of the UK government following the global financial crisis has often been characterised in this way. We note that fiscal austerity is a highly contested policy, which has generated considerable hostility in the literature but also has its defenders. For example, Alberto Alesina, Carlo Favero and Francesco Giavazzi's *Austerity: When it Works and When it Doesn't*[13] examines a number of fiscal measures undertaken by advanced economies since the 1970s and concludes that spending cuts can often be more effective than tax increases in minimising output loss. If the debates about austerity as well as taxation betray a certain optimism about the potential for deliberate policymaking to alleviate the effects of crisis, there is also a strand in the empirical literature that suggests serious constraints on post-crises decision making. For example, Atif Mian, Amir Sufi and Francesco Trebbi argue that countries often become highly polarised after a financial crisis, which they claim reduces the likelihood of major reform.[14] This provides a useful, though pessimistic, reminder that the distributional problems caused by crises may turn out to be intractable in the medium- as well as short-term.

III. Revenues and the Tax State

The first set of issues considered in the present volume encompasses the interactions between crises, revenues and the tax state at a national level. As already mentioned, crises typically widen the gap between states' revenue capacity and their public expenditure needs. This requires governing institutions to make a series of judgements on whether to make short-term tax cuts and to tolerate higher borrowing levels, or instead to increase tax rates, introduce new taxes, reduce spending or target other options such as quantitative easing. Hence crises can influence the mix of revenue, borrowing, money supply and spending, guided by wider views on political and macroeconomic issues. One of the most interesting aspects of previous crises is when they have had such profound effects on revenues as to destabilise states altogether. There is a strong sense of this from Schumpeter's *Crisis of the Tax State*,[15] and particularly his belief that the route to prolonging the existence and success of the Austrian state was to stabilise the tax system. Nevertheless, fiscal crises in English and UK history tend to be associated with

[13] A Alesina, C Favero and F Giavazzi, *Austerity: When it Works and When it Doesn't* (Princeton, Princeton University Press, 2019).

[14] A Mian, A Sufi and F Trebbi, 'Resolving Debt Overhang: Political Constraints in the Aftermath of Financial Crises' (2014) 6(2) *American Economic Journal: Macroeconomics* 1–28.

[15] J Schumpeter, 'The Crisis of the Tax State' in R Swedberg (ed), *The Economics and Sociology of Capitalism*, (Princeton, Princeton University Press, 1991).

transformation rather than outright failure. When the House of Lords famously rejected Lloyd George's People's Budget of 1909, this forged deep and permanent changes in constitutional law but did not precipitate the collapse of the state; the imprint of other episodes such as the IMF bailouts of the 1970s has been slighter still.

These themes are taken up in chapter two of this volume by van Ganzen and Vording, who examine Schumpeter's concept of the tax state and in particular his explanation of how crises influence the development of states. In reviewing Schumpeter's work, the authors conclude that crises tend to increase the size of the state both in terms of the amounts raised and the extent to which the state's role is understood to be redistributive. They argue that the COVID-19 pandemic is likely to follow the pattern of previous crises and to point towards a larger role for government. The chapter also considers the impact of globalisation and the challenges for the state and its tax-raising capacity. The authors observe that globalisation has loosened the connections between states and taxpayers and draw on Schumpeter to argue against the unreflective reuse of expedients from previous crises. Instead, states should take a dynamic approach and respond agilely to evolving circumstances, using new approaches and even new taxes if they are needed.

A similar message is conveyed by Walters in chapter three. This chapter discusses the significance of crisis to taxation in three significant periods of conflict, the Napoleonic Wars and the two World Wars of the twentieth century. Walters observes that these wars placed the public finances of participating states under extreme strain but also acted as such an important impetus to innovation that many of the central features of modern tax systems can be traced to these three periods of history. The chapter starts by reviewing the most significant tax consequences of each conflict, explaining the personalities involved, the practical problems that they faced and the reasons why they decided on certain approaches to taxation rather than others. Walters then pauses to draw some general conclusions from this historical evidence before asking whether there are any relevant parallels with more recent crises such as the financial crash of 2008 and the onset of COVID in 2019–20. He concludes that there are lessons to be drawn from these earlier events but also emphasises the importance of context. There is a much greater role for global responses to public finance problems in 2022 than in 1922, let alone 1822. The need to encourage private spending in the present environment also counsels against some of the expedients employed in previous crises such as greatly increased indirect taxation. There are parallels but also differences between crises. Walters ends his chapter by arguing that, whatever decisions are made on financing the cost of COVID-19, they ought to be visible to and sensitive to public opinion.

In chapter four, Tandon examines the imposition of excess profits taxes in the UK, the US and India in response to super-profits made in the two World Wars, as well as more recent attempts to impose financial transactions taxes. She considers whether these types of measures ought to be reintroduced in the light of the COVID-19 pandemic and what preconditions might be required to make them a success in the modern context. An interesting point raised by Tandon is that the imposition of excess profits tax on India by the British Empire was not an unqualified success and secured much lower support than similar taxes in the UK. This shows that although revenue-raising considerations can be aligned with the consolidation of support for a state more generally, badly conceived taxes can instead have a centrifugal effect, a point not lost on those of us who remember Thatcher's imposition of the Community Charge north of the Scottish border.

The question of revenue-raising is more complicated when a crisis has an unequal impact on different types of activity, an obvious recent example being the general shift from in-person to online shopping during the COVID-19 crisis. Leaving aside for a moment the question whether tax law ought to incentivise one type of shopping relative to the other, this has eviscerated some previously reliable sources of revenue (eg, income, corporation and property taxes from retail and hospitality businesses) whilst creating opportunities for new relatively inelastic revenue streams (eg, online sales and digital taxes). The fundamental point here may be that taxes have long been applied unequally to what are or have become essentially substitutable activities, with COVID-19 transforming this into a serious threat to revenues both by discouraging in-person shopping but also by inspiring new and innovative online offerings (hence creating new opportunities for substitution).

A number of our authors highlight the need for crisis responses in the 2020s to account for the greatly increased role of the digital economy relative to traditional physical businesses. An example is Zu's proposal in chapter eleven for the negotiation of VAT treaties to complement the income tax treaty network. In the author's view, the revenue raising capacity of middle- and lower-income countries is particularly vulnerable to the combination of the rise of the digital economy and the absence of VAT from existing treaties. The COVID-19 pandemic has only exacerbated these problems as transactions shift towards ecommerce. The digital economy is also cited by van Ganzen and Vording in chapter two as an example of the changing context in which tax systems have to operate, with the authors challenging gently the OECD orthodoxy that states ought to phase out unilateral digital services taxes as part of a Pillar 1 agreement.

The challenges of maintaining revenues, when previously established sectors of the economy recede in favour of others, go well beyond ecommerce. This is clearly demonstrated by Panadès-Estruch's review in chapter six of the responses of British Overseas Territories (BOTs) to the financial problems arising from COVID-19. Panadès-Estruch draws attention to the unique challenges facing BOTs owing to their limited economic diversification and heavy reliance on tourism, banking and real estate, their geographical remoteness, their limited sovereignty and their reliance on a narrow range of revenue sources such as tariffs, stamp duties and commercial fees. In the context of COVID-19, these features have contributed to increased poverty and unemployment and have created supply-chain problems that have increased the difficulty of providing public services and especially healthcare. The outcome has been a greater need to rely on external support from the UK and elsewhere, though the position varies widely between different BOTs.

An important point illustrated by Panadès-Estruch's review of BOTs is that crises represent not only a threat to established ways of raising revenue, but also an opportunity to devise new and innovative methods of revenue-raising. This is in line with van Ganzen and Vording's emphasis on the importance of context but also with Tandon's exploration of the possibilities of imposing excess profits taxes or financial transactions taxes on sectors of the economy that have gained from crisis. The same point is brought even further by Prasad Kotha in chapter five, who examines the practice of responding to crises by enacting earmarked or hypothecated taxes, the proceeds of which are dedicated to certain stated public policy objectives. As Prasad Kotha observes, earmarked taxes have already been introduced in Liberia, Uruguay, Argentina and Egypt in order to help with the costs of COVID-19 recovery. She begins her discussion by distinguishing earmarked taxes from ostensibly similar concepts such as Pigovian taxes and user fees, also explaining the differences between 'strong' and 'weak' earmarking and 'window-dressing' whereby revenues are not fully dedicated to the indicated objectives. She evaluates the theoretical justifications for earmarking and draws on this discussion to suggest how the practice might be carried out more effectively especially in the context of COVID-19. The overall tone of the chapter is of gentle advocacy for earmarking, though with a close awareness of the potential difficulties and its greater suitability in some jurisdictions and circumstances than others. Indeed, the idea of earmarking seems particularly apposite in the context of weak institutions and lack of trust in a state, where taxpayers might be more willing to contribute towards specified objectives than state funds in general.

IV. Revenues and Institution Building above the State

If periods of crisis present states with the risk of destabilised public finances but also the opportunity to secure new streams of finance, the same can be said of supranational organisations. The EU is not the only supranational organisation that is being transformed by crisis, but it provides a particularly clear case study of the arguments for and against centralisation as a response to crisis. A number of our authors point out that the EU has been able to provide coordinated fiscal support to Member States in a way that is far from perfect, but significantly exceeds what would have been possible had those states acted independently. The EU's ability to provide this support is constrained by extremely limited 'own resources' upon which it can draw without the need to receive explicit transfers from Member States; hence one of the lessons that might be drawn from recent crises is that these own resources ought to be supplemented by new EU taxes. This attitude is especially prominent in the context of environmental taxes, where of course the underlying crises have serious consequences without regard to national borders.

In chapter ten, Grisostelo and Scarcella begin by citing the COVID-19 crisis as a significant moment of change for the EU. It has required 'exceptional measures' in expenditure terms but might also act as 'a catalyst to rethink the issue of EU taxes'. The authors then provide a brief history of the financing of the EU's budget with a particular emphasis on the development of own resources. There ensues an explanation of the significance of COVID-19 for the EU Budget and the opportunities that it presents to pursue centralising measures and to overcome some of the obstacles that preserve a high degree of Member State control over tax policy in the face of problems that require collective solutions. The centre of gravity of the chapter, though, is the subsequent extended and exceptionally clear overview of the various recent proposals for new EU own resources. This discussion takes in a Plastics Levy, the EU's Emissions Trading Scheme (ETS), the Carbon Border Adjustment Mechanism (CBAM), an EU Digital Levy, the continuing attempts to create a common corporate tax base and a Financial Transactions Tax. The chapter thus comes full circle, showing how the EU's response to COVID-19 might address other crises such as the climate crisis and the ongoing consequences of the 2008 financial crash. The chapter ends with a discussion of unanimity requirements for EU initiatives in the tax field and how these might be managed or overcome in order to make progress on the proposed new resources.

In chapter seven, Hernández González-Barreda considers the role of taxes in constituting the EU as an institution with many if not all of the features of a state. He begins by observing that taxes played a much greater role in the early history of the European Coal and Steel Community (ECSC) as opposed to the European Economic Community (EEC) and Council of Europe. From the 1970s onwards, though, the EEC started to engage more directly with public finance matters, establishing a European Regional Fund, acquiring own resources and budgeting on a multiannual basis. In more recent times, there have been strong moves towards greater coordination, particularly since the decision of the European Court of Justice in *Avoir Fiscal*[16] in 1986 brought into focus the requirement for national direct taxes to comply with European law. This trend has been reinforced by the acute need of some EU Member States for financial support following the global financial crisis of 2008 that culminated in the European Stability Mechanism, an increasingly active approach towards legislating in the direct tax field and most recently the EU's responses to COVID-19. Hernández González-Barreda takes a broad view of these developments, discussing not only tax but also wider public finance matters such as vaccine procurement. He closes the chapter by asking whether these trends in EU taxation might be seen in explicitly federal terms, concluding broadly that they can although the picture is not unequivocal.

A different aspect of this institution building process is highlighted by Pantazatou in chapter eight, who notes that democratic approval and oversight at the EU level is stronger for public expenditure than for revenue raising. This inverts the position in most Member States where the democratic credentials of revenue generation are usually much stronger than of public expenditure. Pantazatou explains that the bulk of the EU's own resources flow from two sources, one based on gross national income and one based on VAT. Although the EU is undoubtedly entitled to these revenues, they bear some resemblance to transfers from Member States. This in turn exacerbates the sense of disconnect between spending (subject to democratic oversight at EU level) and taxation (subject to democratic oversight at national level). It also encourages a belief in some quarters that EU own resources represent a type of subsidy of poorer Member States by richer ones. In any case, the recent financial and COVID-19 crises have greatly added to these strains by prompting the EU to seek substantial funding over short time periods, often without the luxury of going through the normal budgetary processes. This has allowed the EU to react more decisively to crisis but has further widened the gulf between the funding of its activities and the democratic oversight of these finances. Although different views might be taken on how to resolve these tensions, Pantazatou argues that democratic oversight would be best secured by funding EU spending with explicitly EU-based taxes; indeed there are signs of this happening in connection with the ETS, CBAM and OECD Pillar 1 adjustments.

It is not just the EU that is seen as a potential vehicle for more effective coordinated solutions to crisis, and there have been very visible recent attempts to strengthen international tax governance, most notably through the OECD's BEPS project and its

[16] Case 270/83 *Commission of the European Communities v French Republic* [1986] 1 ECR 273.

associated 'inclusive framework' that is designed to increase the voice of developing countries and other non-members within the OECD's decision-making processes.

A more critical outlook on international tax responses to crisis is provided in chapter twelve of this volume by Pushkareva. The author begins by reviewing an article written by Allison Christians in 2009, in the immediate aftermath of the global financial crisis, then proceeds to review more recent events and in particular the international tax consequences of COVID-19. One of the most important responses to these crises has been to galvanise support for measures to mitigate the loss of revenues to tax havens, but as Pushkareva points out, these measures are not always closely connected to the crises that prompted them. The suspicion is therefore that the financial crash was used as a pretext for a campaign against havens that would have been welcomed by wealthy developed states in any case. Besides, many of the supposedly undesirable behaviours of tax havens are also exhibited by European jurisdictions such as the Netherlands, Switzerland and Luxembourg, which have nonetheless escaped most of the controls placed on havens. Pushkareva takes a more optimistic position on coordinated attempts to increase the burden on richer taxpayers and on plans for a 'green recovery', though she warns against the risk that reforms designed with good intentions will in practice bear most heavily on middle-class taxpayers and poorer jurisdictions respectively. This risk might be alleviated by further institutional improvements to ensure that the inclusion of the less wealthy in international tax reform discussions is real rather than merely tokenistic.

Zu's advocacy of VAT treaties is of obvious relevance here, though she stops short of proposing new international institutions for VAT coordination, instead arguing for the perhaps more practical option of agreeing bilateral treaties to mirror the existing income tax treaty network. Conversely, though, it is clear that crises can be extremely helpful to proponents of institutional reform in bolstering their pre-existing agenda, in line with Churchill's famous advice never to let a good crisis go to waste. At least some observers calling for greater EU integration in response to COVID-19 were already in favour of this before the crisis emerged, whilst many of those arguing against integration were already sceptical of it. This illustrates the obvious point that crises can be used as the pretext to pursue pre-existing political and constitutional objectives, but also suggests that seemingly technical arguments around COVID-19 tax treatments may conceal much deeper disagreements about the relationship of the EU with its Member States. It follows that there may be a surprising amount at stake in these technical arguments, so that the ways in which they are resolved are likely to represent victories and setbacks for different respective views about the continent's future.

These disagreements are taken seriously by Pantazatou, whose chapter includes a detailed discussion of the conditions under which EU taxes would be justifiable, before concluding in favour of greater centralisation of revenue-raising within the EU. A much more pessimistic outlook is taken in chapter nine by Garbarino, who explains the convergence of tax policy responses to COVID-19 by reference to the linked concepts of 'biopower' and 'biopolitics'. These ideas are taken from the work of Michel Foucault and describe a shift towards understanding the population of a state at an aggregate level in terms of statistics and trends, identifying and addressing problems at the same aggregate level and in the process changing the way in which individuals within a state are conceived. This approach to governance long predates the present day, but COVID-19 has provided exceptionally strong incentives on states to apply techniques consistent with biopower. This in turn helps to explain the convergence of tax policy responses to COVID-19 as well as aspects of recent EU integration. The chapter begins with a helpful review of tax responses to COVID-19, principally in the EU, before moving on to explain the relevance and usefulness of a Foucauldian framework. The author proceeds to discuss the role of state sovereignty, considering whether to follow Foucault in setting it in opposition to biopolitics, to treat COVID-19 responses as a Schmittian state of exception or to follow Agamben in treating biopolitics and sovereignty as symbiotic. Whilst there are concerns about the authoritarian possibilities of biopolitics, another route of criticism is then pursued by reference to the work of Merrill Singer, along the lines that COVID-19 regulations have not accounted adequately for existing inequalities. The chapter concludes by asking if COVID-19 biopower has prompted a critical juncture in EU taxation.

V. Environment and Regulation

Just as crises generate risks and opportunities for revenue-raising, they also place pressure on existing ways of using taxes to regulate behaviour, potentially making them less effective or more complicated. For instance, attempts to incentivise increased use of public transport through the tax system seem somewhat trivial alongside the perceived risks of COVID-19 contraction from buses and trains, and indeed the outright travel bans imposed by many governments in 2020. Nonetheless, the environmental aims underlying public transport incentives were in fact progressed by the drastic reductions in all kinds of transport. COVID-19 also exposed contradictions in the efforts of governments to support physical retailers struggling with the combined effect of lockdowns, consumer risk-aversion and the boom in online retailing. Many governments provided financial support to affected businesses and emergency relief from property taxes, and designed new taxes on online and digital retailers, but failed adequately to address other tax problems such as the VAT leakage from digital services described by Zu.

The example of COVID-19 also points to a separate question, which is whether government interventions in response to crises such as COVID-19 ought to be carried out through the tax system (eg, vaccine incentives or property tax reliefs for retail premises) or through more direct spending programmes. The choices made here are likely to reflect deeper attitudes towards change, such as whether the government wishes to encourage structural change in the economy (eg, by providing enhanced homeworking reliefs even post-COVID-19), to manage change (eg, by using furlough systems to reduce abrupt unemployment) or to resist change altogether (eg, by incentivising return to in-person office working post-COVID). There may, of course, be concerns around whether some of these options breach other restrictions on government support, perhaps including commerce or free trade clauses in federal constitutions or state aid restrictions in EU law.

A focal point for these types of discussions in the present volume is whether taxes can help to mitigate environmental destruction and indeed whether the dislocations produced by COVID-19 might be used constructively in favour of a 'green recovery'.

This point is made by Pushkareva and is also central to Scuderi, Rizzo and Loucaidou's examination of the 'European Green Deal' (EGD) in chapter thirteen. The aim of the EGD is to encourage climate neutrality by 2050 and the reduction of greenhouse gases by 50–55 per cent from 1990 levels by 2030. The authors of chapter thirteen recognise the EU's pioneering efforts in environmental taxation, but argue that the Energy Taxation Directive and Emissions Trading System could be better targeted to supporting the post-COVID-19 economy and meeting the EGD goals. In essence, the chapter urges the EU to capitalise on the changed attitudes towards pollution during the COVID-19 crisis in a way that addresses negative environmental externalities whilst generating revenues at the same time. This might include a new CO_2 tax as well as potentially the earmarking of revenues for environmental goals.

A different type of environmental tax that has been introduced recently by the EU is the Plastics Levy. Although this is likely to remain small-scale in terms of revenues, Geringer points out in chapter fourteen that it involves many of the challenges of environmental taxation in microcosm and therefore offers an invaluable case study of issues relating to the green recovery more generally. Geringer highlights the difficulties in coordinating EU initiatives and their implementation by Member State governments. In her view, both environmental and EU financing aims could be improved by a centralised approach whereby the design of the tax would be imposed in a Directive and revenues collected by Member States and then passed directly to the EU. This would replace the current approach which involves Member States designing their own taxes and paying increased contributions to the EU. Geringer accepts that environmental and revenue aims may be in tension, in the sense that if taxes on harmful activities succeed in minimising those activities, this will inevitably depress revenues. However, this is hardly a conclusive argument such taxes should not be introduced or that they cannot play a significant role in the post-crisis consolidation of the EU's finances.

VI. Justice, Distribution and Society

Moving to questions of justice and distribution, taxes can certainly be used to redistribute resources from the wealthy to the poor, and from high to low earners. At a more detailed level, they also have a role in constructing the types of societies in which we live. Critical theorists and sociologists point out that social divisions, privilege and deprivation are not independent of tax systems but are shaped and reinforced by tax rules that favour some types of personal and working arrangements over others. As crises themselves tend to have variable impacts on different demographics and sectors of the economy, they can raise these distributional and social questions in particularly acute form. One of the most obvious, already considered above, is whether excess profits taxes should be levied on those businesses and individuals whose financial position has been enhanced by crisis conditions.

A more involved question is how government ought to deal with those who are negatively affected by crisis. Should government provide support, and if so, in what form? Should support be prioritised to those who have lost the most from crisis (even if they had previously been relatively privileged) or instead to the poorest members of society who might be seen as the most deserving under a broader theory of distributive justice? A good recent example of this tension can be seen in the UK's furlough scheme, in which the government subsidised the income of individuals whose labour was surplus to requirements at the height of the COVID-19 crisis and who might otherwise have been made redundant. Although this policy is intelligible in terms of limiting the long-term economic damage of the public health measures imposed to control COVID-19, the individuals involved were often well outside the sectors of society usually considered deserving of public subsidy. This point links closely with the insights of critical theory. By prioritising economic recovery over redistribution, the furlough scheme has robustly reinforced existing social divisions and has arguably missed an opportunity to use the COVID-19 crisis to alleviate pre-existing injustices. Yet this picture is far from monolithic and some such opportunities may remain. For instance, if COVID-19 results in a greater recognition of home-working, through the tax system or otherwise, this may go some way to rebalancing some of the gender disparities associated with childcare, as well as various barriers faced by disabled people.

These issues are discussed by Lind in chapter seventeen in the context of how governments have allocated financial aid to individuals and businesses with costs associated with the COVID-19 pandemic. The author focusses on the connecting factors which qualify a person for aid, whether formal citizenship, previous tax payment, residence, employment or some other economic activity, and explains the fiscal and social implications of relying on each. She also emphasises the importance of designing aid in a way that allows recipients to recover their economic independence after a crisis has abated rather than relying indefinitely on state support. The chapter draws heavily on Denmark's experience during the COVID-19 crisis and concludes with a series of recommendations on how to design financial aid more effectively.

Similar matters are considered in a different context by Cui in chapter sixteen. This chapter contributes to the burgeoning literature on the application of tax and welfare policy to the world of work. The focus is on the policy instruments implemented during the most acute phase of the COVID-19 crisis, including direct payments to workers and wage subsidies. The author calls for various shifts in our approach to policy discussions. First, he argues that the omnipresent concern for how to tax the rich effectively ought to be balanced by a greater emphasis on how to support the non-rich. Second, he points out that the need for COVID-19 support does not always match precisely onto familiar concepts such as employment, self-employment or even 'gig workers'. Instead, some of the most precarious workers are in fact in temporary, part-time and other types of flexible employment. For these reasons, wage support might be more effective in targeting help to where it is needed than is generally recognised, and also has certain other advantages over direct payments to workers. Cui draws on Canadian COVID-19 policies to support his arguments and shows that, whilst sometimes disorganised, they have still had a reasonably high degree of success.

A number of authors point out close links between the distributional implications of crisis measures and other long-running controversies in tax and public finance. The tendency for crisis to increase tax progressivity, at least in the short run, is pointed out by van Ganzen and Vording, Gabarino and others with varying levels of enthusiasm. Likewise, the debate about the taxation of capital relative to labour income is engaged by the UK government's introduction of a 'health and social care levy' partly in response to the healthcare costs of COVID-19.[17] This effectively increases the social security contributions paid by both employers and employees. Leaving aside the point that this levy implies a greater degree of hypothecation than it achieves, the imposition of a new tax on labour as opposed to capital is highly controversial and runs directly counter to the belief of many commentators that some form of wealth tax ought to be introduced.

The tax implications of crisis for the young are considered by Brassey in chapter fifteen. For Brassey, the COVID-19 crisis has taken place against the background of a slow-burn breakdown in intergenerational fairness. The chapter begins with a discussion of the combined effects of decreasing job security, increasing housing costs and changing pensions arrangements, and shows that these systematically disadvantage the young relative to the old. This position is reinforced by tax treatments including the principal private residence relief for CGT, the non-application of CGT on death, the progressive rates of SDLT and the design of IHT. A variety of proposals to alleviate the shortcomings in these provisions have been published over recent years, many prompted by the greatly increased strain that the COVID-19 crisis has placed on the public finances. Brassey evaluates these proposals in turn and with a critical eye, paying particular regard to the ideas of the Wealth Tax Commission. His own preference is for gradual alleviation of the tax disadvantages of younger generations, to be rooted in thorough research by a proposed Fiscal Policy Committee and following a scrupulously rules-based approach.

Brassey's emphasis on rules resonates with a strand in our previous volume, *Tax Justice and Tax Law*, to the effect that it is important to consider the procedures by which tax provisions are imposed and administered. Some of the methods of social control imposed during the COVID-19 crisis are almost unprecedented in the democratic world. They have often been devised at speed, have been approved using accelerated legislative procedures that bypass the usual ways of obtaining scrutiny, and have frequently been enforced by officials with little more than an intuitive estimation of what the rules do and do not permit. These considerations also arise with respect to the tax measures implemented in (or on the pretext of a) response to COVID-19. Although few observers would doubt the necessity for rapid government responses to crisis, it is important to consider how this rapidity has been balanced against the usual need for democratic approval and lawful enforcement of taxation, as well as how to prevent the attenuation of procedural justice from outliving crises and surviving into normal times.

Concern for procedural propriety and democratic inclusion is woven through this volume, as can be seen from the various proposals of Zu, Pushkareva, van Ganzen and Vording, Pantazatou and others for improving the conduct of international and EU taxation. In the final chapter 18, Filipczyk observes that a great deal of emergency COVID-19 legislation in Poland and elsewhere falls well below our usual expectations of procedural propriety, in its enactment, structure, expression and enforcement. She refers to scholarly literature on the rule of law in order to understand in more depth whether COVID-19 legislation should be considered 'bad law' in the light of its

[17] Department of Health and Social Care, 'Health and Social Care Levy to raise billions for NHS and social care' (Press release, 6 April 2022) available at www.gov.uk/government/news/health-and-social-care-levy-to-raise-billions-for-nhs-and-social-care.

procedural deficiencies, and whether this has any consequences for its status as 'law' at all or for the obedience of taxpayers. Filipczyk relies on Fuller's, and to a lesser extent Raz's conception of the rule of law, arguing that Fuller's 'desiderata' for good law should be understood in a gradated rather than binary manner. In the present context, this means that rushed COVID-19 legislation might be regarded as weakly compliant with the rule of law rather than flatly non-compliant. Even elements of tax administration that are impossible to reconcile with the rule of law may nevertheless gain meaning and force from other provisions that do comply, so that 'law' and 'non-law' intertwine. The experience of tax during crises shows the operation of the rule of law to be significantly more complex than is usually appreciated.

VII. Concluding Comments

The methods by which states seek to finance their deficits are likely to define the fortunes of the next generation and beyond. As governments decide how to exist the unprecedented deficit spending of the last few years, it is likely that we will witness significant global turbulence, currency volatility and stagflation.

It is against this background that the contributors to this volume are asking the question 'what role does tax play?'. There is, predictably, no single answer to this, but it is useful to think of taxes as being both constituted and constitutive. They are *constituted* in the sense that they are subject to the legal system and constitutional regime of the relevant state, and, besides, cannot but reflect their political, economic, social and cultural context. If a crisis increases unemployment, then the revenue yield of a tax on employment income is likely to reduce. If a crisis generates widespread public anger against 'profiteers', then demands for an excess profits taxes are a predictable consequence. Yet taxes are also *constitutive*, imposing their own imprint on law and society more broadly. The relative burden of taxation on bricks-and-mortar and online retailers may have serious consequences for the appearance of our cities. Meanwhile, at least some environmental campaigners view tax as a way of helping to construct greener societies post-COVID-19.

If tax law is simultaneously influenced by and influencing wider social trends, unfolding crises, crisis recovery and so forth, this helps to explain the scarcity of legal literature on the interaction of tax and crises. There is no single story or even set of stories about what this relationship is or how it works. Nevertheless, the contributors to this volume have demonstrated clearly that taxes are frequently at the centre of events both during and in the aftermath of crises. As is well known and will not be dwelt upon in depth here, tax responses to crises can lead to critical junctures with lasting consequences. Obvious examples from the UK include the establishment of the income tax during the French Revolutionary and Napoleonic Wars, the remodelling of the House of Lords during the People's Budget crisis and the development of anti-avoidance provisions during World Wars I and II. In other instances, things may largely go back to normal after crises have abated, a UK example being the repeal of special wartime taxes after World War I. It is interesting to speculate which aspects of COVID-19 regulation will outlast the pandemic and which will be reversed and subsequently forgotten.

Whether the tax implications of crises are desirable or not has been a matter of debate between the contributors to this volume, with some taking an optimistic view of the potential for further European integration and environmental protection, and others much more concerned about the drift towards authoritarianism and disrespect for the rule of law. To some extent the normative questions about how to design and implement a tax system are familiar from tax scholarship and discussion outside the crisis context, but with the added urgency that *something* has to be done *immediately* in order to address the crisis or its fiscal implications. In this sense, chapter eighteen is the ideal closing chapter for this volume. How do we organise a tax system in a way that is effective, that respects the rule of law, that reflects the immediate urgency of responding to crises, but that also recognises that crisis expedients can outlive their reasons for existing and become part of the new structure of taxation going forward? What are the implications for tax design if well-organised deliberation about the tax system has to co-exist or is even overshadowed by this type of 'on the fly' reactive reform in the face of crisis? It is well beyond the scope of this project to provide conclusive answers to these questions, but at the very least, this volume poses a whole range of important and fascinating questions which would be well worth considering in more depth before the next crisis arrives.

PART I

Revenues and the Tax State

2

Schumpeter's Crisis of the Tax State, Globalisation and Redistribution

BASTIAAN VAN GANZEN AND HENK VORDING

Abstract

The Austrian economist Joseph Schumpeter regarded taxation as central to state-building. According to him, the 'tax state' both reshapes and reflects the social structure and spirit of a community. He argued that macrolevel shocks do not threaten this tax state, as long as its social order remains intact. Only when the order breaks down, so will the tax state. Indeed, historical evidence shows that wars and economic downturns often caused tax states to expand rather than collapse. The same will probably happen during today's financial and geopolitical turmoil. Much more threatening to modern tax states, however, is the weakening of social ties between taxpayers and their communities in our globalising world. In line with Schumpeter's notions of dynamism and societal change, we argue that the solution to this new 'Crisis of the Tax State' lies not in saving twentieth-century income tax arrangements from twenty-first-century challenges, but in adapting our tax systems to the new social order.

I. Introduction

Using the words 'crisis' and 'tax' in one sentence brings us inevitably to Joseph Schumpeter's essay *The Crisis of the Tax State* (1918). In that essay, Schumpeter analysed taxation as the corollary of the modern state based on market economy and political representation. What underlies his analysis is a Weberian typology of social organisation: the medieval feudal state was based on personal ties and hence, did not need taxation; the modern state relies on bureaucratic formalisation of ties and fully depends on taxation. As long as those ties between members of communities remain intact, Schumpeter suggested, tax states will have sufficient resilience to overcome large macrolevel shocks, including the debt burden crises that several countries faced in the aftermath of World War I. However, he predicted that a successful tax state could eventually crumble under the weight of increasing demands for redistribution.

To him, the tax state is a body that reflects and reshapes the social order of a free market society, and hence requires a distinction between state and market. Once the ties between members of a community are fully socialised and pricing is replaced by planning, this distinction disappears and so does the tax state.

Schumpeter's essay is now over a century old. It is outdated in important respects, for example in its emphasis on socialism as the viable alternative to free market democracy. Furthermore, Schumpeter's world simply did not know many of today's tax challenges: how to tax digital services, how to deal with conflicting national interests concerning cross-border mobility of tax bases. Yet, his work is of continuing relevance. Like his contemporary Austrian economists, Schumpeter was driven by a desire to understand the extensive social, cultural and political changes of his time, in particular the demise of the Austro-Hungarian empire.[1] 'Understand' here means 'Verstehen' in a Weberian sense, being interpretative rather than quantitative and transcending the boundaries of economics, law, history, sociology and political science. Applying this qualitative method to the area of taxation, which he regarded as the central aspect of the modern state, Schumpeter pioneered the academic discipline of fiscal sociology.[2] Central to his work is a notion of dynamism and perpetual change, encapsulated in the well-known phrase 'creative destruction'. This notion relates not only to entrepreneurial innovation as the primary driver of economic progress, but also to the inevitability of change in the entire social order of a community.[3] His definition of a 'crisis of the tax state' is strongly connected to this idea of social change. Therefore, his concept of the tax state is a useful tool for analysing the viability of present tax arrangements both in the light of sudden crises – the debt burden crisis caused by COVID-19 and the recent geopolitical turmoil – and in relation to changes in social ties caused by globalisation.

We first discuss Schumpeter's concept of the tax state in some more detail (section II). Then we turn to Schumpeter's immediate concern: the role of crises in the development of the tax state (section III). We suggest that crises have on balance increased the

[1] E Dekker, 'Left luggage: finding the relevant context of Austrian Economics' (2016) 29 *Review of Austrian Economics* 103.

[2] This field has recently made a comeback with a new wave of multidisciplinary research on taxation: IW Martin, AK Mehrotra and M Prasad, 'The Thunder of History: The Origins and Development of the New Fiscal Sociology' in IW Martin, AK Mehrotra and M Prasad (eds), *The New Fiscal Sociology: Taxation in Comparative and Historical Perspective* (Cambridge, Cambridge University Press, 2009). For an application of the fiscal sociological method to current issues, such as gender equality and global taxation of capital, and for an extensive review of Schumpeter's ideas on taxation, see A Mumford, *Fiscal Sociology at the Centenary: UK Perspectives on Budgeting, Taxation and Austerity* (Cham, Palgrave Macmillan, 2019). Mumford's starting point is Schumpeter's list of central questions of fiscal sociology: 'What does "failure of the tax state" mean? What is the nature of the tax state? How did it come about? Must it now disappear and why? What are the social processes which are behind the superficial facts of the budget figures?'. Her primary focus is the fifth question in a UK context, and she does not propose answers to the first and the fourth questions, which, by contrast, are our main objects of study.

[3] Schumpeter used the phrase 'creative destruction' only in the context of entrepreneurial innovation and not in the context of societal change, but arguably, he regarded both types of progress as two sides of the same coin, not in the least because economic development changes social life. See E Dekker, 'Schumpeter: Theorist of the avant-garde: The embrace of the new in Schumpeter's original theory of economic development' (2018) 31 *Review of Austrian Economics* 177, who shows that an avant-gardist embrace of 'the new' in general, relating to both economic and social change, particularly pervades JA Schumpeter, *Theorie der wirtschaftlichen Entwicklung* (Berlin, Duncker & Humblot, 1919).

weight of the tax state, both in terms of tax burden and of redistributive effort, rather than diminishing it. It seems that an increasingly unstable geopolitical environment and the financial aftermath of the pandemic crisis will just repeat that story. We then turn to economic globalisation as a challenge to the tax state, and one that Schumpeter did not foresee (section IV). Here, the 'fiscal sociology' of social ties illuminates how the tax state may run into trouble as taxpayers lose their connection to it.

We conclude with discussing alternative ways to 'protect' the tax state (section V) along two vectors. One denotes the degree of effectiveness of the tax state: its grip on the tax bases that it wants to address. The other is its economic impact: overall tax burden and redistributive effort. We track the historical path of developed tax states through this vector space and conclude that it was strongly shaped by both the occurrence of crises and the choice of tax instruments. We argue that Schumpeter's world was one in which states felt free to develop sophisticated tax rules of the income/profits tax type and did not have to bother seriously about effectiveness of their taxes; while currently, concerns over cross-border avoidance have grown considerably and we still try to run those sophisticated tax rules. We use Schumpeter's analysis to raise the question how long-run changes in the social fabric may affect the viability of existing taxes – and perhaps give reason to find additional ones.

II. Schumpeter's Tax State[4]

The text of Schumpeter's essay is derived from a lecture that he gave to the Wiener Soziologische Gesellschaft and was originally published in 1918 as *Die Krise des Steuerstaates*.[5] The political context of the time was the imminent collapse of the Austro-Hungarian empire. It had ignited World War I only to become trivial to its outcome – the defeat of Germany at the western front, and the communist seizure of power in Russia. Indeed, quite a number of long-established states were on the verge of disappearance. In his essay, however, Schumpeter flatly denies that there exists a 'crisis of the tax state'.[6]

The immediate concern of his lecture was to respond to Rudolf Goldscheid's *Staatssozialismus oder Staatskapitalismus* (1917), a plea for strong state involvement in market processes. Schumpeter's argument is basically that there is no urgent reason for any move to socialism; acute financial concerns may be solved by a temporary tax on capital. But to undershore that argument, he undertakes a much broader analysis of the 'Tax State'.[7] To some extent, it foreshadows his *Capitalism, Socialism*

[4] See generally: KH Schmidt, 'Schumpeter and the Crisis of the Tax State' in J Backhaus (ed), *Joseph Alois Schumpeter: Entrepreneurship, Style and Vision* (Dordrecht, Kluwer, 2003).

[5] Reprinted as JA Schumpeter, 'The Crisis of the Tax State' in R Swedberg (ed), *The Economics and Sociology of Capitalism* (Princeton, Princeton University Press, 1991). Swedberg offers an overview of Schumpeter's life and work in his introduction. Richard Musgrave, once Schumpeter's student, who translated *Die Krise* in English, summarises and discusses the text in RA Musgrave, 'Schumpeter's crisis of the tax state: An essay in fiscal sociology' (1992) 2 *Journal of Evolutionary Economics* 89.

[6] Schumpeter (n 5) 130.

[7] It has been noted that his analysis was firmly rooted in the German Historische Schule: S Huhnholz, 'Was soll das heißen: Steuerstaat?' (2017) 29 *Ökonomie und Gesellschaft* 15.

and Democracy (1942),[8] especially in its analysis of the state, run by a government based on political contest and competition, as the organisation that matches free-market capitalism. That state *is* the Tax State, as taxation is the link between state and market. When a society relies on planning instead of the market to confront demand for and supply of goods and services, the concept of state becomes useless. That is what happens under socialism – which, for Schumpeter, consistent with his economic interpretation of politics, is not primarily a political doctrine but a non-market mode of organising the economy.

To be sure, the tax system is much more than just the financial flow from market to state. 'The spirit of a people, its cultural level, its social structure, the deeds its policy may prepare – all this and more is written in its fiscal history, stripped of all phrases. He who knows how to listen to its message here discerns the thunder of world history more clearly than anywhere else'.[9] Schumpeter makes no attempt to apply this promising starting point to actual tax policy choices. But he does discuss how the tax state emerged from the dark ages of feudalism.

In the medieval feudal societies of Germany and Austria, he explains, taxes did not exist: peasant-serfs paid dues and vassals made gifts to their prince, but the revenues were not spent in a 'public' sphere by a sovereign state. The prince, the estates and the lesser lords shared power over the same territory, and they used it for their own benefits; their expenses were private affairs. Political power rested on personal ties; we recognise what Max Weber had dubbed *Traditionale Herrschaft* (traditional rule). This system of feudal relations was not too stable by itself, as it had to rely on the intensity of the vassal relationship. But it finally crumbled down under the growing pressure of military expenses in the fifteenth and sixteenth centuries. The prince was unable to finance mercenary armies from his private means and had to rely on the estates for subsidies. In turn, the estates had to raise a revenue stream and spend it in a public sphere, and so the tax state was born. Here we see both a systemic crisis (the loosening ties of the vassal relationship) that induces the demise of an economic system, and a macrolevel shock (war) that leads to an increase in government revenues.

The tax state that, in a gradual historical process, replaced the feudal society, does no longer address collective needs through personal relations; the state assumes that role. But still, there is the idea of 'common purposes', to be served by and through the state.[10] Quite comparable to, for instance, John Rawls's Social Contract, the implication seems to be that the spatial limits of the state coincide with the presence of a sense of cohesion by its inhabitants.[11] Schumpeter denied that the debt crisis left by World War I would necessitate a major overhaul of the pre-war economic order, as he saw no change in the basics of the tax state. If the tax state were indeed to fail, this would be the result of a more structural, societal crisis: 'If the will of the people demands higher and higher

[8] JA Schumpeter, *Capitalism, Socialism and Democracy*, 5th edn (London, George Allen & Unwin, 1976).

[9] Schumpeter (n 5) 101.

[10] Musgrave (n 5) 92.

[11] In his Law of Peoples, Rawls denied the viability of a worldwide Social Contract of the type he had proposed in his Theory of Justice: J Rawls, *The Law of Peoples* (Cambridge MA, Harvard University Press, 1999). The underlying idea that states are the political organisations of people who share a sense of 'belonging' inspires the 'statist' (as opposed to 'cosmopolitan') view of international relations.

public expenditures, if more and more means are used for purposes for which private individuals have not produced them … and if finally all parts of the people are gripped by entirely new ideas about private property and the forms of life – then the tax state will have run its course …'.[12] In line with the notion of inevitable change that pervades his work, Schumpeter regarded this transition to socialism as unavoidable. As he explains twenty-four years later in his *Capitalism, Socialism and Democracy*, it is an inherent result of the internal dynamics of capitalism: innovative entrepreneurship increases people's standards of living and opportunities for leisure, which in turn fosters a class of intellectuals who criticise capitalism because they do not understand its function. Gradually, redistribution will increase to excessive levels and capitalism will destroy itself by replacing entrepreneurialism with bureaucratic decision-making.[13]

Summing up, Schumpeter's tax state is a contingent and context-dependent phenomenon,[14] connected to a free market that accommodates entrepreneurship and to representative government based on the historical notion of no taxation without representation. Its foundation is a desire of a coherent group of people to cooperate. As a social institution, the tax state is stable enough to endure temporary crises. Those should be distinguished from the inevitable structural crisis in which the capitalist and entrepreneurial social order will erode, culminating in a socialist system that is incompatible with the concept of the tax state.

III. Crises and the Tax State

Although the latter prediction is outdated, there may be much truth in Schumpeter's distinction between short-term macrolevel shocks and structural (social) crises. But whereas he formulates the effect of short-term crises negatively, namely, as not posing a systemic threat, evidence shows that they did shape the evolution of today's developed tax states. In particular, they tended to increase taxation and redistribution.

Many of those crises were wars. In fact, warfare was the main driving factor behind the development of European tax systems during the early modern era.[15] The lion's share of government budgets was devoted to the military and much of the remainder consisted of interest payments on war debts.[16] War fostered the growth of the tax state through prolonged 'ratchet effects', as increased wartime tax levels were retained in peacetime and became the 'new normal'.[17] It also incentivised governments to invest in

[12] Schumpeter (n 5) 116.

[13] Schumpeter (n 8) chs XII–XIII.

[14] As de Cogan puts it: 'a modern tax system is not the only way of funding a political community': D de Cogan, 'Public Law and Political Values in Tax Law' in L Parada (ed), *A Research Agenda for Tax Law* (Cheltenham, Edward Elgar, 2022).

[15] C Tilly, *Coercion, Capital, and European States, AD 990–1990* (Cambridge MA, Basil Blackwell, 1990).

[16] PT Hoffman, 'What Do States Do? Politics and Economic History' (2015) 75 *Journal of Economic History* 303.

[17] E Ames and RT Rapp, 'The Birth and Death of Taxes: A Hypothesis' (1977) 37 *Journal of Economic History* 161; E Kiser and A Linton, 'Determinants of the Growth of the State: War and Taxation in Early Modern France and England' (2001) 80 *Social Forces* 411.

legal and fiscal capacity, which, in turn, positively affected future fiscal innovations in both peacetime and wartime.[18]

Admittedly, bellicist theories are insufficient to explain the growth of the tax state in the nineteenth and early twentieth centuries.[19] Consistent with Schumpeter's view of taxation as the central element of the capitalist state, much of that growth can be attributed to the economic development initiated by the industrial revolution, which increased taxable surpluses and stimulated the demand for growth-enhancing public goods.[20] The emergence of a cash and exchange economy fostered the transition from taxes on 'observable facts' to accountants' taxes, which were easier to administer and collect.[21] New transportation and communication technologies enhanced monitoring capacity and facilitated the centralisation and bureaucratisation of tax administrations. Centralised systems largely replaced the patrimonial tax administrations of landed elites, which had been weakened or swept away in democratic revolutions.[22] Relatedly, democratisation paved the way for higher revenues by improving the legitimacy of the state, increasing the credibility of the executive's commitments and fostering 'quasi-voluntary compliance' of taxpayers.[23] Suffrage was slowly extended and political demand for higher taxation and redistribution grew.[24] Even before universal suffrage was adopted, evolving elite views on tax policy-making induced many governments to implement or increase income and profit taxes for equity and efficiency reasons.[25]

But these nineteenth-century developments appear to have amplified rather than negated the effects of warfare, or crises in general, on the size of the twentieth-century tax state.[26] The extreme costs of World War I forced governments to exploit the revenue-raising potential of the new income and profit taxes.[27] These taxes not only turned into

[18] Kiser and Linton (n 17); T Besley and T Persson, 'The Origins of State Capacity: Property Rights, Taxation, and Politics' (2009) 99 *American Economic Review* 1218; M Dincecco and M Prado, 'Warfare, fiscal capacity, and performance' (2012) 17 *Journal of Economic Growth* 171.

[19] See Martin, Mehrotra and Prasad (n 2); PF Andersson, 'Political institutions and taxation, 1800–1945' in L Hakelberg and L Seelkopf (eds), *Handbook on the Politics of Taxation* (Cheltenham, Edward Elgar, 2021).

[20] HH Hinrichs, *A General Theory of Tax Structure Change during Economic Development* (Cambridge MA, Law School of Harvard University, 1966); P Beramendi, M Dincecco and M Rogers, 'Intra-Elite Competition and Long-Run Fiscal Development' (2018) 81 *Journal of Politics* 49.

[21] TS Aidt and PS Jensen, 'The taxman tools up: An event history study of the introduction of the personal income tax' (2009) 93 *Journal of Public Economics* 160. See also Martin, Mehrotra and Prasad (n 2) for alternative accounts of this development.

[22] E Kiser and SM Karceski, 'Political Economy of Taxation' (2017) 20 *Annual Review of Political Science* 75.

[23] M Levi, *Of Rule and Revenue* (Berkeley, University of California Press, 1988); M Dincecco, 'Fiscal Centralization, Limited Government, and Public Revenues in Europe, 1650–1913' (2009) 69 *Journal of Economic History* 48; D North and BR Weingast, 'Constitutions and Commitment: The Evolution of Institutions Governing Public Choice in Seventeenth-Century England' (1989) 49 *Journal of Economic History* 803.

[24] The underlying causal relation is debated: see L Seelkopf et al, 'The rise of modern taxation: A new comprehensive dataset of tax introductions worldwide' (2019) 16 *Review of International Organizations* 239.

[25] Regarding equity, those taxes better reflected people's 'ability to pay' than the existing motley collection of regressive taxes on goods and services: S Steinmo, 'The evolution of policy ideas: tax policy in the 20th century' (2003) 5 *British Journal of Politics and International Relations* 206. As to efficiency, it is plausible that emerging industrial elites realised that income tax revenues could be directed towards public goods that benefitted their industries: Beramendi, Dincecco and Rogers (n 20).

[26] This interaction partly explains why the war–taxation relationship is weaker in modern developing countries: P Emmenegger and A Walter, 'War and taxation: the father of all things or rather an obsession?' in Hakelberg and Seelkopf (n 19).

[27] Steinmo (n 25).

major components of governments' revenue mixes, they also proved useful tools to capture excess profits that individuals and corporations made as a result of the war.[28] As in the pre-modern era, the war had a significant ratchet effect: while top rates were reduced after 1918, they did not return to pre-war levels.[29] The story was repeated during World War II. Besides increasing top rates, governments substantially lowered income tax thresholds. They converted a 'class tax' that had affected only a small number of wealthy taxpayers into to a 'mass tax' that was levied on nearly every income.[30] Average government size increased to an unprecedented level.[31] In many countries, high top rates were sustained well into the following decades.[32]

While financial necessity and institution-building explain much of the early modern relation between war and taxes, the underlying dynamics in the modern tax state are more complex. Political participation in the pre-modern and early modern eras was limited to the upper classes, and medieval princes and peasants would not even have comprehended the idea that they both belonged to the same society.[33] The modern nation state, however, is defined in terms of 'the people', who govern themselves democratically, speak the same language and are exposed to a common culture.[34]

In this context, it is not surprising that severe crises forge a strong national identity. A 'we're in this together' mentality during wartime is likely to increase people's willingness to comply voluntarily with tax obligations, hence allowing the government to set high rates at a relatively low social cost.[35] The political consensus about high tax and redistribution levels in the mid-twentieth century has indeed been attributed to a sense of social cohesion that, plausibly, resulted from World War II.[36]

Relatedly, the democratic idea of treating citizens as equal members of a national community strengthens the role of reciprocity and desert in modern tax policy-making. Demand for high and progressive taxation appears to be positively related to citizens' perception that political and economic circumstances leading to a certain income or wealth distribution are undeserved. This applies particularly in times of mass warfare,

[28] Steinmo (n 25); Emmenegger and Walter (n 26); Tandon, ch 4.

[29] K Scheve and D Stasavage, *Taxing the Rich: A History of Fiscal Fairness in the United States and Europe* (Princeton, Princeton University Press 2016) 56.

[30] Steinmo (n 25); Walters, ch 3.

[31] Scheve and Stasavage (n 29) 91.

[32] ibid 56.

[33] W Kymlicka, *Contemporary Political Philosophy: An Introduction*, 2nd edn (Oxford, Oxford University Press, 2002) 262.

[34] W Kymlicka, 'Solidarity in diverse societies: beyond neoliberal multiculturalism and welfare chauvinism' (2015) 3 *Comparative Migration Studies* 1.

[35] N Feldman and J Slemrod, 'War and Taxation: When Does Patriotism Overcome the Free-Rider Impulse?' in Martin, Mehrotra and Prasad (n 2) *The New Fiscal Sociology*. Or, as noted by Schumpeter: 'In times of patriotic fervour, tax payments are consistent with extreme productive adaptation of strength which normally would make production cease altogether': Schumpeter (n 5) 112. Such a mentality may also reduce tolerance of tax avoidance: see Walters, ch 3.

[36] eg AT Peacock and J Wiseman, *The Growth of Public Expenditure in the United Kingdom* (Princeton NJ, Princeton University Press, 1961); R Putnam, *Bowling Alone* (New York, Simon & Schuster, 2000); S Berman, *The Primacy of Politics: Social Democracy and the Making of Europe's Twentieth Century* (Cambridge, Cambridge University Press, 2006); P Collier, *The Future of Capitalism: Facing the New Anxieties* (London, Allen Lane, 2018). Additionally, the narrative that 'our way of life' was under threat during the Cold War may have fostered this sense of cohesion: T Besley, 'Is cohesive capitalism under threat?' (2021) 37 *Oxford Review of Economic Policy* 720.

because wealthier citizens are more likely to escape conscription or to make business profits out of the hostilities.[37] It has been shown that the twentieth-century increases in both income tax progressivity and inheritance tax rates were indeed related to mass mobilisation for the two World Wars, more than to the extension of suffrage or the emergence of left-wing parties.[38]

Similar fairness arguments shape the relation between non-war crises and taxation. Banking crises have been important driving factors of income tax introductions since the nineteenth century.[39] For instance, the introduction of the US income tax in the 1890s was a direct result of public aversion against rising inequality after the 1893 financial crisis.[40] Economic hardship increases the demand for tax progressivity as well. The tax policy of Roosevelt's New Deal was a clear example; it was largely based on fairness considerations in response to the inequities caused by the Great Depression.[41] According to Schumpeter in his *Lowell Lectures* (1941), the tax increases in the 1930s reflected a 'moral disapproval of high incomes, of capitalist profit making'.[42] The underlying mechanisms of tax increases during financial crises seem to resemble the arguments for taxing the rich in wartime: people will demand compensatory taxation when they believe that the rich caused the crisis or obtained financial benefits from it.[43] This applied particularly during the 2008 financial crisis: the rich were perceived as beneficiaries of the poorly regulated financial markets, while society bore the costs of bank bail-outs; many governments reacted by (moderately) increasing top personal income tax rates.[44]

The remaining pertinent question is how a deadly pandemic affects the tax state. The historical evidence from the modern era is scarce. Due to timing, it would be difficult to distinguish any fiscal policy responses to the 1918 'Spanish' flu from the tax increases related to World War I. However, it is telling that the 1918 pandemic, which killed 2.1 per cent of the world population and led to a 6 per cent GDP loss,[45] was largely ignored by economists.[46] This might reflect people's acquaintance with deadly diseases, or a wanting propensity of the tax state to alleviate social problems caused by macrolevel shocks. In any case, this lack of a fiscal response stands in stark contrast with the stimulus and support packages that governments implemented during the COVID-19

[37] Scheve and Stasavage (n 29).

[38] K Scheve and D Stasavage, 'The Conscription of Wealth: Mass Warfare and the Demand for Progressive Taxation' (2010) 64 *International Organization* 529; 'Democracy, War, and Wealth: Lessons from Two Centuries of Inheritance Taxation' (2012) 106 *American Political Science Review* 81.

[39] J Limberg, 'Banking crises and the modern tax state' (2020) *Socio-Economic Review*.

[40] Technically, it was a re-introduction: illustratively in the light of the present argument, an income tax had previously been in place during the Civil War in the 1860s: ibid.

[41] JJ Thorndike, '"The Unfair Advantage of the Few": The New Deal Origins of "Soak the Rich" Taxation' in Martin, Mehrotra and Prasad (n 2) *The New Fiscal Sociology*.

[42] Schumpeter, 'An Economic Interpretation of Our Time: The Lowell Lectures' in Swedberg (n 5) 366.

[43] Limberg, 'What's fair? Preferences for tax progressivity in the wake of the financial crisis' (2020) 40 *Journal of Public Policy* 171.

[44] Limberg, '"Tax the rich"? The financial crisis, fiscal fairness, and progressive income taxation' (2019) 11 *European Political Science Review* 319; Limberg (n 39).

[45] RJ Barro, JF Ursúa and J Weng, 'Macroeconomics of the Great Influenza Pandemic, 1918–1920' (2022) 76 *Research in Economics* 21.

[46] M Boianovsky and G Erreygers, 'How Economists Ignored the Spanish Flu Pandemic in 1918–1920' (2021) 14 *Erasmus Journal for Philosophy and Economics* 89.

pandemic, which illustrated our demand for tax states that, as Schumpeter would say, penetrate 'deep into the flesh of the private economy'.[47] Besides serving macroeconomic goals, they functioned as insurance schemes that transferred risks and economic losses from the private to the public sector, and they acted as additional instruments of redistribution.[48] As after previous crises, a 'ratchet effect' would occur when they evolve into permanent budget instruments adapted for non-crisis circumstances.[49] For instance, it has been suggested that the EU's support packages provide a window of opportunity for introducing new fiscal competences at the supranational level.[50] Nevertheless, it is notable that state responses to the COVID-19 pandemic, at the time of writing, seem to have been largely debt-financed, and that income tax increases are still small in number and size compared with previous crises.[51] It is not our aim to disentangle the multitude of possible causes, such as Keynesian economic thinking, the recentness of the tax increases following the 2008 financial crisis, the lack of reasons to frame the rich as beneficiaries or culprits, or downward competitive pressure on tax rates. Instead, we will pay attention to one recurring factor in the relation between previous crises and the tax state, namely the social ties between citizens of democratic communities.

IV. Globalisation and the Tax State

It is clear that social ties have loosened as a result of globalisation, at least in some respects. This relates to much more than the salient issues of tax avoidance and evasion, which existed long before the onset of globalisation in the late twentieth century.[52] The key issue here is that globalisation, besides facilitating the avoidance and evasion of national tax liabilities, makes it less evident for individuals or corporations that they owe tax to a specific state or national community in the first place.

This is exemplified first by individuals being increasingly mobile across borders without becoming full members of a community in their new places of residence. Many low-skilled migrant workers perform fungible labour in host jurisdictions where they might pay taxes, but struggle to access welfare benefits or voting rights.[53] On the

[47] Schumpeter (n 5) 111. Through a Foucauldian lens, it seems that we have passed the 'threshold of biological modernity', at which 'the biological processes characterizing the life of human beings as a species [become] a crucial issue for political decision-making': Garbarino, ch 9.

[48] Lind, ch 17.

[49] See text to nn 17 and 29.

[50] Garbarino, ch 9; Grisostolo and Scarcella, ch 10; Hernández González-Barreda, ch 7; Scuderi, Rizzo and Loucaidou, ch 13.

[51] OECD, *Revenue Statistics 2021: The Initial Impact of COVID-19 on OECD Tax Revenues* (Paris, OECD Publishing, 2021); 'Tax and fiscal policies after the COVID-19 crisis' (14 October 2021), www.oecd.org/coronavirus/policy-responses/tax-and-fiscal-policies-after-the-covid-19-crisis-5a8f24c3/.

[52] Offshore tax havens and Swiss banking burgeoned during the high-trust, high-tax post-war decades: V Ogle, 'Archipelago Capitalism: Tax Havens, Offshore Money, and the State, 1950s–1970s' (2017) 122 *American Historical Review* 1431.

[53] Y Lind, 'A Critical Analysis of How Formal and Informal Citizenships Influence Justice between Mobile Taxpayers' in D de Cogan and P Harris (eds), *Tax Justice and Tax Law: Understanding Unfairness in Tax Systems* (Oxford, Hart Publishing, 2020); H Ordower, 'Immigration, Emigration, Fungible Labour and the

high-skilled end of the labour market, the success of the modern knowledge economy depends on the clustering of people and firms with complementary specialisms; jurisdictions therefore bid for such residents by providing them with high-quality public services and attractive tax regimes. As cosmopolitan individuals take into account these options in their location decisions, taxation transforms from a collective instrument that promotes the common goals of a community into a low price paid by mobile citizens for the public services that they enjoy in a particular place.[54] This may not only limit the ability of tax states to raise their desired amounts of revenue, but also decrease electoral demand for progressive taxation. As noted by a recent strand of literature in identity economics, a possible underlying causal mechanism is the increasing salience of job-based identities and the rejection of place-based identities by cosmopolitan elites.[55] Because the existence of a shared identity is a strong determinant of people's reciprocal altruism,[56] the abandonment of a shared attachment to the nation by high-income individuals may be detrimental for the redistributive tax state.

A similar process is taking place – and more pronouncedly – at the level of corporations. The role of FDI in the world economy has continued its secular growth, and it is by now commonplace that the nature of globalisation has changed due to the emergence of e-commerce. As a result, economic life is now dominated by MNEs with limited ties to national 'tax states', that is, those MNEs have few observable 'common purposes' with specific states and the communities that these states represent.[57] This is not just a 'tax' problem – issues regarding ownership of data, access to, and quality of, information, control over AI, etc, are among the other important concerns. As to tax, we should distinguish between perception and empirical fact. Is seems fair to say that the public perception of MNE tax behaviour is negative: newspaper items reading that MNE X pays hardly any tax over its huge profits can hardly be considered 'news' anymore. Empirical fact is more difficult. One reason – which is being addressed with stricter reporting and disclosure obligations – is lack of data. The more fundamental reason is lack of benchmark.[58] When an MNE is compliant with all relevant national rules and is entitled to the treaty benefits that it has – and as a result, pays less tax – what exactly is it avoiding, and to what amount? Obviously, we feel that it should pay (more) tax at the place where it creates value. And yet, it breaches none of its legal obligations. When instead, we claim that it has a moral obligation, we only return to where we started:

Retreat from Progressive Taxation' in de Cogan and Harris, *Tax Justice*. Similar issues arise with respect to the allocation of financial aid in times of crisis: see Lind, ch 17.

[54] T Dagan, 'Re-imagining Tax Justice in a Globalised World' in de Cogan and Harris (n 53).

[55] P Collier, 'Diverging identities: a model of class formation' (2020) 72 *Oxford Economic Papers* 567.

[56] D Rueda, 'Food Comes First, Then Morals: Redistribution Preferences, Parochial Altruism, and Immigration in Western Europe' (2017) 80 *Journal of Politics* 225.

[57] Illustratively, their reputation among the public appears to have no effect on their corporate tax behaviour: L Baudot et al, 'Is Corporate Tax Aggressiveness a Reputation Threat? Corporate Accountability, Corporate Social Responsibility, and Corporate Tax Behavior' (2020) 163 *Journal of Business Ethics* 197.

[58] The economic literature tends to solve the benchmark problem by equating avoidance with reduction of tax burden – an approach that is clearly too broad to tax lawyers. See S Beer, R de Mooij and L Liu, 'International Corporate Tax Avoidance: A Review of the Channels, Magnitudes, and Blind Spots' (2020) 34 *Journal of Economic Surveys* 660; A Cobham and P Janský, *Estimating Illicit Financial Flows: A Critical Guide to the Data, Methodologies, and Findings* (Oxford, Oxford University Press, 2020).

the modern MNE does not necessarily feel much moral obligation to any particular jurisdiction – it has become a 'global enterprise'.[59]

Evidently, Schumpeter did not (and could not) identify the potential effects of economic globalisation and the emergence of huge MNEs. Perhaps, he would have applauded the role of modern MNEs in innovation (AI, settling on Mars, etc), rather than joining the 'intellectuals' in their criticism of increasing tax avoidance. But over the last decades, the emergence of a 'global' tax base not tied to any specific state has been recognised in the literature as a challenge to the Schumpeterian tax state.[60] The common theme is: if national states lose (some of) their grip on tax bases, how do we have to transform the tax state? Multilateral tax policy coordination is by now generally regarded as a logical adaptation. In the field of MNE corporate taxation, much has happened[61] – especially when compared to the taxation of private wealth (personal income, inheritance and estate taxes) where no international action is taking place yet.

V. The Tax State: Effectiveness and Redistribution

It has been argued that in a world characterised by increasing base mobility and competitive tax rate setting, national governments face a 'tragic choice … between joining the game of global competition … while renouncing their sovereign power to unilaterally set tax and expenditure policies, on the one hand, and barricading their borders so as to maintain their sovereign decision-making powers, yet encountering costs in terms of economic efficiency and in terms of their residents' freedom, on the other'.[62] The question is how to broaden the options. Considering that the 'barricading' alternative is utterly unattractive, the core issue that remains is the loss of freedom to follow national preferences in the level and distributive effect of taxation.

In the remainder of this section, we aim to connect this issue with the aforementioned themes, using Schumpeter's concept of the tax state as an analytical tool. We illustrate our argument using a two-dimensional vector space. One vector denotes the existence and effectiveness of a tax state in a Schumpeterian sense, that is, the link between state and market, run by a government based on political competition, as the organisation that matches free-market capitalism and that addresses the common needs of a defined community. By definition, this tax state rests on the pretence (whether or not fully realistic) that it can set its own tax policy. That is to say, it can make choices

[59] S Hebous, 'Global Firms, National Corporate Taxes: An Evolution of Incompatibility' in R de Mooij, A Klemm and V Perry (eds), *Corporate Income Taxes under Pressure: Why Reform Is Needed and How It Could Be Designed* (Washington DC, IMF, 2021).

[60] eg R Paris, 'The Globalization of Taxation? Electronic Commerce and the Transformation of the State' (2003) 47 *International Studies Quarterly* 153; P Genschel, 'Globalisation and the transformation of the tax state' (2005) 13 *European Review* 53; A Cameron, 'Crisis? What crisis? Displacing the spatial imaginary of the fiscal state' (2008) 39 *Geoforum* 1145; Mumford (n 2).

[61] See de Mooij, Klemm and Perry (n 59).

[62] T Dagan, 'The tragic choices of tax policy in a globalized economy' in Y Brauner and M Stewart (eds), *Tax, Law and Development* (Cheltenham, Edward Elgar, 2013) 67.

concerning overall tax burden and distribution of that burden as it wishes; moreover, it is not in any important sense restricted in its choice of tax bases and rates. The second vector is the size of this tax state, that is, how deep it penetrates into the flesh of the private economy, and, strongly related to this, how much income it redistributes. We would expect both effectiveness and size/redistribution to increase with the strength of social ties that connect taxpayers. When people share a sense of 'belonging' they know where to pay tax (effectiveness) and they are prepared to engage in collective action (size/redistribution).[63]

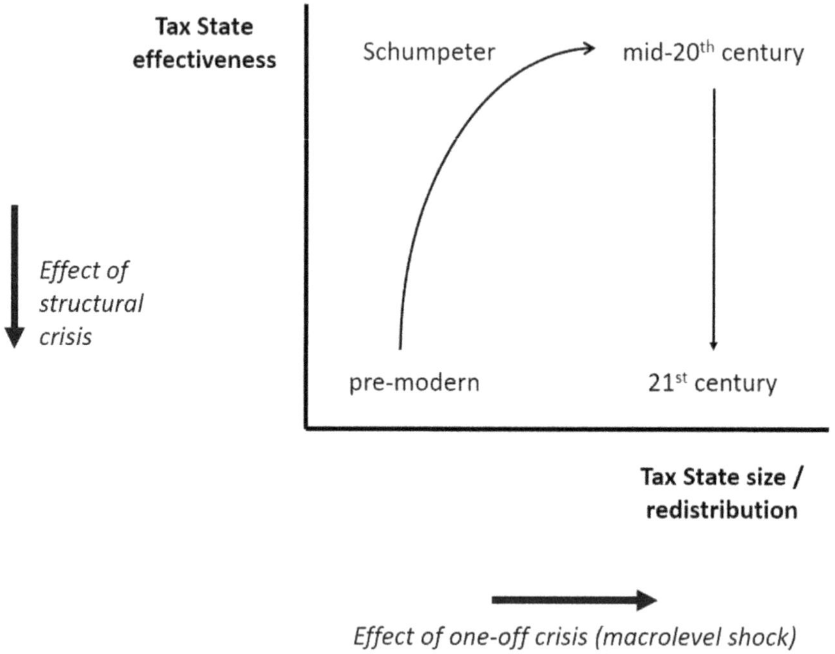

Placing the two respective vectors along a y- and an x-axis, as illustrated in Figure 1, we get a linear space with four quadrants. In the lower left quadrant, denoting little to no existing tax state, we should locate the administrations of the medieval and pre-modern eras. By contrast, the effective, large and redistributive tax states of most western democracies during the decades after World War II are situated in the upper right quadrant. The path they took to reach that point was not a straight line; instead, they followed a curve through the upper left quadrant, which denotes the effective but small Schumpeterian tax state of 1918.

Prima facie, the reason is quite intuitive: a tax state must be effective before it can effectively redistribute. On a deeper sociological level, we learn from the foregoing that

[63] A somewhat similar view is taken by T Besley, 'State Capacity, Reciprocity, and the Social Contract' (2020) 44 *Econometrica* 1307, who argues that 'a strong civic culture' – comparable to our notion of social ties – 'manifests itself as high tax revenues' – similar to our second vector – 'sustained by high levels of voluntary tax compliance' – which is an aspect of our first vector.

the curve through our vector space is shaped by social ties. At the pre-modern starting point of the curve, these ties were formalised by the creation of a public sphere and the centralisation and monopolisation of the means for coercion. In the nineteenth century, they were democratised and bureaucratised, and the tax state started to meet its Schumpeterian definition: a clearly recognisable public sphere now financed the common purposes that 'individual autonomies [were] unwilling or unable to take over',[64] and it finally penetrated 'so deeply into the consciousness of the people … that it was really able to become something impersonal, a machine manner only by serving, not by dominating spirits'.[65] Although warfare did contribute to the development of the Schumpeterian tax state, it was only in this modern democratic context that crises, through identity formation and fairness norms, induced large-scale income redistribution and thus pushed the tax state into the upper right quadrant.

As explained, these crises were one-off macrolevel shocks, in particular wars and economic downturns. Schumpeter would distinguish them from more systemic crises that involve the disintegration of societal structures. In our vector space, the latter would move the tax state downwards, not rightwards. But Schumpeter argued that the most probable cause of a downward shift was, in fact, a rightward shift: the growth of the tax state would lead to its collapse, as the state/market distinction would disappear and the entrepreneurial social structure behind capitalist democracy would erode. In our vector space, this would visually result in a sort of Laffer curve (and perhaps there is a loose resemblance in meaning, as well). Schumpeter's prediction was wrong: the enfranchisement that coincided with the maturing of developed tax states neither lead to serious bourgeois hostility to the free market, nor to class struggle.[66] Illustratively, whenever left-wing political forces questioned the very viability of capitalism during the post-war decades, they failed to win electoral support.[67] Instead, the biggest successes of welfare state expansion were achieved by 'people's parties' that regarded the welfare state as a community project of which all co-nationals were members.[68] Public sectors continued to expand through the 1970s and capitalist tax states thrived in the form of mixed economies, thus persisting in the upper right quadrant of our vector space.

However, it appears that tax states have completed a similar curve for a different reason. Since the late twentieth century, they fail to meet several aspects of their Schumpeterian definition. With MNEs and wealthy individuals being perceived to avoid large amounts of taxes,[69] and burdens increasingly falling on immobile taxpayers,[70]

[64] Schumpeter (n 5) 110.

[65] Schumpeter (n 5) 111.

[66] But see F Caeldries, 'On the Sustainability of the Capitalist Order: Schumpeter's *Capitalism, Socialism and Democracy* Revisited' (1993) 22 *Journal of Socio-Economics* 163.

[67] Berman (n 36).

[68] ibid; Kymlicka (n 34).

[69] Ignoring the legal debates on the meaning of the word 'avoidance', we refer to the public feeling (whatever its base in facts and figures) that MNEs and wealthy individuals do not take the share in the tax burden that they should. Especially relevant is the work of John Prebble, who relates the concept of avoidance to the nature of income taxation.

[70] While revenue-to-GDP ratios have been fairly stable through the last decades, personal and corporate tax rates have declined and countries rely increasingly on regressive revenue sources such as payroll and consumption taxes: S Ganghof, *The Politics of Income Taxation* (Colchester, ECPR Press, 2006).

states can no longer fully address the collective needs of their communities or treat community members as equal democratic participants.[71] Tax states have therefore lost part of their sovereignty in setting their own policies, substantively due to increasing policy spill-overs, and formally because of a growing body of legal and semi-legal international commitments aimed at reducing those spill-overs.[72] We may safely assume that the size of policy spill-overs will continue to grow, as a corollary of further globalisation. And as many mobile taxpayers have lost their connection to particular countries, one may doubt whether the tax state still encompasses a defined community at all. As discussed, the latter issue appears to be a structural crisis of eroding social ties, going beyond tax avoidance and evasion. It also goes beyond class struggle or Schumpeter's prediction that economic development and enfranchisement would erode the structure of the capitalist society. Mobile taxpayers are not simply relocating to jurisdictions with social contracts that better fit their preferences, as a reaction to the excessive redistributive demands of their fully enfranchised co-nationals;[73] instead, they are disconnecting from the very concept of a tax state.

The large but weakened twenty-first-century tax states are, in sum, moving into the lower right quadrant of our vector space. Subsequently, in line with earlier crises, the COVID-19 pandemic and the recent geopolitical turmoil have pushed them further rightwards by necessitating a substantial increase in state expenses. Tragically, this has left them with large debt burdens that will have to be repaid sometime.[74] Although we are at a different point in our vector space and experience a different crisis than in 1918, a striking similarity is the combination of a macrolevel shock, an increased debt burden and the symptoms of a structural crisis. Whether or not we should label that as a 'crisis of the tax state' is a semantical issue. The real issue is whether and how we can steer our tax states safely into either of the upper quadrants, that is, the situation that states can pursue their own priorities whether these include heavy or low taxes, extensive or limited redistribution. We know what shifts the tax state rightwards (a macrolevel shock in a context of strong social ties) and downwards (a structural crisis of eroding social ties), but what shifts it upwards?

The finalisation of the Schumpeterian tax state during the late nineteenth century might give us the key to the answer, which, we argue, is strongly connected to the choice of tax instruments. This period was characterised by the rapid introduction of 'modern' taxes in developed economies: personal and corporate income taxes and social security contributions.[75] Given their low rates and the small size of the state, it is debatable what these taxes could do in reducing income inequality. The major difference between the taxes of the early nineteenth century and those of the post-World War II

[71] T Dagan, 'Re-imagining Tax Justice'. In other words: there is 'a fiscal, sociological disconnect between what citizens expect from tax states … and what tax states currently are capable of delivering': Mumford (n 2) 143.

[72] For an application of Rawlsian 'state sovereignty' thinking in the field of international tax, see P Hongler, *Justice in International Tax Law* (Amsterdam, IBFD, 2019). See also A Christians, 'Sovereignty, Taxation and Social Contract' (2009) 18 *Minnesota Journal of International Law* 99; 'BEPS and the New International Tax Order' (2016) 6 *Brigham Young University Law Review* 1603.

[73] We thank an anonymous reviewer for raising this point.

[74] We ignore the Modern Monetary Theory debate, ie, we assume that governments need tax revenues to keep them moving. That is not to say that a balanced budget is an imperative: see Mumford (n 2).

[75] Seelkopf et al (n 24).

welfare state is how they were levied. Traditional taxes on 'observable facts' like windows and horses, distillery kettles and windmills required a daily battle (sometimes literally) in the streets and marketplaces. New taxes on wages, profits and consumption were accountants' taxes.[76] It might well be argued that the liberal bourgeoisie of the late nineteenth century welcomed the reduction of conflictual forms of taxation but hardly anticipated that the new taxes would reduce opposition to much higher levels of taxation. Schumpeter seems to recognise the point in his Essays: the income tax fitted in with the bourgeois limited state of the later nineteenth century.[77] He believed that it was already outdated in the twentieth century as state interference with economic life had grown – and an expenditure tax would be preferable.[78]

There is no reason to repeat the debate on income taxation in the later twentieth century here: whether income provides a reasonable measure of ability-to-pay, whether tax expenditures infringe upon fair burden distribution, how progressive the income tax should be, and indeed, whether a personal consumption tax would be preferable. The relevant issue is how income taxation is affected by globalising tax bases. The nineteenth-century battles in the streets have been replaced by bureaucratic battles of tax administrations with accountants and tax lawyers worldwide. Those battles are fuelled not just by differences in tax rates, but also by the fact that 'income' and 'profits' are abstract concepts compared to, for instance, 'chimney' and 'steam engine', resulting in many small differences in definitions between countries.

The question then is, whether income taxation is the suitable framework to discuss the reduction of tax policy spill-overs through multilateral coordination. In the Schumpeterian long-run view, are we trying to save twentieth-century tax rules from twenty-first-century challenges? And would that help, or do we need to look for new tax bases? There is now a developing tradition of trying to save income taxes by specifying the obligations they confer on multinational taxpayers. The OECD/IF Pillar 1 and 2 proposals offer a fine example. Conceptually, both Pillars offer interesting answers to globalisation and the emergence of 'global firms'. Pillar 1 is a clear departure from the arm's length principle, allocating part of MNE excess profits to the place where customers reside. On the plausible assumption that customers are less geographically mobile than corporate assets (like IP and shareholdings), the result would be that states increase their grip on the MNE tax base.[79] The Pillar 2 proposal, at the same time, tries to fix the system of cross-border corporate income taxation by introducing an effective minimum rate worldwide.[80] The conceptual advantage is that the debate on 'avoidance' and its legal form, 'abuse', is replaced by an effective tax test.

These are indeed potentially important innovations in the taxation of MNE income. For their effective implementation, however, both proposals rely on the meticulous construction of new flows of information exchange and data sharing between states.

[76] See text to n 21.
[77] See text to nn 20–22.
[78] Musgrave (n 5) 95–96 summarises Schumpeter's views.
[79] This is a quality that the Pillar 1 proposal may have in common with the (much more radical) proposal for a Destination-Based Cash Flow Tax.
[80] MP Devereux et al, 'The OECD Global Anti-Base Erosion ("GloBE") Proposal' (Oxford University Centre for Business Taxation, 2020).

Especially Pillar 2 seems to require sophisticated accountancy rules, which many states and their tax administrations may not be able to deal with.[81] The connected issue is how to find a balance between national tax preferences (bases, rates, revenues and distribution) and the increasing body of international tax obligations faced by states. We cannot draw a sharp line between a national tax system operated by a national tax administration, and a global tax system run by a global tax administration.[82] But we think it is a relevant line, and national states may not want to cross it.[83]

Both Pillars 1 and 2 follow from the BEPS project: a broader attempt to fix the international tax order (as far as MNE profits are concerned) undertaken by the international community since 2013. The results of that project have without doubt exceeded ex ante expectations. They show that OECD Member States, followed by a large number of other countries, feel commitment to 'repairing' international income taxation rather than 'replacing' it. It could hardly be different: any changes to the international tax order may be assumed to be piecemeal, never radical. But a feeling of 'crisis' remains. It is not uncommon for faltering institutions to be shored up by emergency measures – and perhaps that is what we are now witnessing in the field of MNE income taxation.

Again, relying on Schumpeter's long-run analysis of the social and economic context of taxation systems, the question whether new conditions require new taxes makes sense. We do not intend to argue that we should return to pre-income taxes on chimneys and horses. Instead, the appropriate shift in focus is the same one that policy-makers in the nineteenth century made when they were confronted with new technologies and social changes:[84] a shift from asking 'how can we save the taxes that we have had for so many years?' towards 'how can we do something smart with the new conditions that we face?' The attractiveness of the Schumpeterian approach is that it does not assume some permanent 'system' of tax, but rather draws our attention to the ways in which we can adapt to the changing conditions of markets and states. Among those changing conditions we could mention (with no attempt to be exhaustive):

- changes in how wealth is created: increasingly by innovation of services – which shows up, for instance, in the value of intangibles on MNE balance sheets;
- changes in how wealth is spent: consumption of digital services of course, but also travel, and living in a limited number of high-end agglomerations worldwide;
- a notable increase in wealth accumulation, whether in terms of MNE book values, land values or in numbers of billionaires worldwide.

We could then consider apparently unconnected topics like agglomeration effects, digital and financial services to see where new tax handles may be found. Such new tax bases should, we think, cover the ground increasingly being vacated by income taxes: the profitability of cross-border economic activities and the accumulation of wealth. They would necessarily be second-best in comparison to income taxation – that is,

[81] See generally Pushkareva, ch 12.

[82] Or a European tax administration, for that matter; see generally Hernández González-Barreda, ch 7.

[83] This is not to negate the relevance of the 'transnational context … which transcends the conceptual limitations of tax as defined and controlled solely by individual states', as stressed by Mumford (n 2) 193.

[84] See text to nn 21–22.

effective income taxation. Preferably, the relevant tax base definitions should be clearer than the concept of income, thereby reducing perceptions of avoidance and the need for anti-abuse doctrines and/or moral arguments. And preferably, such new taxes, while requiring coordination between countries, would be suited to be run by national tax administrations. We do not claim that such taxes would be able to fully replace income taxation.[85] Indeed, when we want to address private wealth accumulation, we would need a Piketty-style effort to tax private wealth independent of the place where its owner happens to reside at a specific moment in time.[86]

What we do argue is that income taxation can no longer be relied upon to do the job we used it for – not in a world with states pursuing different interests and preferences. We also argue that the Schumpeterian perspective shifts our attention from tax design considerations – that is, the optimisation of tax systems with respect to context-independent benchmarks – to dynamism and pragmatism. Tax design is important, as it focuses on minimisation of economic distortions, and on explanation of the rationale underlying tax bases. But it overlooks the centrality of taxes to state-building,[87] their effect on the evolution of the state, and their public-law character as 'the embodiment … of those principles that shape the right ordering of the state'.[88] Therefore, it may cause us to stick to obsolete ideals.

We may expect governments to be naturally inclined to search for new tax bases, even if paying lip service to obsolete ideals. A recent example – inspired by the 2008 financial crisis – is the development of bank taxes and financial transaction taxes.[89] Whatever their merits in regulating the financial industry, these taxes could also be considered instruments to tackle some of the financial benefits of globalisation. And on the assumption that across the board, personal wealth correlates with pollution, even environmental taxes could qualify.[90] Two other examples deserve brief attention. One is digital services taxes.[91] These have proliferated in recent years as states have attempted to lay their hands on some part of big tech profits. Under a Pillar 1 agreement, such taxes should be phased out.[92] Our question (and probably, the question of many governments

[85] See P Emerton and K James, 'The Justice of the Tax Base and the Case for Income Tax' in M Bhandari (ed), *Philosophical Foundations of Tax Law* (Oxford, Oxford University Press, 2017).

[86] See T Piketty, *Capital in the Twenty-First Century* (Cambridge MA, Harvard University Press, 2014), who argues that his capital tax proposal, before being implemented globally, might serve as a reference point for national states. Mumford (n 2) 127 suggests that this reference point might function as a 'tax principle' in a transnational tax state.

[87] See D de Cogan, *Tax Law, State-Building and the Constitution* (Oxford, Hart Publishing, 2020), who also takes Schumpeter's essay as a starting point.

[88] J Snape, *The political economy of the corporation tax: Theory, values and law reform* (Oxford, Hart Publishing, 2011) 11.

[89] See Tandon, ch 4. A financial transaction tax has also been proposed by the EU as a new revenue source: Grisostolo and Scarcella, ch 10.

[90] Of course, their main objective is to address the climate crisis, which, through a Schumpeterian lens, is another macrolevel shock that may shape the development of tax states, provided that those do not collapse as a result of a social crisis. We expect that green taxes are less sensitive than income taxes to the erosion of social ties within tax states. Addressing the mobility of polluters through international tax coordination is relatively easy, because pollution is better observable than income. For an analysis of EU coordination of environmental taxes, see Geringer, ch 14; Scuderi, Rizzo and Loucaidou, ch 13.

[91] See Grisostolo and Scarcella, ch 10.

[92] At least, the Communiqué of the G7 meeting in London, 5 June 2021, speaks of 'the removal of all Digital Services Taxes, and other relevant similar measures, on all companies'.

who now operate such a tax) is whether this is a clever idea at all. From the tax state's perspective, a DST collected over observable local turnover is more attractive than a tax base allocated by some multilateral formula that still has to prove its viability. The least that could be done is to maintain those DSTs and make them creditable against the P1 market state tax.

The other example is an agglomeration tax. It is not a new idea that agglomeration rents can and should be taxed. The nineteenth-century economist Henry George explains that they accrue as land value appreciations, arising not from the land owner's labour, but from others moving into the city.[93] Schumpeter notes that 'since the motive for the utilization of a piece of land lies in the return to labour and capital which it can yield and which remains even when the ground rent is taxed away, [a land tax] never reflects back on the productive process'.[94] There are no signs of agglomerations disappearing in our digital age; on the contrary, the world is urbanising. As evidence suggests that corporate profits can be taxed at higher rates in economically attractive areas, even under competitive pressure, it seems attainable a fortiori to implement land value taxes, which do not depend on individual income or profits.[95]

As argued elsewhere in this volume, short-term crises could perhaps provide windows of opportunity for the implementation of those new taxes. The housing and inflation crisis could increase political support for land (or perhaps, asset) taxes,[96] the climate crisis now finally paves the way for green taxation,[97] and a plausible consequence of the COVID-19 crisis might be an increased attention for quick personal wealth creation, for example in pharmaceuticals. Although Schumpeter would be the last to argue that history repeats itself, short-term crises might again drive the adaption, evolution and expansion of the tax state.

VI. Conclusion

The lasting heritage of Schumpeter's *Crisis of the Tax State* is that it draws our attention to the meaning of long-term trends for the way we tax. None of our taxes are written in stone; all reflect the social and economic conditions of a specific era.[98] From this

[93] H George, *Progress and poverty: An Inquiry into the Cause of Industrial Depressions and of Increase of Want with Increase of Wealth; The Remedy* (first published 1879, Cambridge, Cambridge University Press, 2011).

[94] Schumpeter (n 5) 114.

[95] H Garretsen and J Peeters, 'Capital Mobility, Agglomeration and Corporate Tax Rates: Is the Race to the Bottom for Real?' (2007) 53 *CESifo Economic Studies* 263; M Brülhart, M Jametti and K Schmidheiny, 'Do Agglomeration Economies Reduce the Sensitivity of Firm Location to Tax Differentials?' (2012) 122 *The Economic Journal* 1069. However, in today's urban populations, significant shares of agglomeration rents are captured by high-skilled workers with low housing demands, rather than by landowners: P Collier and AJ Venables, 'Who gets the urban surplus?' (2018) 18 *Journal of Economic Geography* 523. It remains a challenge to tax those workers using other bases than income.

[96] See generally Brassey, ch 15, who discusses the current asset price boom in the context of intergenerational fairness.

[97] See n 90.

[98] See J Snape, 'The "Sinews of the State": Historical Justifications for Taxes and Tax Law' in Bhandari (n 85).

perspective, we note that the most evident problem of income taxation is, that it results in suspicions of 'international tax avoidance' that are, in the end, untestable. Many legal rules may create moral leeway that is sizeable and perhaps unmanageable in the cross-border context. The challenge is to develop forms of taxation that, using well-defined legal obligations, address those who benefit from the new, globalised social order. We argue that this perspective helps to make sense of what governments are now doing (and perhaps, failing to do) in their tax policies.

3

Lessons of Three World Wars

RICHARD WALTERS

Abstract

The Three World Wars, that is the Napoleonic Wars and the Two World Wars of the Twentieth Century provide good examples of a global shock to the economy and finances of a nation state. The paper shows how the UK controlled the economy and finances in these extreme circumstances and initiated lasting changes to the tax system. Some of the extravagant costs of war were postponed and spread over subsequent years. Whilst relieving immediate economic distress, this caused tensions and, in some cases, civil unrest in the years after the wars ended. The chapter derives lessons which are applied to the present UK economy and tax system in the light of the pandemic.

I. Introduction

The three world wars of the title are the two World Wars of the last century and the Napoleonic Wars which lasted intermittently from 1793 to 1815, which were referred to by Victorians as the Great War.[1] These were generation defining events which brought innovation to the financing of the state in a time of stress. There were also some missteps. These events provide key moments in the history of public finance in the UK as they shone some light on the then current fiscal practices and provoked innovation in the way the government of the time raised money for the war effort. Essentially, the governments had to raise funds in any way they could, but principally through borrowing and taxation. In dealing with these crises, governments also wrestled with questions of control over the national economy, allied to issues of freedom for citizens. The extreme circumstances of these crises left a shadow over the years succeeding these crises.

There are lessons for us today. In 2020 the economic life of the country had to slow almost to a standstill for a prolonged period and substantial subsidies had to be provided by the state for everyday living. This has led to an unprecedented peacetime deficit in

[1] S Dowell, *A History of Taxation and Taxes in England From the Earliest Times to the Present Day, Vol. II* (London, Longmans Green and Co, 1884) 252.

the public finances which is estimated by the Office of Budgetary Responsibility as being £270 bn or 15.2 per cent of GDP.[2] This is an exogenous shock not dissimilar to that of the two World Wars of the Twentieth Century.[3] In what follows, a sketch is given of the effects of these World Wars, followed by a summary of some of the conclusions which may be drawn. Using this perspective, the UK tax system is then examined in the light of these conclusions.

II. The Napoleonic Wars 1793–1815

England and France were rivals and at war with one another for much of the eighteenth century; this rivalry reached a climax in the wars which followed the French Revolution in 1789. The conflict lasted a generation. The general strategy of the UK was to subsidise its continental allies by grants and loans whilst maintaining a strict naval blockade. This required a steady stream of income. The Prime Minister and Chancellor of the Exchequer, William Pitt, initially financed the conflict through borrowing. A crisis was reached in 1797 as the gold reserves in the Bank of England ran low, and Britain came off the gold standard.

The traditional sources of British revenue were from various excise and stamp duties, which were constrained by the reduction of trade resulting from the hostilities. This brought in a new income tax, first promulgated by the Prime Minister Pitt in 1798. This new tax proved unpopular largely due to the intrusive administration which required disclosure of income. It was not as successful as had been hoped and was dropped during the cessation of war following the Peace of Amiens in 1802–3. This truce faltered and hostilities were renewed again in 1803, as was the income tax which was re-introduced by Henry Addington, who had replaced Pitt as Prime Minister and Chancellor. The new and improved income tax, tweaked to distinguish various types of income and providing more protection for the privacy of taxpayers with deduction at source, proved more palatable and a model for the tax going forward, though there were still protests. The tax tended to impact more on landowners than on commercial businesses of the nascent middle class. Addington's income tax was nonetheless a success and the proceeds exceeded expectations. Even so, income tax rates were modest at 10 per cent and the tax only provided (at most) some 20 per cent of the revenue needed by the government.

Where did the rest of the money come from? Apart from traditional imposts, the country continued to borrow on the money markets. It is perhaps symbolic that the government employed, among others, Nathan Rothschild, a nascent international financier, who set up a branch of his bank in the City of London in 1804 at New Court. He was able to raise funds successfully on long dated bonds. (It is perhaps ironic that Rothschild arranged loans from the continent for the British government, so that, in its turn, it could lend the proceeds to its continental allies.) The success of these operations

[2] Office of Budget Responsibility Website, 'Repairing the public finances: the pandemic versus the financial crisis', obr.uk/box/repairing-the-public-finances-the-pandemic-versus-the-financial-crisis/.

[3] Office of Budget Responsibility website, 'Long run drivers of UK government debt', obr.uk/box/long-run-drivers-of-uk-government-debt/.

allowed the Bank of England to pay off the cost of the war over a much longer period of time. Some of the burden was borne by inflation, which reduced the value of the interest that needed paying. The contrast with the financing by France of its war effort is instructive. The bankers, for whom the French Revolution was fresh in their memory, did not trust the Napoleonic regime. As a result, the French bonds had to be backed by gold and most of the burden of the war had to be borne by high rates of taxation. As Bordo and White, economic historians, conclude:

> Given its long record of fiscal probity, coupled with its open budgetary process in Parliament, Great Britain could continue to borrow a substantial fraction of its war expenditure at what were relatively low interest rates … Taxes would not have been greatly increased during the Napoleonic wars except that their duration imposed a debt burden much higher than the eighteenth century norm, requiring a rise in the tax rate to sustain the nation's credibility as a borrower.[4]

Addington's income tax was repealed in 1815 after the Battle of Waterloo effectively ended hostilities the previous year. The government had wanted the tax to continue, but it had been promulgated as a war tax, and there was strong demand from the Parliamentary electorate and the libertarians for its repeal. One lasting legend of this repeal was of Brougham, an MP and a future Lord Chancellor, presiding with delight over the burning of the files of the income tax commissioners in Palace Yard. His view and those of many others was that income tax was an iniquitous imposition and a gross invasion of privacy.[5] The destruction of the files guaranteed, to his mind, the freedom of Englishmen. Despite the destruction of the files and the tax, Addington's income tax remained as a model that was referred to, if not with affection, but as a potentially useful tool in the fiscal armoury.

The interest on the various loans had to be paid, however, and this remained a grievous burden on the exchequer for the next 20 years or so. As Briggs points out, 'in 1815 interest on the national debt accounted for more than half the total of government expenditure'.[6] In addition, the change from a war economy to a peacetime one produced dislocations and hardships, government expenditure declined causing deflation and there was an increase in unemployment due to the return of soldiers and the adoption of new technologies. Initially, the government of Lord Liverpool (1812–27) sought to balance the books by reducing public expenditure but eventually consumption taxes had to be raised, the burden of which fell on largely on consumers through indirect taxes. The general situation was not helped by the Corn Laws (initially enacted in 1802) which protected British agriculture by raising the price of corn. This led to starvation in years of poor harvests. Overall, this was the setting for general social unrest, reform and latterly, the background to the reintroduction in 1843 of the income tax, in the form enacted by Addington in 1804. Income tax remained controversial for the rest of the nineteenth century, with Whigs and Liberals seeing it as an imposition on liberty while property owners naturally wanted to free themselves from the tax. For the government it has provided a steady and reliable stream of income. The principles surrounding

[4] MD Bordo and EN White, 'A Tale of Two Currencies: British and French Finance During the Napoleonic Wars' (1991) 51 *The Journal of Economic History* 303.

[5] A Hope-Jones, *Income Tax in the Napoleonic Wars* (Cambridge, Cambridge University Press, 1939) 2.

[6] A Briggs, *Age of Improvement 1783–1867* (London, Longman, 1979) 170.

income tax were formed during the Napoleonic wars and continue in some ways to this day. There was an inevitable growth in bureaucracy with the rise of the Inland Revenue.

With two centuries of hindsight, it would seem that the government should have either borrowed less and taxed more and also continue to impose income taxation after 1815. Such a solution, however, was politically impossible and the post-1815 generation paid the price.

III. World War I 1914–18

The UK (and its Empire) declared war on the German and Austrian Empires, the Central Powers, on 3 August 1914. The five years before the declaration of war had contained a full measure of political strife with several constitutional crises occurring, not least over Irish independence and, separately, the role of the House of Lords. On the taxation front, there were disputes over increased taxation to pay for some primitive measures of social security, as well as increased defence expenditure. A new land tax had been introduced and also a super tax (or surtax), which brought in higher rates of tax for higher incomes. Nonetheless, tax rates look modest to modern eyes, with a standard rate of income tax of 5.8 per cent reduced to 3.8 per cent for earned incomes, plus surtax of 2.5 per cent for incomes above £3,000. There were also allowances for married men with children under the age of 16. At the end of the war in 1918, the tax-free allowance was reduced to £130, the standard rate of income tax was 30 per cent with a reduced rate of 11.5 per cent with surtax of 22.5 per cent for incomes over £10,000. The top rate for income tax was therefore 52.5 per cent.[7]

The outbreak of war was greeted as a respite from these other problems, especially that of Ireland. It was initially thought that the cost of the war would not be exorbitant as it would be short and that the tactics of the struggle against France in the previous century would, again suffice. It was supposed that the continental allies (France and Russia) would do much of the land fighting, whilst the Royal Navy imposed a blockade which strangled the Central Powers. This vision was optimistic and illusory, and the reality of modern industrial warfare quickly intruded, with its necessity for modern weaponry, much of which had to be purchased from the US. A mass British army was recruited for service in France, Italy and the Middle East. Conscription was not initially used and this made the government peculiarly susceptible to public opinion.

As the historians Michael Anson, Norma Cohen, Alastair Owens and Daniel Todman state:

> Between 1913/14 and 1918/19, government spending rose more than 12-fold to £2.37bn, almost entirely attributable to military expenditures … While tax revenue did quadruple over the same period, war debt was required to finance the remainder. As a result, UK government debt increased from around 25% of GDP to 125% in four short years, requiring bond issuance and debt build-up on a pace unlike anything seen before (or since) in peacetime.[8]

[7] M Daunton, *Just Taxes 1914–1979* (Cambridge, Cambridge University Press, 2002) 47.

[8] M Anson, N Cohen, A Owens and D Todman, 'Your country needs funds: The extraordinary story of Britain's early efforts to finance the First World War', bankunderground.co.uk/2017/08/08/your-country-needs-funds-the-extraordinary-story-of-britains-early-efforts-to-finance-the-first-world-war/.

The government indirectly allowed sterling to come off the gold standard by putting restrictions on the convertibility of bank notes. Despite the political rhetoric of the time, the Bank of England's first war bond in November 1914 was a failure.[9] The Bank had to intervene secretly to buy the unwanted bond – a kind of quantitative easing before its time – though unlike its more recent counterpart it did not keep interest rates low. Nonetheless, appearances were kept up. Care was taken and the next issue was fully subscribed. An offer had to be made to foreign (mostly US and Canadian) subscribers that the interest payable on the bond would not be subject to UK taxation and at what was an appropriately high interest rate, which Lloyd George recognised would cripple generations after the war. This was also the start of the FOTRA bond – a bond which was Free Of Tax to Residents Abroad. Section 47 of the Finance (No. 2) Act 1915 gave the Treasury power to issue these bonds for the duration of the war. (This power was extended in the Finance Acts of 1931 and 1940 – two other crisis points in British economic history – and still exists today.) It made these bonds more acceptable to the principal international markets – the US and Canada. This development was regarded with dismay by some in the city and government as it was thought of as a derogation of sovereignty over taxation matters and a signal that leadership in world finance had crossed the Atlantic. Difficulties in raising funds remained and, in 1917, the new Chancellor of the Exchequer (and future Prime Minister) Bonar Law had to use a good deal of persuasion, including the threat of nationalisation of banks, to get the City to back a new war bond at 5 per cent rather than their preferred rate of 6 per cent.[10]

On the whole, taxation was increased but it was not the extremely high taxation that was seen during World War II. Nonetheless, the better off suffered significantly higher tax than they had in the 20 years before the war and we began to hear the term 'tax avoidance' used for the first time. In 1915 one of the earliest transfer pricing provisions was enacted to prevent the avoidance of higher rate income taxes by overseas companies trading in the UK – Finance Act (No. 2) 1915, s 31(3). One of the drivers of tax policy in the late Victorian and Edwardian era was the teetotal leaseholder who had reasonable employment. Such a figure theoretically did not pay any tax, which was considered wrong as taxation was needed to ensure engagement with the state. This was cured by taxes on tea and sugar. This figure disappeared from view during the war as the tax base was broadened and many were burdened with income tax for the first time.[11]

Arms manufacturers were particular targets of public opinion as they were seen as profiting from the war. This led to an innovation in the excess profits duty (EPD), introduced in 1915. This latter tax was initially aimed at arms manufacturers but was later expanded to include all those who had done well out of the war. In so far as these things can be judged, it was popular and was used to head off a demand by the nascent Labour Party for a capital charge. Under the EPD, profits made during the war were compared to profits made before the war and the excess profits were subject to the special regime.

[9] D Kynaston. *The City of London Vol III; Illusions of Gold* (London, Chatto and Windus, 1999) 11–13. See also N Cohen, 'How Britain paid for war: bond holders in the Great War 1914–32', bankunderground.co.uk/2021/01/18/how-britain-paid-for-war-bond-holders-in-thegreat-war-1914-32. The contrary account given in J Grigg, *Lloyd George 1912–1916 From Peace to War* (York, Methuen, 1985) 190 appears wrong.

[10] Cohen (n 9).

[11] Daunton (n 7) ch 2.

It was initially levied at a rate of 50 per cent but this was increased to 80 per cent in 1917. The high rate of the tax led to a spectacular amount of litigation gathered together in Volume 12 of Tax Cases. In those cases there is often the amusing spectacle of the Revenue seeking to depress, and the taxpayer trying to increase, the pre-war profits, so as to increase (or decrease) the excess war profits.[12]

Rates of estate duty were also increased to 80 per cent but an exemption was quickly enacted in 1914 for soldiers killed in action, echoing a previous provision in respect to the Boer War. Despite these high rates of tax, the economist John Maynard Keynes[13] commented in the 1920s that taxation was not high enough during the war, even though more people paid income tax than ever before.

The transition from war to peace again brought social tensions to the fore, with returning soldiers flooding the employment market. After an initial burst of inflation, there was a severe deflation which led employers to decrease wages and salaries. The government sought to balance the finances through severely cutting public expenditure. Like its predecessors in the 1820s, one of the continuing burdens on the state during the 1920s was paying the war bond interest. The government sought to ameliorate the consequences of repayment by negotiating a loan with the US in 1921,[14] replacing an earlier loan made in January 1916 to forestall a financial crisis at a crucial time. The delicate finances of the time were not helped by a post-war collapse of trade and a recession – not unlike the events of a century before. This was not helped by the failure of a defeated Germany to pay reparations, not only to the UK, but also to the countries that had borrowed money from the UK, causing these countries in their turn to default on their loans. The rampant inflation in Germany was also something that hung over policymakers in the 1920s. All this caused tension with the bankers in New York, and the adoption of the Dawes plan to help German industry, so that that country might pay its war debts. All these problems were exacerbated by the decision to revert to gold standard for the pound sterling in 1925 at pre-1914 rates. This failed to recognise the change in the UK's standing in the world after the war and made British exports and in particular, coal, uncompetitive. The consequent economic strife precipitated general industrial unrest and, ultimately, the General Strike of 1926. The system could not last and following another economic crisis the UK came off the gold standard in 1931. The great depression of the 1930s awaited, only alleviated by the call to arms later in the decade.

The lesson from this war was that although a long-term bond was probably good in practice to spread the costs, higher taxes during the war would have been sensible. The government eventually took greater control of the economy through various regulatory powers,[15] but these provoked a backlash in the inter-war years, seen in such cases

[12] A good example is *Glenboig Union Fireclay Co Ltd v IRC* (1921) 12 TC 427, which remains an important authority on the revenue/ capital divide.

[13] Keynes, 1883–1946, the pre-eminent economist of the time who at various times worked either as an academic or as an adviser to various UK governments.

[14] For the political reception of the agreement see R Jenkins, *The Chancellors* (London, Macmillan, 1998) 232–34.

[15] These were given mainly under the Defence of the Realm Consolidation Act 1914 and the New Ministries and Secretaries Act 1916.

as *Attorney General v Wilts United Dairy*[16] and in Lord Chief Justice Hewart's book, *The New Despotism*.[17]

IV. World War II 1939–45

World War II brought similar issues to the two previous conflicts, but in a more acute form, not least as the military position for a year after the fall of France in May 1940 was perilous. Initially, the financial and economic position, whilst not hopeless, was in some ways weaker than in the previous conflicts. The British Empire (as it then was) was comparatively rich in assets but these assets were widely dispersed and not easily liquidated and, more importantly, not readily available in US dollars in such an emergency.[18] US dollars were needed by the UK as the loss of access to European markets and sources after 1940 led to greater reliance on the US who became one of the main suppliers of armaments and the machine tools to build them. Under the aegis of its neutrality legislation, the US government ensured that arms exports were operated on a strict 'cash and carry' basis whereby supplies had to be paid for in dollars or gold, both of which were in short supply. The Treasury had the power in the Defence (Finance) Regulations 1939[19] to requisition US dollars held by UK citizens or companies. These powers were used quite ruthlessly. For example, the textile firm Courtaulds was forced to sell its US subsidiary, the American Viscose Corporation to New York banks and the dollar proceeds were requisitioned for the war effort.[20]

In the same fashion, and despite pleas from the Prime Minister Winston Churchill, a US destroyer was sent to Cape Town to pick up a large consignment of UK gold. Almost in despair Churchill wrote to President Roosevelt on 7 December 1940[21] to plead the case for credit for the UK, not least as the loss of credit would ultimately cause a loss of business to US factories and businesses. The UK opened its books to the US and, convinced that the UK was not losing, Roosevelt proposed the lend-lease scheme which was passed by the US congress in 1941. This was the basis for financing the rest of the war.

In Autumn 1939, at the start of the war, Keynes wrote two long articles for *The Times* which he later turned into his 1940 pamphlet 'How to pay for the War'. As would be expected, he advocated the measures that would result in full employment but realised they would not be enough to defeat Germany. It would be necessary, he thought, to reduce demand in the economy by increasing prices and reducing disposable income.

[16] (1922) 38 TLR 781, HL.

[17] Lord Hewart of Bury, *The New Despotism* (London, Ernest Benn Ltd, 1929).

[18] See generally D Edgerton, *Britain's War Machine: Weapons, Resources and Experts in the Second World War* (London, Penguin, 2011).

[19] Made under the Emergency Powers (Defence) Act 1939. These Regulations did give rise to issues regarding freedom of the individual echoing some present-day concerns, see HC Deb 31 October 1939 Col 1829 et seq, www.theyworkforyou.com/debates/?id=1939-10-31a.1829.2.

[20] L Olsen, *Those Angry Days* (New York, Random House, 2013).

[21] FL Loewenheim, HD Langley and M Jonas, *Roosevelt and Churchill, Their Secret Wartime Correspondence* (New York, da Capo, 1990) has the text of the note. See also W Churchill, *The Second World War, Volume II, Their Finest Hour* (London, Cassell, 1950) ch xxvii, 'Lend Lease', which dates the memorandum at 8 December 1940.

This would be done by raising both direct and indirect taxes. Issues surrounding the purchase of food and other necessities would be dealt with by price control, subsidy and rationing. In effect, Keynes considered that the government should take control of every aspect of the economy and use it to defeat Germany. In essence, the government adopted Keynes's proposals.[22]

The machinery for some of these changes was already in place in the form of purchase tax introduced by Sir John Simon in his first (and last) war time budget in spring 1940 as Chancellor of the Exchequer. This tax continued in force until its replacement with VAT in 1973. This sales tax was targeted at luxury goods and taxed them by as much as 100 per cent. Apart from producing revenue the tax was designed to save dollars so that they could be used for armaments. It also gave the Treasury a tool by which it had a measure of control over the domestic economy.

As in World War I, an excess profits tax was introduced from the beginning of the war with an initial rate of 60 per cent. With the change of government in May 1940, the new Chancellor, Sir Kingsley Wood brought Keynes into government, despite some opposition from the Prime Minister. The Chancellor in his budget of Spring 1941 proposed the following measures:

> The basic rate of income tax was increased to 50% with a 45% surcharge for investment income. Personal allowances were likewise adjusted downwards.
>
> Excess profits tax was raised to a rate of 100%. It was objected that this gave industrialists little incentive to innovate, so it was designed so that 20% of it would be handed back after hostilities ceased, like post war credits considered below.

As in earlier conflicts, the UK widened the tax base and, in this instance, also relied on higher rates of taxation, for all classes of society. These high rates of tax were to exist for over 30 years until they were gradually reduced in the 1980s and 1990s. For the wealthy, the very high rates of income tax were designed to force them to liquidate their capital so as to keep the economy moving and as such were seen as a more convenient way of imposing a capital charge, which was a continuing concern of the Labour party now in government. This was a people's war and the people suffered taxation on a more general level. The Inland Revenue, a naturally conservative bureaucracy, were reluctantly forced to introduce the Pay As You Earn (PAYE) system which revolutionised the collection of taxes and brought taxation very much to the wider population.[23]

To provide some incentive, a system of post-war credits was operated, whereby taxpayers (both individual and corporate) were promised credit for the tax they paid after the end of hostilities. This was again an idea of John Maynard Keynes, and mentioned in his pamphlet. He suggested the government could use the money from taxes and, after the war, the return of the 'loans' would boost income and the economy with additional spending. In fact, there was not the money to redeem these post-war credits at the end of hostilities. They were only gradually redeemed to those in retirement later in the 1960s and 1970s when inflation had eroded their value. They did not generate much enthusiasm, not least because they did not bear interest and their value diminished with inflation.

[22] R Skidelsky, *John Maynard Keynes, Fighting For Britain 1937–1946* (London, Macmillan, 2000) chs 2–4.

[23] See J Pearce, 'The Impact of the Two World Wars on the UK's Tax Law' in D de Cogan and P Harris, *Studies in the History of Tax Law*,10th edn (Oxford, Hart Publishing, 2021).

Why did taxpayers put up with this? The simple answer was that they recognised that there was a war on which involved them and had to be won. They also saw that there was some fairness and equity as the wealthy were taxed in the same way as they were. The economy was managed so that the basic needs of the population were met. Rates of estate duty remained high at 80 per cent for large estates over £1m. Tax avoidance just six years after the judgment in the *IRC v Duke of Westminster*[24] case was also frowned upon as witnessed by such cases as *Howard de Walden v IRC*[25] where in 1941 the taxpayer got little sympathy from the Court of Appeal ('those who play with fire should not complain if they get their fingers burnt'). This was a complete change in attitude.

One saving grace was that compared to World War I, interest rates were low at around 1.5 per cent. The stock market recovered from 'one of the buying opportunities of the century' in June 1940 to perform tolerably well, especially after the German invasion of the USSR in June 1941.[26]

Nonetheless, by 1945, it was clear that the UK was bankrupt and 'facing an economic Dunkirk'[27] as investment depended upon US fund holders. US aid in the form of lend lease ended abruptly with the sudden end of the war against Japan in August 1945. As in the aftermath of World War I, the UK government needed a loan from the US to give it foreign exchange to finance imports of essential goods. The negotiations were difficult, even though the then ailing Keynes was again among the British party, and the terms proved onerous.[28] In particular, one of the conditions was that sterling should be fully exchangeable with the US dollar from 1947. A system for dealing with exchange rates was put in place at Bretton Woods which would prove a strait-jacket for policymakers in the following 25 years or so. Again, as with the return to the gold standard in 1925, the UK exchange rate was unrealistic and led to devaluation of sterling in 1948 and subsequently in 1967 before the whole edifice of fixed exchange rates was abandoned in the early 1970s, after the US itself got into difficulties financing the Vietnam War. The US loan was a significant part of the financial reality for 25 years after the war until inflation gradually reduced its significance. It was finally repaid in 2006.

With all these difficulties, the transition from war to peace was managed more successfully. The Beveridge Report of 1942 had presaged an expansion of social security including health services. There was comparatively little unemployment, though this remained a worry for policymakers who remembered the 1930s. Social security provided a measure of assistance for less fortunate members of society. Inflation was a problem that was controlled in part by wage restraint and by restricting demand by varying the rates of purchase tax.

However, post-war credits were not such a boon as had been thought. They were only repaid gradually at first to those who had reached the then retirement age (60 for women, 65 for men) and only fully repaid in the 1960s and 1970s. The rates of tax

[24] [1936] AC 1; (1935) 19 TC 490.

[25] [1942] 1 KB 389.

[26] Kynaston (n 9).

[27] Skidelsky (n 22) ch 12; P Hennessey, *Never Again* (London, Penguin, 2006) ch 4.

[28] For a discussion of the immediate post-war prospects and the negotiation of the American loan see E Dell, *The Chancellors* (London, Harper Collins, 1996) ch 1, and at ch 5 for the attempt to break out of the restraints of Bretton Woods in the early 1950s – the ROBOT controversy.

remained high but were increasingly a façade that gave rise to a burgeoning tax avoidance industry, which was tolerated initially at least more generously than during the war.[29] This, in turn, gave rise in the Finance Act 1965 to new taxes on capital gains and corporations. These rates and the central control of the economy, now called planning, gave rise to increasing resentment. The long-term plan was that growth in the economy would provide the wealth to provide for a reduction in taxation. The British economy did indeed grow but at its long-term historic average of 2 per cent rather than at the greater level desired by politicians, who looked enviously at growth in continental Europe.

V. Lessons Learnt

The UK is not experiencing an existential crisis like that of 1940 nor, indeed, 1945; nor are we at the end of 20 years or more of war as in 1815; and, even with the dreadful loss of life in the last year or so, the number of casualties has not reached the levels of 1914–19 from both war and influenza. Nonetheless, the COVID-19 pandemic does resemble these earlier crises as being global rather than local, or even regional. With that in mind there are some general lessons to bear in mind:

- There is no magic bullet. There is no one solution which solves all economic and fiscal problems. A mixture of solutions is required including bond issues, direct and indirect taxes. The government may need to take direct control of some parts of the economy. The crisis does tend to emphasise current issues in the tax system and give some momentum for reform, so we have a new universal direct tax, income tax, new bond issues and a new method of taxing the whole population.
- As with armies there is always a danger of fighting the last war, rather than looking at current issues. At the same time, we should not ignore the lessons of history. Mistakes will be made.
- In many ways the problem lies not in the emergency itself but in the aftermath. How to get back to normal? What is normal? There is an almost irresistible desire to try and get back to the golden age of yesteryear or even of the year before that. We saw this in 1816 with the abandonment of the income tax combined with the full effect of the Corn Laws to return to some seventeenth century pastoral existence, the attempt to return to the gold standard at an unrealistic rate in 1925, and the unrealistic terms of the US loan in 1946. The truth is that the world has moved on and we should look to the future. The emergency may weaken the general health of the economy and provoke or exacerbate financial emergencies which arrive with some regularity.
- There is an international dimension to all the solutions. Even during the Napoleonic wars, there was an international market for government bonds. Their worth depended upon the financial standing of the UK which was climbing in the early

[29] See eg *Vestey v IRC* [1980] AC 1148, HL.

nineteenth century, on a decline in the early twentieth century and dependent on US assistance by the time of World War II. The ability to obtain loans had an effect on the economic health of the country and the ability to raise money through taxation.

- The world seems to suffer an event causing severe economic disruption every decade or so. In the 1960s there was the gradual breakup of the Bretton Woods exchange rate system: in the 1970s/80s we had oil price shocks, trade union issues and inflation; in the 1990s, we had black Wednesday and in 2008–09 we had the banking crisis. There is likely to be another crisis in the next 10–15 years.[30] If one were to speculate, one would say environmental issues will provide the background to an acute issue. However, a crisis is a crisis because it is generally unexpected, as we have seen with the current war in Ukraine and its unexpected consequences.

One clear strategy used in the eras we have examined is to spread the cost of the emergency over many years using long-term loans. This means the great increase in expenditure happens over a number of years and, with the assistance of inflation, reduces the burden on the public treasury. This spares the current body of taxpayers, already reeling from the events following an immediate fiscal shock. It can, however, bring its own difficulties as the years immediately after the world wars continued to be plagued by the need to pay off the debt. These stresses can transform pre-existing problems into acute emergencies such as the general disorders of the 1820s and the unemployment and strikes of the 1920s.

The election of a Labour government in 1945 provides an example of a different approach. It was hoped that sustained growth in the economy would provide a solution. Although the economy did grow it was not at a rate to solve all ills. Strains began to appear and by the 1970s there was a general restlessness towards the post-war approach. Socialists thought the state did not do enough, conservatives thought the state was too big and wasteful. Only with the advent of North Sea Oil did the 1980s bring about a gradual relaxation in the high rates for direct taxation. At the same time, rates for indirect taxes increased.

As for many other things, war brought innovation in taxation with the income tax, FOTRA securities, the PAYE system and purchase tax. It either created a new way of doing things or shook the present bureaucracies into doing something different. The events tend to stir up public opinion and allow issues to be faced, particularly of taxation, which are otherwise avoided. Scheve and Stasavage in their survey of fiscal fairness and taxes on the wealthy in the twentieth century[31] find that public opinion was one of the key factors in allowing higher taxes on the wealthy. The rhetoric in World War I was that if the ordinary citizen was putting his life at risk by volunteering then the wealthy should likewise risk their wealth. This justification was also used in World War II.

[30] In the film *Margin Call* (Before The Doors Pictures, 2011) set during the financial crisis of 2009, one of the lead characters, played by Jeremy Irons, lists the financial crises: 1637, 1797, 1819, 1837, 1857, 1884, 1901, 1907, 1929, 1937, 1974, 1987, 1992, 1997and 2000. 'It's only money.' Available on You Tube, www.youtube.com/watch?v=LtFyP0qy9XU29. He could have added 1721 and 1981, amongst other years.

[31] K Scheve and D Stasavage, *Taxing the Rich* (Princeton, Russell Sage Foundation, Princeton University Press, 2016).

The changes in public opinion possibly allow politicians some room to look with fresh eyes at our tax system and make changes that would otherwise not be possible.

VI. Applying These Lessons to the Present UK Tax Environment

The changes wrought by war often deal with issues which were present before the crisis and what follows is a personal view of some of the issues that arise. The government in an emergency firstly has to deal with this emergency. Then the bills have to be paid. One key question is how the cost should be spread out. Immediate taxation can provide some of the funds but will possibly damage the economy. Long-term bonds are another answer but will encumber future generations with the cost of servicing these loans, but inflation will tend to reduce the debt.

One criticism of the UK coalition's policy after the economic crisis of 2008–09 was that they sought to weather the storms, not through borrowing or taxation but through a reduction in government spending, which resonated with that government's ethos of reducing the state. Whilst this may have put the UK in a better financial position to deal with an emergency such as the pandemic, it would appear that there have been significant social costs. It certainly looks probable that that well is now exhausted, with the evident need to boost health and social care.

At present, interest rates remain at historically low levels, but it is likely that inflation will pick up, given the amount of money that has been pumped into the economy. The usual response to this will be to increase interest rates, but this may choke off any recovery before it has started. The government will hope that inflation is a short-term phenomenon. This will potentially raise the cost of any long-term bond, which will put pressure on the public finances. On the other hand, this will reduce the value of any debt that needs to be repaid. The burden of the 1946 US loan to the UK was high to start with but had become much easier by the 2000s. This pressure will not be eased by uncertain trade prospects and the restrictions on the labour market caused by Brexit. If inflation does reappear in a virulent form, it may be necessary to dust off some of the instruments used to calm it in the 1970s – high interest rates and tax measures to dampen demand, as well as restraint in pay deals.

This is an international crisis which will in the end require a global solution. Similarly, some sort of international agreement on the division of tax due from multinational enterprises is long overdue. Some enterprises have done well from the pandemic. It is encouraging, therefore, that the US (the leader, for better or worse, of international taxation) has signalled its intention to tackle the problem of low tax jurisdiction with a minimum rate of corporation tax. This was accepted by all the G7 nations, even if only reluctantly by the UK. If the nations of the world cooperate one would imagine that this will be to the benefit of all except those in tax havens. This is a counsel of perfection but just as, proverbially, news of a catastrophe is a good day to hide other bad news, so an event such as a pandemic gives us a chance to re-evaluate entrenched positions.

The UK economy has over the last 40 years or so come to rely upon on consumer spending. The lockdown led to spending declining precipitously. There are reports of money being saved by individuals rather than spent, and there are hopes that this money will now fuel a boom in spending: echoing the hopes of Keynes in respect of the repayment of post-war credits. One would suspect that there is an element of wishful thinking in such thoughts, partly as the money saved from staying at home has been spent on internet sales and in paying off past debts. Some of this money will be invested in inflated housing and other costs. With the likelihood of inflation increasing, some of these savings will address the extra costs which have arisen. Nonetheless, it would be helpful if individuals spent money rather than saved it and in so doing kept the economy going and incidentally provided funds for the government, though severe inflation will reduce the value of savings and induce purchases now, which will in turn stoke inflation. In these circumstances, it may be prudent to examine the tax relief given for savings products.[32] Savings have, however, been hit over the last decade by low interest rates. We save for a rainy day – it is raining now. However, we here run into the problems surrounding the provision of social care. There is a dilemma as the elderly wish to have social care without having to liquidate their assets, specifically their houses, into which they have placed their savings. This is a modern version of squaring the circle.

Given the need to encourage spending, generally there would not appear to be a need to introduce a purchase tax such as in World War II aimed at particular types of goods. Indeed, as in the aftermath of the financial crisis of 2008–09 when VAT was reduced temporarily to 15 per cent, there is a case for reducing VAT across the board to encourage spending, as then it would be sensible to add a sunset clause after which there would be a return to normal rates of tax. In the aftermath of Brexit there is no legal restraint to introducing higher rates of VAT in respect of some goods. This would, however, go against the broad-spectrum rate approach of VAT and inevitably give rise to classification disputes. The problem with reducing the VAT rate is that these changes are not passed on to the consumer, or not passed on immediately. Further, if there is a pent-up demand to buy things there may be little need for fiscal encouragement. The work of Professors de la Fera and Walpole[33] shows that the difference in price tends to be pocketed by the businesses selling goods or services, though one would hope that market forces will eventually result in some reduction in prices for consumers.

In the longer term, it is doubtful whether our present indirect taxation profile can bear the burden it has faced in the past 40 years or so. Tax receipts from road fuel duty face a decline in the next 10 years from the introduction of electric vehicles.[34] Similarly, the receipts from tobacco tax are in long-term decline for health reasons – either tobacco kills its customers or they foreswear it. In the same way, as the population has started to take the advice of its doctors, tax receipts from alcohol are in decline, if not quite as steeply as for tobacco. Apart from these taxes (and SDLT discussed below)

[32] For the statistics on savings products see 'Commentary for Annual savings statistics: June 2021', www.gov.uk/government/statistics/annual-savings-statistics/commentary-for-annual-savings-statistics-june-2021. Not the least of these statistics is the fact that there are over 1,000 with ISA holdings worth more than £1million.

[33] R De la Fera and M Walpole, 'Impact of Public Perception on General Consumption Taxes' [2020] *British Tax Review* 637.

[34] See the Report of the HC Transport Committee, 'Is there a case for road pricing in the UK?' (4 February 2022), ukparliament.shorthandstories.com/road-pricing-transport-report/index.html?utm_source=committees.parliament.uk&utm_medium=referrals&utm_campaign=road-pricing&utm_content=organic

the remaining taxes do not provide a significant yield and are used in an attempt to control behaviour, rather than raise money.

In all these circumstances, as in the 1800s more revenue from direct taxes may be a sensible approach. Business generally has had the stuffing knocked from it, apart from certain sectors such as drugs, supermarkets and delivery services, who seem to have profited. The raising of the principal corporation tax rate to 25 per cent does look like an attempt to address this issue, but 25 per cent is a far cry from the 100 per cent excess profits tax of World War II, or even the 80 per cent of World War I. This rate increase is coupled with a super deduction for capital allowances of 130 per cent in the tax year.[35] This presupposes that there are profits to invest. There will also be a danger that this will merely accelerate investment and create inflation in capital assets, rather than increase it over the long term.

The most important source of direct tax revenue is employment tax. The government has, with its furlough scheme, avoided mass unemployment but at a considerable cost, both direct and indirect. Happily, employment seems to have rebounded and with it the relevant tax receipts. Problems remain over the gig economy and various boundary disputes over employment and self-employment.

In the UK, capital taxation has been stagnant over the last 30 years. There is pressure for modernising both inheritance tax and capital gains tax, even if it is only by rationalising exemptions, reliefs and rates of tax. The proposals by both the Office of Tax Simplification[36] and, separately, STEP/APPG[37] in respect of capital taxation indicate a rational way forward. Further to the previous conflicts, public opinion may favour changes in this area. Nonetheless, we are now in a globalised economy with freedom for individuals, especially wealthy individuals, to travel around the world almost as migrating birds. As Professor Dagan made clear in her paper in 2019,[38] states are to a certain extent in competition for the adherence of high-net-worth individuals.

The UK domestic property market has been a shelter from taxation. It is also a lever of last resort when the government has wanted to boost the economy. One of the issues now is that the low rate of taxation on domestic property has been so 'baked into' its value that any sudden increase in taxation could cause a crash in property values. In recent years tax on domestic property has increased, albeit in a haphazard way. We have had an attempt to rein in the buy-to-let market and to discourage second homes with various elaborate rates for Stamp Duty Land Tax (SDLT) which have stood proxy for a tax on property. Offshore ownership has been discouraged by an anti-avoidance tax on enveloped property. The government has sought to encourage the property market by introducing a holiday from SDLT. The weakness of tax on domestic property has created an asset bubble with house prices rising as housing is bought as an investment rather than as dwellings. The problem is that SDLT has discouraged movement in the property market, as the extra cost of stamp duty has been a disincentive and so the properties are

[35] See 'Guidance: Super-deduction', www.gov.uk/guidance/super-deduction.

[36] 'OTS Inheritance Tax Review: Simplifying the design of the tax', www.gov.uk/government/publications/ots-inheritance-tax-review-simplifying-the-design-of-the-tax.

[37] APPG/STEP, 'Reform of Inheritance Tax January 2020', www.step.org/system/files/media/files/2020-05/STEPReform_of_inheritance_tax_report_012020.pdf.

[38] T Dagan, 'Re-imagining Tax Justice in a Globalised World' in D de Cogan and P Harris (eds), *Tax Justice and Tax Law* (Oxford, Hart Publishing, 2020).

not efficiently occupied. It may be that the excessive profits of property developers need targeting with an updated version of the various taxes and levies, such as betterment levy, development gains (and later development land) tax which have accompanied such bursts of property development in the past.

One should add that council tax needs reform. The base valuation for council tax is the value of residences as in 1991 and a revaluation is long overdue with the possible extension of the value bands. Business rates have become more important as a tax on business with the reduction in the rate of corporation tax but some temporary relief is probably needed to smooth the reduction in business rents and value consequent to the desertion of the High Street. This is eventually picked up by the fall in value of business property but not before causing some pain.

Although the tax system was becoming increasingly digitally based before the pandemic, the events of the last year or so will have accelerated this tendency.

VII. A Last Word

Eventually, many of the issues discussed here will become issues of timing. When and how will the costs of the emergency to be paid? There are mechanisms for spreading the cost and it would be sensible if the costs are spread out. The balance between immediate and future taxation is acute in times of crisis. A government also has to judge the level of interference it can make in its citizens' lives. In the end, what impresses from this survey of these past crises is the way in which the various options were discussed. Sometimes decisions were made that in hindsight appear unfortunate, but they did have the virtue of transparency. One would hope that the exigencies of the present emergency will lead to an honest discussion of some of the tax issues involved and an acceptance that some difficult measures are needed.

4

Taxes During Wars and Crises

SURANJALI TANDON

Abstract

During war and economic crises there is pressure to raise tax revenues. Historically, special levies and additional taxes have been introduced to augment the fiscal resources available. After the economic shock caused by COVID-19, the expansion in government budgets created similar pressures to raise higher revenues through an excess profits tax. This chapter details the design of and experience with excess profits tax in politically different contexts. The chapter finds that levying an excess profits tax in addition to existing taxes is difficult and unsustainable over long periods, especially in the current scenario of a broad tax base. The chapter uses the example of the financial transactions tax to demonstrate the present challenges to a proposal to levy an additional tax.

I. Introduction

Income taxes were frequently introduced under compelling circumstances such as war. In England, the financial necessities that arose from war with France led to the famous Pitt Act of 1798, imposing duties regulated by the amount of income a person possessed.[1] Similarly, Italy, France and the US introduced income tax to meet the temporary needs of the government.[2] It is said that governments provide two public goods – justice and defence – the price of which is tax.[3] Therefore, while wars make a compelling case for imposition of a tax, the perpetuity of government creates the permanence of tax. As argued by Ames and Rapp, a tax system once established lasts until the end of the government that instituted it.[4] Yet, there are taxes conceived during exceptional, historic circumstances that have not survived through peacetimes, one of which is the excess

[1] HB Cox, 'Origin and Growth of Income Tax' (1919) 3(1) *Journal of Comparative Legislation and International Law*.

[2] ERA Seligman, 'The Income Tax' (1894) 9(4) *Political Science Quarterly* 614.

[3] E Ames and R Trapp, 'Birth and Death of Taxes: A Hypothesis'(1977) 37(1) *Journal of Economic History* 177.

[4] ibid 177.

profits tax. One reason is prevailing taxes cast a web so wide that there remains a fraction of the base available to apply a new tax. The history of the excess profits tax and the failures of implementing a financial transactions tax are a testimony to the limits to expanding the tax base and unavoidable complexity in tax law.

Instances of exceptional political and economic circumstances are often accompanied by a proposal for tax reforms. For example, during the World Wars excess profits tax was implemented by a wide number of countries, above the existing income tax to cover profits of companies that had benefitted from the war. During the global financial crisis in 2008, the synchronised decline in growth[5] across developed countries revived the need to tax financial services. The rationale for the tax was that there are unregulated financial services that can be regulated by adding a cost to transacting. Similarly, recent economic slowdown after COVID-19 strained the fiscal situation across the world while posing structural challenges from an uneven recovery. The OECD forecasts that the global economic recovery is looking K shaped.[6] That is, the vulnerable are worse off post pandemic. The need for additional revenue and increased focus on sustainable recovery compelled governments to examine the potential for new taxes, particularly through an expanded base. At the beginning of the pandemic the IMF urged countries to collect a solidarity tax on profitable companies and high earners.[7] Similarly, there were suggestions of implementing tax on sectors that have thrived during the pandemic (Avi-Yonah, 2020). While these proposals target specific sectors and may be temporary, a more significant shift has been the recent call for a global minimum tax. The proposal may be seen as a G-20 response to ensuring a sustainable recovery[8] by setting a floor on corporate tax rates. Even though these are only recommendations, it is critical to examine if additional taxes implemented during exceptional economic and political circumstances are successful and whether they can survive through 'normalcy'. Such analysis would be useful for any future approach to tax reform. For this purpose, the fate of taxes proposed during exceptional times such as the excess profits tax (EPT) and financial transactions tax (FTT) is discussed. This is to identify political and economic circumstances that can be propitious or otherwise for additional taxes. While many countries implemented the EPT, this chapter will analyse the experiences of the US, the UK and India in detail. The reasons for their selection are their different design features as well as the context in which they were introduced that allow for comparative assessment of EPT. For example, the EPT in the US, the UK and India were introduced at different times and were in substance very different. The legitimacy of the taxes also derived from different sources – the UK possessed imperial power, while India remained a colony until the end of World War II whereas the US was an influential member of the

[5] T Matheson, 'The Global Financial Crisis: An Anatomy of Global Growth' (2013) *IMF Working Paper Series*, WP/13/76.

[6] S Kennedy, 'What's Happening in the World Economy: A K-Shaped Global Recovery' (*Bloomberg*, 31 May 2021) www.bloomberg.com/news/newsletters/2021-05-31/what-s-happening-in-the-world-economy-a-k-shaped-global-recovery.

[7] C Giles, 'IMF proposes "solidarity" tax on pandemic winners and wealthy' (*Financial Times*, 7 April 2021) financialpost.com/financial-times/imf-proposes-temporary-solidarity-tax-on-pandemic-winners-and-the-wealthy.

[8] G20 Rome Leaders Declaration, (2021), G20 Italia.

allied forces. Thus, their fiscal commitments were not similar. Moreover, this chapter highlights the fact that such additional tax cannot be applied to all sectors or transactions. It is observed that in the application of EPT many exemptions were introduced. The challenge then emerged of tax avoidance and under-reporting of incomes. This is also significant for understanding the evolution of tax law, that is prone to complexities in order to accommodate the investors' demands without generating avenues for avoidance.

Post-war the only comparable tax on a specific tax base is financial transactions tax (FTT). Like the EPT it was conceived as a means to recover fiscal costs of the bail-out while regulating volatile financial markets. Although there are proposals for implementing the tax, it still remains theoretical. This chapter reflects on why a new tax during peacetime may be less acceptable, even though it is to compensate for the greater role of the state. A critical distinction between the two periods is that unlike when EPT was introduced, the tax system is now well formed and capital is fairly mobile. Thus, introducing a new tax can be difficult in a comparatively well-developed tax system that covers a broad tax base and where capital is fairly mobile, especially with sovereign states.

II. Wartime Tax: Excess Profits Tax

Excess profits tax was a wartime measure first implemented during World War I. The rationale for applying such tax was twofold – to fund the wartime expenditure of the government and to curb profiteering[9] while promoting equity. In 1915, Copenhagen reported that a new tax would be levied in Denmark, Sweden and Norway.[10] This tax was made applicable to exporters making enormous profits from the war. The tax received support since it was aimed at exports that serviced Germany's insatiable demand for Swedish iron and Danish butter[11] – a cause for a rise in domestic prices. For this reason it came to be known as *Gulasch* tax. As war proceeded the scope of this tax expanded to sectors such as shipping munition and leather industry. While in principle the tax was to apply to excess returns, over time its scope expanded. In Germany the tax was not regarded as a rod for correction[12] and with its expanded scope it included all increments in wealth. On the contrary, the Spanish Minister articulated the need for tax on profits that were derived at the *cost and injury* of others.[13] The grounds for the implementation of the tax varied across countries but it soon became a popular revenue raising mechanism. The legitimacy of the tax derived from the role of state. As will be seen, the features of the new tax also varied.

[9] M Billings and L Oats, 'Innovation and pragmatism in tax design: Excess Profits Duty in the UK during the First World War' (2014) 24(2–3) *Accounting History Review* 83–101.

[10] JC Stamp, 'The Taxation Of Excess Profits Abroad' (1917) *Economic Journal* 26.

[11] J Hicks, UK Hicks and J Rostas, *The Taxation of War Wealth* (New York, Oxford University Press, 1941) 15.

[12] Stamp (n 10) 27.

[13] ibid 28.

III. The Broad Contours of the Tax During World War I

In the present context, there have been suggestions for applying an excess profits tax. To apply such a tax, it is necessary to objectively define *excess* profits. In the past, a reference was made to a benchmark rate of normal peacetime profits. This rate was not uniform across jurisdictions and neither was the period of reference for determination of peacetime profit. For example, France, Holland and Denmark limited the calculation of average profits to three years preceding the war. New Zealand offered the taxpayer the option of taking an average of any two years of three preceding years. In Germany, the preceding five years were taken as a reference period then the best and the worst year were eliminated after which the average was computed for the remaining three years. In many countries absolute profits were not averaged but instead an alternative to compute this as a percentage of capital employed (Table 1) was made available.

Table 1 Excess profits tax during World War I

Country	Year in which excess profits was applied	Rate of standard profit (% of capital)
Denmark and Sweden	May 1915	6
Italy	November 1915	8
Germany	December 1915	6
Austria	April 1916	6
Russia and Canada	May 1916	8 and 7 (companies and 10% to individuals)
Holland, France and Spain	June/July 1916	6, 6 and 7 respectively
New Zealand	August 1916	7.5
Switzerland and the US	September 1916	6
Australia	September 1917	5% on companies and 6% on individuals
The UK	1915[14]	13[15]

Source: Compiled from Stamp (1917).

By 1917, many countries had adopted excess profits tax to finance the war, and in many cases (as seen in Table 1) it became applicable retrospectively. Italy, France, Germany and Holland introduced the tax in 1916 but it was made applicable from 1 August 1914. While each country sought to tax these returns in its own way, as will be shown in the following sections the features of the tax varied. The EPT in India, the UK and the US are selected for the purpose of comparison. As stated earlier, the reason for this is the UK was an imperial power with the option to expand its tax base beyond its national boundaries, to colonies at its disposal. On the other hand, India was not sovereign and

[14] Preceded by munitions tax of 20% of average profits in the two preceding years. The profits in excess of £200 were taxable.

[15] 'Commerce Reports' (1916) 2 (77) Bureau of Foreign and Domestic Commerce, Department of Commerce.

accepted the EPT. In contrast, the US remained a sovereign and an ally in the War. This chapter therefore compares the experiences of these three countries.

IV. Specifics of the Design and Implementation During the World Wars

A. The UK

With growing evidence of increased profits and the rise in conspicuous consumption during the war, EPT was thought to be the appropriate measure. The proposal received support across political and ideological spectrums.[16] This was caused by widespread public resentment due to a shortage of food, inflation and industrial unrest.[17] As mentioned in the previous section, the basis of the levy was *profiteering* that is conceptually distinct from *profits*. In contrast to Germany, where profits became widely taxed, the UK created a distinction between normal and excess profits. While the concept was simple and had wide appeal, it was not as easy to define. The definition and estimation of profit, the period and industry to which it must apply and its administration were all concerns that received serious consideration.

At first this tax was introduced as a munitions levy[18] in the UK, ring fenced to the industry that perceivably *profiteered* from war.[19] However, later in December 1915 a more general Excess Profits Duty (EPD) was extended to all trading and manufacturing concerns, including to business conducted by ordinary residents abroad.[20] To facilitate its general application, exceptions and flexibilities were made available.

To begin with, the reference period for computing the profits was the best two out of the three preceding years. However, not all companies were in operation or profitable during the year. Therefore, new firms were given the flexibility to select the years for which they operated prior to the war.[21] A fair return to capital was applied where a business was not in operation in the preceding years. Furthermore, to avoid the downward bias in the estimated profits, years of poor economic performance were excluded from such calculation. Yet, strategies for avoiding the EPD soon emerged, including delay in recognition of revenue, write-offs and valuation of closing stock.[22] In some cases, companies merged with others, reporting poor financial records post war.[23]

The standard profit could, as mentioned, be the total value or in relation to the capital employed. Then again, capital used for estimating excess profits was that employed

[16] Billings and Oats (n 9) 6.
[17] ibid.
[18] Administered by the Ministry of Munitions and applied alongside excess profits duty in the UK.
[19] Introduced as the Munitions War Act in July 1915.
[20] Billings and Oats (n 9) 8.
[21] An average of two years for a firm that operated only two years and last year's profit for one year.
[22] Billings and Oats (n 9) 12.
[23] BR Cheffins and SA Bank, 'Corporate Ownership and Control in the UK: The Tax Dimension' (2007) 70(5) *The Modern Law Review* 788.

for the business and the amount taken was that invested by proprietors and not its market value. This was to prevent companies from artificially deflating profit rates. However, this would dampen investments, and to mitigate such risk increments to fresh capital were allowed as deductions from wartime profits whereas depletion was added back[24] while calculating the pre-wartime profit rate.

The flexibility in the application of tax extended to the, often arbitrary, exclusion of professions and sectors. For example, UK professionals were exempted since their incomes were not expected to exceed the limit and bore relation to their health, energy and brain power rather than physical and financial capital.[25] Unlike the progressive tax rates in Denmark, Austria, Sweden and France, a flat tax rate was implemented by the US and the UK. In its first year, the UK levied a tax of 50 per cent, it was later increased to 60 per cent in 1917 and 80 per cent in 1918.

A key feature of the excess profits tax was that a consultative process was made available to a class of trade or business so that taxpayers could appeal before the Board of Referees for an increase in the pre-war rate of profit.[26] The Board, comprising of 29 members, nine of which were accountants and successive senior partners of Price Waterhouse and Co, was constituted to minimise the parliamentary objections to the EPD. The board presided on matters of fact and pronounced rulings, the reasons for which were not published,[27] much like the modern-day advance rulings and pricing agreements. So even though the headline rate of EPT is referred to, the actual rates would have varied widely.

A challenge while implementing high rates of tax is that capital is mobile and can move with ease to jurisdictions with lower tax rates. In fact, it is often suggested that the modern capital controls were invented by belligerents during World War I to maintain a tax base to finance the war[28] and these controls disappeared briefly until the Great Depression in the 1930s.[29] Yet, despite the controls, businesses in the UK carried out cross border flows to avoid taxes. During consultations taxpayers brought to the notice of the Revenue that many businesses had relocated to avoid taxes. In one such consultation it was reported that 45 companies manufacturing jute had moved their operation to India.[30] The tax was applicable to residents and no EPD was applicable, at this time, to companies registered in India. There were further efforts to avoid the tax through lavish use of deductions. In response an anti-avoidance provision was added so as to disallow the deduction in respect of any transaction or operations that appeared to have *artificially* reduced profits.[31] The definition of 'artificial' was not spelt out in the Act or in case law[32] and thus became a contested issue. Nearly 171 appeals were made and

[24] Billings and Oats (n 9) 14.

[25] BM Mallet and CO George, '*British budgets, 1913–14 to 1920–21, Second series*' (London, Macmillan and Co Ltd, 1929) 87.

[26] Initial membership announced on 7 December 1915.

[27] Stamp (n 10).

[28] CJ Neely, 'An Introduction to Capital Controls' (1999) 81(6) *Federal Reserve Bank of St. Louis Review* 13–30.

[29] ibid.

[30] Billings and Oats (n 9) 18.

[31] GSA Wheatcroft, 'The attitude of the legislature and the courts to tax avoidance' (1955) 18 *MLR* 223.

[32] ibid.

considered by the courts[33] in the UK. Nevertheless, the capital controls provided scope for further increasing taxes.

In the years after its application, the number of taxpayers and revenues collected increased manifold in the UK. In 1919, 32.1 per cent of revenue were from EPD, as against 0.04 per cent in 1914, while another third came from income and super tax.[34] The legitimacy of the tax derived from expectations of the government. 'The experience of a more socially active state during the war, and the popularity of Lloyd George's reforms, increased public expectations of the state, legitimising the necessary level of taxation'.[35] However, beyond the social acceptance of the tax, its success was in part attributed to the inflation.[36] The rate of inflation, year on year, in the UK was 25 per cent and 17 per cent in the US in 1917.[37]

In 1920 the Royal Commission appointed experts to study the income tax. The Commission recommended adjustments in the threshold for application of EPD, such as that for married men with children to prop up the birth rate.[38] This was, in a way, the beginning of the end of the EPD. In 1921, despite its revenue raising appeal, the EPD was abolished.[39]

While imagining a similar tax it is important to understand the context. It is seen that there is an implicit and explicit cause for its acceptability. The explicit cause is the greater need for State intervention during war. The implicit rationale for the new tax was that at this time consumption taxes were considered impractical and an excise was only levied on items such as spirits, wine, tea, tobacco and beer.[40] Further, no corporate tax[41] or capital gains tax existed and companies were taxed the same as individuals with deduction for dividend tax made available to individuals. This therefore allowed for an expansion of the tax base. Billings and Oats assess that the tax did fairly well in revenue collection and was able to restore equity while taking economy into consideration.

Experience from World War I was a template for its use of excess profits tax. As a result, the tax made a comeback during World War II. In the years preceding the war, the world economy had also endured the Great Depression. There had been an absence of any effective system of international coordination of national economic policies[42] and the UK, unlike the US, did not resort to budget deficits to fund internal recovery.[43] On the contrary, the expansion in public debt to GDP in the UK (see Figure 1) was

[33] P Ridd, 'Excess profits duty' in D de Cogan and P Harris (eds), *Studies in the History of Tax Law* (Oxford, Hart Publishing, 2004) 138.
[34] Mallet and George (n 25) 390.
[35] *The End of War and Fiscal Change*, The Cabinet Papers, The National Archives (n.d.).
[36] Billings and Oats (n 9) 22.
[37] K Daly and RD Chankova, 'Inflation in the aftermath of wars and pandemics' (*VOX, CEPR Policy Portal*, 15 April 2021) voxeu.org/article/inflation-aftermath-wars-and-pandemics.
[38] Since there had been many deaths during the war. See *The End of War and Fiscal Change* (n 35).
[39] R Douglas, *Taxation in Britain Since 1660* (New York, Springer, 1999) 115.
[40] D Winchand and PK O'Brien, *The Political Economy of British Historical Experience* (New York, Oxford University Press, 2002) 1688–1914.
[41] Corporate tax made a brief appearance in 1920 at 5%, was then redacted and only introduced much later in 1965 along with capital gains.
[42] HW Arndt, *Essays in International Economics* (Brookfield, Aldershot, Avebury, 1996) 221.
[43] ibid 125.

associated with imperial expansion. Nevertheless, the size of the government as represented by its stock of debt increased phenomenally during the war.

Figure 1 Public Debt to GDP

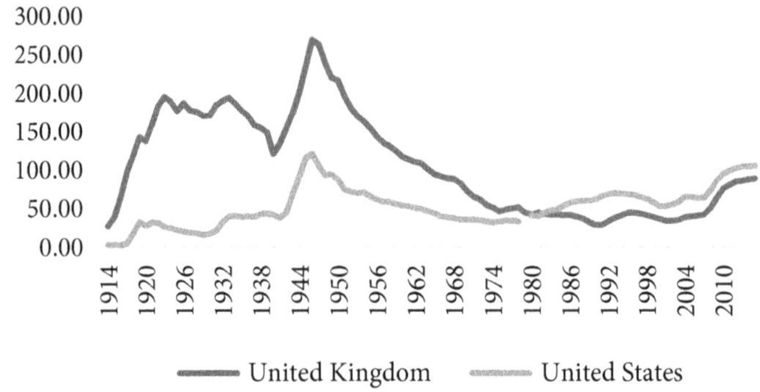

Source: IMF.

In 1939 the armaments profits duty was introduced and later repealed and replaced by EPT in the Finance (No. 2) Act of 1939. This was after proposals for capital levy and mobilisation of wealth were stillborn.[44] Through an emergency budget, the Chancellor of the UK introduced the excess profits tax – more complex[45] in form and subject to fewer exclusions. A national defence contribution was implemented earlier as levy was retained after EPT was introduced. However, the taxpayer received an option to pay NDC or EPT, whichever produced higher liability. EPT was applicable where profits exceeded £1,000 for companies where the director had the controlling interest and £1,500 for companies with one proprietor and £3,000 where there were two proprietors. Though exclusions were kept to a minimum, too many specificities were built into the new law. Thus to compensate for a more stringent tax, more exclusions were permitted.

The standard profits were also to be computed in a more complicated fashion, where the period of reference could be 1935, 1936, or the average of 1935 and 1937 or 1936 and 1937. These profits were to be adjusted upwards or downwards based on a variation in capital employed between a standard period and a chargeable accounting period and tax was calculated at the rate of 60 per cent of the profits. Yet again, there was flexibility in the definition of capital employed. For example, bank balances, already high at this time due to the war, were excluded from calculation since such money was not employed for trade or business. Yet, War Bonds issued by the UK government, that remained essential for funding the war efforts, were included.[46] It is expected that this would have caused a further diversion of funds to finance war. The government's spending plan was quite closely tied to its revenue strategy.

The new EPD was just as contested with 117 cases pertaining to issues such as scope of charge, exemption of professions, adjustments to standard profits and

[44] BEV Sabine, *History of Income Tax: the Development of Income Tax from its beginning in 1799 to the present day related to the social, economic and political history of the period* (London, Routledge, 2013).

[45] ibid.

[46] K Wood, *Excess Profit Tax*, Commons and Lords Hansard, Written Answers, HC Debate, (22 August 1940), vol 364 cc1512-3W.

chargeable period.[47] In May 1940, the tax rate was raised in UK by the Finance Act to 100 per cent.[48] This increase was tenable on the promise a post-war rebate of 20 per cent would be available.[49] Contrary to the understanding that tax at 100 per cent would disincentivise profits, it deterred avoidance of losses[50] so as to reduce the quantum of excess profits. Owing to such practices, EPT collections dwindled and debt accumulated faster during World War II. This was a lesson that new taxes do not yield the same result if applied with exclusions and over a longer period.

B. India

At the time of the wars India was not politically independent. Therefore, the taxes in India were introduced for the purpose of contributing to the cost of the war. While EPD was introduced in the UK, three extraordinary[51] taxes were imposed in India:

1. a super tax on large incomes of individuals, undistributed profits of companies and joint Hindu families,[52] in 1917;
2. a new income tax in 1918, later codified in 1922;[53] and
3. the excess profits tax.

The modernisation of the Income Tax Act in India began in 1914 with graduated tax rates supplementing a rise in excise and customs tax, applicable on items including salt. The intent of such changes was primarily to pay for the European war. While legislature in India was urged to the effect that income tax be treated as one time measure, the tax was not dispensed with and continued. The interest in raising direct taxes may have had to do with the legal changes that permitted Britain to utilise these resources for war. A special sanction in 1916 to the Government of India Act removed the prohibition on financing military expedition outside India from the revenue collected in India.[54] At this time, important export commodities such as jute and cotton were also taxed. Export duty on jute, customs on cotton goods and graduated super-tax on all incomes became an important source of finance for the British government.

This was also a time of uprising against a series of oppressive legislations in India such as the Rowlatt Bill.[55] The prevailing mood did not prove propitious for the excess profits tax. There was severe backlash from industrialists as businesses in India had deteriorated.[56] Nevertheless, in 1919 the excess profits tax was introduced, albeit temporarily,[57] and replaced the super-tax, so far levied on undistributed profits

[47] Ridd (n 33) 139–49.
[48] *The End of War and Fiscal Change* (n 35).
[49] Ridd (n 33) 139–38.
[50] Sabine (n 44).
[51] B Chaudhuri, *Nationalist Movement in Delhi 1911–1932* (Raleigh, Lulu Publication, 2017) 34.
[52] Rebates were allowed to an extent.
[53] JP Niyogi, *Evolution of the Indian income tax* (London, PS King and Son, 1929) 4.
[54] ibid 140.
[55] The Acts allowed certain political cases to be tried without juries and permitted internment of suspects without trial.
[56] Chaudhuri (n 51).
[57] Niyogi (n 53).

of companies.[58] The excess profits in India were to be computed on the basis of profits earned two years before the declaration of the war and two out of the three years preceding March 1919[59] or an assumed yield of 10 per cent, at the discretion of the company.[60] The tax was payable by companies with profits more than INR 30,000 at the rate of 50 per cent and was deductible as a business expense. Similar to the UK, a board of referees was formed in India consisting of at least two non-official members having business experience. An assessee dissatisfied with the assessment could at his discretion appeal to the Chief Revenue Authority of the province or refer such a matter to the Board, thus allowing scope to redefine excess profits. Interestingly, Niyogi notes that unlike the proposal to introduce such a Board in the Income Tax Act 1918, where businesses feared that the presence of a non-official member would expose their state of credit, businesses strongly supported it in the case of the excess profit tax.[61] Soon after its implementation businessmen in India raised concerns such as its impact on the plan to borrow, growth of indigenous companies and its impact on import of capital for reconstruction. Thus, efforts were made to limit the tax, through proposals such as higher profits threshold as well as lower tax rates. Further, the choice was made available between super-tax and excess profit tax, whichever was higher, where credit could be claimed a deduction in computation of income tax.

Unlike EPT in the UK, which was implemented to respond to social pressures, in India the taxes were socially unacceptable in spite of the aforementioned flexibilities and the tax was repealed in 1920. During its brief application INR 92, million were collected from EPT in 1919, INR 19 million in 1920 and INR 2 million in 1921 in India. While these paled in comparison to the collections in the UK – an average of £192,000 per year[62] – the collections are not comparable.

EPT made a brief appearance in India during World War I, but during World War II EPT applied contemporaneously with the UK. The Government of India introduced a bill that proposed the levy of EPT to raise the 'large finances for the prosecution of the war'. Indian businessmen considered this unfair since the underlying premise – businesses profited from war – did not hold true for them. That is, Indian businesses did not receive orders from the government which in turn is a source of profits. Technically, the expansionary fiscal stance of the government through its purchases from business can have multiplier effects for the economy, thus counteracting to some extent the increase in tax rates while redistributing incomes. But this was not the case in India where the applicable taxes increased.

The acceptance of the tax, however, is linked to the structure and dynamics of the jute industry. The Indian Jute Manufacturers Association (IJMA) was comprised of Indian businesses such as GD Birla and the British, represented by Benthall. Since its inception the IJMA controlled the price of jute through controls on output by restraining the number of hours that factories could work. However, with the collapse of global growth in 1929 President Roosevelt raised the tariffs on imports to 40 per cent

[58] ibid 145.
[59] ibid 170.
[60] ibid 170.
[61] ibid 172.
[62] ibid 174–75.

from 10 per cent on gunny bags.[63] This was accompanied by a reduction in demand in Europe, thus wiping off order books in India. To respond to crashing demand, by 1935, wages contracted to a third, smaller businesses shut up shop, retrenching nearly 83,000 workers.

Some businessmen soon began operating factories in *dark corners*.[64] It soon came to light, through an audit initiated by Benthall, that companies were undermining the pact between members of IJMA. The collusion, as it were, was further undermined when in October 1935 GD Birla, along with other prominent members of the association, expressed that he would resign. In response, the constraints imposed by the association were watered down. Benthall called this 'blood-letting' to ensure that some Indian friends were taught a lesson that it is not easy to profit in the jute business. In 1937 the IJMA restrictions were removed and in 1938 prices and profits tumbled, taking with them the rebels that had thus far undermined the market.

Fortunes turned when the government placed an order for 200 million gunny bags with the Indian jute industry, followed by orders for 50 million bags in two weeks of the war,152 million in September. Six months into the war Calcutta mills supplied 923 million bags and 45 million yards of gunny cloth. The profitability of Birla's company became comparable with British companies such as Belvedere (65–78 per cent) and Union Mills (98–110 per cent). Birla's profits were 13 per cent in 1939, 30 per cent in 1940, 40 per cent in 1941, 63 per cent in 1942 and 63 per cent in 1943. Feeding the demand for British goods were machinery imported by Indian businesses between 1933–38.[65] Thus, the support for the EPT in India derived from the handing out of government orders to select companies.

Indian businesses thought such tax would curtail industrial expansion, already ebbing for want of capital and the post-war slump.[66] This sent businesses up in arms, with nationwide protests. The EPT bill was labelled anti-national since the proceeds of this tax were to be used to sponsor an imperialist war in which India was made to participate against her will.[67] Instead, such tax was considered tenable where proceeds funded national reconstruction or revival of growth. Nevertheless, the tax went through and in the Budget of 1941–42, the EPT was raised to 66.6 per cent from 50 per cent. The tax was payable by all businesses and professions, except: (a) life insurance businesses, (b) professions where the earning of profits depended mainly on personal qualifications, (c) profits assessable only on the remittance basis, and (d) profits arising in Indian States after 31 March 1942.[68] Further, super tax and surcharge on income tax was applied raising the rates to 93 per cent, and some argued that it was making its way into standard profits.[69] It was possible to raise taxes since India was not a sovereign.

In addition to the tax, the businesses were required to deposit an additional percentage of the tax which along with a tenth of the EPT were refundable at the end

[63] G Piramal, *Business Legends* (London, Penguin, 2010).

[64] ibid.

[65] ibid.

[66] A Mukherjee, *Imperialism, Nationalism and the Making of the Indian Capitalist Class 1920–1947* (India, SAGE Publications, 2002).

[67] ibid.

[68] 'Report of the Tax Enquiry Commission 1953–54 vol. 2', Ministry of Finance, Department of Economic Affairs, Government of India, (New Delhi, Manager of Publications, 1955) 13.

[69] Mukherjee (n 66).

of the war.[70] The opposition to the tax did not wane until the end of the war and only in 1946 was this tax repealed. Interestingly, GD Birla refrained from participating in agitations against such tax. Birla maintained that such tax was a *sacrifice* that the community would have to make in the short run in the wider economic interest. Birla's support of the tax at the Federation of Indian Chambers of Commerce and Industry meeting in 1940 was based on the argument that the tax was essentially not borne by the capitalist, and to the contrary paid by the customer. The pass forward of the tax allowed the tax to be treated as cost. Although this view remained a minority view, big businesses such Birla lent the necessary support that allowed the tax to continue.

Unlike the legitimacy of the usurious tax in the UK that was based on the government's spending, the tax in India was coercive, deployed to fund the UK's industrial revolution as well as to purchase Indian goods for the UK's consumption.[71] The tax collected in India during World War II was far more robust. The rise in tax and their repatriation as well as the sale of goods made in the UK in India precipitated India's demand for sovereignty.

Table 2 Excess profits tax collected in India 1941–51 (in INR million)

Year	Excess profit charged	Excess profits collected
1941	5.6	5.4
1942	92.2	78.5
1943	262.1	207.8
1944	680.7	603
1945	1140	1021.5
1946	1013.4	883.1
1947	944.6	757.6
1948	370.9	211.9
1949	353	284.9
1950	132.2	75.1
1951	132.7	81.2

Source: 'Report of the Tax Enquiry Commission 1953–54 vol. 2', Ministry of Finance, Department of Economic Affairs, Government of India, (New Delhi, Manager of Publications, 1955) 13.

C. The US

The excess profits tax was also used in the US as a wartime finance measure. A graduated tax rate was applied in the US and peak tax was 60 per cent on companies earning more than 33 per cent. This was subject to deductions for capital invested. Then in 1918, a combination of tax on war profits and excess profits was applied. The EPT was purged

[70] 'Report of the Tax Enquiry Commission 1953–54 vol. 2' (n 68).
[71] J Hickel, 'How Britain stole $45 trillion from India' (*Al Jazeera*, 19 December 2018) www.aljazeera.com/opinions/2018/12/19/how-britain-stole-45-trillion-from-india/.

from the statutes in 1921.[72] The repeal of the excess profits tax was backed by the Treasury's objections in line with numerous representations that 'it encourages wasteful expenditure, puts a premium on overcapitalisation and a penalty on brains, energy, and enterprise, discourages new ventures, and confirms old ventures in their monopolies. In many instances it acts as a consumption tax'.[73] Further, the tax 'discriminated against conservatively financed corporations and in favor (sic) of those whose capitalisation is exaggerated'.[74] It was also suggested that the conditions under which the tax was applied in 1917 were very different. Businesses were thriving as well as labour and capital being profitably employed.[75] In 1940, economies including the US were recovering from the Great Depression and not all industries were operating at capacity or profitably. In fact, there was significant risk aversion. Yet, the tax made a comeback through the National Industrial Recovery Act 1933.

In 1936 the law was amended to disallow the deduction of income tax from calculation of EPT. A graduated rate of 25 to 50 per cent was applied to absolute net profit in 1940. These rates were increased to 35 to 60 per cent in 1941. Graduated scale of tax had existed even during World War I but its efficacy in raising revenue had been limited. The need for steeper rates was expressed by President Roosevelt. The implementation of the tax was not rooted in a single principle. The House Committee stressed the legislation's intent to prevent the rise of 'war millionaires', and the 'substantial enrichment of already wealthy persons'.[76] Thus, much like the UK, the US also yielded to public pressure and the tax was taken up for further examination by the subcommittee of the House Ways and Means Committee.[77]

The Committee's report is considered a compromise between the Treasury, that preferred a capital method for computing excess profits, and the Joint Committee, which was in favour of the income method.[78] But as was later observed the company was to apply either method that resulted in lower liability.[79] In its final form, the highest rate of tax was essentially applicable to all large companies. It was pre-empted that this would result in subdivision of corporations. To stall the effort to avoid tax through such means a graduated rate of tax was applied where corporations subdivided for the purpose of tax avoidance. While there were disincentives to splitting up, corporations were offered the opportunity to file consolidated returns, to ensure that tax law conformed to economic reality,[80] thus benefitting a company whose units out-performed. An allowance of accelerated depreciation or amortisation was also permitted for expenditures on emergency facilities connected with the defence programme. At the time of its implementation the expected revenue in 1941 was US $106 million, which was small in comparison

[72] CJ Hynning, 'The Excess-Profits Tax of 1940: A Critique' (1940) 8(3) *The University of Chicago Law Review* 442.

[73] ibid.

[74] ibid 443.

[75] *Excess Profits Tax: A compilation of Materials on Excess Profits Tax and Bibliography on War Profits and Excess Profits Tax* (New York, Tax Foundation, 1940) 6.

[76] 'The Excess Profit Tax of 1940' (1940) 5 *The Yale Law Journal* 286, openyls.law.yale.edu/handle/20.500.13051/13036.

[77] Hynning (n 72) 444.

[78] ibid.

[79] 'Eccles Proposes a Speculation Tax' (*The New York Times*, 21 February 1945) 22.

[80] Hynning (n 72) 463.

to World War I collections. This in part had to do with the fact that it was applicable to only 13 per cent of total corporations, given the exclusion of mutual investment companies, foreign companies, US companies with foreign operations, air-mail carriers in excess of 95 per cent, corporations with (adjusted net) incomes not more than $5000, personal holding companies and diversified investment companies from this tax. In comparison, the design of the EPT in the US was far more liberal in comparison to the UK.

The 1940 Act also allowed for several adjustments to income and capital, as was applicable, such as exclusion of federal income tax, long-term capital gains and dividends from domestic companies. To those electing for the capital method,[81] casualty loss and abnormal adjustments were also permitted. Then there were adjustments to income for abnormal increases or decreases resulting from, for example, a change in accounting period, resulting from exploration, patents, R&D or dividends from a foreign corporation. The particular reason for exclusion of extractives was that war required them to use up their resources rapidly.[82] Given the complexity and specificity built into legislation, administrative discretion increased, particularly due to the lack of statutory guidance and judicial review.

The Senate estimated that large corporations would end up with an advantage by choosing the income method. Therefore, an additional corporate tax on 3.1 per cent was levied on all corporations with incomes above $25,000 to compensate for this. There were further complications such as preference for debt finance and undistributed profits since accumulated profits, stock rights and borrowed capital were included[83] in computation of the capital stock. Moreover, corporations were allowed to carry forward losses for two years – this was later restricted to small corporations. Standard profits were volatile between industries and Hynning shows using SEC filings that excess profits tax did not fall heavily on most corporations. Therefore, there were sufficient loopholes to avoid paying the tax.

In 1942, the rate of tax was raised to 90 per cent and then again to 95 per cent in 1944.[84] A related impact of the tax was reduction in reorganisations. It was not in anyone's interest to write off loss from bankruptcy that would reduce capital employed and thus increase estimates of excess profit.[85] This had a perverse effect of creating a bull market in companies with losses that in many cases were bought over, provided that the tax status did not change upon purchase. Randolph Paul's observation that 'it is not a natural economic development for a finance company in New York with a large unused excess-profits credit to combine with a war-profitable bus company in Texas'[86] is an example of such perverse effect.

As such practices came to light, the government introduced anti-avoidance legislation just as was attempted in the UK. The benefits of purchase were to be disallowed

[81] Capital was to be calculated by taking an average of daily value.

[82] BU Ratchford, 'The Federal Excess Profits Tax. Part One: Development and Present Status' (1945) 12(1) *Southern Economic Journal* 3.

[83] Adjustments were made for intercorporate transactions and mergers.

[84] ibid 2.

[85] ibid 5.

[86] 'Uneconomic Compulsions of Corporate Taxation: Termination and Taxes' (1944), Papers presented at the Fifty-Seventh Annual Meeting of The American Institute of Accountants, New York, 86.

such as where it was established that acquisitions (after 8 October 1940) were to avoid tax. Even with the income method there were complications. For example, the income in the base year could be inflated by not recognising the losses adequately, long-term capital gains were disregarded and dividends were exempt. Unlike the UK, US had a corporate tax system. Therefore, to accommodate for another tax on corporates, credit was allowed for regular taxes from EPT. This was later resolved by partitioning profits into regular and those subject to EPT. It is not possible[87] to estimate the windfall element and therefore the application of the tax became more difficult.

Just as in the UK's case where the capital employed in war bonds was part of the computation, a company which paid tax in excess of the minimum profit would receive refunds paid through bonds that were non-negotiable and non-refundable till the end of the war. In 1942 only 312 taxpayers within the top five brackets paid 41 per cent of the total tax whereas the smallest taxpayers, consisting of 31,039 taxpayers, paid only 2.3 per cent of the tax. More than a third of the US$17 billion in collections were in tax credits.

Among the rationale for EPT inequality, the most compelling was that it was 'a sine qua non of national unity'.[88] In the US, there was an increase in the share of the bottom 50 percentile in national income from approximately 15 per cent to 20 per cent.[89] The question, and a compelling one, then, is why was the tax repealed? In all countries it was agreed that it was a wartime measure that was to become irrelevant with the war's passing. It was expected that the tax laws would evolve over time expanding the scope of direct and indirect taxes. As it is there were difficulties in defining a normal year and excess profits.[90] Lastly, it was viewed as inconsistent with free private enterprise in the US.[91] As a result, the tax was also repealed in 1945 in the US.[92]

The impact of such increase in taxes is often debated. During World War I the main contention with the tax was its impact on inflation. The rise in prices could in turn raise revenues while there may be inequitable impact on consumers. The tax was not favoured as a peacetime measure. The Finance Committee expressed to the Senate that 'repressive taxes which in time of war are justified for the very reason that they diminish the demand for labour, capital and raw material, are for the very same reason obnoxious and un-desirable in times of peace'. Among the early discussions a common critique of the tax was that it went against the institution of profit, taking away incentive to operate.[93] Some economic evidence suggests higher taxes led to a slump in investment[94] in the US.[95] In the case of India, the political circumstances undermined further its utility in peacetime as much during war.

[87] Niyogi, n53, 175.
[88] Hicks, Hicks and Rostas (n 11).
[89] World Inequality database.
[90] *Excess Profits Tax* (n 75) 9.
[91] Ratchford (n 82).
[92] Reintroduced to finance the Korean War in 1950.
[93] FG Moult, '*The Economic Consequences of the Excess Profits Tax*' (London, s.n., 1943) 37. The author here is discussing the English tax with its 100% rate. For another good discussion of this same topic see Hicks, Hicks and Rostas (n 11).
[94] ER McGrattan, 'Capital Taxation During the U.S. Great Depression' (2012) *The Quarterly Journal of Economics* 127.
[95] ibid.

Ratchford compares the tax as implemented in the US and the UK to find that the tax was less stable in the US than the UK. The reasons for this were three: (i) gradual application in the US rather than the sudden imposition in the UK, (ii) choice between the capital method as well as earnings bases for computing credits, and (iii) the provision for exemptions and relief. In the US, the excess profits were largely the product of railroads and growth of small corporations. As Ratchford suggests, the lack of new investment and lower incomes had a deflationary impact since businesses did not have the leeway to raise prices. Moreover, the revenues were not comparable for these two countries since there were key differences in tax design. Tax-exempt securities, for instance, furnished a very significant part of large investment incomes in the US.[96] Another major difference was between the US and UK tax systems was that dividends were taxable in the hands of the investors in the US whereas in the UK corporate net income was taxed as individual income. It was observed by Musgrave and Seligman that the tax rates in the UK were already very high as opposed to in the US. Thus the scope for raising the taxes further in the UK was possible on the promise of future credits as well as the legitimacy of the government.

Other than the obvious difference observed by authors, the UK's experience with EPT can be compared with the US and India beyond the list of exclusions. For one, such a tax employed in tandem with a variety of other taxes is not without its own complexities. It is quite clear that the EPT had been unpopular in the US during World War I and had also found its way out of the law in the UK, only to re-emerge as a popular fiscal tool during World War II. Nonetheless, the application of tax was under varying economic circumstances. While in World War I there was a rise in inflation, output and thus revenues, World War II began after the Great Depression. The UK possessed the advantage of colonies such as India that it exploited to raise the taxes. It is seen that part of the fiscal plan on which the collections rested was government's spend financed by debt. It is estimated in 1944 that the government alone purchased more than one-half of the total output in the US and UK economy.[97] Taxes increased as a percentage of GDP in the UK (42 per cent) and the US (32 per cent), taxation of the central government declined as a percentage of total expenditure[98] between 1940–44. The composition of taxes also changed during this period.

It was seen that India jute procurement, even though strategically carried out, was able to create a support of some sort for the tax. The non-existence of corporation tax and capital gains tax in the UK allowed the application of tax with fewer exclusions, whereas the US with a corporate tax in place had to account for multitude of exclusions which in turn resulted in subversion through the means discussed above.

The excess profits tax was applied under peculiar circumstances in each country: the nature of fiscal policy pursued and the political autonomy. A relatively complex design in the US weakened the prospects of collection. Excess profits tax thus complemented individual income and corporate income tax. With the tax codes as defined

[96] ibid 22.

[97] RA Musgrave and HL Seligman, 'The wartime tax effort in the United States, the United Kingdom, and Canada' (1943) 36 *Proceedings of the Annual Conference on Taxation under the Auspices of the National Tax Association* 300–23.

[98] ibid.

today an excess profit tax may not be reasonable since it applies to a hard to benchmark circumstance-excess profit. It is reasonable to expect that the calculation of the tax base as being envisaged by the global minimum tax will possibly raise similar computational challenges as EPT alongside the need for a consultative process at an unprecedented scale. The latter has already been seen at play during the drafting of the rules.

V. Excess Profits Tax vs Financial Transactions Tax

A relatively recent economic shock occurred during the global financial crisis of 2008. Like the World Wars, there was a massive expansion in public finance, where governments bailed out entities that were too big to fail. The accumulation of private debt on public balance sheets created the need for an additional source of revenue. Many countries looked at financial transactions tax (FTT) as a viable option – an idea put forth earlier by JM Keynes and James Tobin. Tobin recommended the tax as means to limit cross border capital flows that impair country governments' efforts to regulate aggregate demand. Therefore, the FTT was in some ways like the EPT – meant to achieve multiple goals of revenue, redistribution and regulation. The principal difference however was in regard to capital controls that were a pre-condition for the success of EPT whereas FTT were to substitute for the lack of such controls.

Tax is often viewed as a regulatory tool. The US Supreme Court has deliberated this matter many times. One view is that 'any tax is a discouragement and therefore a regulation so far as it goes(.)'.[99] Thus it is articulated that the Congress '... must inevitably have a purpose other than the raising of revenue since it cannot escape the responsibility of controlling in the national interest – the non-fiscal regulatory effects of its distribution of tax burdens. There can, in short, be no such thing as taxation for revenue only'.[100] However, if one looks at the experience of EPT it was in fact a revenue raising mechanism that exceeded its initial regulatory prerogative. Where a tax is purely regulatory the revenue must decline as the underlying activity are regulated. However, in the US, where a stock transaction tax was applied in the US between 1914 and 1966 at a marginal rate of 0.02 on stock par value was not enough deter the financial crisis in 1929,[101] neither did the rates increases lead to an increase in revenue unlike the EPT. Instead, firms resorted to avoidance through the manipulation of tax base, that is, par value.[102]

With the interlinking of global markets, externalities can result in coordinated market failures as observed during the Great Depression and the Global Financial Crisis. As a result, FTT can potentially divert financial activity to less risky assets while generating additional tax revenues as insurance funds.[103] Revenues collected from regulatory taxes can give effect to desired redistribution.[104] Then there are purely financial

[99] *Pacific Fisheries v Alaska* [1925] 269 U.S. 296.
[100] *Sonzinsky v United States* [1936] 300 U.S. 506.
[101] LE Burman et al, 'Financial transaction taxes in theory and practice' (2016) 69(1) *National Tax Journal* 174.
[102] SA Bank and T Joseph, *War and Taxes* (Washington DC, The Urban Institute Press, 2008).
[103] C Garbarino and G Allevato, 'The Global Architecture of Financial Regulatory Taxes' (2014) 36 *Michigan Journal of International Law* 613.
[104] ibid 615.

reasons for additional taxation of transactions, this includes the special tax treatment of debt, that is, deductibility of interest from profits or that of bad loan reserves.[105] Despite the crisis and the reasons articulated for its application, unlike the EPT, the rationale for FTT has not been as clearly consistent across countries/regions.

In EU the implementation of the FTT was more than regulatory. It was to compensate for the exemption extended to financial and insurance services as per the VAT directive in 2006.[106] The Court of Justice of the European Union (CJEU) has interpreted the VAT exemption as a means to 'alleviate the difficulties in determining the tax base' as well as to 'avoid an increase in cost of consumer credit'[107] which may in turn be disadvantageous for Member States relative to the jurisdictions with no or low rates of VAT.[108] This makes the demand to levy the FTT unique in the context of EU. A more serious concern while levying such an additional tax is the capital mobility. There is a risk of migration of transactions to untaxed markets.[109] Similar proposals have been made for FTT in the US by Senator Bernie Sanders[110] but have been met with resistance.

It is important to verify why the FTT is similar to EPT in that it requires identification and gradation of risks which in turn is in reference to a benchmark. As securities are rated on some standard metric, risk assessment is often backward looking[111] which is similar to the exercise of determining excess profits. Yet, for the tax to be applied successfully, homogeneity is necessary across jurisdictions in market structures, asset classifications and norms. Opponents of FTT suggest that a badly designed tax would result in tax avoidance and would result in cascading.[112]

FTT will apply to financial activity that is mobile and can move to other jurisdictions. This is seen in the case of Sweden's FTT between 1984–91 that resulted in activity moving to London.[113] For this purpose, a supra-national tax would then have to be coordinated. A patchwork of measures would lead to substitution and relocation effects.[114] This can have serious ramifications if the financial sector is critical for the economic strength of a country-GDP, tax revenues and/or the balance of payments.

After the crisis, FTT received support from France and Germany[115] whereas it was strongly opposed by the UK.[116] In the end only 11 of the 27 EU members supported

[105] RS Avi-Yonah, 'Taxation as regulation: Carbon tax, health care tax, bank tax and other regulatory taxes' (2011) 1(1) *Accounting, Economics, and Law* 9.

[106] Council Directive 2006/112/EC of 28 November 2006 on the common system of value added tax [2006] OJ L 347.

[107] Case C-455/05 *Velvet v Steel Immobilien* [2007] ECR I-3225, para 24.

[108] *Group on the Future of VAT 26th meeting* (5 April 2019), European Commission.

[109] C Miller and A Tyger, 'Financial Transaction Tax: The Impact of a Financial Transactions Tax' (*Tax Foundation*, 23 January 2020) www.taxfoundation.org/financial-transaction-tax/.

[110] ibid.

[111] Often a critique of slower rating changes by Credit Rating Agencies.

[112] JH Cochrane, 'Finance: Function matters, not size' (2013) 27(2) *Journal of Economic perspectives* 44.

[113] Miller (n 109). JY Campbell and KA Froot, 'International experiences with securities transaction taxes' in JA Frankel (ed), *The Internationalization of Equity Markets* (Chicago, University of Chicago Press, 1994) 277–308.

[114] Garbarino and Allevato (n 103) 618.

[115] ibid 138.

[116] AV Loon, 'Societal dynamics in European economic governance: A comparative analysis of variation in British and German governmental stances' in M Rewizorski, K Jędrzejowska and A Wróbel, *The Future of Global Economic Governance* (New York, Springer, 2020) 130.

the proposal for enhanced co-operation on FTT.[117] There are two main reasons for disagreement – apprehensions that it would depress activity in national market and *societal expectations* from the government. Van Loon carries out an interesting comparison of responses to economic crisis by the UK and Germany that are comparable financial centres but politically different. The UK is a liberal market economy whereas Germany is a coordinated market economy.[118] It is perhaps for this reason that the UK did not follow through with the FTT. Prime Minister David Cameron balked at the idea of adopting the FTT, citing the European Commission's assessment that it would cost the EU €200 billion and 500,000 jobs. The then Chancellor of the Exchequer George Osborne also argued that the proposal of an EU-wide FTT would be a 'bullet aimed at the heart of London' and an 'economic suicide for Britain and for Europe'.[119] There was fear that London's historically strong financial market would move to Singapore and New York,[120] even though the UK[121] introduced a unilateral bank levy in 2011.[122] This again demonstrates that during peacetime countries do not have a common purpose and respond to demands of the economy and its citizens.

It is observed that a more limited tax on equity or stock market transactions is levied in other countries such as India, China, South Korea, South Africa and the UK. Yet, over the years declining collections along with the dampening effect of tax on activity, securities tax was eliminated in Germany in 1991, Japan in 1999, France in 2009 while in Italy in 2000[123] the tax rate was reduced sharply. In India's case the revenues remain small while the level of activity remains unaffected.

Why is it then that the FTT or a form thereof remains permanently in a small number of countries whereas the EPT was widely adopted, albeit temporarily? One reason for this is that the design of the tax systems varies across countries. In some countries financial services are covered by the indirect taxes and FTT is an add on while in others such as the EU it is meant to fix the exemption extended by the VAT Directive. This in turn is related to the respective size and nature of financial markets. In so far as tax structure is concerned, the applicability of FTT in addition to income tax and VAT is not feasible. While in India it is a third tax, its yield remains low and the impact is mixed.

A more significant cause is that with capital mobility and differences in the rate of return, the tax can change the incentives of investing in a jurisdiction. Therefore, it is important that it is adopted as widely and simultaneously. Yet, the need to encourage domestic financial activity in the FTT remains theoretical despite coordinated economic slowdown in the OECD.

[117] ibid.

[118] ibid.

[119] M Falloon, 'EU financial transaction tax would be "suicide"' (*Osborne*' *Reuters*, 14 November 2011) www.reuters.com/article/uk-britain-osborne/eu-financial-transaction-tax-would-be-suicide-osborne-idUKTRE7AD1E820111114?edition-redirect=uk.

[120] B Waterfield, 'George Osborne rejects EU transaction Tax' (*The Telegraph*, 10 September 2011) www.telegraph.co.uk/finance/newsbysector/banksandfinance/8754834/George-Osborne-rejects-EU-transaction-tax.html.

[121] France adopted a Bonus Tax whereas Germany and Sweden adopted a levy on uninsured liabilities and liabilities less deposits and capital to finance a resolution fund.

[122] Also adopted by: Austria, Belgium, Cyprus, Germany, Netherlands, Latvia, Portugal, Romania, Slovakia and Sweden.

[123] 'Financial Sector Taxation: The IMF Report to the G-20 and Background Material' (IMF, 2010) 147.

VI. The Future of Taxation: Learning from Experience

The two distinct phases of economic and political history shed light on some common features of tax policy during exceptional times. It is seen that during the wars and the financial crisis, the beneficiaries of government's budgetary support – manufacturing and financial industry – are also seen as a potential tax base. In the case of EPT, the underlying principle was that industries that profiteered from government procurement would desirably pay higher taxes. A contributing factor to their adoption in the US and the UK was the glaring inequalities that resulted after the war. Therefore, EPT was meant to be redistributive. A further point that this chapter develops is that an additional tax must be based on fair assessment of existing taxes where an untaxed base leaves scope for introduction of a new tax. However, the main cause for their wider acceptance was that the role and significance of the State was enhanced by the war – a reason that was not applicable in the case of India. The resistance to the tax in India was exacerbated by the political atmosphere. Yet, the monopoly structure of important industries such as jute paved the way for EPT in India where the large firms in receipt of preferential treatment showed support to the EPT. Nevertheless, irrespective of the context, the high tax rates were untenable and did not survive the war – in part because of the exorbitant rates and the loss of purpose. In the years after independence, however, India's income tax rates remained exceptionally high, a fallout of which was chronic tax evasion.

There emerge two other important lessons from the EPT and its comparison with FTT. The first is that any tax that is applied to profits differentiated by a benchmark rate of return or risk can be difficult to design. The law is made more complex with time since the high or even exorbitant tax rates necessitate exceptions.

It is often overlooked that in the case of war, the government's spending plan counteracts the contractionary effect of the tax increase, a consideration for peacetime increases in tax. The second important takeaway, especially derived from the contrast with FTT is that there is a reason why tax increases during war cannot be sustained or replicated in peacetime. Other than the legitimacy, there is need for coordinated implementation of tax policy. The synchronised economic cycle during war and the un-synchronised slowdown accompanied by greater capital mobility weakens the possibility of augmenting taxes. Therefore, any discussion on raising taxes through the application of a new tax would require legislative and administrative effort. Over time avoidance may become rampant as the tax loses its purpose and more so where the economic conditions vary widely across countries. The economic impact of COVID-19 was different across countries.[124] Therefore, any suggestion to implement an excess profits tax is not practical, since it would have to be coordinated. A simpler approach may be to raise the general level of taxes to a level compatible with national economic priorities.

[124] JM Sanchéz, 'COVID-19's Economic Impact around the World' (*Federal Reserve Bank of St. Louis*, 11 August 2021) www.stlouisfed.org/publications/regional-economist/third-quarter-2021/covid19s-economic-impact-world.

5

Earmarking of Taxes for Disruption and Recovery

ASHRITA PRASAD KOTHA*

Abstract

In times of disruption and recovery, raising new taxes may be quite unpopular which may lead governments to instead consider earmarked taxes. However, in such scenarios, earmarked taxes tend to be designed in a non-benefit manner which is contrary to the recommendations in prior literature. This author seeks to provide guidance to a country that weighs all its tax policy options and decides in favour of an earmarked tax. The discussion begins with a deconstruction of the concept of earmarking and a comparison of an earmarked tax with a general/labelled/Pigouvian tax and fee. This chapter reviews the primary theoretical justifications for earmarking to investigate the reasons why earmarking is considered unjustifiable in a non-benefit context which provides crucial learnings for designing an earmarked tax. The chapter also scrutinises the potential merits and demerits of using earmarked taxes as responses in periods of disruption. Finally, the text provides advice to governments and policy makers by outlining the governance structure and key earmarking attributes that need to be borne in mind when designing an earmarked tax, especially in periods of disruption and recovery. The COVID-19 pandemic-induced earmarked taxes are taken as case studies in this regard.

I. Introduction

The pandemic has required governments to look for resources to support vulnerable groups and undertake COVID-19 relief. This is particularly difficult considering countries are facing reduced GDPs. It has been estimated that 85 per cent of the countries around the world will see a contracted GDP resulting from the economic consequences of the pandemic.[1] The International Working Group on Financing Preparedness in the

* The author would like to acknowledge funding from the Austrian Science Fund (FWF): Doc 92-G in support of her research. She would also like to acknowledge the scholarship from Max Planck Institute for Tax Law and Public Finance, where some updates were made during her research stay. Any errors or omissions are her own.

[1] A Tandon, 'Presentation on Economic Impact of COVID-19 on Fiscal Space for "Filling the Coffers Post-COVID." Domestic Resource Mobilization Collaborative, Joint Learning Network' (July 2020) in

context of pandemics recommends that one of the measures that should be considered for domestic resource mobilisation are earmarked taxes 'where they might be an effective way to generate additional resources'.[2] Earmarking or hypothecation of taxes is the act of dedicating a tax to a specific public service.[3] The nuances of the concept of earmarking are discussed in section II.

In the wake of the pandemic, as existing resources may be insufficient, governments will have to weigh various tax and non-tax policy options (such as additional borrowings). When considering tax measures, increases in the aftermath of the pandemic may only be desirable if they are being applied for inclusive growth and social programmes.[4] Raising new taxes is unpopular,[5] more so in times of distress, hence the choice of an earmarked tax. One can already see some real-world examples of earmarked taxes introduced as response measures to the pandemic.

As per a report of the International Monetary Fund, Liberia and Uruguay are using earmarked taxes on wages to finance their COVID-19 fund.[6] In December 2020, Argentina introduced a 'solidarity and extraordinary contribution' to mitigate the effects of the pandemic. The levy took the form of a one-off progressive wealth tax. One-fifth of the proceeds are allocated for the purchase of medical equipment, medicines, vaccines and healthcare. The remaining proceeds are allocated to different purposes and the law also provides the relevant ministry/earmarked fund/state owned public undertaking that will administer the funds.[7] The budgetary treatment and designated authority for this portion of the tax needs to be examined further. In July 2020, Egypt imposed a 1 per cent corona tax on the net salaries of all public and private sector employees earning in excess of a certain threshold (EGP 2,000 per month). Additionally, a 0.5 per cent tax is imposed on all net pensions received. The proceeds

C Ozar et al, 'Health Earmarks and Health Taxes: What Do Know, World Bank Knowledge Brief' (World Bank, Washington, DC, December 2020).

[2] International Working Group on Financing Preparedness, *From Panic and Neglect to Investing in Health Security: Financing Pandemic Preparedness at a National Level* (World Bank, Washington, DC, 2017) 44–47. For more discussions on domestic resource mobilisation, see ch 6 of this volume 'Counting Doubloons. A Critical Assessment of how British Overseas Territories are Funding the COVID-19 Response' by Panadès-Estruch. For discussions on regional or supranational level mobilisations, see chapters on EU taxation such ch 8 'Revising the Justification for an EU Tax in a Post-crisis Context' by Pantazatou, ch 10 'The COVID-19 Crisis as a Momentum for the Creation of a European Tax System?' by Grisostolo and Scarcella, ch 7 'The Role of Crisis in State-Building the European Union through Finance and Taxation: Will COVID-19 and the Russian Attack Trigger Further Union?' by Hernández González-Barreda, ch 9 'Fiscal Evolution and the Syndemic' by Garbarino.

[3] JM Buchanan, 'The Economics of Earmarked Taxes' (1963) 71 *The Journal of Political Economy* 457.

[4] R de Mooij et al, 'Tax Policy for Inclusive Growth after the Pandemic' (Special Series on Fiscal Policies to Respond to COVID-19, International Monetary Fund, 16 December 2020) 3.

[5] AM Rivlin, 'The Continuing Search for a Popular Tax' (1989) 79 *The American Economic Review* 113, 113–17.

[6] F Rahim et al, 'COVID-19 Funds in Response to the Pandemic' (Special Series on COVID-19, International Monetary Fund, 26 August 2020).

[7] The remaining proceeds are pledged for subsidising micro, small and medium enterprises with a view to supporting employment and remuneration of workers (20%), student scholarships (20%), supporting inhabitants of identified neighbourhoods (15%) and natural gas exploration (25%). The designated authorities for some of the proceeds are identified as the Ministry of Education, the Social Urban Integration Fund, Integración Energética Argentina SA which is a state owned entity. Solidarity and Extraordinary Contribution to Help Moderate the Effects of the Pandemic Law 27605, Articles 7, 8 (Argentina).

are to be kept in a separate fund earmarked for health services, medical research and aiding those negatively impacted.[8]

This is not entirely surprising as countries have often introduced new taxes when facing extraordinary circumstances such as war or financial crisis, as is also observed in chapter two of this volume 'Schumpeter's Crisis of the Tax State, Globalisation and Redistribution' by van Ganzen and Hording and chapter three 'Lessons of Three World Wars' by Walters. These immediate examples reveal the introduction of earmarked taxes as likely short-term tax policy responses. Argentina's contribution is explicitly described as a one-time measure. As we move through different phases of recovery,[9] countries will have to evaluate whether earmarked measures are to be introduced and, if so, whether as short-term or long-term measures. What we see from these recent examples is that the contributors pay the tax for benefits accruing to a larger group of beneficiaries – all those in need of healthcare or those negatively impacted by the pandemic, etc. The contributors from the (relatively) wealthy/higher income earning sections of the community may not rely on the public healthcare system and the financial assistance extended by the government. According to prior literature, earmarking is considered to be strong when it manifests the benefit principle, that is, when the contributors receive goods or services in return. The goods have the characteristics of private goods – no external benefits that affect anyone but the users, no claim for special treatment. On the contrary, when the connection between the contributor and beneficiary of the earmarked tax is 'tenuous or non-existent' and the earmarked tax pursues social welfare or redistribution, it is considered weaker.[10]

Hence, earmarked taxes emerging as reactions to the pandemic would be considered weaker earmarks according to existing literature. However, government interventions that take place after a disaster has occurred are typically based on redistributing from those who did not suffer the loss or who have suffered less from the loss.[11] Thus, it may be too simplistic to conclude that strong earmarks readily translate into good earmarks while weaker earmarks ought to be discarded as bad earmarks. Given that earmarking outside the context of the benefit principle is considered contentious and that ordinary budgetary allocations can be used as a means to pursue social welfare goals,[12] there is a need for closer analysis of this tax policy option. This chapter discusses whether there may be some circumstances when so-called weaker earmarks are justifiable and, moreover, if limits can be built to make these arrangements work in favour of the public.

[8] G Essam El-Din, 'Egypt parliament approves CBE, coronavirus tax law' (*ahramonline*, 20 July 2020) english.ahram.org.eg/NewsContent/1/64/374949/Egypt/Politics-/Egypt-parliament-approves-CBE,-coronavirus-tax-law.aspx; L El Baradei, '1% Corona Tax on Public Employees' Salaries in Egypt: How Fair is it?' (*PA Times*, 22 August 2020) patimes.org/1-corona-tax-on-public-employees-salaries-in-egypt-how-fair-is-it/.

[9] See, for discussion on the different phases of the pandemic and the tax policy responses thereto, R Collier et al, 'COVID-19 and Fiscal Policies: Tax Policy and the COVID-19 Crisis' (2020) 48 *Intertax* 794.

[10] W McCleary, 'The Earmarking of Government Revenue: A Review of Some World Bank Experience' (1991) 6 *The World Bank Research Observer* 81.

[11] M Phaup and C Kirschner, 'Budgeting for Disasters: Focusing on the Good Times' (2010) 10 *OECD Journal on Budgeting* 21, 4 See also van Ganzen and Vording, 'Schumpeter's Crisis of the Tax State, Globalisation and Redistribution', ch 2 of this volume, on how crises increase the weight of the tax state in terms of redistribution.

[12] D Bös, 'Earmarked Taxation: Welfare Versus Political Support' (2000) 75 *Journal of Public Economics* 439, 439.

While this chapter does not advocate the imposition of a new tax, it seeks to provide guidance to a country that weighs its tax policy options and decides in favour of an earmarked tax in periods of crisis and disruption. As this chapter only considers the situation of using an earmarked tax for alleviating the revenue needs in periods of crisis and disruption, it does not comment on whether earmarking can be used as a tax policy tool for achieving redistribution, in general.

The second section of the chapter seeks to break down the concept of earmarking and compares an earmarked tax with a general/labelled/Pigouvian tax and fee. The third section reviews the primary theoretical justifications for earmarking to investigate the reasons why earmarking is considered unjustifiable in a non-benefit context. This provides crucial learnings for designing an earmarked tax. The fourth section reviews the merits and demerits of using earmarked taxes as responses in periods of disruption. The fifth section provides guidance for the broader governance structure and key earmarking attributes that policy makers need to bear in mind when designing an earmarked tax suitable for periods of disruption and recovery. The taxes introduced as a response to the pandemic are also looked at more closely to identify potential weaknesses.

II. Earmarked Taxes Compared to Other Tax Policy Options

A. Breaking Down the Concept of Earmarking

There are several variations on the actual implementation of earmarking leading to an understanding that earmarking has become 'less a matter of definition than concept'.[13] One of the quintessential hallmarks of an earmarked tax is that it involves an *ex ante* dedication of tax revenues for a specific public service. Dedication must be undertaken by law. Merely labelling a levy with an indicative purpose not followed up with a dedication under law does not amount to earmarking.

When the tax is earmarked, the proceeds are 'channelled through the general treasury to a specific purpose or paid directly to a dedicated fund'.[14] It is different from general fund financing where all revenues are maintained in a consolidated pool which are *ex post* allocated for public services.[15] General fund financing operates as a two-step process – aggregate level of taxation is decided first which is followed by

[13] HW Batt, 'A General Theory of Earmarking' (1993) 4 *State Tax Notes* 1420, 1422.

[14] K Gwilliam and Z Shalizi, 'Road Funds, User Charges, and Taxes' (1999) 14 *The World Bank Research Observer* 159, 183; See, for an account of the inconsistencies in management and governance of Indian earmarked taxes, AP Kotha, 'Budgetary Treatment of Indian Earmarked Taxes: A Tale of Governance Gaps' (2021) 101 *Tax Notes International* 1419.

[15] H Ashiabor, 'Financing Environmental Expenditures Through Earmarking of Taxes and Charges' in *Tax Expenditures and Environmental Policy* (Cheltenham, Northampton, MA, Edward Elgar Publishing, 2020) 148.

distribution/allocation decisions.[16] The aggregate level of taxation entails deciding the size of the budget/budget constraint. The following vote on distribution decides the budget composition.[17] The separation of decisions means that the opportunity cost of an additional expenditure is not a new tax but reduced expenditure on other public goods.[18]

It must be clarified that another basis to differentiate between earmarking as pure/substantive and symbolic/softer is based on the revenue expenditure link that the earmarking arrangement establishes. Earmarking is pure/substantive when revenue from the tax determines the spending on the service. On the other hand, when earmarking is symbolic/softer, the revenue from the tax does not determine expenditure as transfers from general funds/budget are permissible.[19] This chapter considers the revenue-expenditure linkage aspect as an attribute (in section V(C)(ii)) to be considered by policy makers when designing an earmarked tax.

A country that has decided to opt for a tax policy measure to tackle pandemic relief in the short term or long term will be faced with some choices. For the purposes of this chapter, earmarked taxes are compared to general, Pigouvian labelled taxes and fees.

B. Earmarked Tax vs General/Labelled/Pigouvian Tax

Latham CJ of the High Court of Australia described a tax as 'a compulsory exaction of money by public authority for public purposes enforceable by law and is not payment for services rendered'.[20] A tax is said to have four attributes. First, a tax is a compulsory payment opposed to a voluntary payment. Second, the payment is made for augmenting government's resources for public purposes. Lawmakers have the prerogative to determine which public purposes are to be supported.[21] Third, the payment is made to the government. Fourth, the payment is without the expectation of a quid pro quo or a specific reciprocal benefit.[22] Pigouvian taxes are imposed on activities that cause negative externalities to correct such impact. Such a tax thus has a regulatory goal and the tax revenues are ordinarily transferred to the public in general.[23]

Unlike a general tax, an earmarked tax *ex ante* sets aside proceeds for particular public purpose(s). In the absence of such *ex ante* earmarking, proceeds being available

[16] RE Wagner and DR Lee, 'Chapter 7: The Political Economy of Tax Earmarking' in RE Wagner (ed), *Charging for Government: User Charges and Earmarked Taxes in Principles and Practice* (Abingdon, Routledge, 2012) 115.

[17] EK Browning, 'Collective Choice and General Fund Financing' (1975) 83 *The Journal of Political Economy* 377, 379–80.

[18] RS Teja, 'The Case for Earmarked Taxes' (1988) 35 *Staff papers – International Monetary Fund* 523, 526.

[19] M Wilkinson, 'Paying for Public Spending: Is There a Role for Earmarked Taxes?' (1994) 15 *Fiscal Studies* 119, 125; R Carling, 'Tax Earmarking Is It Good Practice?' (The Centre for Independent Studies, 2007) 1; RM Bird, 'Analysis of Earmarked Taxes' (1997) 14 *Tax Notes International* 2095, 2099.

[20] *Matthews v Chicory Marketing Board* No. (1938) 80 CLR 263 (High Court 9 August 1938).

[21] HD Spitzer, 'Taxes Vs. Fees: A Curious Confusion' (2003) 38 *Gonzaga Law Review* 335, 339.

[22] M Barassi, 'The Notion of Tax and the Different Types of Income' in B Peeters et al (eds), *The Concept of Tax: 2005 EATLP Congress, Naples (caserta)*, EATLP International Tax Series vol 3 (Amsterdam, IBFD, European Association of Tax Law Professors EATLP, 2007) 64.

[23] T Jiang, 'Earmarking of Pollution Charges and the Sub-Optimality of the Pigouvian Tax' (2001) 45 *The Australian Journal of Agricultural and Resource Economics* 623, 624.

for any public purpose would depend on the outcome of the budgetary allocation process in a general fund finance setting. An earmarked tax should also be distinguished from Pigouvian taxes. Pigouvian taxes are imposed on activities that cause negative externalities in order to correct such impact. Such taxes have a regulatory goal and the tax revenues are ordinarily transferred to the consolidated budgetary pool.[24] An earmarked tax, on the other hand, transfers tax revenues to a dedicated or earmarked purpose.[25] An earmarked tax thus is not just a tax levied in pursuit of a particular goal; it goes a step further by *ex ante* dedication of the proceeds for the earmarked purpose. It is also important to distinguish an earmarked tax from a surcharge; the latter is an emergency funding measure for meeting specific spending needs.[26] However, a surcharge may not be specifically earmarked for such ends.

All taxes have names but mostly the name just describes the tax base or taxable event, such as income tax, wealth tax, sales tax, etc. Labelling of a tax in a favourable manner can have a significant impact on the support for the tax.[27] In some instances, taxes may be labelled with a name indicative of the purpose such as solidarity taxes.[28] For example, the German solidarity charge gave the impression that the money was to be spent for solidarity measures. Despite the suggestive/declaratory label, proceeds were not earmarked by law.[29] This is unlike the Argentinian extraordinary solidarity contribution which is labelled and earmarked. A labelled tax which is not earmarked goes into the general fund and can be used for any purpose. Earmarking is meant to be a stronger form of connecting tax revenues to a purpose as it assures spending on the purpose.[30] Some Indian State governments had introduced new measures called COVID tax or COVID fee on alcohol consumption.[31] However, it is unclear if these are earmarked for COVID-19 relief. Labelling a tax without corresponding earmarking by law could positively garner support for the levy but may lead to a misperception which is undesirable, especially in times of crisis.

The process of determining the threshold of expenditure that should be spent on a specific purpose is sometimes referred to as expenditure earmark.[32] Here, the

[24] AJ Hoffer and GR Crowley, 'Chapter 6: Earmarking Tax Revenues: Leviathan's Secret Weapon?' in AJ Hoffer and T Nesbit (eds), *For Your Own Good: Taxes, Paternalism, and Fiscal Discrimination in the Twenty-First Century* (Arlington, Mercatus Center at George Mason University, 2018) 123. For arguments relating to earmarking of environmental taxes, please see ch 13 'A Case for Environmental Taxation as a Response to the Covid-19 Economic Crisis' by Scuderi, Rizzo and Loucaidou.

[25] Jiang (n 23).

[26] J Rogers-Glabush and International Bureau of Fiscal Documentation, *IBFD International Tax Glossary*, 7th edn (Amsterdam, IBFD, 2015) 459.

[27] The authors found greater support for a tax labelled as CO2 tax as opposed to a gasoline tax. Å Löfgren and K Nordblom, 'Puzzling Tax Attitudes and Labels' (2009) 16 *Applied Economics Letters* 1809.

[28] See, for a review of country responses in the form of solidarity taxes, only few of which, as can be seen are in fact earmarked A Waris, 'Solidarity Taxes in the Context of Economic Recovery Following the COVID-19 Pandemic' (May 2021).

[29] Bös (n 12) 440.

[30] J Hundsdoerfer et al, 'The Influence of Tax Labeling and Tax Earmarking on the Willingness to Contribute – A Conjoint Analysis' (2013) 65 *Schmalenbach Business Review* 359.

[31] IANS, '3 Northeast States Hike Duty on Liqour by 25 per Cent to Meet Financial Burden Arising from Lockdown' (*The Statesman*, Guwahati, Shillong, Itanagar, Guwahati, Shillong, Itanagar, 9 May 2020) www.thestatesman.com/coronavirus/3-northeast-states-hike-duty-on-liquor-by-25-per-cent-to-meet-financial-burden-arising-from-lockdown-1502886379.html.

[32] C Cashin et al, 'Earmarking for Health: From Theory to Practice' (World Health Organization, 2017) 8.

expenditure level is not tied to the revenues of a specific tax and, thus, there is no tax revenue earmarking as evident from the examples from Argentina and Egpyt. Contingency funds relying on budgetary allocations to insulate proceeds for contingencies such as disasters, unforeseeable events, etc. constitute an expenditure earmark.[33] However, such contingency funds financed by budgetary allocation should not be confused with the *ex ante* tax revenue earmarking which is the focus of this chapter.

C. Earmarked Tax vs Fee

An earmarked levy may be designed as a tax or a fee. Literature suggests that earmarking exhibits the 'strongest equity rationale in the benefits connection, where it extends the quid-pro-quo concept'.[34]

A fee is a payment for a particular service that the government has monopoly over. If the person demands the service, he has no choice but to pay the fee. Sometimes fees are distinguished from user charges which are imposed on services that are provided by the government but where the government is not the sole service provider.[35] Professor Seligman noted: '... where the government undergoes a certain expense, and actually performs a definite service, for the particular individual, the benefits of which are separably and measurably calculable ... it must be pointed out that such payments do not come under the head of taxes, properly so-called'.[36]

Although fees are in a sense earmarked for the related activity, implementation of a fee and earmarked tax are not the same in terms of efficiency and equity.[37] Earmarked taxes establish a linkage, but at the aggregate level; the total revenues of a particular tax are allocated for spending for the earmarked public task. Unlike in the case of a user charge/fee, earmarked tax does not exhibit a relationship between 'individual tax burden and individual satisfaction from public expenditure'.[38] This is because of the absence of the quid pro quo element in an earmarked tax which is present in a fee. A fee enhances welfare by giving the consumer autonomy to choose a preferred quantity of publicly provided goods to be consumed. In the case of an earmarked tax, the consumer is taxed mandatorily and has no individual entitlement over the publicly provided good or service. Also, earmarked money is spent after the money has been raised – connection is between the expected value of the public good and the tax paid.[39] Fees or user charges are not appropriate when pursuing redistribution goals.[40]

33 Phaup and Kirschner (n 11) 13.

34 F Stocker and S Maguire in JJ Cordes et al (eds), *The Encyclopedia of Taxation & Tax Policy*, 2nd edn (Washington, DC, The Urban Institute Press, 2005) 90.

35 RM Bird and T Tsiopoulos, 'User Charges for Public Services: Potentials and Problems' (1997) 45 *Canadian Tax Journal* 25, 47.

36 ERA Seligman, 'The Progress of Taxation during the Past Twenty-Five Years, and Present Tendencies' (1910) 11 *American Economic Association Quarterly* 331, 341–42.

37 Teja (n 18) 527.

38 Bös (n 12) 440.

39 ibid 460.

40 D Duff, 'Benefit Taxes and User Fees in Theory and Practice' (2004) 54 *The University of Toronto Law Journal* 391, 413.

Economists consider an earmarked tax as a second-best instrument of finance, ranking after a fee.[41] However, there may be some cases where a fee is not advisable. This could be because a fee is impossible to calculate (consumption cannot be monitored or approximated) or is subject to high transaction costs. Healthcare can be priced directly although it may be considered inappropriate to do so, in some cases.[42]

III. Enquiry into Theoretical Justifications for Earmarking

Earmarked or hypothecated taxes can be traced back to ancient times.[43] There are several theoretical justifications for the practice of earmarking. Three primary theoretical justifications (from the public choice theory, behavioural economics/tax psychology and fiscal social contract theory by legal philosophers and public finance experts) are investigated here.[44]

A. Earmarking Enables Individual Participation in Collective Decision Making: Public Choice Theory

The first theoretical justification originates from the public choice theory which perceives earmarking as an instrument for enabling individual participation in collective decision making. This justification comes from the most recent revival of earmarking facilitated by the theoretical framework provided by noble prize-winning economist, James Buchanan. Buchanan's work was inspired by the *New Principle of Just Taxation* written by Knut Wicksell, a noted Swedish scholar.

In the *New Principle of Just Taxation* Wicksell was concerned with tax justice. Despite the title, he was not identifying a new principle but was relying on the benefit principle. He emphasised the need for fiscal matters to be decided by a unanimous legislative vote to ensure voluntary consent. Every expenditure had to be assigned to a definite revenue category, and every public expenditure decision had to be voted simultaneously with alternative tax plans.[45] Whichever proposal of funding secured a unanimous vote (modified to approximate unanimity for practical reasons), it would

[41] Teja (n 18) 527.

[42] Wagner and Lee (n 16) 115.

[43] J Le Grand, 'Chapter 11: Hypothecation' in *Motivation, Agency, and Public Policy: Of Knights and Knaves, Pawns and Queens* (Oxford, Oxford University Press, 2003) 150.

[44] There may be additional justifications. For example, in the context of pigouvian taxes, earmarking has been justified as a transfer medium for mitigating the burden caused by the negative externality. Hoffer and Crowley (n 24).

[45] The tax plan could involve a new tax or an increase in an existing tax. As an example, Wicksell says that the tax plans could involve an increase in the tax on spirits and on beer and wine or an increase in income tax with an increase in inheritance tax. K Wicksell, 'A New Principle of Just Taxation' in RA Musgrave and AT Peacock (eds), *Classics in the Theory of Public Finance* (New York, Palgrave Macmillan, 1994).

be approved. If none of the proposals received the necessary consent, it would not be passed.[46]

This way the consent was truly voluntary, and taxes would not be considered as a burden. Although based on the benefit principle, he conceived that the reformed legislative process would foster a sense of community and persons would occasionally support decisions from which they expect no 'great or direct benefit' or they may contribute 'beyond their own advantage'. His model of tax justice was based on few assumptions – there is justice in the extant distribution of property and income, legislature is truly representative of the society, legislature has full autonomy to accept or reject any public expenditure decision.[47]

Wicksell's emphasis on taking a collective and simultaneous decision on taxes and end uses did not spell out earmarking, but instead inspired Buchanan.[48] Buchanan defined earmarking as the practice of 'designating or dedicating specific revenues to the financing of specific public services'. Unlike prior writing, he studied earmarking as enabling the participation of an individual in collective decision making and not as a restriction on the budgetary authority. For him, the merit of an earmarking system was that it compartmentalised fiscal decisions as the individual can independently vote (directly or indirectly) on funds given the specified revenue sources. In his theory, the median voter-taxpayer-beneficiary has the ability to decide the budget size *and* the budget composition. This is unlike general fund financing where the individual can (albeit through his representatives) only vote on the total outlay of expenditures as the bundles of public services are already decided by the budgetary authorities. Buchanan explains the phenomenon of general fund financing as a tie-in sale where a pre-determined bundle of goods and services are sold and the individual can only choose the units to be bought.

Buchanan argued that the constitution should prohibit earmarking where there is no complementary relationship between the tax base and the public service funded from tax proceeds. Quite categorically, for Buchanan the taxpayer is the beneficiary; he concludes that 'non-complementary dedication of tax revenues does not, and cannot, serve efficiency-enhancing purposes, and should be constitutionally prohibited, in any and all models of fiscal process'.[49] The point on complementarity was also emphasised by other scholars even though they acknowledged the presence of contrary examples.[50] The reason for this emphasis is that it enables taxpayers to reveal their preference, so managers know the quantity of the public good to be supplied.[51] This system allows appropriate allocation of taxpayer sums. Where the contributor-beneficiary nexus is broken or absent, earmarking is mixed with objectives of redistribution and social welfare and is problematic as it signifies a 'straight

[46] ibid.

[47] ibid.

[48] Buchanan (n 3).

[49] JM Buchanan, 'Chapter 10: The Constitutional Economics of Earmarking' in RE Wagner (ed), *Charging for Government: User Charges and Earmarked Taxes in Principle and Practice* (Abingdon, Routledge, 2011).

[50] Bird (n 19); Goetz observes that in practice earmarking may exhibit examples where the 'link between the tax preference and the expenditure preference need not be so direct'. See CJ Goetz, 'Earmarked Taxes and Majority Rule Budgetary Processes' (1968) 58 *The American Economic Review* 128.

[51] Bird (n 19).

transfer' between two groups of citizens. Moreover, earmarking leads to an arbitrary supply of resources.[52] Hence, for Buchanan limits in the constitution were necessary to prohibit earmarks that would result in direct transfers among certain groups of the community or discriminatory practices.

It is pertinent to note that Buchanan's work has met with a lot of criticism. Five important points of critique are made here, about the earmarking model and, more generally, about his theory. First, he himself confessed that his model was far from the real-world and that he does not account for decision making costs. He assumed that earmarking works through a single agent; the fiction of the median voter-taxpayer-beneficiary he introduced. This is quite contrary to earmarking in the real world that involves multiple agents to function effectively.[53] Second, he believed that if the tax base and public service were complementary, there was no need for an external legal constraint that would mandate the government to use the funds for the given public service. However, an earmark must be spelt out in the law, as otherwise, the allocation would happen based on general fund financing. Moreover, for keeping tax systems in check, there is a need for placing content-based restraints which is unlike Buchanan's focus only on consent. As Schoen observed, in the world of Wicksell's (near) unanimity, 'consent fully substitutes for content'.[54] Third and most importantly, Buchanan does not address existing distributional inequities. This is unlike Wicksell who assumed existing societal distribution to be equal when expounding his principle of tax justice.[55] Fourth, when Buchanan uses the term 'constitution', he does not refer to it as a 'narrow legal term', but as the sum total of the fiscal arrangements.[56] Buchanan explains the notion of constitution as the 'set of rules, or social institutions, within which individuals operate and interact with one another'.[57] Hence, when he refers to constitutional limits it is not in a technical legal sense, as lawyers understand it, and the repeated usage of constitutional limits may not point to material restraints. Fifth, Buchanan's writing is also heavily criticised for not accounting for the development of institutions.[58]

B. Earmarked Taxes Usher Greater Taxpayer Support: Behavioural Economics/Tax Psychology

Scholars have studied the relationship between earmarked taxes and taxpayer behaviour. It has been noted that while taxpayers view taxes negatively, earmarked taxes are considered favourably. The reason for the antagonism with respect to taxes is that

[52] McCleary (n 10) 83, 90.
[53] Bös (n 12) 440–41.
[54] W Schoen, 'Taxation and Democracy' (2019) 72 *Tax L Rev* 235, 253.
[55] Wicksell (n 45).
[56] D De Cogan, *Tax Law, State-Building and the Constitution* (Oxford, Hart Publishing, 2020) 8.
[57] G Brennan and JM Buchanan, 'Chapter 1: Taxation in Constitutional Perspective' in *The Power to Tax: Analytical Foundations of a Fiscal Constitution* (Cambridge, Cambridge University Press, 1980) 2–3.
[58] JW Martin et al (eds), 'The Thunder of History: The Origins and Development of the New Fiscal Sociology' in *The New Fiscal Sociology: Taxation in Comparative and Historical Perspective* (US, Cambridge University Press, 2009) 10.

taxpayers have no idea of where the money is spent; they may think that the money is spent wastefully or for purposes they do not support. On the other hand, with earmarked taxes, the knowledge of how the money will be used generates greater support and willingness to contribute. This positive correlation in the mind of the taxpayer implies 'political favour' for financing new services.[59] Earmarking empowers citizens with an instrument to monitor the activities of the government.[60]

From the perspective of the government, providing credible commitments is efficient as it encourages an environment of compliance rather than coercion. Proponents of the fiscal contract theory thus view the state as the provider/seller of services where citizens have the power to withhold revenue.[61] States often use earmarking for politically popular programmes such as education or highly visible public goods such as building highways.[62] In an empirical study, participants exhibited a stronger willingness to contribute to an earmarked tax when compared to a merely labelled tax with an indicative purpose but no actual promise of earmarking. Participants were able to distinguish between the two and exhibited a stronger preference for the earmarked tax.[63]

Although at a high level taxpayers support earmarked taxes, the degree of support may vary based on the precise features. The willingness to contribute is higher when the earmarked tax has contributory attributes. The support may also be garnered when paying for 'manifestly essential programs'.[64] In the context of the pandemic, but also otherwise, this could be significant, as a community may not always agree on what is needed. Though pandemics may help governments to identify financing gaps, taxpayer support would also depend on whether the community believes it to be essential. For example, in the pandemic, some communities may be divided on financing vaccination costs.

Drawing from consumer fairness studies, scholars have likened taxpayers to consumers; taxpayers react positively to earmarked taxes where there is source-use alignment. Source-use alignment can be found when the nexus between revenue source and end use of the revenues accords with familiar consumer fairness norms. This can happen either when the contributors are the beneficiaries or when the contributors are taxed on a particular activity causing a negative externality and the proceeds are applied towards mitigating the ensuing harm.[65] This finding corroborates the emphasis on the complementarity by the public choice theory.

The downside of basing support solely on behavioural justifications is that earmarking may be used for popular programmes which do not need consensus building. Hence, there must be limits to the invocation of this justification.

[59] Rivlin (n 5) 113–14, 116; See Bös (n 12) for a contrary view that a rational taxpayer would make the correlation between taxes paid and public services.

[60] CA Schaltegger and B Torgler, 'Direct Democracy, Decentralization and Earmarked Taxation: An Institutional Framework to Foster Tax Compliance' (2008) 36 *Intertax* 426.

[61] JF Timmons, 'The Fiscal Contract: States, Taxes, and Public Services' (2005) 57 *World Politics* 530, 534–35.

[62] Hoffer and Crowley (n 24) 128.

[63] Hundsdoerfer et al (n 30).

[64] SC Tahk, 'Earmarking: The Potential Benefits' (2006) 4 *Pittsburgh Tax Review* 79–80.

[65] D Hemel and E Porter, 'Aligning Taxes and Spending: Theory and Experimental Evidence' [2019] *Behavioural Public Policy* 1.

C. Earmarking as a Mechanism to Strengthen the Fiscal Social Contract

The fiscal social contract is an 'offshoot' of the social contract. It means that members of society pay tax in return for sharing in the benefit of governance. It also requires citizen engagement in tax matters, harking back to the idea of no taxation without representation.[66]

Citizens rarely get to directly engage or vote on specific revenue and spending decisions. Moreover, citizens pay taxes in the hope of public services for the community at large but could doubt whether the government will keep its promise, especially if trust towards the government is already low. In countries with low trust (caused by a host of factors), repairing the budget contract[67] could be one of the means used to raise trust. This could be done by 'explicitly linking the amounts allocated to the results produced or expected'.[68] Earmarking can achieve this explicit linkage. Victor recommends earmarking of proceeds to a post-pandemic fund in Brazil to renegotiate the vulnerable social contract.[69]

Earmarking can increase the costs to the government for failing to keep up its promise of spending the money for prior pledged purposes. Bird argues that viewing earmarking from a contractual rationale makes sense only when the benefit principle is applicable.[70] However, evidence from countries in Africa and Latin America bears out the moderate positive effects of earmarked taxes when seeking to achieve funding for public purposes such as education and health, in a non-benefit context. Such taxes described as 'progressive fiscal contracts' were found to have a positive impact on levels of poverty, violence, tax revenues and support for development related issues. The countries forming part of the study were described as 'fragile states' with weak fiscal systems and an inability to raise taxes that saw the positive benefits of earmarking.[71]

Having said that, it is important to present contrary evidence. Earmarking may, in some instances, also lead to an erosion of trust. An example in point comes from the historical experience of Britain. While earmarking was popular in the eighteenth century, the high regime of trust took a subsequent beating. In a bid to reform the

[66] MA Umar et al, 'What Is Wrong With the Fiscal Social Contract of Taxation in Developing Countries? A Dialogue With Self-Employed Business Owners in Nigeria' (2017) 7 *SAGE Open* 1, 9. For other perspectives on state-building and social contract, please see ch 7 'The Role of Crisis in State-Building the European Union through Finance and Taxation: Will COVID-19 and the Russian Attack Trigger Further Union?' by Hernández González-Barreda, ch 9 'Fiscal Evolution and the Syndemic' by Garbarino and ch 2 'Schumpeter's Crisis of the Tax State, Globalisation and Redistribution' by van Ganzen.

[67] Wildavsky describes the American budget as a contract; 'a promise to supply funds under specified conditions, and the agencies agree to spend them in ways that have been agreed upon'. AB Wildavsky, *The Politics of the Budgetary Process*, 2nd edn (Boston, Little, Brown and Co, 1974) 2.

[68] A Schick, 'Repairing the Budget Contract Between Citizens and the State' (2011) 11 *OECD Journal on Budgeting* 1, 22–25.

[69] M Victor, 'Taxing for Vulnerabilities' (*AfronomicsLaw*, 20 July 2020) www.afronomicslaw.org/2020/07/20/taxing-for-vulnerabilities.

[70] Bird (n 19) 2105.

[71] P Mosley and A-G Abdulai, 'The Political Economy of Progressive Fiscal Contracts in Africa and Latin America' (2020) 38 *Development Policy Review* 411.

system, William Gladstone abolished earmarking as it signified misuse of tax proceeds by the kings for military expenditure.[72] Hence, in as much as earmarking may help in building trust, its implementation for purposes that the public does not deem fit can potentially threaten the very fabric of the social contract and trust building capacity. Where there is no adequate institutional and infrastructural framework to support earmarking, governments may be better advised to avoid earmarking due to the ill-effects on trust and state-building. If the aim is to introduce transparency and accountability, there may be other ways to achieve the same end.

D. Conclusions from the Theoretical Justifications

The normative emphasis on maintaining a complementary relationship between the contributor and beneficiary is quite strong in prior literature emerging from various disciplines. Buchanan perceived the absence of links as inefficient and discriminatory. However, Wicksell's conception of tax justice was founded on the assumption of justice in the distribution of property and income. Moreover, Wicksell's idea of the benefit principle is based on the process of voluntary consent which includes taxpayer consent for altruistic reasons. However, Buchanan's writings do not address pre-existing distributional inequities. In tax psychology literature while earmarked taxes rank above taxes, within earmarked taxes, there is a preference for earmarking based on the benefit linkage. Support may be possible for non-benefit-based taxes when the cause is considered necessary. The fiscal social contract advocates also limit the beneficial effects of earmarking to situations where the beneficiary-contributor nexus is present.

However, we find practical evidence from Africa and Latin America of progressive fiscal contracts strengthening trust between the citizens and the state even though the tax was levied for redistribution. The public choice theory conception of earmarking does not resolve the question of how governments must achieve their distributional objectives.[73] The so-called nineteenth century conception of the benefit theory does not account for the larger role of the government in achieving redistribution.[74] Real-world tax systems are a blend of taxes based on both the ability to pay and the benefit principle.[75] The differing political, economic and cultural contexts and the relationship between the taxpayer and the government have a bearing on the positive effects of earmarking.[76]

[72] M Daunton, 'Creating Legitimacy: Administering Taxation in Britain, 1815–1914' in JL Cardoso and P Lains (eds), *Paying for the Liberal State: The Rise of Public Finance in Nineteenth-Century Europe* (IFCS, 2010) 31–38.

[73] McCleary (n 10) 85.

[74] V Koukoulioti, 'Chapter 3: User Contribution to Value Creation: The Benefit Principle in the Spotlight' in P Pistone and DM Weber (eds), *Taxing the Digital Economy: The EU Proposals and Other Insights* (Amsterdam, IBFD, 2019) s 3.2.2.

[75] P Elkund, 'Earmarking Appraised' (1972) 25 *National Tax Journal* 227.

[76] J Barrett, 'Democratic Discourse, Taxation and Hypothecation' (2012) 14 *Journal of Australian Taxation* 89, 114.

IV. Reviewing the Merits and Demerits of Using Earmarked Taxes in Periods of Disruption

In times of disruption and recovery, the role of the welfare state as the provider of essential health services is pronounced. This requires governments to implement transparent and justified measures through open communication and cooperation.[77]

This author argues that an earmarked tax has four advantages compared to un-earmarked taxes (general, labelled and solidarity taxes) and fees, especially in times of disruption.

First, earmarking has been found to work well where there are specific identifiable purposes and not when it is used rampantly.[78] Periods of disruption, recovery and crises may act as catalysts in identifying sectors and community groups that require assistance. Such periods can thus identify specific purposes that need urgent financing in the short term and warrant planning for the long term. The merit of earmarking mechanisms is that it can help governments create a framework for committing revenues towards such sectors and groups.

Second, earmarking guarantees support for the chosen purposes despite any financial exigencies (internal or external), political changes, corruption, etc.[79] In periods of disruption and uncertainty, there may be a relevant need, but it may not garner political support because of the financial exigency. Hence, a tax revenue earmark can help secure necessary funds. A contingency fund financed by un-earmarked taxes may be insufficient as rational taxpayers may be concerned that although governments raise taxes when disaster strikes, the costs will have to be financed again as those tax sums were spent elsewhere.[80] One way to mitigate such concerns is to undertake *ex ante* budgeting through an earmarked tax which assures taxpayers that the sums will be available for the relevant crisis.

Third, earmarking helps usher in a system of transparency as the public is made aware of the revenue – expenditure linkage and the transfers between taxpayer groups are made explicit.[81] This can also contribute to greater accountability as stakeholders can hold the government answerable for their promises, which assumes importance in times of crises when tax resources are scarce.[82] With budgetary transfers there is no promise and if transfers are made, these tend to be opaque, making it challenging to seek accountability.

Fourth, in crisis periods such as the COVID-19 induced public health emergency, it may not be possible to compute healthcare services and infrastructure requirements down to an individual taxpayer which is required for imposing a fee. A particular service (such as vaccination cost) over which the government has monopoly of supply may be identified, but this may still be undesirable. In a crisis, access to vaccines is

[77] J Alm et al, 'Tax Policy Measures to Combat the Sars-Cov-2 Pandemic and Considerations to Improve Tax Compliance: A Behavioral Perspective' (2020) 76 *FinanzArchiv (FA)* 396, 416.

[78] Bird and Tsiopoulos (n 35) 47.

[79] Teja (n 18) 531; McCleary (n 10) 85; J Jackson, 'Tax Earmarking, Party Politics and Gubernatorial Veto: Theory and Evidence from US States' (2013) 155 *Public choice* 1.

[80] Phaup and Kirschner (n 11).

[81] G Mulgan and R Murray, 'Reconnecting Taxation' (New York, Demos, 1993) 23.

[82] Tahk (n 64) 59.

required irrespective of availability of financial resources. In times of disruption and recovery, the importance of alleviating the burdens on the community at large should trump efficiency. Tax is the more appropriate route for upgrading medical infrastructure, procuring vaccines and subsidising healthcare and sectors that are suffering from the economic impact.

Like any policy instrument, earmarked taxes also have some demerits. These taxes have been widely criticised in prior literature. It is important to highlight the problems associated with earmarked taxes, more so when introduced in periods of crises.

First, it remains unclear whether earmarking ultimately results in enhanced revenues. Some authors have remarked that earmarks may simply replace funding which would otherwise have been secured through general budgetary funds.[83] Others have pointed to the catalytic impact of earmarked taxes.[84]

Second, one of the most widespread criticisms of earmarked taxes is that it results in budgetary rigidity. Once an earmark is instituted, the budgetary authorities cannot intervene. Scholars support general fund financing as allocation depends on a meritorious evaluation of various competing claims within the available monetary resources.[85] In periods of crises in particular, it may be argued that money should be spent in a judicious manner.

Third, as earmarking is an *ex ante* dedication, it may be tough to estimate the exact amounts that will be collected from the tax revenue source. This may mean that the amount set aside is indefinite which could lead to a 'misallocation of resources'.[86] In the context of extended crises with recurring requirements, initial estimates may not hold out which may require additional funding through extension of an earmarked tax or supplementary grants from general budgetary transfers.

Fourth, a major criticism of earmarked taxes is that these measures often become 'embedded', outliving their purpose.[87] This warning must be taken seriously given various examples of earmarked and non-earmarked taxes introduced during crises as one-time measures that have lived on, some for several years. For example, the German solidarity surcharge introduced in 1991 to fund the German reunification was only being phased out as of 2021.[88] Additionally, a Greek solidarity contribution introduced to assuage the financial crisis was first imposed for five years but was eventually added to the income tax legislation, making it a permanent tax.[89] Perhaps the most famous example comes from the UK; the income tax was historically introduced as a temporary tax, only to have been imposed since 1842.[90]

[83] E Deran, 'Earmarking and Expenditures: A Survey and a New Test' (1965) 18 *National Tax Journal* 354; Browning (n 17); WW McMahon and CM Sprenkle, 'Theory of Earmarking' (1970) 23 *National tax journal* 25.

[84] P Eklund, 'A Theory of Earmarking Appraised' (1972) 25 *National Tax Journal* 223, 225.

[85] F Forte, *Principles of Public Economics: A Public Choice Approach* (Cheltenham, Edward Elgar, 2010) 263; Deran (n 83) 357.

[86] Deran (n 83) 357.

[87] ibid 355.

[88] 'Germany Publishes Law for First Step in Phasing out the Solidarity Surcharge', *Orbitax* (26 December 2019) www.orbitax.com/news/archive.php/Germany-Publishes-Law-for-Firs-40456 accessed 12 April 2021.

[89] K Perrou, 'Greece: "Taxes Covered" – Is an Extraordinary Levy on Business Profits Covered?' in M Lang et al (eds), *Tax Treaty Case Law Around the Globe 2013* (Amsterdam, IBFD, 2014).

[90] G Loutzenhiser, *Tiley's Revenue Law* (9th edition, Hart Publishing, 2019).

Earmarked taxes as instruments to achieve goals of transparency and redistribution may not be completely undesirable given the merits highlighted above. However, the review of the demerits and the theoretical justifications highlight the challenges of earmarking, especially in a non-benefit context. Challenges include inappropriate allocation of resources, earmarked taxes being applied in a discriminatory manner and being reduced to political ploys. Additionally, earmarked taxes are prone to being embedded and have to face challenges arising from *ex ante* dedication. To harness the merits, the challenges identified here should serve as the guiding force in designing the earmarked tax, as discussed in the following section.

V. Designing an Earmarked Tax: Drawing from Past Insights and Reflecting on Pandemic-Triggered Responses

Musgrave observed, 'depending on how it is used, earmarking may thus be an arbitrary procedure leading to budgetary rigidity, or it may be a helpful device for approximating benefit taxation'.[91] Also, Premchand opined that earmarking has its uses and abuses. Its usefulness is directly dependent on the spread of the earmarked funds, the flexibility in their management and their relationship to the budget and national priorities.[92] True to this statement, a deeper study reveals that the devil is in the detail as earmarking comes in various forms. Unfortunately, the theoretical discussions on earmarking do not talk about the implementation of earmarking and what factors determine the suitability of earmarking.[93] However, this is precisely the gap in literature that this author seeks to address.

Designing an earmarked tax involves thinking about four primary aspects: the legal architecture, administrative architecture, tax attributes and earmarking features. Past practices pertaining to earmarking for healthcare, contingencies and disasters are drawn from while reflecting on the design choices made by the recent earmarked tax measures.

A. Governance Framework: Legal and Administrative

The aspects relating to legal architecture determine the extent of permissible earmarking in a country's domestic legal framework (the Constitution or budgetary principles). A country that chooses to earmark must first check if earmarking is permitted.[94]

[91] RA Musgrave and PB Musgrave, *Public Finance in Theory and Practice* (International student edition, 4th ed, 1st printing, New York, NY, McGraw-Hill, 1984) 232.

[92] A Premchand, *Government Budgeting and Expenditure Controls Theory and Practice* (Washington, DC, International Monetary Fund, 1983) 160.

[93] McCleary (n 10) 87.

[94] CD Soares, 'Chapter 6: Earmarking Revenues from Environmentally Related Taxes' in JE Milne and MS Andersen (eds), *Handbook of Research on Environmental Taxation* (Cheltenham, Edward Elgar, 2012) 106.

The efficacy of earmarking as a process depends not just on the legislative pre-commitment device employed but ultimately the time taken for funds to be channelled for a pledged purpose. This depends on the administrative infrastructure and governance systems in place.[95] Safeguards to strengthen the governance framework of earmarked taxes include conducting periodic reviews, audits and dissemination of information on utilisation of proceeds in an accessible, simple manner. While administrative architecture is relevant for earmarking in general, these assume greater relevance in periods of disruption as taxpayer support for new taxes is low which merits greater accountability and transparency.

B. Tax Features

Tax features are tax base and tax rate. Also, the decision could involve whether a new tax or an increase in an existing tax is to be introduced. Quite often, earmarked taxes are added on to existing taxes like the one from Egypt. However, any new tax or tax increase imposed in a crisis must be well thought out and congruent with the existing taxes to avoid confiscatory effects, or an undesirable mix of regressive/indirect taxes in the country.

Examples from Egypt, Argentina, Liberia and Uruguay show a preference for direct taxes. There is support for choosing personal taxes on income, social security, capital or property as the tax base is not shifted and it is clear who pays the tax.[96] A study by the World Health Organization prior to the pandemic noted that 80 countries already have earmarks for health. 62 countries earmark income or payroll taxes along with budgetary transfers for securing financing for health purposes. The suitable tax base would also depend on what is accepted by the public. Sin goods may work in some countries (Philippines and Vietnam) while a non-regressive VAT worked in a country like Ghana.[97]

The choice of the tax base remains important and politically sensitive, more so in periods of crisis. The International Working Group on Financing Preparedness in the context of pandemics recommends industries or activities that may be taxed. The first group is industries that increase the risk of the pandemic such as antibiotic use for growth promotion in meat production. The second are sectors that stand to benefit the most from preventing a pandemic such as tourism.[98] This also includes companies in the digital space that have seen rapid growth and profits owing to the pandemic. Earmarked taxes in the paradigm of the benefit principle are thought to be equitable as the contributor is also the beneficiary.[99] In the absence of a benefit context, these taxes must be fair and non-discriminatory in light of applicable legal principles such as equality. Imposing earmarked taxes on non-residents for local social welfare or on high income earners for the benefit of those affected by the pandemic must thus be

[95] Cashin et al (n 32) 24.
[96] Wilkinson (n 19) 126–27.
[97] Cashin et al (n 32).
[98] International Working Group on Financing Preparedness (n 2).
[99] Bird (n 19).

legally justifiable. Fairness and the perception of it would also have an impact on tax compliance, for example, if the government uses earmarking proceeds to extend similar financial assistance to differently impacted sectors.[100]

Tax rate plays an important role in earmarked taxes, especially in periods of crises when revenue collections tend to shrink despite an increasing demand. Unlike general fund financing, here the sequence of revenue and expenditure decisions is reversed; the revenues garnered essentially drive sums available for expenditure.[101] While the benefit of this system is that it guarantees a revenue source for the desired purpose, the quantum of revenues is tied to the tax rate and tax base. In the absence of a periodic revision, in periods of crisis the revenues will fall. This leads to an anomalous situation as periods of crisis require higher revenues.[102] Lack of a periodic review of the tax rate will entail reliance on general budgetary sources.[103] Upward revision of tax rates must be done in a systematic manner, in accordance with established legal and constitutional principles and procedures.

C. Key Earmarking Features of Relevance

This sub-section discusses certain key features pertaining to earmarked taxes that assume relevance when designing an earmarked tax, more so in periods of disruption and recovery.

i. Temporal Aspects: When and for How Long?

One of the crucial questions when earmarking is to decide whether this must be done before or after the period of disruption. Countries that have had a propensity to higher risk from disasters have adopted long-term budgeting measures. Prior budgeting is more consistent with long-term planning. As explained earlier, long-term planning in the form of contingency funds may still leave taxpayers wondering if they must pay taxes again when a crisis arises because the money was already expended.[104] A solution to address this concern is to undertake *ex ante* budgeting through an earmarked tax which assures taxpayers that money will be available for the relevant crisis.

The length of pre-commitment in an earmarking arrangement can be varied; earmarked levies may be in force for short or long periods. As discussed, one of the criticisms of earmarking measures is that these measures often become 'embedded' in a tax system, outliving their purpose.[105] Argentina's solidarity contribution is described as a one-off tax and thus gives the impression of being a short-term measure. However, based on examples from different countries, there is no guarantee that such a tax cannot be extended by subsequent legislative action. When designing an earmarked tax, the

[100] Alm et al (n 77) 20.
[101] Bird (n 19).
[102] Cashin et al (n 32).
[103] McCleary (n 10) 90.
[104] Phaup and Kirschner (n 11).
[105] Deran (n 83) 355.

choice of temporal aspects would depend on whether the recognised purpose requires short-term or long-term support. For long-term measures, regular reviews of utilisation patterns and revenue goals must be undertaken.

ii. Revenue – Expenditure Linkage

As explained earlier, the linkage between revenue and expenditure may be varied. In the case of pure/substantive linkages, funding comes only from the earmarked revenues; there is no reliance on general budgetary funds.[106] However, symbolic/softer earmarking occurs when funding is also supplemented by budgetary allocations.[107]

The COVID-19 funds set up by Liberia and Uruguay are financed by other revenue sources making it a form of symbolic/softer earmarking which may be described as 'window dressing'.[108] The problem with such measures is that the earmark serves political rather than legal goals as taxpayers may favour earmarked taxes but the impact on financing the ultimate goal is minimal. One may argue that such softer/symbolic earmarking is not so bad as it helps secure electoral support, and most people may not care about the details of the earmarking arrangement implemented. However, it is important to underscore that softer/symbolic earmarking may build support for additional taxation but misses the mark on long-term trust building. The trade-off is essentially between short-term support and long-term trust and credibility. One may further argue that there may be no adverse impact on trust as citizens may not take notice of the details. However, this may not be the same during crises where individuals are already facing an economic hardship and may scrutinise any additional taxation with much more caution. An initial study of the impact of the COVID-19 pandemic revealed loss of trust in institutions.[109] This may be one of the reasons for taxpayers to be extra circumspect about details.

iii. Extent of Earmarking

A levy may earmark the entire proceeds or only a designated portion of the total revenues. Moreover, the proceeds can be apportioned between multiple purposes, such as Argentina's solidarity contribution, which is applied towards several causes. Some purposes are closely related to COVID-19 relief while others seemingly pursue broader goals in the public interest. In this event, while the entire proceeds are earmarked, only a part of the proceeds are earmarked for pandemic-related financing. This could once again mean that the pandemic-related financing is only nominally supported by the

[106] Wilkinson (n 19) 125.

[107] J Michael, 'Earmarking State Tax Revenues' (Policy Brief Research Department, Minnesota House of Representatives, 2015) 3.

[108] Canada earmarked its GST to make it more appealing to the public. However, this was merely a window dressing exercise as the costs for financing the earmarked public service were larger than the revenue from the GST. RM Bird, 'Visibility and Accountability: Is Tax-Inclusive Pricing a Good Thing?' (SSRN Scholarly Paper, Rochester, NY, 23 November 2009).

[109] D Gianmarco et al, 'When Economic and Health Crises Collide: The Effect of Covid-19 on Political Attitudes' (Max Planck Institute for Tax Law and Public Finance Working Paper 2020–18, Munich, December 2020).

earmarked tax and that budgetary transfers will still be required. The danger once again is that the earmark looks more like an instance of symbolic/softer earmarking and a political ploy.

VI. Conclusion

Country level responses to the pandemic reveal that some countries have imposed an earmarked tax for pursuing social welfare. This ties in with earlier practice involving countries employing earmarks for public health, contingencies and disaster relief. In the post-pandemic world, governments may find earmarking of taxes an easier and more popular route for domestic resource mobilisation. Earmarked taxes levied in periods of crises tend not to be based on the benefit principle which is cautioned against in prior literature, since such taxes may lead to inappropriate allocation of tax resources, have discriminatory effects or may act as a political ploy. This author argues that these potential pitfalls should guide the designing of an earmarked tax.

While the introduction of earmarked taxes during periods of disruption has certain merits, governments choosing to go down this route must think about many crucial aspects. First, whether such tax is really required and whether the legal and administrative infrastructure can support appropriate implementation of the tax. Second, the motivations for the tax, whether it is a move towards long-term trust and credibility or for mere short-term political and electoral support. Third, countries choosing to earmark will also have to consider when to introduce the tax and whether it should be designed as a short or long-term measure. Fourth, the government must also think about the framing of the tax, in terms of labelling versus earmarking and that labelling without earmarking is undesirable. Fifth, the design of the tax must facilitate content-based restraints such as periodic reviews, audits and dissemination of information on utilisation of proceeds to harness the merits of earmarking. This author argues that design choices should be guided by long-term trust and credibility while also the legal dimension of fairness, the overall legal and administrative architecture, the tax and earmarking attributes. A review of the taxes introduced by Argentina, Egypt, Liberia and Uruguay reveal soft earmarking. The discussion on the design choices has a broader appeal, even when designing a benefit-based earmarked tax.

Unlike what was conceived by Wicksell and Buchanan, real-world earmarks connect tax and expenditures, but parliamentary deliberations do not simultaneously consider several alternative tax proposals. Also, not all domestic systems appear to prohibit non-benefit earmarking which is evident from the examples discussed here. It is hoped that the guidance helps an earmarked tax not to be reduced to a fiscal sleight of hand at the expense of the taxpayer, more so in times of disruption. Like any other fiscal instrument, there is scope for abuse, and the goal is to steer away from such a consequence and build a tax that truly bridges the revenue and expenditure sides of the budget.

6

Counting Doubloons. A Critical Assessment of how Caribbean British Overseas Territories are Funding the COVID-19 Response

LAURA PANADÈS-ESTRUCH

Abstract

As tax neutral jurisdictions, Caribbean British Overseas Territories (BOTs) have faced the financial impact of COVID-19 without a recourse to traditional revenue raising methods. This chapter critically assesses the solutions that Anguilla, Bermuda, British Virgin Islands, the Cayman Islands, Montserrat and Turks and Caicos Islands applied. COVID-19 pressures have strengthened the diplomatic links between the UK and its overseas territories, credited to the UK's medical and technical support. However, the crisis exaggerated patterns in financial performance; countries with resilient financial governance frameworks scored well; financial dependencies were exacerbated. All countries increased their public debt. Sophisticated methods to raise finance, like issuing government bonds and setting up commercial lines of credit, were sometimes considered but seldom implemented. Lessons learned in this chapter will assist Caribbean BOTs keep their doubloons safe in the foreseeable future.

I. Introduction

In the fight against COVID-19, the Caribbean is carefully counting both its blessings and its doubloons. Viewing the region as a unit, however, disguises great disparities in managing the health crisis and how to fund it. This chapter critically analyses the COVID-19 response in Caribbean British Overseas Territories (BOTs). The chapter's claims are based on a critical, comparative analysis of these countries' financial responses to COVID-19.

This chapter reasons that there is a link between a measured crisis response in line with good governance based on a portfolio of measures to respond to COVID-19 and optimum results. Caribbean BOTs have learned, first, that good governance frameworks set up in advance of the financially distressing event are a crucial part of a successful financial response. Countries committed to good governance prior to the pandemic managed the crisis effectively. The Cayman Islands had set up financial frameworks in the 2010s and, with a good combination of policies and public health at the helm, was able to brave the storm. Second, rising public debt is unavoidable. Third, those with more resilient governance systems have had access to more sophisticated means of raising public finance, such as issuing bonds or setting up commercial lines of credit. Fourth, financial dependencies prior to COVID-19 have been exacerbated and prolonged. The pandemic exaggerated the poor results of those that had not invested in their governance frameworks. In particular, Montserrat, already financially dependent on the UK, saw its economic problems deepen exponentially during the pandemic.

Pirates searched the Caribbean for treasure as early as the 1700s, but academics have yet to research the region in any detail. BOTs are unique in their revenue-raising models, based on coercive fees: most charge little to no personal income and corporation taxes and, as a result, have faced revenue-raising challenges during the pandemic. Scholars will be familiar with many journals that have published a special issue studying the financial impact of COVID-19 on the major economies. Its impact on smaller economies, however, remains largely uncharted, with no pan-Caribbean studies. The United Nations has published a series of reports on Caribbean economies, but these are country studies covering COVID-19 macroeconomic and human impact assessment data. Unfortunately, they cover only two Caribbean British Overseas Territories (BOTs): Anguilla and British Virgin Islands.[1] Scholarly, Benwell, Clegg and Pinkerton conducted a study on the COVID-19 response in BOTs; however, only one Caribbean BOT was included. Their study concluded that 'Britain has afforded some assistance to [the] territories [but there] is a feeling, rightly or wrongly, in the [British Virgin Islands] and other Caribbean OTs that skin colour does make a difference in how they are treated.[2]

This chapter starts setting up the scene, with critical comments on Caribbean BOTs and their public finances. It is structured in four main sections, covering UK and BOTs' relationships, critical public finance considerations of the UK-Caribbean BOT links and their financial response to COVID-19, followed by its critical assessment. The author is based locally and has spared no effort in engaging with local sources and fieldwork.

[1] S Naitram, 'Anguilla – COVID-19 macroeconomic and human impact assessment data' (UNDP, UNICEF and UN Women Eastern Caribbean 2020) www.gov.ai/documents/finance/Human%20Economic%20Impact%20Data%20-%20Anguilla%202020.pdf; S Naitram, 'British Virgin Islands – COVID-19 Human and Economic assessment of Impact' (UNDP, UNICEF and UN Women Eastern Caribbean 2020) www2.unwomen.org/-/media/field%20office%20caribbean/attachments/publications/2020/covid-19%20heat%20report%20-%20human%20and%20economic%20assessment%20of%20impact%20-%20british%20virgin%20islands.pdf?la=en&vs=3511.

[2] MC Benwell, P Clegg and A Pinkerton, 'COVID-19 and the British Overseas Territories: a comparative view' (2021) 110 *The Round Table – The Commonwealth Journal of International Affairs* 166–67.

II. Caribbean British Overseas Territories as a Group of its Own Right

Caribbean countries and BOTs are ripe for historical research as alternative models of financial responses to COVID-19. This chapter looks at Caribbean British Overseas Territories' (BOTs) financial response to the pandemic, taking stock of the public financial developments and critically assessing their COVID-19 response. Caribbean BOTs include Anguilla, Bermuda, the British Virgin Islands, the Cayman Islands, Montserrat and Turks & Caicos Islands. These countries are often ignored. In the few occasions where they are studied, tax studies often eclipse the study of their societies and rules; at other times, they are mixed with Latin America; or simply, these countries are omitted due to their low populations in comparison to major world economies. This chapter remedies that, arguing that these countries follow common patterns that justify their study as a unit. Such common patterns comprise qualified sovereignty, smallness, limited economic diversification and taxation choices.

First and foremost, the sovereignty of BOTs rests within the UK. All Caribbean BOTs are governed by a UK Governor, who represents HM The King locally, and the Caribbean desk of the Foreign and Commonwealth Development Office. However, BOT governments act largely independently, with UK intervention kept to a minimum. Locally, Caribbean BOTs have set up different combinations of a local Cabinet or Executive Council, normally comprising the Premier or Chief Minister (as the top elected authority on island), a number of Ministers ranging from three to six, plus the Deputy Governor and the Attorney General (AG) as *ex officio* members (or the AG and the Financial Secretary in Turks & Caicos).[3] Local Constitutions are enacted by UK secondary legislation but, locally, they are the supreme source of law. The longest Constitution in force is that of Bermuda, from 1968. BVI, Cayman, Montserrat and Turks & Caicos enacted their currently in force Constitutions during and after the Global Financial Crisis (2007–11). Article 73 of the United Nations Charter frames the relationships between the UK and its former colonies. The article commits the UK to 'promote […] the well-being of the [BOTs'] inhabitants' in varied areas, for instance, cultural respect; political, economic, social and educational advancement; and to develop self-government'. In this vein, the UK is 'able to make laws for the Overseas Territories [and holds] separate powers to make Orders in Council for most of the OTs'.[4] However, it intervenes only when necessary. The six territories have been acquired by settlement, but they are not British settlements for the purposes of the British Settlements Acts 1887 and 1945.

Second, small Caribbean economies face extreme challenges. Their small size, both geographically and in population, their remoteness and their 'islandness' remain surprisingly uncharted. COVID-19-related risks included difficulties in 'securing

[3] Data on local government extracted from I Hendry and S Dickson, *British Overseas Territories Law* (Oxford, Hart Publishing, 2018) 315–81.

[4] Foreign and Commonwealth Office, 'Written evidence from the Foreign and Commonwealth Office (OTS0103)' (The Future of the UK Overseas Territories inquiry, London) data.parliament.uk/writtenevidence/committeeevidence.svc/evidencedocument/foreign-affairs-committee/the-future-of-the-uk-overseas-territories/written/90142.pdf, para 22.

essential goods and services, including inbound logistics for their value chains'.[5] Even in the best of times, the Caribbean has 'reduced investment in health and research and fragile public health systems'.[6] In addition, the Caribbean region is exposed to heightened environmental risks, such as hurricanes and, most recently, earthquakes.[7] This has made their regular risk management even trickier than usual.

Third, limited economic diversification makes these six countries susceptible to greater impacts from internal and international crises. These economies are largely dependent on international finance and banking, tourism and real property. All Caribbean BOTs are associated members of the CARICOM, the regional body for the advancement of regional economic integration, foreign policy coordination, human and social development and security.[8] The COVID-19 pandemic has enhanced the challenges of poorly diversified economies, especially for tourism-dependent economies: the World Bank has stated that most were maintaining positive growth rates but have been 'badly impacted' by the pandemic, with economic downturn, job losses and rising poverty headcounts.[9] Several tourism-dependent Caribbean countries have seen their sovereign ratings downgraded.[10] With COVID-19 having shut down most of the tourism industry and some countries having closed their borders, in some cases for over a calendar year, COVID-19 has had an impact on the public finances of many of the sampled countries.

III. Public Finances in Caribbean British Overseas Territories

The main reason why tax scholars should study Caribbean BOTs is that they represent alternative models to those of mainstream, Western economies. Coercive revenue is the basis of their public budgets, instead of the income or corporation tax. Coercive revenue is that collected by government's powers and without providing a good or a service in exchange.[11] Tariffs, stamp duty, work permit fees, private funds fees and corporation registration fees also assist greatly in providing stable public revenue. Mainly, tariffs are charged on most products. Caribbean countries which rely on

[5] UNCTAD, 'COVID-19 in the Caribbean and the Central America region: Identifying blue pathways to move forward in a COVID-19 context and beyond' (23 July 2020) unctad.org/es/node/26953.

[6] AA Escobedo, AJ Rodríguez-Morales, P Almirall, C Almanza and R Rumbaut, 'SARS-CoV2/COVID-19: Evolution in the Caribbean Islands' (2020) *Travel Medicine and Infectious Diseases* 37.

[7] See a briefing on hurricane history in the American continent here: National Hurricane Center and Central Pacific Hurricane Center, 'Hurricanes in History', www.nhc.noaa.gov/outreach/history/.

[8] Treaty establishing the Caribbean Community, art 4, caricom.org/wp-content/uploads/Final-Act-Declaration-and-Resolution-ALONG-with-The-Treaty-Establishing-The-Caribbean-Community-with-signature.pdf.

[9] The World Bank Group, 'The World Bank in the Caribbean. Overview', www.worldbank.org/en/country/caribbean/overview.

[10] A Haroon, 'S&P hits 5 LatAm economies with outlook revisions, downgrades on COVID-19 woes' (*S&P Global Market Intelligence*, 17 April 2020) www.spglobal.com/marketintelligence/en/news-insights/latest-news-headlines/s-p-hits-5-latam-economies-with-outlook-revisions-downgrades-on-covid-19-woes-58072067.

[11] As an example, see The Cayman Islands Public Finance and Management Act (2020 Revision).

tariffs include Anguilla, Bermuda, the Cayman Islands, Montserrat, Turks & Caicos Islands and US Virgin Islands.[12] That makes them different from mainstream, Western economies.

Caribbean BOTs are mostly known as tax-neutral jurisdictions, but their story is much richer than the 'treasure island' trope. With little to no income or corporation tax, they attract thousands of companies and inhabitants into their small nations. 10 out of the 26 worldwide offshore financial centres are in the Caribbean.[13] The EU is one the loudest critics of these countries and has subjected them to careful scrutiny. Specifically, the EU lists four out of 12 Caribbean countries as non-cooperative jurisdictions for tax purposes, with Anguilla as the only BOT among them.[14] Cayman was included on the February 2020 list and removed in the next revision in October.[15]

Legal developments beyond the letter of the law are worth of study. Beyond the core obligations of Article 73 of the Charter of the United Nations, as previously discussed, the UK provides technical assistance and support, particularly in promoting good financial governance, but only intervenes when strictly necessary. Largely, the territories are responsible for managing their financial affairs: revenue is raised according to their own legislation, expenditure is 'regulated by standard provisions in [their own] Constitution' and they have 'substantial authority to borrow or lend money'.[16] That understood, the UK has occasionally needed to intervene in the affairs of Caribbean BOTs. Notably, the 2008 Global Financial Crisis exposed weaknesses in economic development and management. A consultation commissioned by the UK Parliament found that the 2008 Global Financial Crisis was one of the greatest challenges to economic development in BOTs.[17] This triggered 'reduced activity in financial services and falls in tourist arrivals and construction' leading to fiscal deficits.[18] The UK insisted that BOTs implement Frameworks for Fiscal Responsibility.[19] For instance, under UK supervision

[12] L Panadès-Estruch, 'Small States, High Stakes: a policy proposal to deliver welfare via public purchasing' 6 *International Journal of Procurement Management* 2020; Cayman Islands Customs Department, *Customs Tariff and Law* (Cayman Islands Customs Department, 2019); Government of Anguilla, *Anguilla Customs Duty Calculator* (Government of Anguilla, 2021) www.gov.ai/customs; Government of Bermuda, *Bermuda Customs Tariff 2016* (Government of Bermuda, 2016); Government of Montserrat – Customs and Excise Department, Publications (Government of Montserrat, 2021) www.gov.ms/government/ministries/ministry-of-finance-economic-management/montserrat-customs-revenue-services/; Government of the Virgin Islands, *Customs Management and Duties Act 2010, Law 6 of 2010* (Government of the Virgin Islands, 2021) bvi.gov.vg/sites/default/files/resources/Customs%20Management%20and%20Duties%20Act%202010%20plus%20Ammendments.pdf; Turks and Caicos Customs Department (*Tariff search*, 2019) customs.gov.tc/cltr.

[13] International Monetary Fund, 'Past IMF Staff Assessments on Offshore Financial Centers (OFCs)' (3 October 2019) www.imf.org/external/np/ofca/ofca.aspx.

[14] Council Conclusions of 26 February 2021 on the revised EU list of non-cooperative jurisdictions for tax purposes (OJ 2021/C 66/10).

[15] Council Conclusions of 7 October 2020 on the EU list of non-cooperative jurisdictions for tax purposes – Report by the Code of Conduct Group (business taxation) suggesting amendments to the Annexes to the Council conclusions of 18 February 2020 (OJ 2020/C 331/03) 3–5.

[16] Hendry and Dickson (n 3) 231, 235.

[17] TruffleNet, 'Independent analysis for public consultation on the overseas territories' (2012) assets.publishing.service.gov.uk/government/uploads/system/uploads/attachment_data/file/12248/ots-consultationreport.pdf.

[18] I Ioannides and J Tymowski, 'Tax evasion, money laundering and tax transparency in the EU Overseas Countries and Territories – Ex-post impact assessment' (*European Parliament Research Service*, PE593.803) 170–71.

[19] UK government, 'Foreign Office and Cayman Islands sign new fiscal responsibility framework' (*Foreign and Commonwealth office*, 23 November 2011) www.gov.uk/government/news/foreign-office-and-cayman-islands-sign-new-fiscal-responsibility-framework.

and despite some local opposition, Cayman implemented the Framework for Fiscal Responsibility in 2011, which became binding in 2013 via the Public Management and Finance Act and triggered internal policies towards responsible fiscal management.[20] The BVI also implemented 'Protocols for Effective Financial Management', agreed in 2012 and still contentious.[21] This push for good governance is not specifically set out under Article 73 of the UN's Charter but has emerged in practice.

IV. Caribbean BOT'S Policy Response to the COVID-19 Pandemic

Caribbean BOTs may enjoy similar levels of sunshine, but the financial weather is due to be very changeable in their responses to COVID-19. Six small countries have shown different levels of success in policy response, as well as different approaches to financial responses. A prolonged pandemic has brought longer border closures and more stipends and PPE costs than anybody could have foreseen before it started. The table below summarises the findings of this chapter.

Table 1 Summary of financial instruments used to fund COVID-19 across BOTs

BOT		**Anguilla**	**Bermuda**	**BVI**	**Cayman**	**Montserrat**	**T&C**
Financial response		UK emergency funding, CDB loan, commercial overdraft facility	Public bonds and refinancing current debt	Increased public debt	Increased public debt, line of credit with local banks' consortium	UK funding	Cash reserves, cost containment, line of credit and long-term loans
Financial response	**Cash reserves**				X		X
	Public debt		X	X	X		X
	Commercial line of credit/ overdraft	X			X		X
	Bond		X		?		
	UK funds	X				X	
	Other funds	X (Caribbean Development Bank)					

[20] The current version of this law is the Cayman Islands Public Finance and Management Act (2020 Revision).

[21] Benwell, Clegg and Pinkerton (n 2) 164.

On a public health note, Caribbean BOTs responded to COVID-19 from a public health perspective in broadly the same way with similar policies. Murphy et al have identified common patterns in the Caribbean public policy response to COVID-19.[22] Based on their primary research, the following patterns can be identified. First, all applied full border closures, except for Montserrat's partial closure. Second, all controlled gatherings by limiting public gatherings, closing public services and shutting down schools. Third, there is no clear pattern in mobility restrictions. Cayman had the most extreme response, having combined mobility restrictions, curfew and full lockdown; in contrast, Anguilla had the weakest approach, applying only a full lockdown. These have kept the small countries mostly safe, but at a high economic and financial cost.

From a financial perspective, there has been very limited coordination among Caribbean BOTs: each one has decided to take its own course. A combination of increased public debt, public bond issuance or commercial lines of credit, funding from UK or other external entities or cash reserves form the catalogue of measures available to them. All have had to increase their debt. Particularly for Caribbean BOTs, this is the only way to square the circle of coercive revenue as the main source of income and little to no personal taxation. Other than with public debt, the pool of countries considered shows no common pattern. However, four countries have set up commercial lines of credit or overdraft to make sure that they have access to cheaper credit in times of need.

Links between the UK and its BOTs have overall strengthened during COVID-19, despite unearthing some of their intrinsic problems. On the one hand, UK-BOT interactions remain alive but are subjected to time-consuming decision-making processes and a feeling of guardianship, rather than true partnership. Fabian Picardo, Chief Minister of Gibraltar since 2011, affirmed in May 2020 that the UK and its BOTs had 'not acted as a British family' early in the COVID-19 crisis.[23] Benwell, Clegg and Pinkerton have argued that the COVID-19 crisis has come at the most difficult time since the 1990s because of the confluence of the UK's decision to leave the EU, the weak response to Hurricane Irma in Anguilla and British Virgin Islands, the introduction of reinforced Anti-Money Laundering legislation and the legal recognition of civil partnerships signed by the Governor in the Cayman Islands when its legislators failed to pass a bill to that effect. Thus, the BOTs sometimes question whether the UK regards them as equal to the mother country. However, the UK would deliver later on by providing significant COVID-19 assistance on four main fronts: healthcare and vaccination support, security assistance, repatriation and other funding.[24] In particular, the UK offered political support to make sure such small and remote territories had access to 'UK supply chains for key medicines and medical devices'.[25] The UK pledged to provide free vaccinations

[22] MM Murphy, SM Jeyaseelan, C Howitt, N Greaves, H Harewood, KR Quimby, N Sobers, RC Landis, KD Rocke and IR Hambleton, 'COVID-19 containment in the Caribbean: The experience of small island developing states' (2020) 2 *Research in Globalization* 7.

[23] Friends of the British Overseas Territories, 'Impact of COVID-19 on the Overseas Territories Webinar' (Fabian Picardo, 5 May 2020).

[24] C Mills and P Loft, *Coronavirus: UK support to the Overseas Territories* (HC 2020–21, 9021) 2–5.

[25] L Sugg, *British Overseas Territories: Coronavirus – question for Foreign, Commonwealth and Development Office* (London, HL 2020–21, UIN HL8985).

to British Overseas Territories.[26] It also offered assistance including a 24/7 telephone hotline for medical questions, equipment to boost testing in BOTs and support from the armed forces with RFA Argus being deployed to the Caribbean.[27] Beyond Caribbean BOTs, Gibraltar also benefited from a sovereign loan through the UK to maintain the flow of shipments and cover transportation needs.[28]

V. Lessons Learned from the Caribbean BOTs' Financial Response to COVID-19

Having set out the context, the question is: what worked? What lessons have we learnt from the Caribbean BOTs' response to COVID-19? This section focuses on the most notable financial instruments, either due to their common use or to the common lessons learned.

A. Financial Governance has Become a Prerequisite for Good Results

Good governance pays off. There is a link between good governance and success in managing COVID-19. This trend applies across the Caribbean, exemplified in some non-BOT countries as well. Recently, Jamaica and Grenada have developed fiscal responsibility laws or equivalent provisions in related legislation, Antigua has prepared fiscal risk assessments and St Lucia is in the process of doing the same, according to the IMF's Fiscal Management in the Caribbean programme.[29] The Bahamas is also working on a Fiscal Responsibility Bill that will eventually become law.[30] They are setting a trend for good fiscal governance in the Caribbean.

Caribbean BOTs that had set up comprehensive fiscal responsibility frameworks have scored better in times of financial distress such as that during the COVID-19 pandemic. Cayman worked in conjunction with the UK to set up such a framework

[26] E Dugan, 'Cayman Islands awash with COVID vaccines' *The Times* (24 January 2021) www.thetimes.co.uk/article/cayman-islands-awash-with-covid-vaccines-762l5z9tz.

[27] Foreign and Commonwealth Office, 'UK Armed Forces step up support to the Caribbean Overseas Territories during coronavirus pandemic', www.gov.uk/government/news/uk-armed-forces-step-up-support-to-the-caribbean-overseas-territories-during-coronavirus-pandemic; 'UK supports overseas territories in coronavirus (COVID-19) battle' (10 June 2020) www.gov.uk/government/news/uk-supports-overseas-territories-in-coronavirus-covid-19-battle.

[28] Friends of the British Overseas Territories, 'In Conversation with Vice Admiral Sir Adrian Johns, KCB CBE KstJ DL, Former Governor of Gibraltar' (22 April 2021) 14:30.

[29] S Joshi, R Allen and B Imbert, 'PFM reform in the Caribbean' (2018), blog-pfm.imf.org/pfmblog/2018/06/pfm-reform-in-the-caribbean.html.

[30] Government of the Bahamas (2018a). 'Fiscal Responsibility Bill, 2018', www.bahamas.gov.bs/wps/wcm/connect/ebf7a997-b11e-416a-b222-f048c48f2f4a/DOC12_56_4409_24_18.pdf?MOD=AJPERES; A Wright, 'The Bahamas' in D Beuermann and M Schwartz (eds), *Nurturing Institutions for a resilient Caribbean* (Inter-American Development Bank, 2019); A Wright and K Grenade, 'The Bahamas Fiscal Responsibility Bill 2018: Some Observations and Practical Guidance for Implementation Effectiveness' (Inter-American Development Bank, 2018).

and was thus prepared to withstand the high expenditure linked to COVID-19. BVI is in the middle of the financial responsibility scoreboard, where compliance with fiscal principles was tough and required some temporary exemptions, but still proved of value to avert a lengthier crisis. On the other hand, Turks & Caicos Islands was preoccupied with a constitutional and political crisis during 2012, a crucial time in the set-up of fiscal responsibility, and thus needed a further bending of the rules to shoulder COVID-19 related expenses. Anguilla, at the bottom of the scoreboard, was subject to a deep local banking crisis and a devastating hurricane, and the local fiscal rules could not take more pressure by the time COVID-19 arrived.

The UK, via the FCDO, exercises specific financial controls. These vary from country to country and are largely political safeguards.[31] Cayman, Montserrat and Turks & Caicos Islands have made some of those UK financial controls legally binding, subjecting themselves voluntarily to the risk of further penalties.

Having signed up to the UK-led principles of financial management in 2011, Cayman took a further step and chose to make these principles legally binding on itself in 2013 through local legislation.[32] Of no concern for several years, Cayman's self-imposed financial safeguards have recently come to frustrate government officials in some respects. The pandemic forced Cayman to breach these rules for the first time ever when it breached the principle of government surplus when, in 2021, the government accounts forecast a deficit. As a consequence, the breach triggered FCDO oversight and meant that all Cayman's major expenses and financial decisions now required FCDO approval.[33] The need for FCDO approval and enhanced monitoring by its Caribbean desk appear to have frustrated local officials by slowing down decision making precisely when quick decisions followed by swift action was of the essence. As an example, the government needed to request FCDO approval to award its vital CI$330.5 million line of credit (£315 million) to a consortium of local banks and, later, to spend that credit.

Montserrat and Turks and Caicos Islands also gave some legal force to similar provisions via their respective Constitutions, whereby the issuance of guarantees or indemnities by local governments or raising loans needs to be in line with any borrowing guidelines agreed with the UK government.[34] This shows an increasing trend in UK-based controls.

Though BVI has been able to pass a raft of economic measures, it has done so late and under a cloud of diplomatic conflict with the UK. BVI reacted to the COVID-19 crisis with an economic stimulus package in May 2020 that came too late, due to some degree to UK-imposed financial restrictions. In 2012, the UK negotiated the 'Protocols for Effective Financial Management' with BVI. Such protocols were put forward by the UK in response to the public finance weaknesses exposed by the 2008 Global Financial

[31] Hendry and Dickson (n 3) 235.

[32] The principles were made binding via the Cayman Islands Public Management and Finance Law (2020 Revision), s 14(3). Such principles include positive operating surplus, positive net worth, debt servicing not exceeding 10% of core government revenue, net debt not exceeding 80% of core government revenue, cash reserves covering not less than 90 days and prudent management of financial risks.

[33] The Cayman Islands Public Management and Finance Law (2020 Revision), s 34(3)(a)(iii).

[34] Montserrat Constitution, s 98(2) and Turks and Caicos Islands Constitution, s 119(2).

Crisis: the protocols restricted BVI's ability to borrow and would require the UK's consent if the borrowing limits had to be raised.[35] There were calls for the 2012 protocols to become more flexible in response to COVID-19 because plenty of countries, including the UK, have needed to bend some fiscal responsibility rules to accommodate its impact. At the height of the crisis, the UK Governor and local Premier came into conflict over the protocol, the Governor being in favour of strict adherence to it and the Premier claiming it unduly restricted his ability to respond to the crisis.[36] As a compromise, the BVI legislature passed Resolution 16 to authorise further expenditure for most public entities to help them bear the brunt of the pandemic.[37] Many countries took similar steps to respond to the pandemic, but diverging from the financial framework when convenient may have set a dangerous precedent for the BVI the next time it wishes to break its own rules.

Turks and Caicos Islands continues to struggle with governance issues, which made its pandemic experience more difficult. During Misick's premiership in 2009–12, the UK government was forced to suspend the parts of the Constitution granting self-government so it could clear up the financial mess. Investigations conducted by Sir Robin Auld concluded that there was a 'high probability of systemic corruption in government and the legislature', namely via bribery to public officials; serious deterioration of governance; serious dishonesty and systemic weaknesses in legislation.[38] Misick unsuccessfully challenged the UK's intervention.[39] During COVID-19, cash reserves in Turks and Caicos have been kept only slightly above the common 90-day requirement for Caribbean BOTs, allowing USD73 million (£57.7 million) to fund the budget shortfall for the 2020–21 period: this measure 'buys [them] more time but would eventually fade'.[40] Turks and Caicos plans to set up an Economic Council, a group that will engage government, the Opposition, major stakeholders, the private sector, civic groups and others to find a way forward.[41] After the cash has been reduced to the legal minimum, all other strategies will follow. However, no concrete details on how or when this will happen have been made public at the time of writing.

Anguilla implemented a framework for fiscal responsibility but has not been able to comply with it. Even before the pandemic, Anguilla had been battered by a series of fiscally catastrophic events: the 2008 Global Financial Crisis, another banking crisis in 2013–16 (at a cost equivalent to 45 per cent of its GDP), then Hurricane Irma in 2017 (causing losses valued at 100 per cent of GDP).[42] Anguilla's Fiscal Responsibility Act and its Framework for Fiscal Sustainability and Development state that net debt

[35] Government of the Virgin Islands, 'Protocols for Effective Financial Management' (23 April 2012) bvi.gov.vg/sites/default/files/resources/PROTOCOLS%20FOR%20EFFECTIVE%20FINANCIAL%20MANAGEMENT.pdf.

[36] Benwell, Clegg and Pinkerton (n 2) 164.

[37] The House of Assembly of the Virgin Islands, Resolution No 16 of 2020 (13 August 2020).

[38] R Auld, *Turks and Caicos Islands – Commission of Inquiry 2008–2009*, assets.publishing.service.gov.uk/government/uploads/system/uploads/attachment_data/file/268143/inquiry-report.pdf.

[39] See *R (Misick) v SoSECA* [2009] EWCA Civ 1549.

[40] Government of Turks and Caicos Islands, 'Approved Budget 2020-21 – The Appropriation (2020/21) ordinance 2020', online.fliphtml5.com/pejq/ueiy/, 10.

[41] ibid 11.

[42] S François and K Greaves, 'Impact of the COVID-19 pandemic on our economy and finances' (Radio Anguilla, 3 June 2021) www.facebook.com/watch/live/?v=215591860205326&ref=watch_permalink, 10:14–11:17.

should remain below 80 per cent of recurrent revenue, debt service payments below 10 per cent of recurrent revenue and liquid assets above 25 per cent or 90 days of recurrent expenditure. The country was not in compliance with the framework before the pandemic.[43] Naitram has recommended that the framework be made flexible to allow Anguilla to breach it in times of national crises.[44] Some suggestions include allowing temporary breaches of the framework, setting less strict intermediate limits on net debt, debt service and liquid assets and to return to the framework when possible. This flexibility seems a good compromise to allow Anguilla to undertake the necessary COVID-19 recovery effort whilst maintaining the government's commitment to comply with the framework at the earliest opportunity. Regardless of the specific developments on the framework, Anguilla needs to rethink its strategy.

B. Public Debt

All Caribbean BOTs kept throwing tomorrow's doubloons at today's expenditures during the pandemic. This is unsurprising, especially when put into the regional context. Data shows that the Eastern Caribbean, as a region, has seen rising levels of public debt to GDP: in 2019, it was estimated around at 67 per cent; it rose to 86 per cent in 2020.[45] Except for Anguilla, all have seen increased public debt. Anguilla's public debt was rising before the pandemic, despite local and UK efforts. Its debt to GDP ratio was 49.9 per cent in 2019.[46] Thus, the country had to moderate its response to COVID-19.

Bermuda's financial response to COVID-19 was to reach for its figurative platinum credit card. The country chose to fund its fiscal response 'largely […] by increased Government borrowing'.[47] Bermuda's latest budget describes 'increased spending resulting from the pandemic and funding economic recovery is driving further near-term deficits and increased pressure on public finances'.[48] Indeed, current account expenditures for 2020–21 were 7.7 per cent higher than budgeted, amounting to USD1 billion (£0.79 billion). However, fiscal prudence is one of the principles that could lead the way out of the crisis: Bermuda's budget considers that 'fiscal discipline will continue to be exercised in managing the government's finances mindful of existing borrowing levels'.[49] Other guiding principles are combatting COVID-19 as a priority, reducing the cost of living, fairness and equity to guarantee access to economic growth and opportunity, financial viability of small and medium-sized businesses and timeliness in execution of plans.[50] It is not clear whether the total debt of USD3 billion (£2.37 billion) for the Bermuda government is sustainable.

[43] Naitram (n 1) 6.
[44] ibid 22.
[45] François and Greaves (n 42) 9:52–10:36.
[46] Naitram (n 1) 3.
[47] Government of Bermuda, '2021–2022 Budget Statement' (26 February 2021) www.gov.bm/sites/default/files/Budget%20202122_Statement_Web.pdf, 3.
[48] ibid 9.
[49] ibid 13.
[50] ibid 12–13.

C. Sovereign Bonds and Commercial Credit

Bermuda and Cayman have pushed financing options to the limit by advocating for instruments that are uncommon in Caribbean BOTs. Bermuda and Cayman are developing a taste for bonds. Bermuda has issued 30-year bonds and Cayman is considering doing likewise. The Cayman Islands government sought to procure consultancy services for a potential 30-year maturity bond issuance of USD400 million (£316.34 million) in 2022.[51] The consultancy services would cover legal, independent advice for all stages in issuance, bond rating and underwriting.

So, how will Bermuda square the circle of putting together skyrocketing debt with fiscal prudence? By issuing 30-year public bonds and refinancing current debt by taking advantage of the lower interest rates available in the height of COVID-19. Bermuda's government attributes this to a good timing in the pandemic, when credit was more widely available, and its own risk profile: Bermuda achieved 'record low spreads to Treasuries, but demand was such to allow Bermuda to upsize the issuance to refinance more debt than initially planned at much lower interest rates'. Bermuda realised a 0.58 per cent reduction in interest rates and an 8.4-year extension of Bermuda's debt maturity.[52] A sinking fund sits to the side as a separate facility to make sure that Bermuda will be able to repay its growing debt.

While initially intended as a safeguard, the Cayman Islands government's commercial line of credit has become an essential emergency raft. Cayman set up a CI$330.5 million (£315 million) stand-by line of credit early in the pandemic. The rationale was to provide for extra financial resources should the need arise and 'to mitigate the effects of government's loss of revenue and increased [COVID-19-related] expenditure'.[53] Roy McTaggart, then Minister for Finance and Economic Development, expressed that 'what [he] would like to see is all Cayman-based banks doing a national effort and presenting a bid together'.[54] His wish came true: the winning bidder was a consortium made up of five of the largest local banks.

Setting up the line of credit was an early move intended to optimise the cost of financing, but it did not come for free. The facility operates under a specific timeline: the line of credit will be on stand-by for 18 months. Afterwards, 'any amount advanced and unpaid under the [line of credit] will be converted to a 15-year fixed rate amortising loan'. Both the amounts advanced in credit and the resulting loan are at an annual interest rate of 3.25 per cent,[55] which is the prime rate offered in Cayman – the lowest the government could achieve. McTaggart, who negotiated the line of credit, stated that

[51] Cayman Islands Government, 'CIG-MOFED-RFI-012022 Notice of potential bond issuance of US$ 400 million in 2022', cayman.bonfirehub.com/opportunities/57754.

[52] Government of Bermuda (n 47) 18.

[53] Cayman Islands Ministry of Finance and Economic Development, *Pre-Election Economic and Financial Update Government of the Cayman Islands* (Cayman Islands Government, 2021) mof.gov.ky/portal/pls/portal/docs/1/13060582.PDF, 17.

[54] R Ragoonath, 'Gov't issues RFP for $500m line of credit' (12 June 2020) www.caymancompass.com/2020/06/12/govt-issues-rfp-for-500m-line-of-credit.

[55] ibid.

'so far, we hope we don't have to use it but it is there as a backup'.[56] When arguing why it had been set, he replied that '[t]he best time to go and look for money is when you do not need money. Whenever you are desperate for money is when you would break your saw'.[57] Having achieved a prime rate with no add-ons should shield the government from the risk of rising costs if many nations require access to credit. However, additional costs are high, at a staggering fee of USD2.4 million (£1.90 million) just to set it up plus a stand-by fee of 70 basis points per annum for all amounts not used from the line of credit.

In April 2021, the General Election resulted in a change of government and the line of credit would soon become the new government's lifesaver. Days after the new government's formation, Saunders, the new Minister for Finance and Economic Development, expressed that the new 'Government will continue to refrain from borrowing as long as possible, but it may become necessary if the borders remain closed and the economy is not operating at its full potential'.[58] Two months would go by that reflected a radical shift, whereby 'the Government intends to utilise the established CI$330.5 million line of credit in order to fund forecast capital expenditure'.[59] The Auditor General is currently examining COVID-19 expenses and only time and in-depth financial analysis will tell us the effectiveness of the set-up and use of the line of credit.

D. Financial Independence

The least financially resilient BOTs have been the most concerned about redistributing wealth in times of crisis at the expense of long-term financial dependence. The UK advocates for self-government and expects all BOTs to be financially independent. While providing support and guidance, the UK leaves space for BOTs to implement their own legal frameworks for raising revenue, monitoring spending and auditing public finances. This has remained the case during COVID-19, where the UK did not provide widespread financial assistance to BOTs.

Not many BOTs have ever depended on the UK financially, but those that have will do so for some time because of COVID-19. Montserrat is the only case of long-term financial dependence among Caribbean BOTs, having needed UK financial assistance since 1995 when the *Soufrière Hills* volcano destroyed almost half the island, and will not become financially independent in the foreseeable future following COVID-19. This is shown via the UK contribution for the financial year 2021–22 and its COVID-19 policy measures in which Montserrat receives an annual allocation from the UK's development assistance budget. It received £23.6 million for the financial year 2021–22, with the UK having maintained 'core support at the same level as the previous year'.[60]

[56] Cayman Islands government, 'COVID-19 Update 5 May 2021', www.youtube.com/watch?v=HwU7PMyY5i0, 1:50:20–1:50:45.

[57] ibid.

[58] M Klein, 'Government finances better than budgeted' (6 May 2021) www.caymancompass.com/2021/05/06/government-finances-better-than-budgeted/.

[59] The Cayman Islands government, '2022-2024 Strategic Policy Statement', www.caymancompass.com/wp-content/uploads/2021/07/2022-2024-Strategic-Policy-Statement.pdf, 16.

[60] Government of Montserrat, '£23.6 million confirmed for Montserrat's 2021/22 budget' (30 April 2021) www.gov.ms/2021/04/30/23-6-million-confirmed-for-montserrats-2021-2022-budget/.

Montserrat has put costly measures in place to assist its citizens throughout the pandemic. Reduced tariffs on essential products and one-off payments to families, children and businesses are hoped to bear some of the weight of the crisis. Montserrat has made payments to private citizens, such as to guarantee a minimum threshold for the unemployed, one-off payments to children and assistance to pay utilities[61] and made one-off payments to businesses up to a maximum of ECD10,000 (£2,390) to cover overhead expenses.[62] These measures are necessary for the wellbeing of its inhabitants but cast doubt over Monserrat's ability to provide for itself for some time to come. Recently, Montserrat has decided to follow the Keynesian way out of the COVID-19 crisis. It is developing its port, which should lead to improved sea transportation and a smoother shipping experience. The UK is currently investing £14.4 million, representing approximately 54 per cent of the current design and build phase, and expected to reach a total contribution estimated at £28.3 million.[63] While this might open future paths towards financial independence, in the short and medium term it keeps Monserrat firmly in the UK's pocket.

Not even external support has helped Anguilla to recover. Since 2016, the UK has provided £60 million to assist Anguilla to rebuild critical public infrastructure following Hurricane Irma.[64] The National Commercial Bank of Anguilla also gave the government a USD7.2 million (£5.70 million) overdraft facility. In 2018, the Caribbean Development Bank supplied a USD9.3 million (£7.35 million) loan to implement a reform programme for fiscal sustainability and enhance resilience against natural disasters.[65] Recently, Anguilla received additional emergency support from the UK to 'keep essential public services running and ensure [it] can respond to the impacts of the pandemic'.[66] The pandemic caused an estimated GDP contraction of 27 per cent due to its dependence on tourism, strongly diminished by border closures.[67] Significant action must be taken to boost their local economy and reverse its increased dependency on the UK.

E. Other Measures

Anguilla deserves praise for its bravery in regulating markets. Anguilla acted in both the public and the private sectors, was right to make such an unexpected move. The local government prohibited price gouging for a range of essential items. In April 2020, the government passed regulations setting maximum markups on essential pandemic products including, but not limited to, hand sanitiser, bleach, toilet paper, milk, vegetables, fruits and water.[68] The Premier at the time justified this on the basis of complaints

[61] Ministry of Finance of Montserrat, 'Government COVID-19 support package for residents and children' (26 February 2021) www.gov.ms/2021/02/26/government-covid-19-support-package-for-residents-children/.

[62] Ministry of Finance of Montserrat, '$10k one-off grant available for businesses' (25 February 2021) www.gov.ms/2021/02/25/10k-one-off-grant-available-for-businesses/.

[63] Government of Montserrat, 'Design build contract signed for Montserrat's port project', www.gov.ms/2022/05/19/design-build-contract-signed-for-montserrats-port-project/.

[64] Naitram (n 1).

[65] ibid, 6.

[66] Sugg (n 25) para 1.

[67] François and Greaves (n 42) 11:19–12:22.

[68] Government of Anguilla, Distribution and Price of Goods (Maximum Price Order) Regulations 2020, beatcovid19.ai/downloads/Distribution-and-Price-of-Goods-(Maximum-Price-Order)-Regs-2020.pdf.

from citizens and residents about unfair pricing at some grocery retailers.[69] This was among the most notable actions in the midst of COVID-19 and a necessary one: the remoteness of Caribbean BOTs and the low number of grocery store chains often make it too easy for cartel-like structures to form, especially when the opportunity arises.

VI. Conclusion

Caribbean BOTs have left behind the 'treasure island' trope to become a kaleidoscope of countries with their own responses to events on the world stage. The fortunes of each territory now and in the immediate future are linked directly to the quality of their financial response to COVID-19. Their responses are different to those in mainstream, Western countries because these coercive revenue-based systems cannot raise personal income or corporation taxes to correct inequalities and raise government revenue. As an alternative, Anguilla, Bermuda, British Virgin Islands, the Cayman Islands, Montserrat and Turks and Caicos Islands had a set of tools comprising burning up cash reserves, raising public debt, issuing sovereign bonds, setting up lines of credit, and, ultimately, financial aid from the UK.

COVID-19 has been a challenging time for Caribbean BOTs, whose local economies were put under strain due to lockdowns, high public health expenses and border closures shutting out tourism income. Each BOT chose a different combination and a critical analysis of their choices led to identifying some lessons learned.

Good governance paid off. BOTs that had UK-led and locally tried-and-tested frameworks for fiscal responsibility such as Bermuda and Cayman were in an advantageous position. Having done their homework, they had cash reserves and enough space to allow public debt to rise whilst also being able to reach out to private markets via sovereign bonds and commercial lines of credit. Turks and Caicos is middling, as it, despite a constitutional crisis leading to the emergency replacement of Premier Misick by the Governor right when fiscal responsibility was being negotiated, still managed to implement a wide catalogue of measures to finance COVID-19. Anguilla and Montserrat, already in a precarious financial situation prior to COVID-19, partly due to natural disasters, have cemented their financial dependence on the UK.

There are early signs of change, even in islands that time forgot. Government intervention is on the rise, local online shopping has finally picked up and there has even been some minor redistribution of wealth to correct severe imbalances. However, a radical change in political and social culture would be necessary for these interventionist measures to stay in place in such US-modelled, small, non-diversified economies.

What are the regional implications of increasing debt? Will interest rates increase regionally, leading to unaffordable levels of debt for Caribbean BOTs? If so, it would prove right those that negotiated lines of credit and overdraft facilities.

[69] V Banks, 'Honorable Premier press statement on price gouging COVID-19' (*COVID-19: Anguilian Response*, 20 March 2020) beatcovid19.ai/hon-premiers-press-statement-on-price-gouging-covid-19/.

What is the future of the Frameworks for Fiscal Responsibility, that the UK helped to set up after the 2008 Global Financial Crisis? Can the Caribbean BOTs show they are fit to be trusted by the UK, leading to more flexible frameworks? Rigid fiscal frameworks were designed to remedy Caribbean BOTs' pre-2008 proclivities for skyrocketing spending with little scrutiny. Would their current enhanced scrutiny lead to a flexibilisation or reversal of rigid fiscal frameworks?

As for the future relationship between the UK and its overseas territories, will the UK reward those that did not require its financial assistance? Only if Caribbean BOTs learn today the lessons from this chapter, will they be able to watch over their doubloons in the future.

PART II

Revenues and Institution Building above the State

7

The Role of Crisis in State-Building the European Union through Finance and Taxation: Will COVID-19 and the Russian Attack Trigger Further Union?

PABLO HERNÁNDEZ GONZÁLEZ-BARREDA

Abstract

The European Union tax and finance sovereign character has been frequently denied. However, the analysis has often been one-sided on economic stability or resorting to quantitative arguments. Thus, the evolution and qualitative side of the issue has been overlooked. Following the academic works on the tax state, this chapter aims at reviewing how the interaction of crisis/wars, tax and sovereignty has contributed to the sovereign status of the European Union. The chapter concludes that despite the competences and financial resources of the EU remaining limited, crises have reinforced the sovereign financial status of the EU allocating increasing competences on taxation, financial supervision, financial stability and redistribution. This shows the sovereignty reinforcement-follows-crisis character of sovereign entities. In addition, it also shows that despite the low EU budget, its value is worth more as it is targeted at projects where national budgets are constrained and it has a redistributive function across the EU as a sovereign function. It concludes that current crisis funding allocation may be also an indication of further sovereign development of the Union.

I. Introduction

Whether or not the EU is a state has been a major question in academic literature since almost the beginning of the European Economic Community (EEC).[1] However, the

[1] R Koslowski, 'A Constructivist Approach to Understanding the European Union as a Federal Polity' (1999) 6 *Journal of European Public Policy* 561; J Caporaso, 'The European Union and Forms of State: Westphalian,

works dealing with the finance status of the Union are mostly biased towards economic stability developments. They overlook its impact on state building and there are few comprehensive works.[2]

Developments in the EU in respect of taxation powers, financial stability and budgetary controls, especially those following the Great Recession, may have affected the constitutional core of the EU as well as that of its Member States. Additionally, the EU response to the economic challenges posed by COVID-19 seems to point towards a more relevant role of the Union in finance and tax law. Taking into account the role of taxation, state finance and war and crisis in shaping sovereignty and states, one wonders how the EU has been evolving and has been affected by crisis, and how current crises may continue shaping it.

This chapter aims at analysing how the development of tax law and public finance law in the European Communities and the EU has impacted its constitutional status, particularly during times of crisis.

In section II, the chapter analyses how finance impacts the concept of a state. In section III, the chapter deals with the role of finance, budget and taxation in the original design and early times of the Community, as well as the attempts to expand its competences with little success. Section IV asks whether the economic shock of the Great Recession forced the expansion of EU competences in finance, budgetary and tax law. Section V analyses the role of the EU in tackling COVID-19 challenges and the Russian attack on Ukraine, and asks whether the unprecedented amount of budgetary resources and tax legislative impetus has enlarged EU powers. Finally, Section VI summarises the tax and finance sovereign characteristics of the European Union and its evolution, and applies the lessons from the historical evolution of the EU in tax and finance matters to recent and forthcoming challenges.

II. The Finance Elements of a (Federal) State

The intimate relationship between the state and taxation can be seen in their development between the eighteenth and early twentieth centuries. Among other issues, taxes, new concepts of ownership, democracy and state were feeding each other to build up contemporary nation states. On the one hand, the development of the nation-state, and the reaffirmation of national identities was done through war.[3] Taxes, in turn, played their role in financing war and reinforcing state power.[4] On the other hand, the

Regulatory or Post-Modern?' (1996) 34 *Journal of Common Market Studies* 29; A Moravcsik, 'Federalism in the European Union: Rhetoric and Reality' in K Nicolaidis and R Howse (eds), *The Federal Vision: Legitimacy and Levels of Governance in the United States and the European Union* (Oxford, Oxford University Press, 2001); G Majone, *Regulating Europe* (Abingdon, Routledge, 1996).

[2] H Hofmann, *The Metamorphosis of the European Economic Constitution* (Cheltenham, Edward Elgar, 2019).

[3] E Kiser and A Linton, 'Determinants of the Growth of the State: War and Taxation in Early Modern France and England' (2001) 80 *Social Forces* 411, 411–12.

[4] Kiser and Linton (n 3); SH Steinmo, *The Leap of Faith: The Fiscal Foundations of Successful Government in Europe and America* (Oxford, Oxford University Press, 2018).

development of the liberal and quasi-absolute concept of ownership was attached to the new concept of democracy.[5] Taxation again was essential to the new democratic state and in tension with the absolute concept of ownership.[6] And democracy was essential to taxation.[7]

The second half of the twentieth century saw well-established nation-states with increasing tax powers enjoying the longest period of peace in Europe. The experience of the tax state in war showed smaller amounts of money could produce a welfare state in times of peace.[8] The development of the liberal state also provided universal education and healthcare, which in turn needed taxation to fund it.

The development of modern welfare-state taxation played a core role intimately linked to ownership, welfare services and the concept of nation itself. This is the reason why taxation appears inextricably united with the concept of state as we know it.

The result is that taxation is seen as one of the key elements of a sovereign state, to some even the key element.[9] Taxation is a state-building driver and at the same time an expression of state power.[10]

Less clear is the content of such power. Authors frequently include among sovereign state tax elements the right to establish taxes, collection, enforcement, hold the revenues and use them for public expenditure, with exclusion or pre-emption over other political entities.[11] Moreover, the ability to enforce them is for some paramount among tax powers.[12] Such a view assumes that only a political entity that is able to enforce taxation can be considered a sovereign state, at least from a financial and tax perspective.

However, tax powers as related to sovereignty are not as solid and single-sided as most see them. There are several cases in which the tax power is not exclusive within a single subject or object.[13] This is common in international transactions, especially recently, regarding the digital economy.[14] There are cases in which a state may not exercise its tax power to its full extent, or even not tax at all and fund its expenditures from other sources. Moreover, a state that relies exclusively on hard enforcement will have difficulties in becoming a state as we know it, as increasing tax compliance relies on trust and voluntary contribution.

Thus, analysing how and whether a political entity has the tax and finance characteristics of statehood cannot be done against a defined set of characteristics. Rather, we should analyse how a set of elements related to the economic functions of state contribute

[5] TE Kaiser, *The French Idea of Freedom: The Old Regime and the Declaration of Rights of 1789* (California, Stanford University Press, 1994).

[6] R Nozick, *Anarchy, State, and Utopia* (New York, Basic Books, 1974) 169; L Murphy and T Nagel, *Myth of Ownership* (Oxford, Oxford University Press, 2004) 44–45.

[7] P Boria, *Taxation in European Union* (New York, Springer, 2017) 190.

[8] A Briggs, 'The Welfare State in Historical Perspective' (1961) 2 *European Journal of Sociology* 221, 227.

[9] JA Schumpeter, 'The Crisis of the Tax State' in J Backhaus (ed), *Navies and State Formation: The Schumpeter Hypothesis Revisited and Reflected* (Berlin, Lit Verlag, 2012); A Christians, 'Sovereignty, Taxation and Social Contract' (2009) 18 *Minnesota Journal of International Law* 99, 104.

[10] D de Cogan, *Tax Law, State-Building and the Constitution* (Oxford, Hart Publishing, 2020) 1–30.

[11] ibid 25; Moravcsik (n 1) 170; Boria (n 7) 190.

[12] D Strasser, *The Finances of Europe*, 7th edn (European Commission, 1992) 91–92.

[13] Christians (n 9) 107.

[14] ibid.

to the specific set of political tools the relevant political entity aims at performing, and whether the combination of these elements can be considered a sort of sovereign entity.

The fact that most legal, economic and political scholars put the spotlight on hard power or enforcement characteristics may explain why the European Union has not been considered a state from a tax perspective, taking into account the lack of hard tax competences.[15] To my view, the assessment has to be done on the power/competence and the income-expenditure function, jointly with the aim of the political entity.

In terms of the hard power abilities of a sovereign state, the ability of the bodies of the political entity to define the amount of resources of the total of the economy for the public sector to perform its activity is one of the elements most scholars relate to sovereign characteristics of a state in relation to finance.[16] Also the ability to collect and enforce the revenues through own bodies.[17] The amount of resources allocated to welfare state expenditure is also seen as a sign of tax sovereignty.[18]

In economic or functional terms, it is widely accepted that redistribution, macroeconomic stabilisation and regulatory functions are the main goals of the financial and economic constitution of a state.[19] Though these functions can be done through several different tools, the use of taxation and the budget to attain them is one of the most relevant.

III. Finance, Budget and Taxation in the Birth and Evolution of the European Communities (1951–2007)

A. The Evolution of the Budget and the Finance of the Communities and its Contribution to Shaping the Constitutional Role of the Union

i. The Role of Member States and Other Institutions on the EEC/EC/EU Budget

Finance and the budget was not a key issue at the birth of the European Communities and was probably merely seen as an instrumental issue to achieve a political integration through a Common Market. This apparent secondary role was not because the European Communities' founding fathers were not aware of its significance. Contrarily, the important role of state finance as an element of sovereignty probably avoided the spotlight of political integration as placing it in the first row of integration would have

[15] See Majone (n 1) 54; Moravcsik (n 1) 169; F Laursen, 'The EU and Federalism: Constitutional Equilibrium or Continued Federalization?' in *The EU and Federalism: Polities and Policies Compared* (Farnham, Ashgate 2011) 267; N Groenendijk, 'Federalism, Fiscal Autonomy and Democratic Legitimacy in Europe: Towards Tax Sharing Arrangements' [2011] L'*Europe en formation* 5; Boria (n 7) 192. Moravcsik (n 1).

[16] Boria (n 7) 190.

[17] Arnold in Christians (n 9) n 25.

[18] Moravcsik (n 1).

[19] Majone (n 1) 54.

encouraged Member States to reject the project.[20] Following the Schuman idea of soft economic integration that would drag political integration,[21] European Communities finance would follow the Common Market.

Paradoxically, the European Coal and Steel Community (ECSC) enjoyed a high level of financial independence at its early stages. The High Authority of the ECSC was able to establish its own scheme of resources and to determine the expenditure within the limits of the treaty. Only on administrative expenditure and outside the limits of the treaty or in certain cases could the Committee of four presidents overrule the High Authority decisions. More surprisingly, the High Authority was able to contract loans to give loans, with almost no limit from Member States. However, the broad financial independence of the ECSC contrasts with its limited focus on the coal and steel market, and consequently, in the amount of the budget.

As compared to the ECSC, the European Community and the European Community of the Atomic Energy enjoyed little to no financial independence from Member States at the beginning. The budget was decided by the Council, which left the size and content of its action directly dependent on the trade-off negotiation with Member States. The Assembly as a body independent from Member States had no direct decision-making power.

However, the Treaties of Rome foresaw the establishment of a Community System of own resources in parallel with the development of a proper European Parliament (EP) directly elected by citizens, which took place in 1970. The Treaty of Luxembourg gave the EP actual decision-making power on the budget by giving the ability to override Council decisions as regards expenditure derived from obligations contained in the treaty. Moreover, the budget was to be proclaimed by the President of the EP, increasing its political status as a symbol related to the Parliament.

In 1975, the Parliament increased again its powers, being able to decide on non-compulsory expenditure subject to certain conditions. In addition the European Court of Auditors was created. In 1979 Europe held the first direct elections to the EP. This, together with the increasing competences of the Parliament on the budget and the new own resources structure, gave the EC's budget more legitimacy and increased ideas of EU sovereignty.

In the 1980s, subsequent conflicts on the budget between the Parliament and the Council prompted the establishment of a new system of competences.[22] Following the agreements around the Single European Act, the European Council subjected the European Communities budgets to a multiannual expense ceiling system that continues today, subject again to the approval of the Council by unanimity, and to national Parliaments, constraining the ability of the Community bodies to decide on finance and economic-political capacities over long periods. On the other hand, it increased the size of the budget.[23]

[20] P Wattel and B Terra, *European Tax Law*, 6th edn (Alphen aan den Rijn, Wolters Kluwer, 2012) 4.

[21] R Schuman, 'Declaration of 9th May 1950 Delivered by Robert Schuman' [2011] *European Issue* 1.

[22] G Benedetto, *The History of EU Budget* (Policy Department for Budgetary Affairs, Directorate General for Internal Policies of the Union, 2019) PE 636.475 6.

[23] ibid.

The result of the modifications of the financial and budget competences of the 1980s was that the European Communities lost part of the institutional budgetary independence gained in the 1970s as the total expenditure was again directly subject to the will of Member States in the Council, which left the decision of the total expenditure as a mere trade-off.[24] At first instance, the setting of a ceiling subject to a great extent to the Council may be seen as a loss to the EC's budgetary sovereignty in terms of an ability to set the budget amount different from Member States' will.[25] However, once the ceiling has been settled, the system defined in the Treaty of Brussels established a system of checks and balances between the institutions of the Union that enables them to depart from the trade-off negotiations of Member States and obtain a different result. To put the ceiling in a different and previous negotiation limits the influence of Member States outside the negotiation table of each year budget.

ii. The Amount of the Budget

The EU budget has increased from less than 5 billion in 1967 to an annual average in payments of 91.64 billion in 2006. Some authors have argued that the evolution of the 'tax state' in the twentieth century, in connection with social welfare, made a tax total of 25–50 per cent GDP a measure of the power of a state as such.[26] The size of the European budget of around 1 per cent of GNP leaves it far from an amount necessary to show sufficiency and ability to sustain services as characteristic of states. Moreover, some authors have pointed out the amount is 'irrelevant' from a macroeconomic point of view.[27]

iii. The Right to Revenue and Collection Powers

The levies established by the ECSC directly accrued to and were collected by the Authority, providing a hard indication of being a sovereign supranational organisation, even more taking into account the high level of independence given to the High Authority.

However, the EEC was born with no resources accruing directly to the new political organisation. At the beginning, the Community was funded exclusively with transfers from Member States. Early in 1970 the EEC established the custom tariff on imports, agricultural and sugar levies, and a percentage of VAT as own resources. In this first period, such duties rose from 50 per cent of the total resources of the Community in 1970 to almost 100 per cent in 1987. In 1988, a so-called fourth resource supplementary contribution, based on a percentage of GNP/GNI, was introduced. In 1985, the VAT contribution was introduced and first increased up to the early 1990s, and then decreased from then on until 2007.

[24] Groenendijk (n 15) 11; C Fuest and J Pisani-Ferry, 'Financing the European Union: New Context, New Responses' [2020] *Policy Contribution* 1, 4.

[25] The previous ability of the Parliament to break the interinstitutional agreement as a bargaining power was eliminated in the TFEU. See Groenendijk (n 15) 10.

[26] Moravcsik (n 1) 169.

[27] M Buti and M Nava, *Towards a European Budgetary System* (European University Institute, 2003) 1.

Customs duties, agricultural and sugar levies are where the Community is closer to a state tax power. In all of those cases, the Community established the duties, accrues the revenue directly to the Community, and enjoys the revenue. However, though they are called 'own resources', collection remains in bodies of the Member States. Moreover, the establishment of customs duties is one of the few competences of the Community that is exercised by the Council alone. This leaves competence in the hands of Member States and outside other institutional checks and balances of the Union. Member States account for the custom duties in their budgets and account for the payment to the Union as a transfer, though this can be seen as a mere accounting issue.[28] On the enjoyment of the revenue, the increase in collection costs to 25 per cent has increasingly eroded the indirect 'collection powers' and enjoyment ability of the Community.

As regards VAT, the definition of the part of its collection accruing to the Community as own resource belongs to the Council and Member States. In addition, collection is fully in hands of the Member States and the Community has very little room in that regard, leaving the VAT resource close to a transfer.[29]

Last, as regards the fourth resource or GNI-based own resource, the Community has no decision on how amounts are obtained and its accrual is based on a decision by the Council. Hence, this resource cannot be said to vest any taxation powers in the institutions of the Community. Consequently, some authors do not speak about 'collection' regarding these resources but 'putting at disposal' of the Union.[30]

In sum, the accrual, collection and enjoyment of Community tax resources depends heavily on transfers by Member States. Even in the case of so-called traditional own resources – the ones considered closer to European taxes – the level of independence of EU institutions from the collection and revenue establishing powers of Member States is very low. Moreover, the structure of funding has eroded the resources that have a stronger independence from Member State tax powers, and increased the role of resources dependent on Member States. Namely, the increasing role of the GNI contribution in the budget 'encourages thinking about the EU budget in terms of net balances' which is quite the opposite of a single sovereign state.[31]

iv. The Expenditures in the Budget

In the early history of the European Community, between 60 and 80 per cent of the budget accounted for the ECSC and European Development Fund. However, after the Common Agricultural Policy emerged as an area of expenditure in 1962, the European Agricultural Fund progressively increased its share of the ECs budget to reach an average level between 70 and 80 per cent of European Communities expenditure in the period between 1968 and 1980. Within the rest of the budget, more than 10 per cent on average accounted for the ECSC and the EDF, and the rest was allocated to research, external action, administration and structural funds.

[28] See P Butzen, 'Notable Trends in the EU Budget' (2006) *Economic Review* 50, 50; G Cipriani, *Financing the EU Budget: Moving Forward or Backwards* (Centre for European Policy Studies, 2014), 8–9.

[29] W Coussens, 'Financing the EU Budget: Time for Reform' (2004) 57 *Studia Diplomatica* 73, 76; Cipriani (n 28) 9.

[30] Cipriani (n 28) 9.

[31] Fuest and Pisani-Ferry (n 24) 4; Cipriani (n 28) 9–10.

After the enlargement of the European Community in the 1980s, structural funds gained an increased share of the European Budget. The increase in structural funds was mirrored by a decrease in the share of the agricultural funds.

The budget structure of the European Union shows it has little to no direct expenditure, but relies largely on transfers to Member States and their regions.[32] Direct transfers or expenditure directly related to citizens are limited.[33] The largest part of the transfers relates to infrastructures and investment. However, agricultural, research, cohesion and development funds are still redistributive policies, which are directly related to state characteristics.[34] Though such a redistributive function is limited by the size of the European Budget,[35] its value is high as it takes income from high-earning countries to invest in low earning countries, with an enormous purchasing power parity (PPP) impact. The stability and inflexibility of national budgets, combined with the relative flexibility of European funds, may allocate the additional funds to new investments that will result in higher marginal results in state objectives. As suggested by literature, European funds may leverage additional public and private investment.[36] EU funds may be more effective and/or efficient for certain policies, achieving results that domestically may only be achieved with higher amounts.

On the other hand, the fact that the largest portion of the budget is allocated to agricultural and cohesion policies shows the value of the EU budget in terms of redistribution. The EU budget is one of the very few public instruments of cross-border redistribution in Europe, increasing its qualitative value. The extraction of resources from wealthy Member States to fund cohesion programmes in less wealthy Member States increases the EU budget value PPP.

B. Taxation Powers in the European Communities

i. Exclusive Competence in Custom Duties and Abolition of Duties between Member States

First, on the Common External Tariff and in custom duties between Member States, competence was exclusively given to the European Community. As early as 1968 the Council adopted Council Regulation (EEC) No 950/68 of 28 June 1968 on the Common Customs Tariff.

The main issue as regards competence in the Common External tariff and decisions on custom duties and measures between Member States is that its approval and modification is done by the Council by unanimity, and the Parliament only holds consultative status. At first sight, the allocation of powers on Customs Tariff and duties to the Council seems to leave such powers in hands of Member States. This means that such decisions

[32] Moravcsik (n 1) 170.
[33] Majone (n 1) 66.
[34] ibid 54.
[35] ibid 77.
[36] P Wostner and S Slander, 'The Effectiveness of EU Cohesion Policy Revisited: Are EU Funds Really Additional?' (2009) European Policy Research Paper 69, 20, www.researchgate.net/publication/228427571_The_effectiveness_of_EU_cohesion_policy_revisited_are_EU_funds_really_additional.

may be subject to a trade-off negotiation rather than the type of checks and-balances decision that might be expected of a sovereign state.

Nevertheless, the role of the European Court of Justice also reinforces the sovereign status of the EU in these matters. Since very early on, the ECJ recognised the ability of the Court to scrutinise the decisions of the Council and Member States on measures regarding the Common Tariff and duties between Member States.[37] The result is that even when Member States reach an agreement on changes to the Custom Tariff and related measures, it is subject to ECJ scrutiny under EU law and principles, which makes the Custom Tariff and duties subject to EU checks and balances decision-making rules and to some extent independent from the will of Member States.

ii. Shared Competences with Pre-emption in Indirect Taxation

In the Treaty of Rome, there was no direct conferral of taxation powers to the European institutions outside the scope of the Common Tariff. However, the treaty prohibited any type of measures distorting the internal market (including tax measures) and enabled the Council to adopt legislative measures to approximate legislation, subject to unanimity, to prevent such distortions.

However, even before its birth the Community was aware of the significance of indirect taxes to the realisation of the common market, and Article 99 of the EEC Treaty mandated the EC to analyse and propose the harmonisation of turnover taxes, excise duties and other forms of indirect taxation, including countervailing measures. In 1967 turnover taxes were harmonised under a European VAT. This was followed in the 1970s by Directives on the raising of capital and tobacco and in 1992 by Directives on excise duties on mineral oils, alcohol and tobacco.

The exercise of such competence by EU institutions since 1992 has largely turned indirect tax matters into an EU exclusive competence, at least to the extent of abolishing limits to the internal market.[38] However, the Treaties require unanimity in the Council and the Parliament continues to have a limited consultative status. The unanimity requirement limits the chances of modification as any Member State may veto any change.

Vetoes makes difficult any direct attempt by Member States to modify general rules or policies in such matters, or even abolish them, with the effect that such rules have crystallised in EU law. Though formally dependent directly on the aggregated will of Member States in the Council, the practice is that changes do not (only) follow political decisions fostered by Member States, making it an EU competence in practice.

Negative harmonisation by the CJEU has also strengthened EU competences in VAT even more than in relation to the Custom Tariff and custom duties. The ECJ/CJEU has been active in interpreting harmonised rules on indirect taxes in the light of secondary law, as well as non-harmonised areas under primary law, to an even greater extent than in the custom duties field.[39]

[37] eg Case 7/68 *Commission of the European Communities v Italian Republic* [1968] ECR 562.

[38] R De la Feria, 'Towards an [Unlawful] Modernized EU VAT Rate Policy' (2017) *EC Tax Review* 89; M Aujean, 'Tax Policy in the EU: Between Harmonisation and Coordination?' (2010) 16 *Transfer* 11; Wattel and Terra (n 20) 9.

[39] P Genschel and M Jachtenfuchs, 'How the European Union Constrains the State: Multilevel Governance of Taxation' (2011) 50 *European Journal of Political Research* 293, 301.

iii. The Slow Progressive Expansion of EU Competences in Direct Tax Matters: Anti-sovereignty?

The Treaties on the European Communities did not have specific rules on harmonisation of direct tax matters, as there were and are on indirect tax matters.[40] However, as early as in 1962 and in 1970, the Neumark and Van den Temple reports called for harmonisation of tax matters, including direct taxes.[41] Nonetheless, the allocation of almost complete harmonisation competence on custom duties to the Union, and broad competences in indirect taxes, made Member States highly reluctant to also allocate competence in direct tax matters.[42]

Tax measures were also within the scope of elimination of market distortions, prohibition of anti-competitive measures, and free movement competences of the Union. Though it took almost 21 years to pass them due to the reluctance of Member States, the Parent-Subsidiary Directive and the Merger Directive were approved under these headings in 1990. There were no other positive harmonisation acts in EU law until 2003, when the Interest and Royalties Directive was passed. Though several other proposals were issued in the 60 years between the birth of the Communities and the Treaty of Lisbon, only the three mentioned Directives succeeded, showing the slow pace of EU law competences in direct tax matters and the reluctance of states to give up sovereignty in this field.[43]

This does not mean the EU did not advance at all in competences in direct tax matters. In an early relevant case in 1986, *Avoir Fiscal*, the ECJ ruled that the fact that the laws of Member States have not been harmonised cannot justify the difference of treatment between residents and non-residents.[44] From then on, the Court ruled in several aspects of tax matters as far as they were considered compatible with EU rules on freedoms or state aid rules.[45]

However, EU limits to taxation in direct tax matters were largely confined to cross-border cases or cases affecting the internal market, which may lead us to consider Member States' ability on domestic tax matters up to the Treaty of Lisbon as almost unlimited. However, the increasing interrelation in the internal market makes it progressively more and more inconceivable that domestic tax law decisions have no wider impact; hence, EU law has been expanding to cover more and more aspects of tax law.

As regards the specific competence of positive harmonisation of taxes through competences to approximate and harmonise the internal market, former Article 95 of the Treaty also required unanimity.[46] As direct tax matters have been subject to little

[40] Aujean (n 38) 13.

[41] F Neumark, 'Report of the Fiscal and Financial Committee (Neumark Report)' in H Thurston, *The EEC Reports on Tax Harmonisation* (IBFD, 1963); AJ van den Tempel, 'Corporation Tax and Individual Income Tax in the European Communities' (Commission of the European Communities, 1970) Approximation of Legislation Series 15.

[42] Wattel and Terra (n 20) 4.

[43] See CHJI Panayi, *European Union Corporate Tax Law* (Cambridge, Cambridge University Press, 2013) 4–30; M Gammie, 'Corporate Tax Harmonisation – Stage I: The Struggle for Progress' in CHJI Panayi et al (eds), *Research Handbook on European Union Taxation Law* (Cheltenham, Edward Elgar, 2020); Wattel and Terra (n 20) 198 ff.

[44] Case 270/83 *Commission of the European Communities v French Republic* [1986] 1 ECR 273.

[45] See a summary in Panayi (n 43) 123 ff; Wattel and Terra (n 20) 881–1060.

[46] Wattel and Terra (n 20) 22.

harmonisation, the unanimity requirement largely leaves the subject to the will of Member States at the Council. To be able to reach harmonisation in such matters, a strong political pressure, joint willingness or a large trade-off game has to take place, which leaves the field largely in the hands of Member States.

The harmonisation of direct tax matters has been largely done through negative harmonisation where the ECJ interprets the limits of Member State sovereignty in direct tax matters. This implies that the EU institutions have very little positive strong sovereign power on direct tax matters, but they have an important influence in a negative sense.[47] Moreover, contrary to what has been said by some scholars, in the medium term negative harmonisation leads to positive harmonisation power, because it can progressively bring the Member States to a point where positive harmonisation is necessary.[48] And once harmonised, the unanimity lockdown makes it a strong EU competence.

iv. The Administrative Regulation of Taxes in the EU

On the administrative regulation side, the EU competences were limited until the Great Recession. On indirect taxation, the removal of internal borders was a major issue. Also Custom Union and VAT administrative cooperation development took place to some extent, but not as fast as the development of the substantive regulation in such matters. In 1977, mutual assistance in direct tax matters was approved. In 2003, the Savings Directive also introduced cooperation among Member States on exchange of information for direct tax matters, with limited results. Also, an agreement on cooperation in transfer pricing has been introduced.

C. Budgetary Control in the European Communities

The EEC design was aimed at a progressive political integration through economic integration. However, a common market with different monetary and fiscal policies was severely distorted.

In 1992, the Treaty of Maastricht established a public debt ceiling of 60 per cent of GDP, and a maximum of 3 per cent deficit in the European Union as a counterpart to the development of the European Monetary Union in order to maintain stable fiscal positions towards the currency and economic stability.[49]

States lost to some extent their ability to govern their finance and debt in favour of the Union, though the enforcement of such rules was largely in the hands of Member States in the Council. The Commission had limited powers on such issues even after Maastricht (such as name and shame) and even in the most severe cases, could only enforce indirect coercive measures but no direct enforcement competences.

[47] Boria (n 7) 189–206.

[48] Gammie (n 43); L Cerioni, 'Corporate Tax Harmonisation – Stage II: Coordination to Fight Avoidance and Harmful Tax Competition' in Panayi et al (eds) *Research Handbook on European Union Taxation Law* (n 43).

[49] See A Verdun, *Ruling Europe: The Politics of the Stability and Growth Pact* (Cambridge, Cambridge University Press, 2010).

In relation to debt, since the very beginning the Treaties prohibited EU institutions and Member States from incurring debts or liabilities for another Member State, effectively barring mutualisation of debt, and as a preventive measure placed pressure on each state to manage and be responsible for its own debt in order to enforce debt limits. With strong currency powers allocated to the Union, soft powers allocated to the Union on budget stability, and with no powers on common debt, several economists and some EU institutions feared the EU would have had no tools in the case of severe economic recession.[50]

In 1997 and within the Treaty of Amsterdam scheme, the Growth and Stability Pact (GSP) supplemented the EU rules with medium term objectives for Member State stability, and not just annual objectives, and strengthened EU enforcement procedures and abilities in the event of breach of stability rules, including mandatory sanctions. In 2005, amendments to the GSP somehow relaxed the conditions and broadened the exceptions in case of severe economic downturn and extended deadlines. Conversely, they introduced stronger requirements by requesting a minimum annual improvement of 0.5 per cent GDP.

Within this period, it can hardly be said the European Union had a strong finance sovereign competence on the finance of the public sector of the Union. The rules were based on name and shame, indirect enforcement sanctions, and were subject to the Council exclusively, making it subject to the aggregate political will of the Member States.

IV. How the Great Recession Fostered EU Powers in Finance and Taxation

A. The Treaty of Lisbon Changes in the Budgetary Rules

Though not properly triggered by the Great Recession, changes to budgetary rules took place at the same time. The Treaty of Lisbon consolidated the multiannual expense planning, now officially included in the Treaty, excluded the ability of the institutions to withdraw the mechanism, and relabelled it as the Multiannual Financial Frameworks (MFF). It also provided for a new give and take exchange on the finance and budgeting abilities of the then new Union.

On the one hand, the Treaty provided the community institutions with more independence from Member State decision-making bodies, by removing the subjection of the MFF to national parliaments.[51] In addition, it subjected disagreements on budgetary matters to a joint committee of the Council and the Parliament. On the other hand, it eliminated the ability of the EC, Council and EP to cancel the multiannual planning and return to annual budgeting, restricting the capacity of the Union to act more

[50] A Verdun, 'A Historical Institutionalist Explanation of the EU's Responses to the Euro Area Financial Crisis' (2015) 22 *Journal of European Public Policy* 219, 222.
[51] Benedetto (n 22) 10.

dynamically on its finance and economical-political action, and limiting the bargaining power of the Parliament in terms of threatening to terminate the agreement.[52]

In sum, it might be seen the Treaty of Lisbon formally put the European Union closer to a sovereign entity on the budgetary side. However, some may argue that the actual procedure of approval and/or implementation still submits European institutions to the willingness of Member States. The negotiation of the recent MFF 2021–27 may be seen as indicative of such submission through the European Council.[53] In my view, the increasing complexity of the procedures establishes a new set of rules where neither the Member States, EC nor EP hold the absolute power of decision. In the end, the budget procedure is developing into a checks and balances system that is precisely the core of an independent sovereign body. Moreover, as suggested by Benedetto, the loss of agenda setting power by the Parliament has been compensated for by gaining veto power.[54]

B. The European Powers on Member States' Budgeting and Finance

i. The New Ability to Rescue Member States in Financial Distress

When the Great Recession kicked the European economy in 2008, events which several academics and experts had been dreading took place.[55] A sharp pressure on the debt of some Member States put the stability of the Euro at risk. The European Union was prohibited from bailing out any country with its funds or by borrowing funds in the market.

At first instance, the bailout of Greece was done through a pool of coordinated bilateral loans with the EC acting as coordinator, but where the funds were not formally given by the EU.[56] Later, the Union used Article 122 for financial assistance of Member States under severe difficulties caused by natural disasters to establish the European Financial Stability Mechanism, with a view to preserve the financial stability of Member States, which was clearly against the purpose of the Treaties.

However, this was just a temporary measure, limited by their own resources ceiling, and unable to solve the increasing problems some Member States were facing.[57] Thus, an institution at the borders of the EU institutional frame was created. The European Financial Stability Facility (EFSF) was put in place in 2010 as a temporary mechanism to bailout euro area Member States that were unable to fund their finance

[52] ibid 10. MW Bauer, JD Graham and S Becker, 'The EU Budget System after Lisbon: How the European Parliament Lost Power and How It May Compensate (Somewhat) for It' (2015) 13 *Journal for Comparative Government and European Policy* 479, 485; *cf* G Benedetto, 'The EU Budget after Lisbon: Rigidity and Reduced Spending?' (2013) 33 *Journal of Public Policy* 345.

[53] R Drachenberg and M Vrijhoeven, 'The Role of the European Council in Negotiating the 2021–27 MFF' (European Parliament, 2021) PE 662.611.

[54] Benedetto (n 22) 350.

[55] Verdun (n 50) 222.

[56] ibid 225; M Ruffert, 'The European Debt Crisis and European Union Law' (2011) 48 *Common Market Law Review* 1777, 1778–79.

[57] ibid 1779.

at reasonable rates.[58] Later, the need for a permanent mechanism boosted the creation of the European Stability Mechanism.[59]

The main issue regarding the facilities established during the Great Recession to bailout countries facing financial problems was its coherence with the rule prohibiting liability or assumption of the EU or other Member States on the debt of other Member States laid down in Article 125 TFEU. Though controversial in the beginning, it has been settled and now widely supports the EFSF and the ESM being fully compatible with the Treaty for two reasons. First, a restrictive reading of Article 125 provides for a prohibition of guarantee of debt of other Member States, but not of providing loans or credits.[60] Second, a swift modification of Article 136 introduced a new paragraph allowing EMU Member States to establish mechanisms of assistance.[61]

In addition to bailout mechanisms, the European Central Bank enabled quantitative easing mechanisms. Breaking some dogmas, the ECB helped as a European institution to consolidate financial stability as a core constitutional principle of the EU.

The result of the establishment of the EFSF, the ESM and the modification of Article 136 was that the EU constitutional framework gained a new competence: the euro area stability through loans and other financial mechanisms. Before 2011, EU stability rules, including debt limitation rules and prohibition of bailouts, were aimed at maintaining price stability within the EU. After the 2011 modification of Article 136, the financial stability of the euro area as a whole was an EU matter. Through a last resort mechanism a new EU competence was laid down in the Treaties.

ii. The Allocation of a True Power to Enforce Stability Rules on the EU

As the reverse of the new stability competences of the Union, the so-called 'six pack' was approved in 2011. The six pack introduced preventive measures and severe financial sanctions on euro area Member States that do not comply with the recommendations on excessive deficit. More interestingly, it allocated new competences to the EC including monitoring, warning and the proposal of measures to the Council. Moreover, the inaction of the Council could lead to the adoption of the proposal of the EC unless rejected by the majority of the Council.

It also strengthened the 60 per cent debt-to-GDP ratio by permitting the excessive deficit procedure to be opened on the sole basis of the debt criterion, and by requiring a reduction of a twentieth part of the difference between the debt ratio and the 60 per cent per year, otherwise subjecting the Member State to the excessive deficit procedure.

In 2013 the so-called two-pack enhanced surveillance in the euro area, and a common budgetary timeline and budgetary monitoring measures of Member States incurring an excessive deficit.

[58] ibid 1780; Verdun (n 50) 226.

[59] Ruffert (n 56) 1782.

[60] Judgment of the Court of Justice of 27 November 2012. Case C-370/12 *Pringle v Ireland* [2013] 2 CMLR 2. G Bianco, 'The New Financial Stability Mechanisms and Their Poor Consistency with EU Law' (European University Institute, 2012) RSCAS 2012/44 12–14. Against, Ruffert (n 56) 1785–87.

[61] Council Decision 2011/199/EU of 25 March 2011 amending Article 136 of the TFEU with regard to a stability mechanism for a Member State whose currency is the euro. In theory this is just a confirmation. 'The Court of Justice Approves the Creation of the European Stability Mechanism Outside the EU Legal Order: Pringle' (2013) 50 *Common Market Law Review* 805, 843.

These changes have without any doubt modified the financial constitution of the European Union, enlarging EU financial competences. First, the bailout prohibition ended up being modulated by changes in the Treaty and by new institutions, allowing secondary bailouts while prohibiting direct assumption of debt. Second, this new approach introduced the concept of financial stability as an objective of the Union, enlarging prior mere price stability. Third, Member States are now subject to a permanent and strong surveillance of their finance by a European set of checks and balances of the EC, the Council and the Parliament, and not just the Council. And fourth and last, these concepts may have modified to some extent the economic and social principles enshrined in Article 3.3 TFEU, supplementing a mere market constitution with a social and finance constitution that to some extent has developed finance solidarity.[62]

C. Consolidating (Direct) Taxation into EU Competences

From the beginning of the European Communities until 2008, only 17 instruments were passed on the topic of direct taxation. Since 2008, in a period of 10 years, at least 10 directives in direct tax matters have been enacted. There is a similar pattern in the jurisprudence of the Court of Justice of the EU. On this basis, there is no doubt the EU has increased the exercise of its competences in direct tax matters after the Great Recession.[63]

As mentioned, EU harmonisation in direct tax matters took place mainly through the prohibition of discrimination, the development of freedoms and prohibition of state aid. The role of jurisprudence in harmonisation has been of utmost importance, with two effects. On the one hand, through negative harmonisation, there has been the setting of the areas limited to the direct tax sovereignty of Member States. On the other, by limiting the scope of action of Member States and putting the spotlight on the internal market, it has brought Member States to the Council table to develop positive harmonisation in the field to clarify the scope of action in direct tax matters and prevent distortions. Not surprisingly, most harmonisation directives have followed the jurisprudence of the Court in the matter.

Probably the field in which the Court has mostly developed its jurisprudence in direct tax matters is the prevention of abuse. This is particularly of importance because of the special role and diversity of anti-avoidance rules and principles within tax law systems. Owing to CJEU jurisprudence on anti-avoidance rules there might be a significant convergence among Member States on the treatment of avoidance, reinforced by rules enacted through directives.[64] In other words, EU law has engaged with a core element of all Member States' tax systems and incorporated it within the EU tax constitution.

Not limited to defining the negative limits on Member States' prevention of tax avoidance, the jurisprudence of the Court triggered harmonisation of certain rules.

[62] Ruffert (n 56) 1792.
[63] Cerioni (n 48).
[64] See J Freedman, 'General Anti-Avoidance Rules (GAARs) – A Key Element of Tax Systems in the Post-BEPS Tax World? The UK GAAR' [2016] *Legal Research Papers* 22.

Following the financial pressure on domestic budgets during the Great Recession, the spotlight moved to international tax avoidance, which can only be properly tackled through international coordination. On this premise, the European Union implemented a significant development of secondary legislation on this matter and it also influenced international developments at the OECD and the G20.

The Court of Justice also has continued ruling on several subjects, especially tax avoidance, with rules and principles that have been followed by several Member States, and most recently have been harmonised through directives.[65]

In the case of state aid, even though the assessment of tax under state aid rules has been achieved since the beginning of the Communities, it gained an enormous significance after 2013. As mentioned previously, case law has introduced a set of rules concerning tax incentives at the heart of the EU tax constitution, undermining the sovereignty of Member States.[66]

Regarding the European Charter of Fundamental Rights, the Court has assessed the compatibility of the actions of tax authorities in relation to taxpayers. In this regard, one of the main issues is the expanding exchange of information procedures in relation to rights to privacy and effective judicial remedy. The result is that the EU tax constitution recognises a set of taxpayers' rights that is progressively being defined.

On positive harmonisation, after the Treaty of Lisbon anti-avoidance directives, a recast of the parent subsidiary directive and a merger directive were passed. But perhaps the area where largest harmonisation has been developed in this period is exchange of information and mutual assistance. Such directives have an extraordinary impact on domestic tax systems. The use of common information and rules of assessment in certain areas leads to a soft convergence of tax law which is stronger than immediate appearances may suggest.[67] In addition to already passed directives, a directive on minimum tax is likely to be passed imminently.[68] Its importance is paramount, as it will bring an important element of sovereignty on corporate tax rates into EU competence.

The active role of the European Union in the Base Erosion and Profit Shifting (BEPS) Action Plan led to the inclusion of several of the proposals previously contained in EU drafts in the final reports of the Plan, making the EU external action in tax matters a vital area and impacting not only Member States but also third countries. The active role of the EU in leading the implementation of such rules among Member States, mainly through the Anti-Tax Avoidance Package, as well as the commitment of EU countries to the plan, has also impacted their domestic tax law and policy.

Although the abovementioned competences in tax matters are not EU own competences, the Union has operated under the subsidiarity principle, and by doing so, it has gained competence by exercise. The result is a significant enlargement of the European finance and tax constitution.

[65] See, as an example, exit taxes in Aujean (n 38).

[66] E Fort, 'EU State Aid and Tax: An Evolutionary Approach' (2017) 57 *European Taxation*.

[67] PA Hernández González-Barreda, 'The Economic Allocation of Income and the Disregarding of Narrowly Held Entities Following the OECD/G20 Base Erosion and Profit Shifting Project: Coordination of the Work on Exchange of Information and Income Allocation Rules' (2022) 76 *Bulletin for International Taxation*.

[68] Proposal for a Council Directive on ensuring a global minimum level of taxation for multinational groups in the Union COM (2021) 823 final.

V. Will a New Crisis Trigger Further Union: COVID-19 and the Russian Attack on Ukraine

A. The EU Role in the COVID-19 Outbreak: Strengthening Competences in Health and Economic Crisis Matters

i. Health Measures

Following the sudden COVID-19 outbreak, the EU took measures under existing instruments. But very soon, the Union took decisions that enlarged its abilities and competences in order to tackle the crisis.

A new Health Programme (EU4Health) was adopted reserving 2.4 billion euros for the health programme, including common procurement and grants, with a possible increase of up to 2.9 billion. It also furthered joint procurement regulation, enabling the EC to act as wholesaler by buying, stocking and reselling or donating supplies and services for Member States or partner organisations as opposed to the previous Joint Public Acquisitions (JPA) where its powers were subjected to a Steering Committee. Moreover, under the new procedure, the EC does not only act on behalf of the Member States but can only do it on its own behalf in a Joint Public Procurement (JPP) competence.[69]

The procurement of vaccines, however, despite being arranged under the legal framework of Council Regulation (EU) 2016/369, has been organised as an Advance Purchase Agreement with vaccine manufacturers, and not as an actual Joint Procurement. This is probably the consequence of Member States wishing to retain decision power on the tender as well as benefiting from the advantages of a joint action. Regarding materials for COVID 19 treatments, several tenders on ventilators, needles and medical treatments have been organised by the EC.

Joint procurement is not new as the European Union has already tendered medical supplies or influenza vaccines. Still, the COVID-19 threat has strengthened EU abilities and competences in procurement, enlarging its effective competences, mainly through new abilities on own purchase as wholeseller. Moreover, the increase of the EU4Health programme budget from around 450 million to 5.4 billion is a major sign of the increased power of the European Union in health matters, a competence that is strongly linked to Welfare States. However the amount is very limited and largely allocated to mere promotion of health.

ii. Finance Support: rescEU, SURE, CRII, EUSF, EGF

Since the beginning of the crisis, the EU adapted existing mechanisms and adopted new ones to cover the wide range of needs triggered by the unprecedented crisis, including cohesion policy, the EU Solidarity Fund, the Coronavirus Response Investment Initiative, the Emergency Support Instrument, the rescEU budget and the European

[69] See Art 9.1(c) Regulation (EU) 2021/522.

Guarantee Fund. The Council also enacted a new mechanism to support unemployment risks of the COVID-19 emergency under Article 122, even though social security is a national competence. The SURE mechanisms enabled financial assistance of up to 100 billion euros in the form of loans, backed by solidarity bonds.

All such measures were immediate responses to the crisis and made significant amounts available to citizens, enterprises and Member States.

All these measures put the EU at the very spotlight of the management of the public finance crisis of the COVID-19 pandemic with an unprecedented amount of budget. In this regard, it consolidated its constitutional powers as regards supporting Member States' finance in difficulties, that decades ago were inconceivable.

B. The 2021–27 MFF, REACT and Next Generation: Enlarging the Budget and New Resources

i. Doubling the Own Resources Ceiling

The heavy decrease in EU GDP fostered the adoption of an expansive EU financing plan through the multiannual financial framework for 2021–27. This is probably the largest and most important multiannual budget of the European Communities history, which aimed to guide the recovery from the deepest European recession since World War I, allocating 2.018 trillion to the 2021–27 MFF, amounting to up to 2 per cent of the EU GNI annually.[70]

An important point as regards the MFF 2021–27 is that it doubles the EU own resources' ceiling to 2 per cent of EU GNI.[71] Though most of the increase accounts for temporary expense on loans repayments, the increase in the budget is significant. It represents a complete change from the pre-existing trend and on some metrics exceeds the size of the Marshall Plan.

ii. New Own Resources

On the revenue side, the MFF provides a new national contribution based on non-recycled packaging waste, in addition to traditional own resource. This new contribution is again a transfer based on non-recycled plastic packaging waste, but is not a true European tax. Some countries have introduced a tax on plastic packages to fund it, but there is no direct link, accrual, collection or revenue enjoyment by the Union.

The MFF agreement also proposes the establishment of new resources from the Emissions Trade System, Carbon Border Adjustment and Digital Levy/Pillar 1 by 2023. In addition, financial transaction taxes and financial contributions are sought for 2026.

All such proposals are based on a participation in the share of the revenue collected by Member States on such instruments, making it in the end a transfer. They will

[70] 'The EU's 2021–2027 Long-Term Budget and NextGenerationEU' (Directorate General for Budget (European Commission), 2021) 24.

[71] ibid 24.

also have only a limited impact on the estimated revenue of the EU. The Financial Transaction Tax and the corporate sector contribution, which is less defined, may lead to a small increase in the budget in the long term. Compared to previously mentioned items, these contributions seem permanent as those are seen as limited to Next Generation finance. But again, the budget will still be far from the commonly argued budget of a sovereign state.

However, the more harmonisation that takes place in tax matters, the more EU competences in tax matters will crystallise, which in turn will be consolidated in the hands of EU institutions by the unanimity rule.

C. The EU Reaction to the Russian Attack on Ukraine

Among the political decisions taken to counteract the brutal Russian attack on Ukraine, the EU allocated loans to Ukraine, funds to buy weapons to deliver to Ukraine, delivered humanitarian materials to Ukraine, funded support to the Ukrainian government, and supported Member States' asylum of Ukrainians. Regarding the amounts, the EU has allocated more than €19 billion.[72]

These measures represent an actual change in EU state status, as it is using its funds to behave as a true state in the international arena, not only using a single voice but a single budget and common agreed expenditure. The use of public finance power and a single voice of the EU in the Russian attack on Ukraine could therefore be a major milestone in the advancement of EU state-building.

VI. The EU as a Financial State: Current Proposals and Final Remarks

The birth of the modern state was shaped as a four-sided concept relying on identity, taxes, ownership and liberal democracy. In such development, crisis and war played a major role.

Leaving aside detailed discussion of the nature of a state and new pluralism trends, the state status of the EU has always been challenged as regards its tax and finance powers. However, such assumptions are based on limited finance models and on a single-sided tax power concept.

Before the Great Recession, it is doubtful that the EU was a sovereign entity taking into account competences on the budget and taxation, the size and quality of the budget, revenue collection and finance control.

Regarding the budget, competence can be regarded as the EU's as opposed to the mere aggregation of Member States' wills. Regarding competences in taxation, before the Treaty of Lisbon, the Union only had strong competences on indirect taxes and custom duties. The Union had very few competences as regards direct taxation despite

[72] 'EU Solidarity with Ukraine' (EC, 2022), ec.europa.eu/info/strategy/priorities-2019–2024/stronger-europe-world/eu-solidarity-ukraine/eu-assistance-ukraine_en.

several attempts. As direct taxation is a key element in a tax state as related to individuals, modern taxation and redistribution function, the lack of competence on such matters was a key issue in defining the lack of tax state abilities. However, though subject to unanimity in the Council, the lock-in effect of this, combined with the activism of the Court of Justice, allocated a significant tax power to the Union, especially in anti-avoidance matters, at the very core of a tax system.

Regarding the size of the budget, the small size of the budget of the Union does not approach the level most scholars consider for a sovereign entity of 25–50 per cent of the economy output. However, this view does not take into account the qualitative side of the budget. The EU budget plays a significant role in macroeconomic stability, redistribution and economic conversion, even more in some cases than national budgets, such as in macroeconomic changes.[73] From this point of view, the EU budget plays a significant role in key constitutional matters.

Finally, the heavy and increasing reliance on transfers does not resemble hard state powers. However, confederal states may allocate tax powers to the Member States and from an international point of view that does not question their sovereign status.

The role of crisis in shaping the EU also shows indicia of a political entity. In the first stages of the development of the Union, the main driver was to avoid wars such as those of the nineteenth and twentieth centuries.

It could be also argued the Bretton-Woods collapse and the First Oil Crisis of the 1970s contributed to the 1970s and 1980s developments of the European Union. Though the first years of the 1970s have been seen as an impasse in the development of European institutions, the late 1970s and 1980s saw an enormous development of the Community including new own resources design, the furthering and completion of the VAT directives, new indirect taxes directives, the enlargement of the Union, the introduction of cohesion policies, the Single European Act, and several others.[74] These developments cannot be attributed solely to crisis, but this was one of the key factors as European countries become aware that not being a key player left them in the hands of other larger countries.[75] Moreover, some authors suggest that crises boosted European identity.[76]

In the 1990s, the road to EMU pushed the Union forward even more. The Growth and Stability Pact and the budgetary control was enacted, and fiscal convergence was sped up. It cannot be said that the EMU and the GSP were just driven by crisis, as several previous proposals took place in the 1960s, but it is likely that what previously failed succeeded in the 1990s because of the new global economic scenario.

Before the Great Recession, the EU had several characteristics of a sovereign entity from a financial point of view, though such analysis cannot be done from a monolithical

[73] Benz argues the size hardly reflects the relative powers of EU and national levels: A Benz, 'The EU's Competences: The "Vertical" Perspective on the Multilevel System' (2010) 5 *Living Reviews in European Governance* 1, 17.

[74] H Marhold, 'How to Tell the History of European Integration in the 1970s A Survey of the Literature and Some Proposals' (2009) 3–4 *L'Europe en Formation* 13.

[75] A Gfeller, *Building a European Identity: France, the United States and the Oil Shock, 1973–1974* (New York, Berghahn Books 2012) 1–18.

[76] See ibid 10, 13 and pieces quoted in fn 84.

point of view, as has been done frequently in literature, but from a functional pluralist one.

The Great Recession allowed the EU to take actions and develop competences that Member States would have not allowed at other times.

The new ESM provided the EU institutions, namely the EMU, with a key core competence such as market stability that qualifies as a key sovereign characteristic. Moreover, the procedures for such mechanism were reinforced in the hands of EU institutions and subjected to checks and balances, separating the competence from the direct will of Member States. As macroeconomic stabilisation is less effective at lower levels, this could probably lead to further union.[77]

As regards direct taxation, the period between 2007 and 2020 saw an unprecedented development in the harmonisation of direct taxation. As direct taxation is so intimately related to sovereignty as personal taxation and because of its redistributive role, the increase in the EU powers on the matter reinforced the tax and finance sovereign characteristics of the Union. In addition, tax harmonisation in direct tax matters has taken place in a core area of taxation (anti-avoidance). Again, the crisis and the high pressure on public budgets put the spotlight on revenue, and the EU took advantage of the political momentum to tackle tax avoidance. More importantly, the EU played an enormous role in shaping the BEPS project, consolidating the external action role of the EU in the tax area. The fact that international tax avoidance can only be tackled through international instruments also ensures future developments in EU. Anti-avoidance rules having been harmonised, a core element of domestic tax system is now driven by European institutions, and has entered EU constitutional matters.

Conversely to all such developments, the budget and associated competences did not show advancements in this period. The budget remained limited to 1 per cent of the GNI and the Treaty of Lisbon limited the competences of the EP.[78] However, some authors argue the new set of competences gives slightly more bargaining power to the EP as its agreement is more difficult to achieve.[79]

On the redistribution function, the enormous pressure on the Member States' budgets increased the value of the European Funds. If before 2007 European Funds had a larger value than its numbers show because of its leveraging capacity, its multiplier effect, its redistributive function across the Union and Member States own budget limits, the crisis made European Funds even more important than before.

In sum, the Great Recession strongly developed EU tax and finance competences, and made the Union closer to what we might regard as a state.

From its evolution, the European Communities have been enlarging their tax and finance sovereignty, sometimes slowly, but continuously. Though the amount of the budget has been limited for a long time, or even decreased, the value and impact of the budget has increased in importance and relative value. Moreover, its redistribution value is of utmost importance for European economies. The lack of collection and enforcement powers, in turn, despite reducing its sovereignty status do not necessarily

[77] Groenendijk (n 15) 14.
[78] Bauer, Graham and Becker (n 52).
[79] Benedetto (n 22) 348–49.

eliminate it, because if its persuasive power is enough to make it through its lower levels, it may still be indicative of a power. The doubtful power on collection and enforcement may be compensated by the constant enlargement of tax regulatory powers. Even though subject to the unanimity of the Council, negative harmonisation and the lock-in effect of positive harmonisation has hastened the allocation of tax powers to the communities, especially after the Great Recession.

The evolution of the EU in finance and taxation also shows crisis has an important role in shaping it. Most tax and finance developments have occurred during or after crises. It is likely that the enormous number of resources allocated to economic rebalance after the COVID-19 crisis is a sign of a new move and will trigger further developments. Proposals on new resources to fund such expenditure such as the financial transaction tax, the emission trading system, the corporate contribution or the French and Italian proposal on own resources indicate this. The proposals on Coronabonds may also consolidate new finance powers.

The role of the EU in the Russian attack on Ukraine could also help to consolidate the finance and tax sovereignty of the Union. The enormous amount of resources to help the Ukrainians will trigger new funding needs. Moreover, the fact that such funds are being used on military expenditure, a function related to the concept of state, will contribute to the idea. If the war turns into a severe and deep economic crisis, the need for further integration will likely boost more finance integration as the other option would be a split, which is unlikely to occur without devastating consequences at the current point of harmonisation.

Moreover, the increase in the European budget could trigger further political integration if the economy is stabilised in some years, as the Union could have shown it is able to raise a certain level of resources without compromising other funding or the economy. In that regard, as happened with the birth of the welfare state, the extra funds once crisis has been passed could fund a (limited) Welfare Europe.

However, more integration will face a major challenge, as the lock-in effect of unanimity in most finance and tax matters may lead negotiations to a dead end and a threat to European integration. This, together with the EU's limited legitimacy in finance and tax matters due to the reduced role of the Parliament, could likely raise further debate and development on the role of representation in the Union in tax and finance matters.

8

Revising the Justification for an EU Tax in a Post-crisis Context

KATERINA PANTAZATOU

Abstract

The possibility of the EU budget being financed by 'genuine' EU taxes re-emerged recently, after the COVID-19 pandemic created the need for a coordinated financial intervention by the EU. Literature, so far, has focused on whether this is legally possible and politically desirable and if so, what form these taxes should take. This chapter discusses a largely ignored question, the justification for raising such taxes. In this bid, it tests the two predominant theories, the benefit and the sacrifice theories by reference to both the EU revenue-raising side (the 'own resources system') and the EU spending side (the EU budget) and observes an imbalance between the two sides in terms of democratic legitimacy. The chapter describes how in crisis times 'new types' of financing the EU and the EMU budget emerged that did not necessarily comply with democratic legitimacy and accountability. It is, thus, argued that granting the EU the possibility to raise its own EU taxes would, under conditions, comply with both predominant justification theories and would allow for democratic legitimisation and increased democratic accountability.

I. Introduction

As Member States are unable to deal with the economic consequences of the ongoing pandemic, a discussion on the possibility for the European Union (EU) to introduce its own tax re-emerged recently.[1] The ground was fertile for such a discussion as 2020 was not only the year of the breakout of the COVID-19 pandemic, but also the year that the main decisions on the reform of EU budgetary and fiscal law were to be taken.[2]

[1] See for instance F Vanistendael at al, 'European Solidarity requires EU taxes' (*Op-Ed EU Law Live*, 21 April 2020) eulawlive.com/op-ed-european-solidarity-requires-eu-taxes/.

[2] I am referring to the regular revision of the Multiannual Financial Framework (MFF) and the revision of the Own Resource Decision.

In this context, it became obvious that the EU did not have sufficient 'own resources' to finance the EU budget in order to deal with the economic consequences of the pandemic. The weaknesses of the EU budget and its institutional set up were witnessed, however, already in the financial crisis of 2008, amidst which the EU and especially the Economic and Monetary Union (EMU) looked for ways to finance Member States in a dire economic state.

In light of these developments, the discussion whether the EU should be able to raise taxes and if so, in what form, became topical, in an effort to enhance the EU budget and shelter the Union from future crises. The main questions addressed in this context focused on whether the EU Treaties allow for the introduction of such a tax and, if so, what type of tax should be introduced.[3] A largely ignored question, however, has been the justifications for raising taxes. If the EU were to raise an EU tax, would this tax be justifiable and if so, on what basis? This is not only a moral and ethical question, it is also a question of legitimacy of the tax(es) to be introduced as well as the public spending linked to the revenue arising from these taxes.

This chapter aims to discuss, in light of the connection between a potential EU tax and the EU budget, the possible directions the justification an EU tax could/would take and what these justifications would depend upon. To underline that point, it will depart from briefly examining the different theories of justifications of taxes, notably the benefit and the sacrifice theories, before it explains how the EU budget is financed and spent. It will, then, analyse how the different crises (economic and COVID-19) have changed both spending and financing by and within the EU.

The close relationship between revenue and public expenditure and the different expressions of the principle of 'no taxation without representation' and 'no representation without taxation' will undergo the entire analysis, which will be informed (also) by public economic theory and moral philosophy considerations. This contribution departs from the premise that the institutional framework establishing the EU budget and the way it is financed is deficient and has proved to be unable to deal with the financial and COVID-19 crises. The deficiency does not only relate to the insufficiency of EU funds to cope with the crises but also to the need that emerged therefrom to devise new 'revenue sources' and new 'spending priorities' of questionable legality and legitimacy. While the introduction of an EU tax and/or EU taxes is advocated throughout this contribution, as a means to enhance democratic legitimacy in financing and spending in the EU, the purpose of this chapter is much more modest than providing a comprehensive analysis of why EU taxes should be introduced. It instead aims to understand how the justification(s) for 'EU revenue' or an EU tax would be shaped in relation to the EU budget as it currently stands and at a normative level.

II. A Brief Overview of the Justifications for Taxation

No unequivocal answer exists with regard to the fundamental questions of why one should pay taxes – and the necessary (or not) connection of these taxes to fairness

[3] See G Bizioli and A Martinez (eds), *A tribute to Frans Vanistendael* (Madrid, EU Law Live Press, 2023 forthcoming).

and justice. The reason is that not only different moral, political and economic considerations, methodologies and appraisals affect the answer but also that this fundamental question is often nuanced by a number of other sub-questions (emphasised to a greater or lesser extent) that will, inevitably, contribute to shaping the answer. In addition to the special canons of taxation and of justice that may play a role not only to the formulation of the justifications for taxation but also to the choice of the design of the tax at issue, one, for example, may further consider to *whom* should the taxes be justifiable? As Rawls argues 'if a man knew that he was wealthy, he might find it rational to advance the principle that various taxes for welfare measures be counted unjust; if he knew that he was poor, he would most likely propose the contrary principle'.[4] Such welfare questions, however, become even more complex in a context, or a geographical area, that comprises not only fundamentally different – at least from an economic point of view – states, but also that is governed by complex multi-level governance networks. Who is to decide under these conditions and is the institutional set up able to accommodate the majority's decision and guarantee (some) degree of accountability and legitimacy?

Throughout the years, two theories of justification(s) for taxation have prevailed; the benefit and the sacrifice (or ability to pay) theories that have attempted to answer the question of *why* or *under what conditions* one should pay taxes.[5] In other words, they have endeavoured to provide a rationale for allocating tax burdens in societies. The benefit theory views taxes as a 'price' or consideration to be paid by all taxpayers for the public goods and services provided in a state[6] whereas the sacrifice or ability to pay theory provides that a tax is equitable only if the tax law levies an equal sacrifice on all citizens.[7] Accordingly, each of the two theories – including their many variations across time – embodies its own ideals of tax justice, and is built around different canons of justice and taxation. On this basis, the distinction between the justifications for taxes and tax justice itself becomes blurred, assuming that a tax must be just to be justified.

Musgrave and Peacock present the ability to pay approach as a 'disregard of public expenditures'.[8] Thus, according to the *economic analysis*, the ability to pay principle falls short of providing an answer to the determination of budget policy as it only deals with the tax side of the picture.[9] The disconnection of the ability to pay (or equal sacrifice) principle from public expenditure has been criticised by other scholars who have denounced this principle as myopic for treating the justice of tax burdens as if they could be separated from the justice of the pattern of government expenditure.[10]

[4] J Rawls, *A Theory of Justice – Revised Edition* (Cambridge MA, Harvard University Press, 1999) 17.

[5] J Dodge, 'Theories of Tax Justice: Ruminations on the Benefit, Partnership, and Ability-to-Pay Principles' (2005) 58 *Tax L Rev* 399, 399.

[6] ibid 402, who titles this version as the 'contractarian benefit principle' due to its connection to the necessary cost everybody pays to secure the benefits of entering into the social contract.

[7] JS Mill, *Principles of Political Economy* Abridged with Critical, Bibliographical and Explanatory Notes and a Sketch of the History of Political Economy by J Laurence Laughlin (New York, D Appleton and Company, 1884) 622 et seq.

[8] RA Musgrave and AT Peacock (eds), *Classics in the Theory of Public Finance*, 4th edn (New York, Macmillan, St Martin's Press, 1967) ix.

[9] ibid xi.

[10] L Murphy and T Nagel, *The Myth of Ownership: Taxes and Justice* (Oxford, Oxford University Press, 2002) 25.

In contrast, according to the traditional benefit theory, people are required to contribute to government on account of the benefits obtained from it on the latter's spending side. Thus, the expenditure side is necessary to legitimise taxation and to link it with the core role of the government. Several variations of the benefit theory have been put forward by many scholars, most notably by Buchanan, who distinguished between its 'organic' and its 'individualistic' version.[11] For Buchanan, the latter was ethically superior in that in the quid pro quo transaction between the government and the taxpayers, *all* individuals were *collectively* considered.[12] The new and expanded version of the benefit principle (NBP), in turn, deviates from Buchanan's choice in that it postulates that the measure of a person's benefit from government is none other than their financial well-offness, which is made possible by what the state offers.[13] Importantly, in all variations of the theory, the 'spending side' is central to the justifiability of taxes.

This implies that taxation is closely connected to the different functions (or purposes) of government, and accordingly the different functions taxes may serve; the allocation of resources, redistribution and stabilisation.[14] These basic functions have found different expressions throughout public economics literature and they have been divided into the fiscal function that serves to provide (part of) the revenue for the states' budgets, the regulatory function and the promotion of a regulatory objective, as very often happens with environmental taxes (eg. 'plastic tax'), and the 'social welfare' or distributional function of taxation, serving as an expression of the ability to pay principle.[15] As purported by Wagner, and despite the critics' view of the dissociation of the sacrifice theory from public expenditure, the 'social welfare' function of taxation intended to distribute the tax bill in a way (more or less) proportionate to income, represents (albeit distantly) the ability to pay principle.[16] Accordingly, it is not unconvincing, in the author's view, that the ability to pay principle may also be linked to public finances through the (re)distributional function of taxation which is effectuated, in turn, through public expenditure directed towards social welfare purposes.

Public expenditure or public finance, therefore, affects the justifiability of taxes, regardless of the chosen theory to apply. How would taxes be justifiable to the taxpayer (in the first instance) if the revenue raised therefrom were to be spent and distributed in an arbitrary manner? Hence, the question then moves quickly to questions of distributive justice as well as its sub-constituents, economic justice entailing a *fair* distribution of economic burdens and benefits and tax justice encapsulating the ability to pay principle and guaranteeing a fair distribution of the tax burden among the taxpayers.[17]

[11] J Buchanan, *Fiscal Theory and Political Economy, Selected Essays* (North Carolina, The University of North Carolina Press, 1960) 7 ff.

[12] ibid 8. Buchanan contrasts this more 'modern theory' with the traditional one, whereby, in his view, the quid pro quo relationship was individual and not collective. In this sense, Buchanan's 'individualistic' theory does not depart much from the 'social welfare' theory discussed below.

[13] Dodge (n 5) and references listed therein.

[14] RA Musgrave, *The Theory of Public Finance* (New York, McGraw-Hill, 1959).

[15] A Wagner, 'Three Extracts on Public Finance' in Musgrave and Peacock (n 8).

[16] ibid 8–9.

[17] For a discussion on these concepts see S Dusarduijn and H Gribnau, 'Balancing Conflicting Conceptions of Justice in Taxation' in D de Cogan and P Harris (eds), *Tax Justice and Tax Law: Understanding Unfairness in Tax Systems* (Oxford, Hart Publishing, 2020) 35–56.

Whether seen from the perspective of the state, how much the state ought *in justice* to take from the taxpayer and under what conditions the state ought to take it,[18] or whether approached from the taxpayer's side, under what conditions and towards what purposes should the taxpayer contribute to the state, the distinction between the justification *for taxation* and the justification *for public finances* becomes blurry and epitomises questions of fairness and justice.

The incorporation of fairness and justice and ethical considerations in the justification for taxation was purported by Vogel in his seminal 1988 article.[19] In an effort to (re-)assess the basis or the justification of the tax burden – rather than the actual distribution of the burden – Vogel argued that the early justifications for taxation should be revisited and should be tested against a more contemporary economic and political context whereby, for instance, the tax rates on (personal) income are much higher than those in the late nineteenth century (when those theories were first created). Besides the different context, Vogel argued that the justification question itself is different in that '[w]hereas in the past the question of justification for taxation focused initially on whether taxation is justifiable as such and later on what standards for tax rates follow from this justification, the emphasis today [...] should lie on the limits within which taxation remains justifiable'.[20] Thus, Vogel invites the reader, whether a lawyer, an economist or a policy maker, to look beyond the mere positivistic analysis of fiscal policy, usually grounded on economic theory, but rather to insert moral and ethical considerations in order to create a more tenable tax system *lato sensu*.

In this contribution, I would add the element of democratic legitimacy and I will explain below why I find this additional element of the utmost importance. For the reasons stated above, fiscal federalism which attempts to answer which is the most *efficient* distribution of competences (*in casu*, at the multilevel governance of the EU), will be discussed only to a limited extent as a determinant/factor in the attribution of tax raising powers to the EU.[21]

III. Taxation and Public Finance in the EU

A. The Principles of Legality and Legitimacy in EU Taxes and Public Finances

Traditionally, the maxim 'no taxation without representation' suggests that a tax cannot be levied without the consent of the persons subject to that tax. Related expressions of this principle are the principle that public expenditure is (usually) financed through taxation (the 'no public expenditure without taxation' principle), the principle that the

[18] T Carver, 'The Minimum Sacrifice Theory of Taxation' (1904) 19(1) *Political Science Quarterly*, 66–79, 67.
[19] K Vogel, 'The Justification for Taxation: A Forgotten Question' (1988) 33 *The American Journal of Jurisprudence*. 19–59.
[20] ibid 23.
[21] W Oates, 'An Essay on Fiscal Federalism' (1999) 37 *Journal of Economic Literature* 1120–49; W Oates, 'Towards A Second-Generation Theory of Fiscal Federalism' (2005) 12(4) *International Tax and Public Finance* 349–73.

one who imposes the tax (should) decide(s) how the tax will be spent and that one level of government cannot impose a tax that is specifically intended to be spent by another level of government. All these expressions demonstrate the close relationship between taxation and public expenditure, characterised by Menendez as 'democratically imperative'.[22]

Accordingly, taxes, in order to be legal, have to be democratically consented upon. In modern societies, this happens, traditionally, through democratic representation. While the legality of taxes is fundamental in their justification, the decision about which goods are to be financed through taxation is left out of the political agenda on the grounds that this is a technical and/or scientific question,[23] and, therefore, does not necessarily entail democratic legitimisation. This results in the paradoxical situation that while the first part of the equation (taxation) is democratically controlled, the second part that of public expenditure is not.[24] The situation is reversed in the EU context, as the European Parliament 'is the only parliament in the world that *debates* expenditure but has no competence to determine the revenue that must be collected in order to finance that expenditure'.[25]

Consequently, besides meeting the legality principle,[26] if an EU tax were to be raised, it should be ensured (by the EU institutions in charge) that the levy of this tax is democratically exercised. While at a national level it would be strange if taxation imposed by the representatives of the interested parties should not result in taxation according to interest,[27] the EU situation is peculiar due to the particular nature of the EU institutional and constitutional set up, including the limited involvement of the European Parliament in adopting legislation – even the legislation relating to the own resources system and the way the EU budget will be spent, as well as the limited participation of EU citizens in the European elections.[28] Thus, at present, in the EU set up, public expenditure, which is not financed by EU taxes, is only partly democratically legitimised.

At a national level in non-federal states, taxation and public finance are reserved for the central level. The administration of public finance may also take place at regional or local level. At EU level, while the EU increasingly engages in domestic tax policy making,[29]

[22] AJ Menendez, 'Taxing Europe: Two Cases for a European Power to Tax (with some comparative observations)' (2003–04) 10 *Colum J Eur L* 297, 300.

[23] See AJ Menendez, *Justifying Taxes – Some Elements for a General Theory of Democratic Tax Law* (Berlin, Springer Science+Business Media Dordrecht, 2001) 99.

[24] Although one could argue otherwise if they consider the possibility of outvoting the government in the next elections. This is however, an indirect and distant connotation of democratic legitimacy.

[25] S Goulard and M Nava, 'A More Democratic System for Financing the EU Budget' mimeo (2002) (emphasis added).

[26] The discussion on whether an EU tax would meet this principle is long and inconclusive, especially with regard to issues of competence and legal basis. For a thorough analysis of this see H Kube, 'Competence to Levy EU taxes' in Bizioli and Martinez (n 3).

[27] K Wicksell, 'A New Principle of Just Taxation' in Musgrave and Peacock (n 8) 77.

[28] See for instance, A Moravcsik, 'In Defence of the "Democratic Deficit": Reassessing Legitimacy in the European Union' (2002) 40(4) *JCMS* 603, 604.

[29] I am referring here not only to the secondary EU law, adopted under the special legislative procedure that obviously shapes EU tax law (eg the Anti-Tax Avoidance Directives (ATAD) and the Directives on Administrative Cooperation (DACs)) but also the European Court of Justice's case law as well as the Commission's investigations of tax rulings and their compatibility with state aid law.

it *arguably* still has no power to raise taxes.[30] This is partly concomitant with the EU's limited EU budget, both in terms of net numbers but also in terms of proportionate numbers to national budgets.[31]

B. The EU Budget and its Financing from Own Resources

The EU budget is governed by the principles laid out in Article 310 TFEU and is adopted in accordance with the procedure in Article 314 TFEU. Its spending must comply with the Multiannual Financial Framework (MFF), which is adopted following the procedure in Article 312 TFEU. For the adoption of the five-year MFF, the Council acts unanimously after obtaining the *consent* of the European Parliament. The MFF aims to ensure that Union expenditure develops in an orderly manner and within the limits of its own resources. The MFF Regulation sets annual 'ceilings' for EU expenditure as a whole and for the main categories of policy areas where the EU budget will be spent.

Article 311 TFEU provides that the EU shall 'provide itself with the means necessary to attain its objectives and carry through its policies'. As per Article 311(2) TFEU, '[w]ithout prejudice to other revenue, the budget shall be financed wholly from own resources'. The same provision does not exclude the possibility that new categories of own resources may be established, in accordance with a special legislative procedure, or existing categories may be abolished.[32]

Consequently, the EU budget must be made up from own resources. The own resources required are determined *ex ante*, pursuant to the expenditures specified in the MFF and the respective yearly budgets.[33] In its formal understanding, own resources are all resources that are called own resources in the respective Own Resources Decisions (ORD), while there is no *numerus clausus* of admissible own resources.[34] Is there anything, then, that prevents the EU from establishing an EU tax or tax-based own resources? This depends largely on whether the EU has competence to introduce such new taxes.

Currently, the ORD 2020 is in force for the period from 2021–27.[35] According to this decision, the total amount of own resources may not exceed 1.40 per cent of the sum of all Member States' gross national incomes.[36] The total amount of annual

[30] Besides the discussion on the legal basis and the constitutionality of raising EU taxes, also note the discussion on VAT and customs duties as an 'EU tax'.

[31] According to the Own Resources Decision, the total amount of own resources that finances the EU budget may not exceed 1.40% of the sum of all Member States' gross national incomes.

[32] Article 311(3) TFEU.

[33] M Schratzenstaller, A Krenek, D Nerudová and M Dobranschi, 'EU Taxes as genuine own resource to finance the EU budget – pros, cons and sustainability-oriented criteria to evaluate potential tax candidates', FairTax Working Paper Series no 3 (*diva-portal.org*, June 2016) www.diva-portal.org/smash/get/diva2:934128/FULLTEXT01.pdf.

[34] Kube (n 26).

[35] Council Decision (EU, Euratom) 2020/2053 of 14.12.2020 on the system of own resources of the European Union and repealing Decision 2014/335/EU, Euratom, OJ 2020 L 424/1; for a detailed account of the political process leading to the decision, see A D'Alfonso, 'Own resources of the European Union. Reforming the EU's financing system', Briefing (European Parliamentary Research Service, June 2021) 2, www.europarl.europa.eu/thinktank/en/document/EPRS_BRI(2018)630265.

[36] According to Article 6 of the Decision, this ceiling 'shall each be temporarily increased by 0,6 percentage points for the sole purpose of covering all liabilities of the Union resulting from the borrowing referred to in Article 5 until all such liabilities have ceased to exist, and at the latest by 31 December 2058'.

appropriations for commitments shall not exceed 1.46 per cent of the sum of all Member States' gross national incomes. The democratic financing of the EU budget is, purportedly, guaranteed by the process laid out in the aforementioned provisions, including Article 311 TFEU that requires that Member States approve the decision relating to the Union's own resources, in accordance with their respective constitutional requirements.

In addition to the existing own resources – custom duties from imports outside the EU, the so-called traditional own resources, Gross National Income (GNI)-based and VAT-based own resources[37] – a new own resource was introduced – that of a plastic levy.[38] In 2020, the vast majority of the EU revenue came from the GNI-based own resource, which represented almost 80 per cent of the total revenue.[39]

The slow but steady replacement of the traditional own resources as a means of financing the EU budget by the VAT-based own resources and even more so by the GNI own resource, has raised concerns as to whether the EU budget is indeed financed by own resources and not by national contributions.[40] While technically VAT is an EU tax, the formula according to which the transfer of resources takes place reinforces the perception by EU citizens of a direct national transfer.[41] This is not only because VAT is collected by the Member States, but also because the percentage to be transferred by the states to the EU is calculated by reference to a *hypothetical* VAT base.[42] Similarly, while the GNI per capita could reflect the Member States' ability to pay and could be viewed as an effort to embed fairness and distributive justice criteria within the Union,[43] empirical research for past periods shows that Member States' national contributions per capita only very roughly correspond to their GNI per capita as an indicator of their ability-to-pay.[44] Ranking Member States according to their net contributions in percentage of GNI against their GNI per capita further shows that the distribution of net financial benefits across Member States follows GNI per capita only roughly, similar to national contributions.[45] This has led to the division of contributing Member States into 'net contributors' and 'beneficiaries', that – in light of the overwhelming reliance on GNI for the financing of the EU budget and the increasing need for additional revenue due to the recent crises – has further exacerbated the *juste retour* argument of some Member States.[46] Accordingly, especially the net contributing Member States

[37] The VAT-based own resource is capped at 0.30% of the Member States' VAT base, which in turn is capped at 50% of each Member State's gross national income.

[38] A uniform call rate of EUR 0.80 per kilogram is applied to the weight of plastic packaging waste generated in each Member State that is not recycled.

[39] For a breakdown of the numbers on both the revenue and the spending sides, see ec.europa.eu/info/strategy/eu-budget/long-term-eu-budget/2014-2020/spending-and-revenue_en.

[40] Schratzenstaller et al (n 33) 17.

[41] Menéndez (n 22) 312.

[42] ibid.

[43] ibid 310; F Heinemann, P Mohl and S Osterloh, 'Reform options for the EU own resources system: Abstract and executive summary' Research Project 8/06 (2008) ZEW Gutachten/ Forschungsberichte, Zentrum für Europäische Wirtschaftsforschung (ZEW), Mannheim, according to whom '[t]he GNI resource has favourable characteristics with respect to most principles of taxation'.

[44] Schratzenstaller (n 33) 14.

[45] ibid 15–16.

[46] A Iozzo, S Micossi and MT Salvemini, 'A New Budget for the European Union?' CEPS Policy Brief 159 (2008).

perceive EU expenditure as an EU membership right or at times even as a *juste retour* based on the national budget contribution.[47]

In December 2021, the European Commission proposed three new sources of revenue for the EU budget:

(1) an Emissions Trading System own resource that, in an effort to reduce net greenhouse gas emissions in the EU, would direct 25 per cent of the revenues from emissions trading in the EU to the EU budget;[48]
(2) a Carbon border adjustment mechanism (CBAM) own resource that would transfer 75 per cent of what EU countries collect under CBAM to the EU budget; and
(3) an own resource based on the reallocation of profits of large multinational companies (MNEs) that will materialise under OECD's Pillar 1 framework.

It is suggested that the Commission will propose additional new own resources in 2024, possibly including a financial transaction tax (FTT) and a contribution by the corporate sector, possibly based on a new common consolidated corporate tax base (CCCTB).[49] It is doubtful how these sources of revenue, including the digital levy already proposed by the Commission, distinguish themselves from EU taxes. Own resources, in their original sense, are fiscal resources levied on companies and/or individuals, whose proceeds are attributed directly to the EU even if the collection is done at national level. In contrast, to qualify as an EU tax, the tax must, thus, be established by EU law, levied by the European Union, that would also be responsible to set the rates, and the revenues that arise therefrom must accrue at EU level.[50] Such a tax may be administered by Member States or by EU agencies. Midway between a genuine own resource and a national contribution, the High Level Group on Own Resources places the VAT-based own resources, as well as an FTT-based own resource or a carbon tax. These, as the High Level Group specifies, are often mistaken for 'EU taxes', but they are in fact *a share of national taxes* that Member States decide to transfer to the EU level, once there is a sufficiently harmonised approach concerning such taxes.[51] Thus, the main difference, or alternatively, what these taxes are lacking to qualify as EU taxes, is that these taxes exist or are created at national level and they are not levied by the EU.[52] The main impediment in introducing such an EU tax lies with the competence of the EU to do so and the (in)existence of the appropriate legal basis/es in the Treaties.

A brief overview of the potential legal bases for the adoption of an EU tax suggests that the provisions giving the EU taxing competences (must) serve substantive policy

[47] R Crowe, 'The European Council and the Multiannual Financial Framework' (2016) 18 *Cambridge Yearbook of European Legal Studies* 69–92.

[48] Commission, 'The next generation of own resources for the EU Budget' (Communication) COM (2021) 566 final.

[49] A Schwarz, 'Reform of the EU Own Resources', In Depth Analysis requested by the BUDG Committee of the European Parliament (March 2021) 11, www.europarl.europa.eu/RegData/etudes/IDAN/2021/690963/IPOL_IDA(2021)690963_EN.pdf.

[50] High Level Group on Own Resources, 'Future Financing of the EU, Final report and recommendations of the High Level Group on Own Resources' (December 2016) 24, ec.europa.eu/info/strategy/eu-budget/long-term-eu-budget/2014-2020/revenue/high-level-group-own-resources_en.

[51] ibid.

[52] Although, as already stated, the EU provides for the harmonising basis of these taxes.

aims, such as environmental protection,[53] regulating the energy industry,[54] or protecting the functioning of the internal market.[55] Thus, tax-related directives and regulations based on Articles 192, 194, 113 and 115 TFEU (as well as Article 116 TFEU, of course) may not primarily aim at financing the EU.[56] Only if the provisions based on the aforementioned competences can be justified by substantive policy aims, then the unified tax bases established by these provisions can – according to an own resources decision pursuant to Article 311(3) TFEU – be used as assessment bases for the calculation of own resources.[57]

C. The Pre-pandemic EU Budget

The EU has a long-term budget of €1,082.5 billion for the period 2014–20 and of €1,074.3 billion for the 2021–27 period. The budget amounted to approximately €148 billion for 2019, representing 2 per cent of the combined national budgets of all EU countries (€7,524 billion) in 2019.[58] Despite its relatively small size, the EU budget allows the EU to pursue its policies, notably economic, social and territorial cohesion; sustainable growth (including Common Agricultural Policy (CAP), fisheries and the environment); competitiveness for growth and jobs (including research and education); security and citizenship (including justice, border protection, migration and citizenship) and global Europe (including priorities relating to external action, development and humanitarian aid). Among the many policy objectives of the EU budget, some aim to serve regulatory goals (eg, in relation to the environment), whereas the two main expenditure categories, namely cohesion policy and CAP, serve a redistributive purpose as they aim to foster economic convergence within the EU. Consequently, in lack of an EU fiscal capacity whereby redistribution would depend largely on the revenues arising from taxation, redistribution via the EU budget is currently effectuated through regulation, as the example of the EU Cohesion policy demonstrates. Indicatively, in the 2014–20 period, 39 per cent of the EU budget was allocated to sustainable growth and natural resources (including the Common Agricultural Policy (CAP) and 34 per cent on economic, social and territorial cohesion (EU cohesion policy), the most 'redistributive policy of all'.[59] The allocation did not defer much for the previous periods, for which the funds were earmarked before the breakout of the financial crisis.

The EU cohesion policy has an important place in EU philosophy and is governed by the 'redistributive idea' which stems from the intuitively reasonable assumption that the 'less favoured' regions are in need of 'EU funding' in order to be able to compete in the common market against the more favoured ones.[60] As a redistributive idea, the EU

[53] Article 192 TFEU.
[54] Article 194 TFEU.
[55] Articles 113–115 TFEU.
[56] Kube (n 26).
[57] ibid.
[58] ec.europa.eu/info/strategy/eu-budget/eu-budget-added-value/fact-check_en.
[59] For a specific breakdown of the spending for this period, see www.consilium.europa.eu/en/policies/the-eu-budget/long-term-eu-budget-2014-2020/.
[60] Note, however, the 'neoliberal' objection, according to which the EU cohesion policy's objective is to create an internal market insulated from political and governmental interferences. In this respect, cohesion

cohesion policy is intrinsically linked to the development of the EU budget. Together with the CAP, EU cohesion policy constitutes the second policy area, where the EU has an impact as an independent allocator of resources.[61]

Even prior to the discussion that emerged during the COVID-19 pandemic regarding an increase in the EU budget and the introduction of an EU tax, the EU budget allocations were not unanimously endorsed. Traditionally, national interests in the amounts and the allocations involved are divided, with the 'traditional net payers' or, in other words, the 'richer' Member States opposing more spending and the traditional 'beneficiaries' or the poorer states aiming for even more financing to compete with the richer ones on equal grounds.[62] This opposition to a larger EU budget for redistributive purposes was later exacerbated because of the crisis, expressed as a divide between the 'profligate south' and the 'prudent north'.[63]

D. Public Finances after the Financial Crisis

Since the financial crisis of 2008, a number of economic governance measures were introduced that allowed for different EU institutions, notably the Commission, to monitor and 'have a say' on the spending of national budgets and their policy objectives.[64] Thus, for the first time after the Maastricht criteria were introduced,[65] the EU could now lawfully participate in the spending of the budget, what was until recently the traditional bone of contention of national tax politics.

In addition to this and pursuant to the financial crisis, the European Central Bank (ECB) employed several unconventional monetary policy measures to 'save the Euro'.[66] Besides their contestable legitimacy[67] these measures allowed Eurozone Member States to have access to a wider pool of funds, albeit under strict conditionality. This raised questions as to whether the Euro area Member States are in a 'privileged position' in

policy has more an allocative rather than a distributive function, whereby it aims to stimulate growth and competitiveness in the market by increasing GDP per head rather than redistributing income to poorer regions. See specifically, G Marks, 'Exploring and Explaining Variation in EU Cohesion Policy' in H Liesbet (ed), *Cohesion Policy and European Integration: Building Multi-Level Governance* (Oxford, Clarendon Press, 1996) 388–421, 391.

[61] F Vanistendael, 'The European Union' in G Bizioli and C Sacchetto (eds), *Tax Aspects of Fiscal Federalism – A Comparative Analysis* (Amsterdam, IBFD, 2011) 603.

[62] J Bachtler, C Mendez and F Wishlade (eds), *EU Cohesion Policy and European Integration – The Dynamics of EU Budget and Regional Policy Reform* (Farnham, Ashgate, 2013) 130.

[63] K Pantazatou, 'Promoting solidarity in crisis times: Building on the EU Budget and the EU Funds' (2015) 7 *Perspectives on Federalism* 49–76, 57.

[64] See for instance the 'European Semester', the 'Six Pack' and the 'Two Pack'.

[65] In brief, in order to comply with the 'Maastricht criteria' Member States should not have an excessive deficit defined as more than 3% of GDP, except in severe recessions. The corrective arm of the Stability and Growth Pact (SGP) mainly prescribes how governments should react in case the deficit limit is breached. Such a breach would trigger the Excessive Deficit Procedure (EDP), a step-by-step procedure for correcting excessive deficits that occurs when one or both of the rules that the deficit must not exceed 3% of GDP and public debt must not exceed 60% of GDP are broken, as described in Article 126 TFEU and Regulation 1467/1997.

[66] Speech of the ECB President, Mario Draghi, at the Global Investment Conference in London who claimed that the ECB is prepared to 'do whatever it takes to save the Euro […] and believe me, it will be enough', referring to the Outright Monetary Transactions (OMT) Programme (26 July 2012).

[67] The adoption of these measures created doubts as to whether the adopted measures fell within the ECB's mandate as well as whether they complied with the TFEU provisions, notably the prohibition of monetising debt under Article 123 TFEU and the no bail out clause under Article 125 TFEU.

comparison to the other EU states, for being able to rely on the ECB for funding. Giving a clear answer to this requires further elaboration, notably understanding how close are the conditions under which the ECB purchases government bonds in the secondary financial markets to the 'private investor principle' (see, for instance, the Outright Monetary Transactions Programme (OMT)). The question becomes more complex if one considers that these purchases come under strict conditionalities that may, eventually, result in fiscal entrenchments in the states at issue. Despite these conditionalities, one may argue, however, that Euro area countries have readily available a 'lender of last resort', leading to an additional 'para-budget' for those states, in addition to the 'traditional' EU budget.

Furthermore, the establishment of the ESM, a *permanent* mechanism, designed to provide financial assistance to Euro area states,[68] allowed those states experiencing or being threatened by severe financing problems to receive loans within a macroeconomic adjustment programme (as in the cases of Cyprus, Greece, Ireland and Portugal) and loans for indirect bank recapitalisation (as in the case of Spain). In the first case, the disbursement of funds is subject to strict conditionalities upon the implementation of macroeconomic reform programmes prepared by the European Commission, in liaison with the European Central Bank (ECB) and, where appropriate, the International Monetary Fund (IMF). Eligible ESM members for such loans are members in significant need of financing, and which have lost access to the markets, either because they cannot find lenders or because the financing costs would adversely impact the sustainability of public finances.[69]

In general, the three institutions that issue bonds at EU level, and thus, can provide for funding to the Member States – whether in the form of loans or grants – are the European Commission, the ESM and the European Investment Bank (EIB). The ESM and the EIB are both funded *with capital provided by Member States*. The capital acts *as guarantee* for borrowing money on the capital markets, and the Member States' capital contribution is proportional to voting rights in the relevant decision-making bodies.[70]

E. The COVID-19 Crisis Stimuli and the EU 2020 Recovery Package

Next to the new ORD and the 2021–27 Multiannual Financial Framework (MFF), the EU institutions have set up a large Recovery Package. It provides for extra spending of the Union – partly through temporary and partly through permanent programmes.

[68] Treaty Establishing the European Stability Mechanism (2012).

[69] ESM Treaty, above, Recital 13.

[70] For their credit rating see A Zoppe and S Lenzi, 'Credit Rating for Euro Area Member States and European supranational institutions' (Briefing) European Parliament 2020, www.europarl.europa.eu/RegData/etudes/BRIE/2020/651351/IPOL_BRI(2020)651351_EN.pdf.

On 14 December 2020, the Council finalised and adopted its Decision on the system of own resources of the European Union,[71] replacing its 2014 predecessor.[72] The ORD is based on Article 311(3) TFEU that imposes both the authority and an obligation upon the ECOFIN Council to adopt a decision laying down the provisions relating to the system of own resources of the Union. The ORD requires *consultation* of the European Parliament, the observance of the rules on a special legislative procedure, and unanimity in the Council. Moreover, it requires approval by the Member States in accordance with their respective constitutional requirements. The own resources will continue funding the 'traditional' EU budget.

By way of a temporary stimulus, the Next-Generation EU programme (806 billion Euro) consists of future-oriented spending. Two essential pillars, a Recovery and Resilience Facility (RRF, 672.5 billion Euro) and a Recovery Assistance for Cohesion and the Territories of Europe (REACT-EU, 47.5 billion Euro), are supplemented by five minor pillars; the programmes Horizon Europe (5 billion Euro), InvestEU (5.6 billion Euro), Rural Development (7.5 billion Euro), a Just Transition Funds (JTF, 10 billion Euro) and the new RescEU programme (1.9 billion Euro).

The NextGenerationEU, a temporary instrument, will inject up to EUR 806 billion – 5 per cent of EU GDP – into the EU economy in the form of expenditures and loans. The Commission will, on behalf of the EU, borrow the initial amounts through funding operations on international capital markets in the years 2021–26. The financing raised by the EU will be *repaid by Member States* either directly (for loans) or through the *EU budget (for the grants)* by December 2058 at the latest.[73] To back this borrowing and raise funds under favourable market conditions, the EU will use the EU budget and its headroom, that is, the difference between the Own Resources ceiling of the long-term budget and the actual spending.[74] Indicatively, for the funding of the RRF, the EU will borrow from capital markets to finance up to €672.50 billion in expenditures in all EU Member States, approximately half (€312.5 billion) of which will be *grants* – and thus not be recuperated from Member State recipients.

Thus, so far the EU budget funded through own resources is used to cover 'traditional' expenses, such as the funding of the EU cohesion policy,[75] but also since 2021 to fund the grants to be issued in the context of the Next Generation EU.[76]

[71] Council Decision 2020/2053/EU, Euratom of 14 December 2020 on the system of own resources of the European Union and repealing Decision 2014/335/EU, Euratom, OJ L 424/1 of 15 December 2020 (hereinafter ORD).

[72] Council Decision 2014/335/EU, Euratom of 26 May 2014 on the system of own resources of the European Union, OJ L 168/105 of 7 June 2014.

[73] Communication from the Commission to the European Parliament and Council on a new funding strategy to finance NextGenerationEU COM(2021) 250 final, 14.4. 2021.

[74] To ensure sufficient headroom, the EU is increasing the Own Resources Ceiling of its budget by 0.6 percentage points of the EU's Gross National Income (GNI). The permanent Own Resources ceiling of the budget is currently being increased to 1.4% of EU's gross national income. The additional ceiling of 0.6 percentage points will come on top and it is limited in time, until 2058, so as to be used in the context of the recovery from the COVID-19 pandemic. See ec.europa.eu/info/strategy/eu-budget/eu-borrower-investor-relations/nextgenerationeu_en#guaranteeing-of-the-borrowing.

[75] For a breakdown of the 'spending' and the own resources for 2020, see ec.europa.eu/info/strategy/eu-budget/long-term-eu-budget/2014-2020/spending-and-revenue_en.

[76] For the MFF 2021–2027 breakdown in 2018 prices, see ec.europa.eu/info/sites/default/files/about_the_european_commission/eu_budget/mff_2021-2027_breakdown_2018_prices.pdf.

20 Member States had received (non-repayable) grants (out of the EU budget) and loans under the RRF on 31 December 2021. Although the grants are not repayable, the loans are to be repaid by national budgets, creating, thus, an asymmetry between the EU budget (the guarantor), the payers (the national budgets) and the liabilities in case of default (the other states). Accordingly, and on a temporary basis, revenue is spent following the EU budget process, yet the revenue (to be) spent is not provided through the own resources procedure.

The increase in EU spending necessary to cover the reimbursement of the loans for subsidising the Next Generation EU programme means that *additional new own resources* should be mobilised for the EU budget. This becomes all the more imperative since, after Brexit, the contribution based on UK GNI disappeared. The ORD adopted on 1 June 2021 provides that additional own resources should not be based on existing VAT and GNI contributions from Member States, but on new levies *and taxes*.[77] In this vein, the European Council invited the Commission to put forward a revised proposal on the EU Emissions Trading System, possibly extending it to the aviation and maritime sectors. It concluded that the Union will, in the course of the multiannual financial framework for the period 2021–27 ('MFF 2021–27'), work towards the introduction of other own resources, which may include an FTT.[78]

Next to these programmes, the temporary SURE programme (Support to mitigate Unemployment Risks in an Emergency) is available for Member States that need to mobilise significant financial means to fight the negative economic and social consequences of the COVID-19 outbreak on their territory. It can provide financial assistance of up to €100 billion in the form of *loans* from the EU to affected Member States to address sudden increases in public expenditure for the preservation of employment. These loans are governed by a system of *voluntary guarantees* from Member States. Each Member State's contribution to the overall amount of the guarantee corresponds to its relative share in the total gross national income (GNI) of the European Union, based on the 2020 EU budget.

IV. The Many 'Sources of Funding' and the Relevance of Taxes

A. EU Sources of Funding

Looking at the spending side from a chronological perspective, one can note that the *pre-crises EU spending* focused on (re)distributional policies and objectives, notably CAP and EU cohesion policy. These first years were governed by (very) poor democratic safeguards attached to the own resources system on the revenue side, and the adoption of the MFF on the spending side.[79] Within these two re-distributional policies, the

[77] See below for the Commission's proposals on the new generation of own resources.

[78] ORD (n 71) recital 8.

[79] Note that according to Article 312(2) TFEU, the Council has to obtain the consent of the European Parliament (expressed via a simple majority of its component members) in the adoption of the MFF; however, pursuant to Article 311 the Council has to only consult the European Parliament before adopting the own resources decision.

juste retour argument has been traditionally invoked, especially among the 'net donor' states, negating, effectively, the benefit principle and any input legitimacy due to the particular institutional set up of the Union.

The financial crisis of 2008 resulted in the creation of 'para-budgets', of questionable legality and legitimacy, that were available to the Euroarea states. These additional para-budgets *lato sensu*, have resulted in asymmetrical spending from a budgetary perspective in that the financial assistance granted to Euroarea states by the ESM is to be reimbursed by funds from the national budgets of the Member States. Similarly, the loans granted by the ESM are guaranteed by contributions from the national budgets of the Member States and any eventual losses are at the charge of national budgets. Access to these funds, as well as the funds arising from the ECB's unconventional monetary policy measures,[80] comes with strict conditionalities, usually in the form of macro-economic adjustment programmes. In case of failure to repay the loans, it is the (other) Euroarea states that would bear the budgetary risk, becoming, thus, liable for the non-repayment. In this sense, despite the prohibitions in EU primary law, they would assume the debt of another state. Thus, while strictly speaking the available funds under these schemes appear to serve redistributive purposes, the strict conditionality their release is attached to, partly refutes this purpose.[81]

The subsequent COVID-19 crisis further revealed the need for a bigger EU budget and additional financing to deal with the long-term repercussions, such as unemployment and bankruptcies. In light of this dire need, the EU budget and its high credit ranking is used as a 'guarantor' *lato sensu* to back up further borrowing of the EU, and the European Commission, specifically. In this case, thus, the contributions of the Member States 'feed' the redistributive effects of the EU budget in times of emergency. This additional revenue – in the form *of debt for the Union* – will allow to enlarge and modernise the policy areas funded by EU spending. Thus, the focus is shifted to green and digital economy as well as unemployment and policy areas with regulatory significance that complement the re-distributional purposes of the EU budget.

Both crises revealed that the EU budget and the current institutional setting have proved to be insufficient to deal with the increasing need to resort to EU financing. In view of the difficulty in amending the Treaties, the EU showed that it can bend the rules, in cases of emergency. The imminent need for funding to cope with the pandemic or to save the common currency resulted in the introduction of temporary or 'emergency' measures towards the weakest economies/Member States, which, however, did not satisfy (input) democratic legitimacy. In the case of the *financial crisis* specifically, it is doubtful whether those measures could be characterised as being of a redistributional nature, not only because of the strict conditionalities attached to the release of funds but also due to the alleged reason(s) behind the establishment of these emergency mechanisms, that is the potential domino effect the default of a Member

[80] K Pantazatou and I Asimakopoulos, 'Conventional and Unconventional Monetary Policy' in F Fabbrini and M Ventoruzzo (eds), *Research Handbook on European Economic Law* (Cheltenham, Edward Elgar, 2019).

[81] The CJEU, in its seminal *Pringle* (Case C-370/12 *Pringle v Ireland* [2013] 2 CMLR 2) and *Gauweiler* (Case C-62/14 *Gauweiler and Others* [2016] 1 CMLR 1) judgments, found these conditionalities to be the main backstop to the alleged moral hazard the access to these funds would entail. However, the conditionalities attached to the bailout programmes often impinge upon the social policies of the Member States and they often require the introduction of measures detrimental to the welfare state.

State could cause to the Eurozone, and, consequently, the absence of solidary or altruistic motives.[82]

Furthermore, while according to the TFEU and the High Level Group on Own Resources the EU budget cannot be financed by debt, under emergency conditions debt can finance other (generated) EU revenue, what we called 'para-budgets', that does not necessarily have to fall within the EU budget scope. Consequently, the institutional setting that, allegedly, prevents the adoption of EU taxes, has been tested in crisis times and can change. This, in turn, has resulted in multiple sources of 'EU revenue' that are financed via different means (own resources, debt), spent in different policies but following *the EU budget-process*, which appears to remain the only constant in the changing nature of EU funding and spending.

B. EU Spending and Democratic Legitimacy

Both crises have revived the discussion regarding the introduction of an EU tax. Based on similar grounds as the scholastic philosophers' view that taxation was permissible (only) as an emergency measure and in cases of extraordinary need,[83] the emergency plans proposed amidst the (financial) crisis revolved around the transfer of budgetary powers from the Member States to the EU, and the possible establishment of taxing powers at the EU level.[84] The proposed emergency and temporary transfer, in the context of the financial crisis, would encompass: (i) a transfer of decision-making powers from the state in distress to an authority at the EU level which would be responsible for taking and enforcing the necessary fiscal and budgetary decisions. Such a shift of sovereignty could be perceived as a more effective 'sanction' for the indiscipline and incompliance of this particular state with the legal framework, and (ii) an unconditional obligation of solidarity of all the other Eurozone states.[85] These points would entail an amendment of the national constitutions regarding the transfer of the budgetary sovereignty, but also the abolition of the 'no bail out clause' for the states in distress that have surrendered this power. Such an 'activation of a democratic economic and fiscal federation by exception'[86] would suffer from several limitations, especially in terms of democratic legitimacy and political accountability.[87]

[82] C Fried, 'Distributive Justice' (1982) 1 *Social Philosophy & Policy* 42, who considers redistribution to be permissible only when it is based on 'sympathy' and Pantazatou (n 63) criticising the lack of an EU solidary reaction to the crisis.

[83] See Vogel (n 19) 24–25 and references listed therein.

[84] Commission, 'A blueprint for a deep and genuine economic and monetary union Launching a European Debate', (Communication) COM(2012) 777 final/2 (30 November 2012) and Van Rompuy et al, 'Towards a Genuine Economic and Monetary Union', Report EUCO 120/12 (2012), both advocating a fiscal Union or at least the introduction of a 'fiscal capacity' of the EMU.

[85] Vanistendael (n 61).

[86] JC.Trichet, 'Reflexions on Unconventional Monetary Policy Measures and on European Economic Governance: Towards an Economic and Fiscal Union by Exception', Mandeville Lecture 2012 – Erasmus University, Rotterdam (6 June 2012): '[…] in order to comply with the subsidiarity principle, the interventions and the measures taken by the federal institutions would so rely on the principle "as little as possible in normal times, but as much as necessary in exceptional times"'.

[87] To counter the democratic and political accountability of the central authority, Vanistendael (n 61) suggests the creation of a new mechanism either under the enhanced cooperation procedure or the establishment of a new Treaty between the Eurozone States that would postulate the transfer of precisely defined and

The 'EU taxation by exception', because of its temporary and exceptional character, lends itself to resolving the main objections that have arisen throughout the years with regard to EU-revenue raising and spending. Notably, as the EU was expanding, and in light of the perception of direct contributions by Member States to the EU budget, EU citizens have felt alienated from EU spending, despite their feeling that they have been contributing to it. The financial crisis that affected 'only' some Member States exacerbated the *juste retour* argument and also contributed to discrediting the benefit principle. The same applied with the post-pandemic raise of capital and the expressed dissatisfaction of some Member States in the context of the EU Recovery Package.[88] Both the 'quid pro quo' and redistribution were perceived to apply to/benefit some Member States only, spurring a general feeling of dissatisfaction to those that contributed the most, whether through own resources, or as guarantors of loans that could default.

It is inevitable that in light of the very diverse economies across the Union, the EU budget will always be governed to a larger or lesser extent by redistributive purposes. The promotion of such 'welfare' priorities and commitments would fit best with a justification for an EU tax based on the ability to pay. Yet, both the benefit principle and the ability to pay principle in the EU (budgetary) context will (continue to) be disproved as long as the 'social benefit', however it is defined,[89] or the *juste retour*, attached to the benefit principle, are not considered to apply on an EU-wide basis. The lack of European demos, and – more pragmatically – the lack of the sense of contributing (substantially) to the EU budget and receiving from it accordingly also contributes to the discreditation of the benefit principle at EU level.

The same applies in case of redistribution – and if we accept its connection to the ability to pay principle, also to the latter. This is because the trade-offs required for the redistributive state to perform entail, in most cases, the choice among different levels and quality of supply of public (or quasi-public) goods, different taxation systems and rates and different state intervention levels. These decisions usually take place at the national level and they are shaped in accordance with each state's traditions, culture and preferences, represented at a higher level by the elected governments. This way these choices enjoy democratic legitimacy. Naturally, these national preferences and benchmarks are then transposed to the EU level, creating different expectations and different dispositions towards the associated 'trade-offs' among people who are united by a certain degree of economic integration, but not by any sense of demos or identity.[90] This became all the more obvious in the case of 'net donor states' (whether within or outside the crisis context) which, representing the interests of their constituencies, were often against the spending of the 'EU revenue' on purposes foreign to their own interests.

enumerated taxing and spending decisions in times of crisis to the designated centralised institution, and a reorganisation of the European Parliament to enable it to exercise effective and democratic political control over this institution. See also F Vanistendael, 'The Crisis: A Window of Necessity for EU Taxation' [2010] *European Taxation* 397.

88 '"Frugal four" chief Mark Rutte leads opposition to EU recovery plan' *Financial Times* (18 June 2020) www.ft.com/content/8e30fd89-4958-491e-9f30-8c0b5f8b4cef.

89 Buchanan (n 11) 9.

90 Pantazatou (n 66) 53.

These arguments are further supported by economic theory as well as from a political perspective, as both fiscal federalism and the subsidiarity principle adhere to a (rebuttable) decentralisation presumption, yet they both leave plenty of room for centralised intervention. It is doubtful, however, whether the subsidiarity principle can be used as a sufficient anti-centralisation argument. This is not only because of its vague and political nature,[91] but also because of the obvious inability of several Member States to cope with the financial and/or COVID-19 crisis effects from a budgetary perspective.[92]

V. Conclusion: A Case for an EU Tax?

This chapter departed from the introduction of different possibilities for EU-revenue raising in the face of different crises. These different possibilities of financing were followed by a 'non-traditional' funds' allocation. In light of these changes, a discussion on the introduction of an EU tax emerged which, in turn, prompted the important question when designing completely new tax regimes of the choice of justification of the taxation system.[93] In search of this justification, this contribution argued that the spending side cannot be considered independently from the revenue side, and vice versa, both in terms of *justification* and *legitimisation*. A state's claim for taxes is *legitimised and justified* because taxation returns to the state a portion of the economic value that the state, for its own part, has assisted in producing (benefit principle) or because it is used for welfare or redistributive purposes, purposes traditionally attached to 'fairness' and the ability to pay principle.

Putting aside the existing institutional and constitutional obstacles and without considering any fiscal federalism arguments, granting the EU fiscal capacity would contribute to the much-needed increase of the EU budget. For the purposes of this contribution, however, importantly, the introduction of an EU tax would complete the equation between revenue and public finances, raising money and public spending by providing for an accountability and democratic control tool of public institutions and public decision making. In other words, it would complete the 'no taxation without representation principle' by satisfying, its adjacent principle 'no public expenditure without taxation', thus legitimising EU spending.

As it has been shown, the current system of own resources, the revenue side, and the spending side, the EU budget, are lacking democratic legitimacy and accountability. This is not only because of the missing direct and visible fiscal link between EU citizens

[91] G de Burca, 'The Principle of Subsidiarity and the Court of Justice as an Institutional Actor' (1998) 36 *JCMS* 218.

[92] If one applies the 'subsidiarity calculus' and the test of comparative efficiency in the context of the two crises, they would probably conclude that the action at issue – whether it relates to saving the common currency, or the different regulatory purposes advanced in the context of COVID-19 – would be better/only achieved by the EU. See also Trichet (n 86).

[93] T Eskelinen and A Laitinen, 'Taxation: Its justification and application to global contexts' in H Gaisbauer, G Schweiger and C Sedmak (eds), *Philosophical Explorations of Justice and Taxation* (Heidelberg, Springer, 2015) 219, 220.

and EU institutions that undermines democratic accountability,[94] but also because under the current system of own resources the taxpayers' 'translated' individual contributions cannot be assessed either vis-à-vis the benefit principle or vis-à-vis the 'social welfare' aspect of the ability to pay principle. Even in the case of the GNI-based own resources system, which, supposedly, divides the total (contributions') burden in a *just* manner across all contributors, it has been shown that the individual taxpayers' ability to contribute is not accurately represented.

It follows that the transfer of tax raising powers to the EU, provided it is democratically exercised, would also 'democratise' the EU's spending powers. Thus, a 'pure EU tax' would repeal both the perception of own resources as domestic, yet not individual, contributions and would enhance the connection between raising revenue and spending it, fulfilling the principle 'no public expenditure without taxation'. This argument is further reinforced by tax fairness concerns. As Menendez argues, in the US the reason for a dramatic increase in the federal power to tax[95] was the political mobilisation to ensure greater fairness in the distribution of the tax burden and greater economic justice in general.[96]

Besides the advantage of enhancing democratic legitimacy and accountability, such an EU tax would also be justifiable and legitimised on grounds of either the benefit or the ability to pay principle. Yet and despite its contribution to the building of an EU demos, one cannot overlook the fact that the introduction of EU taxes could backfire. The spending priorities or even EU financing and spending altogether have not been unanimously endorsed across Member States and their citizens, within or outside the crisis context(s). These tensions, governed primarily by the *juste retour* argument, have been documented throughout this contribution. Does this imply that a total overhaul is needed to prepare the ground for an EU tax? That, despite the many benefits EU taxes bring about, they should be introduced only if the EU becomes more economically homogeneous and politically and democratically mature?

I believe that this is a matter for the meta-EU tax question(s), notably the specific design of the EU tax and the yardstick(s) or canon(s) this tax would be designed upon, that would have to be carefully selected from a list of many possibilities.[97] This is because the EU budget (and the own resources system) already exists and has contributed in several ways to the development of the EU and its Member States. The recent crises have, however, revealed that the current institutional setting cannot cope with the emerging challenges. This leaves three possible options: (i) to eliminate the EU budget altogether, (ii) to re-design it to make it more functional, less prone to institutional manipulation and arbitrariness and democratically legitimised, or (iii) to establish

[94] Schratzenstaller (n 33); High Level Group on Own Resources (n 50) 16; J Le Cacheux, 'Funding the EU Budget with a Genuine Own Resource: The Case for a European Tax' (Paris, Notre Europe, 2007) 5 and 24; G Cipriani, *Financing the EU Budget. Moving Forward or Backwards*? (London, Rowman & Littlefield, 2014).

[95] Note that until the early twentieth century the three main sources of US federal revenue were customs duties, excises on alcohol and tobacco and proceedings from the sale of land.

[96] Menéndez (n 22) 331.

[97] Among the most prominent ones, one can find *fairness, equity, reciprocity, redistribution, solidarity,* neutrality, certainty, convenience, administration and simplicity, efficient allocation of resources and many more.

some sort of an 'emergency framework', an 'EU budget' by exception. While the answer to this question will, inevitably, be informed by one's predisposition towards the EU project, in the author's view, the current framework should be amended by establishing a clear framework of connected EU revenue raising and spending that allows for a wider participation of EU citizens. As the EU spending is currently earmarked, both the benefit and the ability to pay principle would be able to justify EU taxes in that EU and EMU revenue (EU budget and the different 'para budgets') contribute to the (financial) 'well-offness' of the taxpayers individually or collectively[98] and they pursue redistributive policies, notably the EU cohesion policy and CAP.

[98] Several examples can be listed here, from (product-), (health-), (environment-) regulation to the correction of market failures.

9

Fiscal Evolution and the Syndemic

CARLO GARBARINO

Abstract

Since its inception the COVID-19 crisis revealed that EU countries' immediate responses did not follow a clear path. There is however growing evidence that tax measures naturally converged and this chapter hypothesises that this was a downstream effect of a common political framework of 'COVID-19 exceptionalism' based on biopolitics, a convergence that defies the initial expectations of fragmented reactions to the emergency but which also poses critical challenges. Section I sets the stage of the evolutionary analysis and indicates that the COVID-19 crisis led to a convergence of tax policies. Sections II and III briefly describe the concept of 'biopolitics' and 'state of exception' as they emerged in seminal contributions mainly by Foucault and Agamben and show how these concepts can be understood in a novel fashion to explain convergence of tax policies in the context of the COVID-19 emergency. Section IV concludes showing that COVID-19 biopower, biopolitics and exceptionalism also constituted the institutional cause for the sudden adoption of the Next Generation EU, a measure that directly implies investments but which has the essential mark of being a fiscal turning point.

I. Setting the Stage of the Evolutionary Analysis

The regulatory landscape of how states responded to the contagion of COVID-19 varies from health measures in the strict sense to differentiated socio-economic measures. In this chapter I will refer to tax measures implemented as responses to the COVID-19 crisis as a *proxy*, that is, I will use evaluation of one variable – the tax measures – as an indicator for the evaluation of another variable – the broader regulatory responses aggregated at EU level. My goal is to advance possible explanations about the institutional evolution of the EU fiscal architecture that emerged as a result of the recent COVID-19 crisis.

The mode of the chapter is initially descriptive as I will provide a summarised account of the tax policy dynamics that unfolded during the COVID-19 crisis in this section I, but there will be several normative implications when, in sections II–IV, I will discuss the implications of biopower, biopolitics and the state of exception on EU fiscal policy.

In doing that I will weave together four different themes that at first glance do not appear to be correlated. These four different themes are the following. First, a process of convergence of tax measures during the COVID-19 crisis (section I) that is somehow unexpected in light of the fact that the EU countries' immediate responses seemed to be corona-nationalistic, hence the term 'Coronationalism' was proposed.[1] Second, the hypothesis that biopower and biopolitics – two structural phenomena that will be described in detail – are the overarching causes of tax convergence (section II). Third, the assessment of a pervasive state of exception that animated COVID-19 tax nationalisms (section III). Finally, the sudden emergence at EU level of a major holistic strategic move – the *Next Generation EU* – which appears to be causally related to biopower and biopolitics (section IV).

Weaving together these – apparently separated – four themes obviously requires some signposting. In this direction one should consider that this chapter presents an attempt to explain the convergence of tax policy responses to COVID-19 as an effect of 'biopower' and 'biopolitics'. These ideas are taken from the work of Michel Foucault and describe a shift towards understanding the population of a state at an aggregate level in terms of statistics and trends, identifying and addressing problems at the same aggregate level and in the process changing the way in which individuals within a state are conceived.

This approach to governance long predates the present day, but COVID-19 has provided exceptionally strong incentives on states to apply techniques consistent with biopower. This in turn helps to explain the convergence of tax policy responses to COVID-19 as well as aspects of recent EU integration. The chapter begins with a concise review of tax responses to COVID-19 principally in the EU, before moving on to explain the relevance and usefulness of a Foucauldian framework. I will discuss the role of state sovereignty, considering whether to follow Foucault in setting it in opposition to biopolitics, to treat the COVID-19 response as a Schmittian state of exception or to follow Agamben in treating biopolitics and sovereignty as symbiotic.

Whilst I will highlight concerns regarding the authoritarian possibilities of biopolitics, another route of criticism will be pursued by reference to the work of Merrill Singer, along the lines that COVID-19 regulations have not adequately accounted for existing inequalities. The chapter concludes by asserting that COVID-19 biopower has prompted a critical juncture in EU fiscal juncture with the enactment of the Next Generation EU project.

The tone of my analysis may sound somehow pessimistic, as the responses of governments to COVID-19 are treated not as obstacles to greater European unification as in chapter ten of this book,[2] but rather as examples of a wider approach to governance that could well outlast the acute phase of the COVID-19 crisis. The recourse to certain philosophical categories mainly used by Giorgio Agamben may appear to be possibly

[1] See G Bouckaert, et al, 'European Coronationalism? A Hotspot Governing a Pandemic Crisis' (2020) *Public Administration Review* 765–73.

[2] See Grisostolo and Scarcella (ch 10).

not relevant in a financial piece, but the contribution of this author is very helpful in understanding the structural sense of the changes that are under way. I am aware that the sense of foreboding derived from Agamben contrasts strongly not only with more optimistic contributions to this book but even with other chapters with a critical flavour such as Pantazatou's search for justifications for EU taxation in chapter eight.[3]

This pessimism towards the measures described in terms of 'biopower' and 'biopolitics' is not shared by the majority of commentators in so far as many COVID-19 responses, at least initially, appeared to be sensible health measures which were made significantly more effective by being targeted at the population at an aggregate rather than individual level.

A very good argument that is generally advanced regarding the benevolent purpose of COVID-19 measures is that, all else being equal, a citizen would in theory prefer to be treated as an individual rather than as an integral part of the mass of the population drastically subject to biopower, but this citizen has to be alive in order for this treatment as an individual in a liberal democracy to matter. So the point which is generally highlighted is that if biopower helps to keep this individual citizen alive, then that biopower seems to be a positive and unavoidable first step. Foucault's answer to this would be that critical analysis aims at showing the structure of power rather than justifying the possible rationale of the emergency measures that are the outcome of the exercise of such power: section II will discuss this in detail.

The key point of the discussion that follows is not whether recourse by governments to biopower during a public health crisis was feasible or acceptable, but whether governments will retain biopower techniques after the crisis to deal with other policy objectives in a new context of ecopolitics and ecopower that will emerge as responses to structural ecosystemic crises such as climate change. As highlighted in the Introduction to this volume, crises can be used as the pretext to pursue political and constitutional objectives which can be only understood when viewed in the long-term evolution.[4]

Indeed, for COVID-19 to be truly 'exceptional', it would have to have fundamental consequences for taxation and public finance that are comparable to previous crises such as the World Wars, Great Depression and Napoleonic Wars. Time is not yet ripe to make such quantitative assessment but a fair assessment of the COVID-19 crisis needs to consider that the COVID-19 situation is not only a contagious epidemic that affects the entire planet in a specific period, rather it is a so called 'syndemic', a structural feature of society that indeed has fundamental consequences for taxation and public finance in terms of a significant change of the underlying political process, rather than only in a change that is readily measured and captured by economic indicators.

The notion of a syndemic was first conceived by Merrill Singer, a medical anthropologist, who evidenced that a syndemic is not merely a comorbidity because it is characterised by biological and social interactions between pre-existing health conditions and interactions that increase persons' susceptibility to worsen their health.[5]

[3] See Pantazatou (ch 8).
[4] Introduction (ch 1).
[5] M Singer, *Introduction to syndemics: A critical systems approach to public and community health* (Hoboken, John Wiley & Sons, 2009).

Within the COVID-19 crisis two categories of disease are interacting: a communicable infection with severe acute respiratory syndrome which can be lethal (SARS-CoV-2) and an array of non-communicable diseases. These conditions are clustering within social groups according to patterns of inequality deeply embedded in our societies that are not necessarily captured by the epidemic models developed by infectious disease specialists, who have framed the present health situation in terms of a contagious disease and by economists who attempt to measure the impact of COVID-19 on national accounts.

The aggregation of these diseases on a background of social and economic disparity exacerbates the adverse effects of each separate disease and is a structural feature of society. If the COVID-19 situation is part of a syndemic – ie a structural condition – then the 'exceptional' dimension of the COVID-19 crisis morphs into a structural feature which is bound to persist in the future.

Singer argued that a syndemic approach reveals biological and social interactions that are important for prognosis, treatment, and health policy: 'A syndemic approach provides a very different orientation to clinical medicine and public health by showing how an integrated approach to understanding and treating diseases can be far more successful than simply controlling epidemic disease or treating individual patients.'[6]

Limiting the harm caused by COVID-19 will demand far greater attention paid to non-communicable diseases and socioeconomic inequality than has hitherto been admitted. In the case of COVID-19, addressing non-communicable diseases such as hypertension, obesity, diabetes, cardiovascular, chronic respiratory diseases and cancer will be a prerequisite for successful containment.

The most important consequence of seeing COVID-19 as a syndemic is to underline its *social origins*. This points to the fact that certain classes of citizens are more vulnerable depending on a complex and variable societal matrix (senior; Black, Asian, and minority ethnic communities; key workers, and so on). So the pursuit of a purely biomedical solution to COVID-19 based on vaccines will fail if proper welfare protections are not implemented.

Unless governments devise policies and programmes to reverse profound disparities, our societies will never be truly COVID-19 secure. As observed in the Introduction to this volume, crises often have direct fiscal effect as they depress tax revenues whilst increasing the need for public funds, thus increasing fiscal deficits, but significantly, in indirect terms, crises can have uneven consequences for different demographics and sectors of the economy, disadvantaging some, leaving some relatively untouched and advantaging others. Moreover, crises can also exacerbate existing social problems, making the need for solutions to those problems even more pressing.

If the COVID-19 crisis requires structural social interventions, the premise of the current narrative that the state has the responsibility to ensure in the short term the healthcare of its citizens with stringent biomedical measures can be misleading. Rather the state has the responsibility to address the syndemic problem systemically. If that is the case, it is not true that the state is entitled to the enforcement of a superior mechanism of control and surveillance.

[6] M Singer, N Bulled, B Ostrach and E Mendenhall, 'Syndemics and the biosocial conception of health' (2017) 389(10072) *The Lancet* 941–50.

As we will see at section III, Agamben advances the claim that the 'bare life' of citizens has become a government concern to the detriment of everything else. The extent to which the state has a right to override other basic liberties is clearly crucial in bringing Agamben to the fore and potentially invites a discussion over for example mandatory vaccines (in a number of settings) as well as the ethically difficult decision in respect of children's vaccination and many other critical situations we encountered in the COVID-19 crisis generated by biopower and biopolitics.

A discussion about who ought to be determining risk management and what the parameters are in this respect would be fundamental. Yet the main objective of this chapter is not a fully-fledged discussion of civil liberties and the destiny of liberal democracies – which would obviously be worth a separate chapter – but more humbly to attempt to explain the connection between the dynamics of the COVID-19 crisis and an unexpected fiscal convergence.

So in light of these preliminary clarifications, the aim of this chapter is to contribute to categorising the various ways in which states have provided financial help to individuals and businesses, and in situating taxation within this wider public finance context: the focus of this volume may be taxation, but it is helpful to have this sense of where tax 'fits'. Tax policy has in fact played and continues to play a central role both in circumscribing the economic impact of the COVID-19 crisis and in alleviating the negative consequences of the lockdowns and other restrictions.

The data about tax measures adopted by states within the EU is overwhelmingly complex and extremely detailed. In light of this fact this chapter eschews an attempt to provide a comparative taxonomy of tax measures but adopts the hypothesis of 'spontaneous convergence' according to which measures converge even if there is no actual or deliberate transfer of policies by governments.

This hypothesis has the advantage of showing that national tax responses, irrespectively from the sheer variability of details and idiosyncratic constraints, were a mix of containment, mitigation and recovery that required tax policy to focus on liquidity, solvency and income support. Temporarily national tax systems morphed from revenue raisers to revenue mitigators. Tax policies were mainly characterised by containment measures which reflected three goals:[7] (i) increasing cash flow, (ii) reducing the tax burden and influencing behaviour, and (iii) providing legal certainty.[8]

When contrasted with the haphazard way in which individual Member States addressed the COVID-19 challenge, the EU approach has been more proactive. This role of the EU is evoked in the Introduction to this volume, in so far as it highlights that the EU has been able to provide coordinated fiscal support to Member States in a way that is far from perfect, but far exceeds what would have been possible if those states

[7] Other criteria may also be used to classify the short-term tax responses to the crisis. See, eg, the fivefold classification used by the OECD: OECD Centre for Tax Policy and Administration, *Tax and Fiscal Policy in Response to the Coronavirus Crisis: Strengthening Confidence and Resilience* (Paris, OECD Publishing, 2020) 12. See also the IMF report that distinguishes between 'spending-side measures', 'revenue-side measures' and 'government-supported liquidity measures': IMF, *Fiscal Monitor: Policies to Support People During the COVID-19 Pandemic*, www.imf.org/en/Publications/FM/Issues/2020/04/17/Fiscal-Monitor-April-2020-Policies-to-Support-People-During-the-COVID-19-Pandemic-49278, 17–18.

[8] See Centre for Tax Policy and Administration, *Tax and Fiscal Policy* (2020); A Pirlot, J Vella and R Collier, 'Tax Policy and the COVID Crisis' (2020) 48 *Intertax* 794–804.

had acted independently.[9] This appreciation of the EU role also resonates with other contributions to this volume.[10]

In addition to immediate relief measures, to ensure that recovery is sustainable, inclusive and fair for all Member States, on 27 May 2020 the EU Commission presented a Recovery plan for Europe: specifically, it proposed to create a new recovery instrument, ie *Next Generation EU*[11] (NGEU) embedded within a powerful, modern and revamped long-term EU budget.[12]

II. Biopower and Biopolitics as Overarching Causes of Tax Convergence

The conjecture of this chapter is that these COVID-19-related tax measures occurred *without* actual transfers of policies among countries because overwhelming structural factors levelled off any real feature of regulatory competition. The consequence was that national tax measures spontaneously converged and were one – among many – of the direct effects of a *radically changed political framework, that shifted from traditional tax politics to tax biopolitics*. In this context there was no top-down coordination at EU level, let alone at global level *because regulatory measures were instead compelled at national level by the 'invisible hand' of the global phenomenon of biopower and biopolitics*. So tax measures as a proxy of broader regulatory measures were contingent on biopower and biopolitics.

Michel Foucault's notions of biopower and the related notion of biopolitics provide a formidable support in understanding the overarching convergence triggered by the COVID-19 crisis that impacts also on tax policies. These notions are found in his work in the mid-1970s. The term 'biopower' encompasses a disciplinary power focused on the individual body. Foucault claims that biopower emerged as a rationality of power which is distinguished from sovereign power because it places the new political subject of the population, rather than individuals, at the centre of governmental policies in terms of fostering of life.

Foucault argued that the emergence of 'life' as an object of politics at the end of the eighteenth century marked a definitive shift in political rationality by contrasting it with the sovereign right of death that characterised political power up until the nineteenth century. Sovereign power, he argued, operated as a 'subtraction mechanism', such that it was 'essentially a right of seizure: of things, time, bodies, and ultimately life itself; it culminated in the privilege to seize hold of life in order to suppress it'. With biopower this right of death of the sovereign morphed into a new type of power that 'aligns itself with the exigencies of a life-administering power': Foucault states, 'the ancient right

[9] Introduction (ch 1).

[10] See Hernandez in ch 7 of this volume who eg provides a helpful history of a legacy of past and recent crises in providing an impetus to state-building activities of the EU. By contrast see Grisostolo and Scarcella in ch 10 who review in detail the existing and possible 'own resources' of the EU.

[11] European Commission, Communication from the Commission (EU) COM/2020/456 final of 27 May 2020. Repair and Prepare for the Next Generation. COM (2020) 456 final.

[12] M Motta and M Peitz, 'The EU recovery fund: An opportunity for change' in A Bénassy-Quéré and B Weder di Mauro (eds), *Europe in the Time of Covid* (London, CEPR Press, 2020).

to *take* life or *let* live was replaced by a power to *foster* life or *disallow* it to the point of death'.[13]

Foucault clarified that biopower operates at *the level of the population* and attempts to control the phenomena of the mass, such as birth rates, rates of mortality and morbidity and longevity across a population. The late eighteenth and early nineteenth century thus saw the emergence of policies about the ordinary and permanent factors of the health of the population, giving rise to public hygiene and institutions to 'coordinate medical care, centralize power and normalize knowledge'.[14]

The other seminal term coined by Foucalt – 'biopolitics' – focuses specifically on the new political subject of the population, rather than on the disciplinary aspect of biopower. Thus, biopolitics denotes the emergence of the vital phenomena and generally the health of the population as the primary focus of politics. In Foucault, biopolitics operates to both 'foster life or disallow it', so that its manifestations are not necessarily bad.[15]

According to Foucault, biopower and biopolitics can be understood by looking at their historical development. The first of these forms – biopower – emerged at the end of the seventeenth century as 'anatomo-politics of the human body' through discipline which treated the human body as a machine in order to optimise and control its capacities through the 'parallel increase of its usefulness and its docility'.[16] The second of these forms – biopolitics of the population – emerged in the eighteenth century and focused on the species-body and its biological characteristics of mortality, birth rates, morbidity and longevity to subject them to measurement and regulatory control.

Over time, biopower and biopolitics became coexistent within the polity: biopower focused on the bodies to individualise and manipulate them, while biopolitics was 'centred not upon the body but upon life' in the sense that 'bodies were replaced by general biological processes', so biopolitics was focused on statistical dynamics of the population.[17]

In conclusion, coining the notion of biopower and biopolitics, Foucault emphasised what he calls a society's '*seuil de modernité biologique*' ('threshold of biological modernity'). Our society crossed such a threshold when the biological processes characterising the life of human beings as a species became a crucial issue for political decision-making, a new 'problem' to be addressed by governments, not only in 'exceptional' circumstances (such that of an epidemic) but in 'normal' circumstances as well. This gradually became a permanent concern which defined what Foucault calls the '*étatisation du biologique*' (the 'nationalization of the biological').

In light of the illuminating anticipations of Foucault about biopower we can thus define at the current COVID-19 juncture 'COVID-19 biopower' specifically as the discipline deployed during the COVID-19 crisis focused on the individual bodies of the mass

[13] M Foucault, *The History of Sexuality: An Introduction, Volume 1*, trans R Hurley (New York, Vintage Books, 1990) 136–38.

[14] M Foucault in M Bertani and A Fontana (eds), *Society Must Be Defended: Lectures at the Collège De France, 1975–6* trans D Macey (London, Palgrave Macmillan, 2003) 244.

[15] Foucault (n 13).

[16] ibid 139.

[17] ibid 249.

of the population through all sorts of regulations and restrictions, ranging from social distancing to pervasive social control through new technologies. As highlighted in the Introduction to this volume, some of the methods of social control imposed during the COVID-19 crisis are almost unprecedented in the democratic world.[18]

We can also define as 'Covid-biopolitics' the emergence of the vital phenomena and generally the health of the population in connection to the spread of the virus as the overwhelming focus of politics. The crossing of the *threshold of biological modernity* and *nationalisation of the biological* mentioned by Foucault in respect to the *fin de siecle* certainly occurred in a macroscopic way in the 'exceptional' circumstances of the COVID-19 crisis.

To understand COVID-19-biopower one needs to juxtapose it with the traditional understanding of *political power in terms of sovereignty*, and adopt a different approach and conceive power in general as a mobile set of relations that take different configurations. COVID-19-biopower is in fact a power different from the sovereign conception of power exercised within traditional sovereignty in legal studies.

The sovereign conception of power has three principal features. First, in the sovereign conception, power is understood as being imposed upon subjects from 'above'; this view typically presupposes that the individual exists independently or prior to power and is then subject to its effects in the form of limitations. Second, the sovereign conception assumes that power is both totalising and uniform, in the sense that it operates in the same manner across all aspects of the social field (principle of equality). Third, the sovereign conception supposes that the principal tool of power's operation is the law, and the characteristic of power is legal use of force and the distinction between licit and illicit.

Against this backdrop, Foucault proposes what he calls an 'analytics' of power or a 'grid for historical decipherment'[19] that is very important to understand the latest transformations of power during the COVID-19 crisis. First, in antithesis to ordinary exercise of power, COVID-19 biopower does not presuppose that the individual exists independently or prior to power, but rather *power constitutes the individual as its effect through normalisation and homologation*. Second, COVID-19 biopower does not operate in the same manner across all aspects of the social field, rather it *percolates within the social compacts in different forms forgetful of the principle of equality*. Third, COVID-19 biopower *operates above and beyond the law and relies on new constraints*, such as tightened social norms that the population is assumed to self-impose, backed by technological measures: a distinction is normal/abnormal rather than licit/illicit.

Foucault's statement, when read in the light of the COVID-19 crisis, is foreboding:

> It is a mistake to think of the individual as a sort of elementary nucleus, a primitive atom or some multiple inert matter to which power is applied, or which is struck by a power that subordinates or destroys individuals. In actual fact, one of the first effects of power is that it allows bodies, gestures, discourses, and desires to be identified and constituted as something individual. The individual is not, in other words, power's opposite number; *the individual is*

[18] Introduction (ch 1).
[19] Foucault (n 13) 90.

> *one of power's first effects*. The individual is in fact a power-effect, and at the same time, and to the extent that he is a power-effect, *the individual is a relay: power passes through the individuals it has constituted*.[20]

So the individual is one of COVID-19 biopower effects, which passes through the individuals it has constituted, so that the individual must conform to the norm, intended as the statistical normality of the population as a whole and of each individual within it.

Take for example EU mobility of individuals. Before COVID-19 this mobility was guaranteed for all individuals on the basis of the preexisting condition of being EU citizens. During a certain period of the COVID-19 crisis only those holding the 'EU Covid Vaccine Passport/Certificate' that attested a set of normal biomedical conditions were entitled to travel throughout Europe without the need to quarantine or test for COVID-19.[21]

Previously being an EU citizen was the only condition to hold the right of mobility, while during that period the COVID-19 biopower passed through the individuals it had constituted by way of the EU Covid Vaccine Passport/Certificate, and being a political subject – ie an EU citizen – was just an additional condition. During this period of the COVID-19 crisis the individual holding the right to mobility was constituted by COVID-19 biopower, but did not exist prior to it.

This constitutive effect of COVID-19 biopower was also quite apparent during the COVID-19 crisis in which bodies' conduct was a direct effect of COVID-19 biopower, from lockdowns to social distancing and all other sorts of normalised behaviour. The tracking of COVID-19 spread and social distancing behaviour of the public has generated new opportunities for even greater biopower surveillance and control.

Foucault insisted on a multiplicity of force relations and techniques at work in different fields of biopower's operation, which do not necessarily constitute a unity. As he argued, *power is always relational*, such that the term 'power' is only a 'name that one attributes to a complex strategical situation in a particular society',[22] or shorthand for a network of relations[23] that do not emanate from a centre, nor are organised according to a single overriding strategy. Rather, the ways in which power operates in different fields, such as the economic, the domestic, and so on, may vary at a local level, and should be analysed at that level.

So the principal mechanism of COVID-19 biopower is not law, but a relational concept, the 'norm', intended as the statistical normality of the population as a whole and of each individual within it, and the mark of COVID-19 biopower is *normalisation* rather than interdiction: normal and abnormal rather than licit and illicit: '[a] normalizing society is the historical outcome of a technology of power centred on life'.[24] So we

[20] Foucault (n 14) 29–30.

[21] The certificate proves that its holder has been vaccinated, has been tested for COVID-19 with PCR or Rapid Antigen test and resulted negative, or has recently recovered from COVID-19, while also containing additional information on the vaccine, such as when the doses were administered, who is the manufacturer, etc.

[22] Foucault (n 13) 93.

[23] M Foucault, 'The Ethics of Concern of the Self as a Practice of Freedom' in P Rabinow (ed), *Ethics: Subjectivity and Truth, The Essential Works of Michel Foucault, 1954, Volume 1 84* trans R Hurley (London, Penguin, 1997) 291.

[24] Foucault (n 13) 144.

can say that the *normalisation induced by COVID-19 policies fittingly is the outcome of a new technology of power centred on life, rather than on political subjects as such.*

Accordingly COVID-19 biopower operates simultaneously at the level of both individual bodies and the concurrently emergent political subject of the population as a whole; it is concerned both with singularity and the group. Normalisation is a technique of COVID-19 biopower, which is intertwined with the institutions and force of the law but irreducible to them. Within a COVID-19-normalising society legal apparatuses are 'increasingly incorporated into a continuum of institutions (medical, administrative and so on)', the function of which are 'for the most part regulatory', such that the mode by which the law operates is increasingly that of the norm, intended as the statistical normality of the population as a whole and of each individual within it.[25] To be outside the 'norm' in the COVID-19 juncture is to be the recipient of restraining measures to fall within the norm.

This clearly does not mean that law itself is superseded; rather as a regulatory apparatus, the law continues to operate within the regime of COVID-19 biopower, but in a different mode than previously. Norms intended as the statistical normalities of the population effectively become the operative condition of law in COVID-19 biopower, since they allow the law to operate in conjunction with apparatuses such as medicine, which are themselves increasingly regulatory. In the COVID-19 crisis, the required statistical normality of the population gives the law access to the body in an unprecedented way, that is, as a continuous regulatory force rather than as a repressive and constraining instrument of sovereignty.

Thus, the management of life geared toward the regulation of the individual body in the discipline of collective well-being at the level of the population in a COVID-19 biopolitics of population fundamentally shapes power relations. This has two broad implications. First, it necessitates a reconsideration of the central tenets of political philosophy to the question of political power. In this context power is no longer primarily exercised through the hierarchical mechanisms of the sovereign, but through networks that include non-state institutions. Second, the free subject no longer stands in opposition to the sovereign, but is instead constituted by the operation of COVID-19 biopower.

III. The State of Exception and COVID-19 Nationalisms

The formulation of biopower and biopolitics by Foucault is essential to understanding the overarching political implications of the COVID-19 crisis, but it is Giorgio Agamben, a living philosopher, who contributed most to the understanding of the concept of 'COVID-19 exceptionalism', and this actually happened in a quite heated polemic context. Giorgio Agamben mainly in his book *Homo Sacer* and in other writings propounded ideas that were conveyed into a polemic thesis in respect to the COVID-19 crisis.

[25] ibid.

It is however essential to clarify that *Homo Sacer* offers a paradigmatic understanding of the nature of politics and is not an attempt to describe a historical process, particularly that of the current juncture. As Agamben explains, his philosophical method focuses on the recognition and articulation of 'paradigms' that elucidate the present without positing causal or historical claims'.[26]

The importance of Agamben's thoughts on the COVID-19 crisis was highlighted by Agamben himself in a series of articles and publications in which he explicitly manifested his idea that in times of ecosystemic crises modern state power resorts to the 'state of exception' in which the bare life of citizens is subject to unmediated power. More explicitly: in Agamben's view in the COVID-19 crisis the 'bare life' of citizens has become a governmental task that overrides everything else, so the life of citizens runs the risk of being reduced to 'bare life'.

Agamben characterised COVID-19 policies and practices of state control over the bodies of citizens as the 'biopolitical paradigm of the modern', a 'concealed matrix' of contemporary political life that usually hides behind the civilized mask of liberal democracy.[27] Agamben's position obviously sparked fierce reactions, for example by Slavoj Žižek[28] and Tim Christiaens.[29]

Agamben's analysis in *Homo Sacer* is dedicated to explain how the 'life' of political subjects is captured within the political sphere, and this is particularly important at the juncture of the COVID-19 crisis. He claims that 'life' constitutes the 'inclusive exclusion' that provides the foundation for the political sphere and that biopolitics is linked to the structure of sovereignty, to such an extent that Western politics has always been biopolitical.

In Agamben the inclusive exclusion is essentially a *state of exception* that excludes something and that at the same time again includes that something within politics. The something that is excluded is specifically the *biological life* of human beings which is then included in politics in the form of what Agamben calls *bare life*. The process is the following: simple biological life is excluded from the *polis* in the strict sense and remains confined – as merely reproductive life – to the *oikos*, 'home', while its remnants in the form of bare life are included in politics.[30]

In this formulation, 'life' is excluded from the sphere of politics (biological life), and simultaneously included in the sphere of politics (bare life). This 'inclusive exclusion' forms for Agamben the foundation of Western politics. In more simple terms the individual is exposed – included – in politics through bare life. In even more simple terms,

[26] M Foucault, *The Ethics of Concern* (New York, New Press, 1997) 32.

[27] G Agamben, *L'invenzione di un'epidemia* (26 February 2020), www.quodlibet.it/giorgio-agamben-l-invenzione-di-un-epidemia; see also www.journal-psychoanalysis.eu/coronavirus-and-philosophers/ for an English translation. Agamben's contributions on COVID-19 are collected in N Bassani et al and G Agamben, *A che punto siamo? L'epidemia come politica* (Macerata, Quodli-bet, 2020).

[28] S Žižek, 'Monitor and Punish? Yes, Please' (16 March 2020), www.thephilosophicalsalon.com/monitor-and-punish-yes-please; T Christiaens, 'Must Society be Defended from Agamben?' (26 April 2020), www.criticallegalthinking.com/2020/03/26/must-society-be-defended-from-agamben/.

[29] G Agamben, 'Chiarimenti' (17 March 2020), www.quodlibet.it/giorgio-agamben-chiarimenti; G Agamben, 'Contagio' (11 March 2020), www.quodlibet.it/giorgio-agamben-contagio.

[30] G Agamben, *Homo Sacer: Sovereign Power and Bare Life* trans D Heller-Roazen (Stanford, Stanford University Press, 1998).

the basic biological life is stripped of its core features to become the simulacre of an individual – her bare life – who in such a modality is subjugated to the power.

The category of bare life is neither biological life nor political life, but rather the politicised form of biological life. Agamben argues that overcoming biopolitics requires the formation of what he calls 'form-of-life', that is, a life in which the separation of the biological life and the political life is no longer possible. Only then will the machine of biopolitical violence be stilled.

By contrast, in the current situation bare life indicates the exposure of natural life to the force of the law, the ultimate expression of which is the sovereign's right over biological life. Thus, as neither biological life nor political life, bare life emerges through the irreparable exposure of life to the sovereign, such that the politicisation of life is ultimately nothing other than its exposure to sovereign use of force.

Agamben also claims that the *sovereign power* is itself founded on a similar exclusion, because the sovereign both includes and excludes itself from the rule of law. Agamben's conception of sovereignty in fact draws on Carl Schmitt, who famously argued that '[s]overeign is he who decides on the exception'.[31] In this formulation, the very possibility of juridical rule and the meaning of state authority is in fact the exception. According to Agamben, in deciding on the state of exception 'the sovereign creates and guarantees the situation that the law needs for its own validity'.[32] Or, as he also puts it, 'what is at issue in the sovereign exception is … the creation and definition of the very space in which the juridico-political order can have validity'.[33]

The sovereign thus operates as the threshold of order and exception, determining the confines of the law. The sovereign determines the suspension of the law vis-à-vis an individual or extraordinary case and simultaneously constitutes the efficacy of the law in that determination. Under the state of exception what is excluded from the law continues to maintain a relation to the rule precisely through the suspension of that rule.

According to Agamben, what is 'excluded' is not merely set outside the law and made indifferent or irrelevant to it, but rather it is thoroughly subjected to the force of the law while the law simultaneously withdraws from its subject. So sovereignty 'is the originary structure in which law refers to life and includes it in itself by suspending it', and the 'originary relation of law to life is abandonment'.[34]

Essentially, the idea here is that Western politics is founded on biological life which is excluded from politics, and then brought back into politics as bare life, so the original task of the sovereign is the production of the *biopolitical body*. In *Homo Sacer* and the associated text, *State of Exception*[35] there is little distinction between sovereignty and biopower, since according to Agamben the Western political tradition has been

[31] C Schmitt, *Political Theology: Four Chapters on the Concept of Sovereignty* trans G Schwab (Cambridge, MIT Press, 1985) 5.

[32] Agamben (n 30) 17.

[33] ibid 19.

[34] ibid 28–29.

[35] G Agamben, *State of Exception* trans K Attell (Chicago, University of Chicago Press, 2005).

biopolitical from its inception. In this respect Agamben differs from Foucalt, who distinguishes between sovereignty and biopower. According to Agamben Western politics has always been biopolitical because it is *founded on a state of exception*, a relation of 'inclusive exclusion'. By contrast, according to Foucault, Western politics *became* biopolitical when it moved to regulate the health of the population.

Agamben places sovereignty at the centre of biopolitics, and in contrast to Foucault, he claims that 'the inclusion of bare life in the political realm constitutes the original nucleus of sovereign power. *It can even be said that the production of a biopolitical body is the original activity of sovereign power.* In this sense, biopolitics is at least as old as the sovereign exception'.[36]

This claim that biopolitics is as old as the sovereign exception supports the thesis that Western politics is originally biopolitical. This implies that there was no politics prior to sovereignty, and that sovereignty is by its nature exceptional. Significant doubts have been raised about the historical plausibility of this account of biopolitics, but Agamben clarifies that figures such as that of *homo sacer* are understood as paradigms, where a paradigm is a 'singular object that, standing equally for all others of the same class, defines the intelligibility of the group of which it is a part and which, at the same time, it constitutes'.[37]

Agamben's approach to biopolitics substantially revises central aspects of Foucault's. First, he claims that sovereignty is foundational to biopolitics and that Western politics is biopolitical from its inception. Second, Agamben claims that bare life is simultaneously expelled from the political sphere and integrated into it, so that life cannot resist a biopolitical capture.

For example in a lockdown the 'bare life' of the locked down citizens became a governmental task that overrode other entitlements of the citizens. Lockdowns were strict emergency measures, but this aspect is more evident for example with the 'EU Covid Vaccine Passport/Certificate' a document that attested a set of normal biomedical conditions which entitled the citizens to travel throughout Europe without the need to quarantine or test for COVID-19: the 'bare life' of the would-be mobile citizen became a governmental task that overrrode the right of mobility.

While Foucault's contribution to the understanding of the COVID-19 crisis is that biopower and biopolitics have entered into an unprecedented phase, Agamben's thought contributes to explain how nation-states, squeezed by globalisation, reasserted their authority in a general situation of 'COVID-19 exceptionalism' by producing an overwhelming narrative of pervasive power. This narrative is articulated as follows. The *premise* is that the COVID-19 situation is a state of exception concerning healthcare and that the nation-state is responsible for ensuring the healthcare of its citizens. The *conclusion* is that in this state of exception the nation-state is entitled to the enforcement of a superior mechanism of control and surveillance that pervades the lives of the masses.

[36] Agamben (n 30).
[37] G Agamben, *The Signature of All Things: On Method* trans L D'isanto (New York, Zone Books, 2009) 17.

IV. Biopolitics as a Possible Explanation of the EU Fiscal Evolution

The implications of COVID-19 biopower, biopolitics and state of exception as explained by relying on Foucault and Agamben are far reaching. I have discussed them in this context not just for the sake of philosophical investigation, but to provide a robust foundation for the attempt to provide an explanation at EU level of what I called 'spontaneous convergence'.

So more specifically the question is: what are the implications of COVID-19 biopower, biopolitics and state of exception on tax relations, certainly a basic aspect of politics? The main finding of this chapter is that the hypothesis of regulatory competition did not work at all in the COVID-19 juncture, but at the same time there was no hint of actual coordination. Basically, national tax measures converged, temporarily reversing national tax systems from revenue collectors into revenue mitigators. Why then already in the summer of 2020 was there a unitary moment of the EU fiscal evolution, the approval of the NGEU? Is there a causal connection between biopolitics and the fiscal aspects of the NGEU?

My thesis is that COVID-19 biopower, biopolitics, and exceptionalism constituted the institutional cause for the sudden adoption of the NGEU, a measure that directly implies investments but which has the essential mark of being a fiscal turning point.

The NGEU plan amounts in total to 750 billion Euros, financed through a debt issue of unprecedented importance. The European Council of 17–21 July 2020 endorsed the agreement of national governments on this structure and stated that the Commission shall be empowered in the Own Resources Decision to borrow funds on the capital markets on behalf of the Union up to the amount of EUR 750 billion in 2018 prices; new net borrowing activity will stop at the latest at the end of 2026. The Union shall use the funds borrowed on the capital markets for the sole purpose *of addressing the consequences of the COVID-19 crisis*. The funds borrowed may be used for loans up to an amount of EUR 360 billion in 2018 prices and for expenditure up to an amount of EUR 390 billion in 2018 prices.[38]

The European Council of 17–21 July 2020 stated that the Council Decision on the system of own resources of the European Union will clarify with regard to NGEU financing the cases in which the Commission may provisionally call more resources from Member States than their respective relative share, without increasing the ultimate liabilities of the Member States, and set out the conditions thereof. It will provide that any such contribution will be compensated without delay in line with the applicable legal framework for the EU budget, without prejudice to other own resources and other revenues.[39]

As of July 2020 it was decided that the repayment shall be scheduled in accordance with the principle of sound financial management, so as to ensure the steady and

[38] For details on this process see C Garbarino, 'Tax Convergence and the Next Generation European Union' (2022) 48 *European Taxation* 319–28.

[39] Before calling such resources, the Commission will meet these needs through active cash management and, if necessary, recourse to short-term financing via the capital markets under its diversified funding strategy consistent with the limits of the Own Resources Decision. Only if such measures were not to generate

predictable reduction in liabilities *until 31 December 2058*. That date should be used retrospectively to understand the NGEU in terms of institutional evolution.[40]

Some commentators have called the NGEU a Hamiltonian moment for the EU in monetary terms, but there are no clear perspectives in terms of full tax coordination, in light of the fact that unanimity is still required for tax revenue matters. The NGEU is clearly debt in its structure. However, the repayment will only be in 2058 and a big portion will not be paid back by recipient Member States. This means that the NGEU grants are, in a significant part, directly created and made available at EU level.

This NGEU process confutes the conventional wisdom of 'fiscal austerity' that expenditures must be paid for by tax revenues, because the NGEU expenditures and related grants paid to Member States are created before taxes are collected. This reversed process partly addresses the concern highlighted in the Introduction to this volume that the EU's ability to provide financial support is constrained by extremely limited 'own resources' upon which it can draw without the need to receive transfers from Member States.[41] So the lessons that might be drawn from recent crises are that these own resources ought to be supplemented by new EU taxes or otherwise, as epitomised by the NGEU by innovative forms of financial mobilisation.

In practice the EU funds infrastructural expenditures through a kind of fiat money constituted by that part of the NGEU funds made available to Member States but which must not be paid back. It would have been anathema at the end of 2019 to even conceive of such a programme at the level of individual Member States, in the climate of dire fiscal austerity, and at the beginning of 2020, by magic, this was possible. So I argue here that the immediate cause of the NGEU as a fiscal turning point is COVID-19 biopower, biopolitics and exceptionalism.

With the COVID-19 crisis, biopower and biopolitics entered into an unprecedented phase that led governments within the Council to reach unanimity on 17–21 July 2020 on a matter – the NGEU – which is in essence a fiscal structural measure. At the same time these nation-states reasserted their authority on the basis of 'COVID-19 exceptionalism': as a convergence of tax measures toward mitigation was already in progress and bound to last in the medium term, the solution was a form of hybrid long-term debt plus non repayable grants.

The explanation of this unpredictable change can be found in evolutionary studies where the term 'exaptation' was proposed by Stephen Jay Gould to describe a shift in the function of a trait during evolution: a trait can evolve because it served one particular

the necessary liquidity could the Commission provisionally call more resources from Member States as a last reserve. The amount of additional resources which can be called annually from Member States in such circumstances shall be on a pro rata basis and, in any case, limited to their share of the temporarily increased own resources ceiling, ie 0.6% of Member States' GNI.

[40] Amounts not used for interest payments as foreseen will be used for early repayments before the end of the MFF 2021–27, with a minimum amount, and can be increased above this level provided that new own resources have been introduced. The amounts due by the Union in a given year for the repayment of the principal shall not exceed 7.5% of the maximum amount of EUR 390 billion for expenditure. The amounts of the own resources ceilings shall be temporarily increased by 0.6 percentage points for the sole purpose of covering all liabilities of the Union resulting from its borrowing to address the consequences of the COVID-19 crisis, until all these liabilities have ceased to exist, and at the latest until 31 December 2058.

[41] Introduction (ch 1).

function, but subsequently it may come to serve another function.[42] Bird feathers are a classic example: initially they may have evolved for temperature regulation, but later were adapted for flight.[43] Of course, institutions are not subject to the same laws of natural evolution so I will just use the concept of exaptation as a metaphor to explain NGEU from a constitutional tax viewpoint and to conclude the chapter.

So if one assumes that the current function of the NGEU (as of 2022) is to address the structural consequences of the COVID-19 crisis, this proves that the immediate cause of the NGEU is COVID-19 biopower, biopolitics and exceptionalism and that once the NGEU will have exhausted its effect (and by that time COVID-19 will be gone) its function will cease to exist. It is also reasonable to think that the NGEU subsequently may come to serve *another function* through exaptation, and specifically a *fiscal function*, ie *the formation of an initial core of genuine own EU tax resources* because EU own resource needs to be collected to pay back the debt part of the whole operation.

Therefore, this is a path different from the one usually discussed in academic and political circles: rather than first creating own EU tax resources to fund investments (a mission impeded by the unanimity rule in fiscal matters), the EU first makes investments by unanimity on non-tax matters (the NGEU) and then creates its own tax resources, as already indicated by the Council of 17–21 July 2020.

Let us now find ourselves in 2060, when the repayment of NGEU funds will be completed. Perhaps historians will in that year affirm that the NGEU initially evolved to address the consequences of the COVID-19 crisis, but later was adapted for creating own EU resources. They will perhaps conclude that when the NGEU was initially used to address the consequences of the COVID-19 crisis it was doing so because of a unique historical juncture. However, since the NGEU in its 2020-state will have evolved in 2060 to be the pivot for EU own tax resource formation, so it can be inferred that the NGEU in 2060 will be regarded as an *exaptive evolution of the EU toward a common tax system*.

[42] SJ Gould and ES Vrba, 'Exaptation-a missing term in the science of form' (1982) *Paleobiology* 4–15.

[43] When feathers were initially used to aid in flight they were doing so exaptively, but since that moment they have been shaped by natural selection to improve flight, so in their current state they are adaptations for flight.

10

The COVID-19 Crisis as a Momentum for the Creation of a European Tax System?

FRANCESCO EMANUELE GRISOSTOLO AND LUISA SCARCELLA*

Abstract

The aim of this chapter is to examine the possible impacts of the recent COVID-19 crisis on the tax integration process in the EU. The incisive spending measures taken during the crisis are an incentive to strengthen the European budget also on the revenue side and to create new own resources of a tax nature. Hence, after a brief overview of the current financing system of the Union, the chapter illustrates the new own resources of a tax nature proposed to finance the repayment of the public debt that the Union resorted to in the context of the health crisis. Finally, the chapter analyses the limits of the Union's competences and the procedural reasons that have so far hindered the establishment of own resources of a tax nature.

I. Introduction

In the aftermath of COVID-19, the dramatic situation has required exceptional measures and a direct intervention at the supranational level. However, the need to overcome the economic crisis due to the pandemic could also be seen as a catalyst to rethink the issue of EU taxes.

Even though the new Decision on the EU own resources[1] does not contemplate new types of resources, the Interinstitutional agreement reached in December 2020 by the Parliament, the Council and the Commission seems to point in a different direction and refers to new own resources to be adopted following a precise roadmap.

* Dr Scarcella contributed to the chapter in her personal capacity. The views presented in this chapter are her own and do not necessarily represent the institutional ones of the International Chamber of Commerce.

[1] Council Decision on the system of own resources of the European Union and repealing decision 2014/335/EU, 24 September 2020.

The new suggested EU own resources initially suggested within Annex II of the Interinstitutional agreement included: a levy based on the consolidated corporate tax base (CCTB), which lately has been transformed into BEFIT, a digital levy on big tech companies, carbon border adjustments and a financial transaction tax. However, after the historic OECD/G20 Inclusive Framework on Base Erosion and Profit Shifting agreement of October 2021,[2] the Commission has put forward a proposal to modify the measures included in Annex II.[3] These amendments included the removal of the proposal for a digital service tax and the introduction of a new own resource based on a share of the residual profits of the largest and most profitable multinational enterprises.[4]

In this chapter, the brief analysis of the initial and modified proposals will focus on two aspects: (a) an overview of the main characteristics of such proposals, and (b) the justifications for their adoption, also considering their reinvigorated saliency due to the COVID-19 crisis.

Second, the chapter investigates one of the main reasons why these proposals have not already been implemented. The current institutional architecture of the EU requires a 'double unanimity filter' both for legislating in tax matters (Articles 113, 115, 192.2 TFEU) and to include new taxes within the EU's basket of own resources (Article 311 TFEU). However, it is hard to see how the binding nature of the Interinstitutional agreement[5] proposing new EU own resources will reconcile with the unanimity requirement. Indeed, achieving majority voting in taxation and strengthening the role of the EU Parliament in the design (and selection) of new EU taxes would be a substantial step forward for the EU integration process.

As the new EU own resources are expected to be allocated to the repayment of the European debt that has been essential to finance the Next Generation EU Plan, Member States might not have any other options than to finally reconsider the EU tax architecture to strengthen the EU fiscal capacity.

II. The Current Financing System of the EU Budget and the Past Tax Proposals as EU Own Resources

The new Decision on the EU own resources, approved in 2020 by all 27 EU Member States, not only made it possible for the EU to borrow for the Next Generation plan but also introduced new changes to the EU budget. The current system, as regulated by the Council Decision 2014/335/EU, provides for three main sources of revenues: Traditional Own Resources, a Value Added Tax-based Own Resource and the Gross National Income-based Own Resource (GNI). Under the rules agreed for the period 2014–20,

[2] OECD, *Statement on a Two-Pillar Solution to Address the Tax Challenges Arising from the Digitalisation of the Economy* (Paris, 8 October 2021).

[3] European Commission, 'Proposal for a Council Decision amending Decision (EU, Euratom) 2020/2053 on the system of own resources of the European Union', COM (2021) 570 final.

[4] European Commission, 'Communication From The Commission To The European Parliament, The Council, The European Economic And Social Committee And The Committee Of The Regions. The next generation of own resources for the EU Budget', COM (2021) 566 final (22 December 2021).

[5] Article 295 Consolidated versions of the Treaty on European Union and the Treaty on the Functioning of the European Union [2016] OJ C202/1 (TFEU).

the EU could mobilise its own resources for payments up to a maximum amount of 1.20 per cent of the sum of all Member States' gross national income (GNI), a cap which was then reduced to approximately 1 per cent. While Traditional Own Resources are a direct source of revenue to the EU budget and have been identified as a 'genuine' EU Own Resource, the latter two categories are, in essence, national contributions to the EU budget.

Traditional Own Resources are customs duties, for which the EU has exclusive competence regarding the determination of the scope and structure. However, since customs are an essential element of the internal market and the external commercial policy, legislation in the area of customs duties is not considered as having a fiscal nature and, therefore, is jointly adopted by the council (with a qualified majority) and the parliament under an ordinary legislative procedure (Article 294 TFEU).

The other two EU resources consist of compulsory national contributions by the Member States to the EU budget. The VAT-based own resources are calculated based on a uniform rate of 0.3 per cent applied to the corrected value-added tax base of each Member State with the VAT base capped at 50 per cent of each country's GNI and a reduced rate of 0.15 per cent applying to Germany, the Netherlands and Sweden. Finally, the GNI was established as a 'residual' keystone of the Own Resources system to ensure full funding of the agreed expenditure. However, over time it has become the system's predominant component and now accounts for more than 70 per cent of EU revenue.

The current EU system of own resources primarily resting on contributions from EU Member States certainly has the merit of providing steady and predictable revenues to finance EU expenditures.[6] From a subsidiarity principle perspective, this system also leaves the decision to distribute the financial burden among individual taxpayers to the Member States.[7] Nonetheless, the increasing dominance of direct contributions out of a Member State's national budgets into the EU budget curtails the EU's financial autonomy and reinforces a retour-logic.[8] Moreover, this opaque own resources system would prevent EU citizens from assessing their individual and respective country's contributions to the EU budget and the connection between EU revenues and expenditures.[9] The own resources system has also been criticised as neither reflecting nor directly supporting core EU policies, such as sustainable growth and development.[10]

[6] A Hudetz, A Mumford, D Nerudová and M Schratzenstaller, 'Reform needs and options in the EU system of own resources' (2017) 44 *Empirica*, 609–13; High Level Group on Own Resources – HLGOR, Future Financing of the EU (Brussels, December 2016) ec.europa.eu/info/sites/default/files/about_the_european_commission/eu_budget/future-financing-hlgor-final-report_2016_en.pdf.

[7] V Lipatov and A Weichenrieder, 'The subsidiarity principle as a guideline for financing the European Budget' in T Buttner and M Thone M (eds), *The future of EU finances* (Tubingen, Mohr Siebeck, 2016) 15–29.

[8] European Commission, 'Financing the EU budget: report on the operation of the own resources system. Accompanying the document proposal for a council decision on the system of own resources of the European Union, Commission Staff' COM (2018) 325 final (2 May 2018); S Richter, 'Facing the monster "Juste retour": on the net financial position of member states vis-à-vis the EU budget and a proposal for reform.' (2008) The Vienna Institute for International Economic Studies, Research Report No. 348/2008, wiiw.ac.at/facing-the-monster-juste-retour-on-the-net-financial-position-of-member-states-vis-a-vis-the-eu-budget-and-a-proposal-for-reform-p-456.html.

[9] M Schratzenstaller, 'The EU own resources system – reform needs and options' (2013) 48(5) *Intereconomics* 303–13; C Fuest, F Heinemann and M Ungerer, 'Reforming the financing of the European Union: a proposal' (2015) 50(5) *Intereconomics* 288–93.

[10] Schratzenstaller, ibid 303–13; European Commission (n 8).

Concerns have been raised in particular on the perception that in this way, the bulk of the current own resources remain pure national contributions.[11] Thus, Member States would be induced to measure the benefits derived from the EU budget in terms of net financial contributions. Consequently, the current structure of the EU system of own resources could represent an obstacle to further European integration.[12]

Before the COVID-19 pandemic, the Commission has already suggested amending the current EU financing system. The Commission proposed to modernise existing own resources, maintain the own resource based on GNI, simplify the VAT-based Own Resource while also introducing a basket of new own resources. Even though the process was constantly on a deadlock, COVID-19 gave new impetus to the possibility to reform the current system of EU own resources by introducing new EU levies.

III. The 'Potential' Role of Taxation in Financing the Union's Response to the Crisis

The pandemic erupted at a very sensitive time for EU finances, namely close to the approval of the new MFF 2021–27. However, before the pandemic, even though the Commission was already moving in the direction of introducing new own resources, the discussion conducted by the representatives of national governments in the Council of the Union did not lead to fruitful results. Crucial was the extraordinary European Council of 20–21 February 2020 on the new multiannual budget where the Finnish EU Presidency prepared a Negotiating Box proposing new EU own resources.[13] Nonetheless, the states' positions were still too far apart: the President of the Council declared that European leaders needed 'more time'.

Less than a month later, Italy was subjected to a total lockdown dealing with the pandemic and progressively adopted by all other European countries. The social and economic consequences were immediately evident, and the European institutions intervened promptly, for example, by suspending the Stability Pact and the rules on state aid or through monetary interventions by the European Central Bank. However, it soon became clear that the Union's response would have to be structural.

Therefore, on 27 May 2020, the Commission presented an updated legislative package for the European multiannual budget, based on a dual structure.[14] On the one hand, the Multiannual Financial Framework (MFF) which is financed by the usual system of own resources. On the other hand, the well-known Next Generation EU plan consists of the Recovery and Resilience Plan (the so-called 'Recovery Fund') and other plans, amounting to 750 billion Euros, financed through a debt issue of unprecedented importance. However, debt financing of the Next Generation EU also became an opportunity

[11] Hudetz et al (n 6).

[12] European Commission (n 8); as reported by Hudetz et al (n 6).

[13] Council of the European Union, 'Multiannual Financial Framework (MFF) 2021-2027: Negotiating Box with figures' (Brussels, 5 December 2019) www.consilium.europa.eu/media/41630/st14518-re01-en19.pdf.

[14] European Commission, 'Europe's moment: Repair and Prepare for the Next Generation', COM (2020) 456 final (27 May 2020).

to take a step forward for European taxation. From 2021 onwards, the EU budget started to be expected to amortise the debt by repaying principal and interest before 31 December 2058. Article 6 of the new Own Resources Decision thus foresaw that these increased outflows from the budget will be financed through an increase of up to 0.6 per cent of the ceiling of the own resource based on GNI: at first glance, it would seem, therefore, that there is no significant change in the financing system of the Union.

However, additional data pointing at an evolution of the system should be taken into account. Recitals 6, 7 and 8 of the Decision, in fact, indicate some new own resources, more aligned with the strategic priorities of the Union and aimed at reducing the contributions based on GNI. Specifically, Recital 7 provides for a resource calculated based on non-recycled plastic packaging waste: this is the only new resource that is already implemented and specified within the provisions of the Decision (Article 2(1)(c) and (2)). Recital 8, on the other hand, describes the possible new 'additional' resources cumulatively, committing the Commission to submit proposals on this point: it explicitly mentions a carbon adjustment mechanism at the border, a digital levy, an EU emission trading system and a tax on financial transactions, but the list is not intended to be exhaustive.

Recital 8 is reflected in the subsequent Interinstitutional Agreement on budgetary matters of 16 December 2021 whose Annex II includes a roadmap spelling out the link between new own resources and the Union's financial effort for the Recovery and Resilience Plan. These new resources should be sufficient to cover the expenditure foreseen for the repayment of the debt financing the pandemic plan. In other words, they should progressively replace the ad hoc increase in the GNI-based own resource now provided for in Article 6 of the Own Resources Decision.

Type of Resource	Proposal	Approval	Enter into force
Levy based on the quantity of non-recycled plastic packaging waste		2021	1.1.2021
Carbon border adjustment mechanism (CBAM)	June 2021	1.7.2022	1.1.2023
Digital levy	June 2021	1.7.2022	1.1.2023
EU Emission Trading System (ETS)	June 2021	1.7.2022	1.1.2023
Financial Transaction Tax	June 2024	1.7.2025	1.1.2026
Levy based on a common consolidated corporate tax	June 2024	1.7.2025	1.1.2026

In addition to this quantitative objective, Annex II also sets out some 'substantive' guiding principles for the new own resources: their link with the Union's priorities – and especially the fight against climate change, the circular economy, digitalisation, tax fairness and the fight against fraud and evasion – simplicity, transparency and fairness, the stability and predictability of the revenue generated, and limited bureaucratic implementation burdens for States and businesses (Part A no 2). Particularly interesting is point (g), which indicates as a principle 'of preference, to generate "new" revenues', which seems to express a preference for own resources that have a direct link with a (new) fiscal effort as opposed to simple 'new' transfers, albeit calculated with a different criterion from the traditional ones. Fiscal resources, in fact, are a more obvious expression of a duty of European citizenship and, in the future, a step in the direction of the fiscal sovereignty of the Union.

However, it is not yet definite whether all these deadlines will be met. While in July 2021 the European Commission had published a series of legislative proposals in the area of climate action, including the revision of the ETS[15] and more information on the introduction of a CBAM,[16] the proposal for a digital levy tax (as described in section IV(D)) has been momentarily dismissed and replaced by a new proposal for a measure related to corporate taxation and subsequent to the international tax agreement on a minimum global tax. Indeed, the developments in tax policy negotiations at OECD level are strongly influencing the Commission's legislative initiative, and in December 2021 the Commission presented a proposal for amendments to the Decision on own resources,[17] introducing an own resource based on the Global Minimum Tax for multinational companies, not provided for in the Interinstitutional Agreement, but agreed with the OECD/G20 Inclusive Framework in October 2021.[18]

Furthermore, it must be excluded that the conclusion of the agreement can really guarantee the approval of the new resources envisaged therein. In fact, the conclusion of the Agreement cannot avoid the need to comply with the unanimity rule provided for the amendment of the Own Resources Decision and the adoption of rules of a tax nature. The Agreement is still a secondary act, which cannot derogate from the procedures laid down in the provisions of the Treaties. Second, the Agreement itself states that: (a) it 'does not affect the respective budgetary and legislative powers of the institutions' (No 3); (b) the introduction of the new own resources must, in any case, be 'carried out by means of a limited number of revisions of the own resources decision' (All., II, Preamble, point K) and, consequently, (c) 'in accordance with the procedures applicable under the Treaties and subject to the approval of the Member States in accordance with their respective constitutional requirements'.

Therefore, the agreement can bind the institutions – for instance, the Commission to present its proposals in time or the Council to discuss them – but it cannot oblige national governments to reach an agreement.

IV. Planned New EU Own Resources

In the initial package that was proposed in 2020, it is possible to distinguish three different categories of EU own resources proposals and all these proposals can count on an

[15] European Commission, 'Proposal for a Directive of The European Parliament and of the Council amending Directive 2003/87/EC establishing a system for greenhouse gas emission allowance trading within the Union, Decision (EU) 2015/1814 concerning the establishment and operation of a market stability reserve for the Union greenhouse gas emission trading scheme and Regulation (EU) 2015/757' COM (2021) 551 final.

[16] European Commission, 'Carbon Border Adjustment Mechanism: Questions and Answers' (14 July 2021), ec.europa.eu/commission/presscorner/detail/en/qanda_21_3661.

[17] European Commission (n 3).

[18] More precisely, the OECD/G20 Inclusive Framework on BEPS, Pillar One, affirms that – for Multinational Enterprises (defined as enterprises with global turnover above 20 billion euros and profitability above 10%) – 25% of residual profit defined as profit in excess of 10% of revenue will be allocated to market jurisdictions with nexus using a revenue-based allocation key.

additional justification beyond the need to finance for the EU budget. The presence of this second aim not only offers a second legal basis for their adoption but also raises a question mark on whether some of these proposals (which in the past had already been put forward) will now finally be adopted.

The first group relates to environment, energy and climate and it includes a revised EU Emission Trading System (ETS), a Carbon Border Adjustment Mechanism (CBAM) and the plastic levy.[19] Additionally to environmental and economic reasons, as claimed by Scuderi, Rizzo and Loucaidou in chapter thirteen of this volume, given the changes in people's approach to the environment, economic and investment decisions, the post-pandemic could represent the right moment to introduce such green taxes. The second group of EU own resources can be justified by their role in contributing to the better functioning of the single market since they are believed to potentially combat tax fraud, evasion and avoidance, and ensure fair taxation. This second category originally included a proposal to introduce a common consolidated corporate tax – more recently turned into a 'Business in Europe: Framework for Income Taxation' (or BEFIT) – and a financial transaction tax. Finally, the third group is constituted by the digital levy, leading to a fairer taxation of digital business.[20] However, after the international tax agreement reached in October 2021, the last two categories seem to have merged, despite the different purposes they were aimed to fulfil. The new measure based on the international agreement will not in fact be limited only to digital businesses but represents a broader revolution in the area of corporate taxation.

A. Plastic Levy Resource

The plastic levy consists of a national contribution based on the quantity of non-recycled plastic packaging waste (calculated as the difference between the weight of the total plastic packaging waste generated and recycled) in the Member State with a uniform call rate of €0.80 per kilogram. It is accompanied by an adjustment mechanism, which reduces Member States' contributions with a GNI per capita below the EU average by an annual lump sum corresponding to 3.8 kilograms of plastic waste per capita.[21] The political aim is to urge the Member States to introduce fiscal measures of their own to reduce the consumption of single-use plastics, foster recycling and boost the circular economy. Besides growth in the proportion of plastic packaging recycling, another desired effect is a reduction in the production and use of plastic packaging.

The estimated revenue is around €7 billion annually (corresponding to approximately 4 per cent of the budget) but the revenues generated should decrease in time as non-recycled plastic packaging waste gradually disappears.[22]

[19] These proposals are described in detail by Geringer in ch 14 and Scuderi, Rizzo and Loucaidou in ch 13.

[20] A similar categorisation is present in European Parliament, 'Reform of the EU own resources' (Policy Department for Budgetary Affairs Directorate-General for Internal Policies, March 2021) www.europarl.europa.eu/RegData/etudes/IDAN/2021/690963/IPOL_IDA(2021)690963_EN.pdf.

[21] Article 2, Interinstitutional Agreement between the European Parliament, the Council of the European Union and the European Commission on Budgetary Discipline, on Cooperation in Budgetary Matters and on Sound Financial Management, as well as on New Own Resources, Including a Roadmap Towards the Introduction of New Own Resources [2020] Official Journal L 433 I/28.

[22] ibid.

B. EU Emission Trading System (ETS)-Based Own Resource

The ETS consists of a so-called 'cap and trade' system aimed at gradually reducing the cap set on the total amount of greenhouse gas emissions, while emission allowances can be traded among emitting companies. The cap and its reduction shall ensure the reduction of the total greenhouse gas (GHG) emission by incentivising emissions reduction in sectors or production methods where it is most economically viable, reducing the cost of greening by creating a market and putting a price on the externalities.

Both the new own resources based on the ETS mechanism and the Carbon border adjustment mechanism (CBAM)[23] have been confirmed by the EU Commission communication on the EU own resources of December 2021. The EU ETS was first launched in 2005, and during its phase 3 (which ended in 2020), it introduced a single, EU-wide cap (instead of national ones) and made auctioning the default method for allocating allowances (instead of free allocation). Previously, the possibility of transferring a part of ETS revenue of EU budget had been considered and abandoned in 2010 because of the different economic impact on EU countries.[24] More recently, the European Green Deal prompted a revision of the EU ETS, putting forward an increased GHG emission reduction target. Its current objective is to help achieve a climate-neutral EU by 2050 and reduce greenhouse gas emissions by at least 55 per cent by 2030. An EU own resource based on EU ETS revenues fulfils two aims, the one relating to the financing of the EU budget through its own resources while contributing to climate goals and strengthening the internal market.

In the case of the ETS mechanism, the Commission has proposed that 25 per cent of the revenues generated by EU emissions trading become an own resource for the EU budget which are estimated at around EUR 9 billion per year over the period 2023–30. A share of them will enable the financing of the Social Climate Fund.

In December 2021, the Commission has additionally proposed a temporary solidarity adjustment mechanism to ensure a fair emissions trading-based own resource contribution from all Member States. In particular, until 2030, an upper and lower boundary for the EU emissions trading own resource contribution will apply, in relation to the gross national income key.

C. Carbon Border Adjustment Mechanism (CBAM)

As also recognised in Annex II of the interinstitutional agreement, the CBAM and the EU Emissions Trading System are thematically interlinked.[25] However, despite the EU ETS effort carbon leakage can still occur as long as international partners are not introducing similar pricing on environmental externalities for example when emission rules are more relaxed, or EU production is replaced by imported products from countries with

[23] Section 4.3.
[24] HLGOR, Future Financing of the EU (n 6) 44.
[25] Interinstitutional Agreement (n 21) Annex II, Part B, 7.

lower carbon prices.[26] Thus, the EU internal efforts in creating more environmental-friendly industries will be in vain.

A CBAM would counter carbon leakage by putting a price on the GHG content of imports through limiting the price advantage of offshoring or outsourcing carbon-intensive production to third countries and, at the same time, reducing the competitive disadvantage of EU companies paying for their emissions. In terms of revenue, to avoid discrimination, the CBAM will put a price on the CO2 content of the imported product that is equal to the price an EU producer would pay for its CO2 allowance in the EU ETS. Therefore, the revenue resulting from this source would be as volatile as that from the EU ETS.

One of the criticisms that has been raised in relation to this proposal is the compatibility of such a system with the World Trade Organization (WTO) rules or other EU international obligations.[27] The introduction of a CBAM would affect the EU itself and its trading partners since it will make carbon-intensive imports more expensive. However, it would contribute to achieving global climate goals by indirectly promoting the adoption of stricter emissions standards and investment in climate-friendly technologies by the EU's trading partners.[28] However, even if the CBAM was fully WTO-compliant, respecting the principle of non-discrimination and the most favoured nation clause, it could still lead to trade disputes with trading partners. As noted by Geringer in chapter fourteen of this volume, it should be kept in mind that environmental protection and the consequences of climate change go beyond EU's external borders and that environment-related revenues will only constitute one component in a multi-faceted strategy to fight the climate crisis.

In the case of CBAM, the Commission proposes that 75 per cent of the revenues generated will become an own resource for the EU budget which are estimated at around EUR 0.5 billion per year over the period 2023–30.

D. EU Digital Levy

Digital businesses have revolutionised the tax and international tax panorama. While discussions are still ongoing at OECD level, the EU Commission in March 2018 had put forward two proposals. The two proposals included a Council Directive laying down rules relating to the corporate taxation of a significant digital presence and a Council Directive on the common system of a digital services tax on revenues resulting from the provision of certain digital services (DST).[29] Indeed, digital services can generate

[26] EU Parliament 'Towards a WTO-compatible EU carbon border adjustment mechanism' (Report 2020/2043(INI), 10 March 2021) www.europarl.europa.eu/doceo/document/TA-9-2021-0071_EN.html.

[27] For a complete analysis of the concerns arising in the area of international trade, please refer to A Pirlot, *Environmental Border Tax Adjustments and International Trade Law. Fostering Environmental Protection* (Cheltenham, Edward Elgar, 2017); T Falcao, 'Toward Carbon Tax Internationalism: The EU Border Carbon Adjustment Proposal' (2020) 98(9) *Tax Notes International.*

[28] EU Parliament – Policy Department for Budgetary Affairs Directorate-General for Internal Policies, Reform of the EU own resources (March 2021) 14.

[29] On the European DST see among many: G Kofler, 'Editorial: The Future of Digital Services Taxes' 2021 (30(2) *EC Tax Review* 50–54; C Dimitropoulou, 'The Proposed EU Digital Services Tax: An Anti-Protectionist Appraisal Under EU Primary Law' (2019) 47(3) *Intertax* 268–81; G Kofler and J Sinnig, 'Equalization Taxes

income from online advertising, the online sale of goods and content, digital intermediary activities, the sale of user-generated information etc. Nevertheless, the current set of rules seems not to be able to capture profits generated in a country without the provider being physically present.

The idea behind these proposals was to create a level playing field between digital services and traditional providers, between EU-based and third-country multinationals, between multinationals and SMEs and between the Member States with different corporate and consumption tax schemes. Nonetheless, there were some adverse effects, such as the implications from a global trade relations perspective. Since major players in the digital services market are homed in the US and China, those countries might adopt measures in response to the adoption of a European DST. Another paramount concern is that if drafted as a consumption tax, providers might incur double taxation, being liable to pay for a consumption tax on their digital services while also having to pay a corporate income tax on the profits gained from the same services. The EU DST proposal was foreseeing a tax on revenues derived from specific digital services: online advertising, intermediary services between users for selling goods and services, sale of user-provided data. Companies with annual revenues above €750 million worldwide and €50 million in the EU would be subject to this tax to exempt start-ups and scale-ups. If a digital services tax is introduced as an intermediary measure, applying a 3 per cent rate according to the Commission proposal, the annual revenue is estimated at around €5 billion.

In the past few years, some Member States have unilaterally introduced or are planning to introduce taxes on digital services. However, these have still not been adopted at EU level. Initially, the proposal of a DST as an EU own resource has been postponed to 2022 and then was again put on hold after an agreement at international level was reached in October 2021.

E. Financial Transaction Tax (FFT)

Another suggested new EU own resource was a Financial Transaction Tax (FTT). An FFT proposal was already presented in 2011 and rejected by the Council.[30] Afterwards, it was revived in the form of 'enhanced cooperation' in 2013, with the participation of 11 Member States.[31] Despite this second unsuccessful attempt, negotiations have been

and the EU's "Digital Services Tax"' (2019) 47(2) *Intertax* 176–200. Differently, on the legality of the digital taxes under EU law adopted by Member States, refer to R Mason and L Parada, 'The Legality of Digital Taxes in Europe' (2020) *Virginia Tax Review* 175–217.

[30] On this first proposal, please see among many: J Kaiding, 'The Financial Transaction Tax: The Way Forward for the European Union?' (2014) 23(1) *EC Tax Review* 30–42; O Henkow, 'The Commission's Proposal for a Common System of Financial Transaction Tax: A Legal Appraisal' (2012) 21(1) *EC Tax Review* 5–16; B Cortez and T Vogel, 'A Financial Transaction Tax for Europe?' (2011) 20(1) *EC Tax Review* 16–29; L Denys, 'Why a Financial Transaction Tax?' (2012) 21(1) *EC Tax Review* 2–4.

[31] Belgium, Germany, Estonia, Greece, Spain, France, Italy, Austria, Portugal, Slovenia and Slovakia. On the FFT under the 'enhanced cooperation' framework, see the comment by R Ness, 'An Analysis of the Financial Transaction Tax in the Context of the EU Enhanced Cooperation Procedure' (2015) 24(6) *EC Tax Review* 294–30.

ongoing, and the latest proposal for discussion was submitted by Germany in 2019. Meanwhile, at least seven Member States[32] have introduced domestic FTTs, adopting different scopes and tax rates.[33]

An FTT consists of a very low-rate tax applied to the exchange of securities, bonds, shares and derivatives between financial institutions. In the aftermath of a financial crisis, the main aims of an FTT should be ensuring that the financial sector makes a fair contribution, preventing further fragmentation of the Single Market, and discouraging risky trading activities. Moreover, it shall not cover every day retail bank transactions of private individuals, households or businesses.[34] In the negotiations, the main questions debated among the Member States concerned the taxation of derivatives transactions, the taxation principles and the method of tax collection.[35] At the same time, the application of uniform (0.01 per cent) rates instead of minimum rates was suggested together with the creation of uniform methods of collection and the partial allocation of the revenues to the Union budget as genuine own resources. Thus, the idea of an FTT as EU own resource is not an absolute novelty.

In terms of revenues, in 2011 the Commission claimed that the tax could raise approximately €57 billion per year if implemented in all Member States[36] while in the case of the 'enhanced cooperation' proposal between €4 billion to €33 billion.[37]

F. Own Resources Based on the Corporate Income Tax: From CCCTB to BEFIT

The idea to establish a common (consolidated) corporate tax base in the EU has been on the agenda for decades. The differentiation in the corporate income tax (CIT) among the Member States concerns not only the application of different rates but also that the methods of calculation for profits and losses that form the basis of the tax are different. The reasons for adopting a CCCTB are many. It would simplify tax administration, reduce obstacles for companies operating across borders and enhance legal certainty. The harmonisation of rules would make tax systems more transparent and provide symmetrical information to all players on the effective tax rate. A CCCTB would also help counter tax avoidance by eliminating preferential regimes. Having a common consolidated tax base is also a precondition for a corporate tax-based EU own resource but a uniform method of calculation is necessary. The Commission proposal of 2018

[32] Belgium, Finland, France, Ireland, Italy, Poland, Spain.

[33] There has been also a decision by the European Court of Justice that upheld the compatibility of the Italian FTT with the principle of free movement of capital and services.

[34] Central Bank of Ireland, 'The EU financial transactions tax proposal: a preliminary evaluation' (April 2012) www.esri.ie/system/files?file=media/file-uploads/2015-07/BKMNEXT217.pdf.

[35] European Parliament, 'Deeper and fairer internal market with a strengthened industrial base' (Legislative train schedule, 20 May 2022) www.europarl.europa.eu/legislative-train/theme-deeper-and-fairer-internal-market-with-a-strengthened-industrial-base-taxation/file-financial-transaction-tax.

[36] Central Bank of Ireland (n 34).

[37] D Nerudová et al, 'The Financial Transactions Tax as Tax-based Own Resource for the EU Budget', Fair Tax Policy Brief no. 2 (September 2017).

contains a calculation using a call rate of 3 per cent for the EU budget,[38] which would result in annual revenue of around €12 billion, equivalent to around 7 per cent of the budget.

According to Annex II, a new EU own resource based on the corporate income tax was planned to see the light in 2024 and be adopted in 2025/2026. Nonetheless, already on 18 May 2021, the European Commission adopted a Communication on Business Taxation for the 21st century, which contains a so-called framework named 'Business in Europe: Framework for Income Taxation' (or BEFIT) replacing the old CC(C)TB proposal.

For the long term, the EU Commission Communication has presented a new framework for business taxation in the EU, aiming at reducing administrative burdens, removing tax obstacles and fostering a more business-friendly environment in the Single Market.

This new proposal builds on global discussions on the Pillar One and Two discussions at OECD level. According to the EU Commission Communication, BEFIT will consolidate the profits of the EU members of a multinational group into a single tax base, which will then be allocated to the Member States using a formula to be taxed at national corporate income tax rates. As recognised by the Commission, the key points to be discussed concern how to give appropriate weight to sales by destination, as well as how the business market and assets (including intangibles) and labour (personnel and salaries) should be reflected, to ensure a balanced distribution of corporate tax revenue across the EU Member States with different economic profiles.[39] The difficulties in reaching an agreement in this area also emerge in the international context which explains why a levy based on the corporate income tax as a new EU own resource is chronologically the last measure to be adopted.

G. Implementing the International Tax Agreement on a Global Minimum Tax and its Relevance as a Source of EU Own Resources

On 8 October 2021, 137 countries that are members of the OECD/G20 Inclusive Framework on Base Erosion and Profit Shifting agreed on a two-pillar solution on the re-allocation of profits of multinational enterprises and on an effective global minimum tax rate. 'Pillar One' of the agreement provides for the re-allocation of a share of

[38] The European Commission's proposal for a 3% 'call rate' on the Common Consolidated Corporate Tax Base (CCCTB), to be introduced after the CCCTB itself, has been submitted for the first time with the draft budget for 2021–27 for allowing the EU to rely on a new 'own resource'. Previously, scholars have considered the proposal for a 3% call rate as a step forwards the 'European Union Company Income Tax' (EUCIT), one of the alternatives for a comprehensive business taxation scheme. L Cerioni, 'The European Commission Proposal for a 3% "Call Rate" as a New Suggestion for a EUCIT: An Assessment Against the Criteria for a Fair Taxation' (2018) 27(5) *EC Tax Review* 237–49; B Peeters, 'EUCIT: For How Much Longer Will Political Objections Outweigh the Advantages?' (2015) 24(3) *EC Tax Review* 128–31.

[39] Other concerns that have been raised by scholars with reference to the previous 2016 proposals – one on a Common Corporate Tax Base (COM (2016) 685 Final) ('the CCTB Draft') and one on a Common Consolidated Corporate Tax Base (COM (2016) 683 Final) ('the CCCTB Draft') – refer to the international taxation framework. See E Raingeard de la Blétière and D Gutmann, 'CC(C)TB and International Taxation' (2017) 26(5) *EC Tax Review* 233–45.

the residual profits of the largest and most profitable multinational enterprises to end market jurisdictions where goods or services are used or consumed. The global minimum effective tax rate of 15 per cent is at the core of 'Pillar Two' which has been one of the main drivers for the international tax deal of October 2021. However, the practical implementation aspects of the agreement are still being finalised. The Commission has committed in its 2022 Work Programme to table a proposal for a Directive giving effect to the agreement in compliance with EU law and in line with the requirements of the Single Market. As all EU Member States signed up for the tax deal, the European Commission presented a proposal for an EU directive to implement the minimum tax uniformly across the EU. Nevertheless, reaching an agreement on the Directive does not seem an easy task as shown in the case of Poland which has recently vetoed the adoption of the implementing directive.[40]

In its communication of December 2021, the Commission has also proposed an own resource equivalent to 15 per cent of the share of the residual profits of the largest and most profitable multinational enterprises that are reallocated to EU Member States under the agreement on a reform of the international tax framework. Under the Commission's own resources proposal, Member States would provide a national contribution to the EU budget based on the share of the taxable profits of multinational enterprises re-allocated to each Member State under Pillar One. According to the Commission, pending the finalisation of the agreement, revenues for the EU budget could amount to up to EUR 2.5–4 billion per year.[41]

V. Unanimity under the Treaties on Own Resources and Tax Legislation: A 'Double Obstacle' to Introducing Own Resources Having a Fiscal Nature?

As has emerged in the previous paragraphs, there has been an increasing awareness of the need to revise the current EU own resources system. In the past, many proposals have been put forward to create a system that relies more heavily on taxation. Then why does the system appear to be 'unreformable'? This question cannot be answered without highlighting the peculiarities of the path that led to the approval of the 2021–27 Multiannual Financial Framework (MFF). At the same time, we should also ask ourselves whether the health crisis (and its economic consequences) can push for a real change in the Union's fiscal policy.

Among the various angles, the main determinant is, in our opinion, the set-up of powers and the procedures as currently established in the Treaties. Indeed, the path to be followed to establish new own resources of a fiscal nature is particularly difficult. The difficulty is mainly due to what can be described as the double rule of unanimity among the representatives of the national governments and the absence of any real power in the

[40] As reported in newspapers, eg 'EU Push for Global Minimum Tax Falters Again as Poland Blocks' *Bloomberg* (5 April 2022) www.bloomberg.com/news/articles/2022-04-05/eu-push-for-global-minimum-tax-falters-again-as-poland-blocks.

[41] European Commission (n 4).

area of taxation by the EU. For instance, to introduce an FTT intended to finance the EU budget, it is necessary, on the one hand, to include in the Decision on the EU own resources a provision establishing that part of the revenue of the Union's annual budgets will be made up of the proceeds of this tax. On the other hand, it is also necessary to approve a directive which will govern the tax, to be then implemented by the Member States. To approve both acts, unanimity is required within the Council of the European Union.

The importance of these procedural constraints would be reduced in the presence of a homogeneous socio-economic context and a strong common political will. However, in markedly plural contexts, characterised by the coexistence of strong national identities, such as that of the EU, consensus can only be achieved through a system of trade-offs between the interests of the various national players, who assess the impact of regulations keeping in mind their own economic system. In this sense, the unanimity rule makes the political costs of a common decision very high. Moreover, what is perhaps worse, it consolidates a way of thinking that is more attentive to not 'losing control' over areas considered strategic for national policy than to achieving the advantages that can only be obtained through a European tax and financial policy.[42]

The first aspect to be considered when trying to address these types of concerns is indeed the EU Own Resources Decision. From a formal point of view, this is a decision of the Council of the European Union adopted unanimously after consultation with the European Parliament, which must then be approved by the Member States 'in accordance with their respective constitutional requirements' (Article 311 TFEU). It is in substance an agreement between states. The national passage cannot be considered purely formal: this is confirmed by the tensions that accompanied the approval of the most recent Decision 2020/2053, for example, in Finland and in Germany (in this case, with the intervention of the Constitutional Court).[43] To change the Union's own resources structure by introducing tax-based resources, it is, therefore, necessary to reach an agreement that not only satisfies all national governments but also, in most cases, withstands the scrutiny of national parliaments and constitutionality checks.

In practice, a new own resources decision is adopted simultaneously with each new regulation laying down the Union's Multiannual Financial Framework, that is, every seven years. The decision and the regulation govern, respectively, the revenue that can be established and the level of expenditure that the EU can commit to when approving the Union's annual budget. The MFF also has to be approved unanimously by the Council, but unlike the own resources decision, the regulation also needs the approval of the European Parliament. Thus, in relation to the expenditure, since the entry into force of the Lisbon Treaty (2009) the two branches of the EU budgetary authority – the European Parliament and the Council – are on an equal footing, at least in formal terms.

[42] On the advantages of introducing new EU own resources, see also Pantazatou, ch 8 of this volume.

[43] About the Finnish case, see P Leino-Sandberg, 'Who is ultra vires now? The EU's legal U-turn in interpreting Article 310 TFEU' (Verfassungsblog: On matters constitutional, 18 June 2020). In Germany, an application in front of the Constitutional Tribunal (Bundesverfassungsgericht) against the domestic act ratifying the EU Own Resources Decision was unsuccessful: for more information, see the press release of the Tribunal on the Order of 15 April 2021, 2 BvR 547/21 (www.bundesverfassungsgericht.de/SharedDocs/Pressemitteilungen/EN/2021/bvg21-029.html).

The Commission, which holds the power of initiative, has taken on board the need to make the resources system more transparent and in line with the Union's objectives for a long time. It has also underlined that if the European budget is to be endowed with broader functions (such as economic stabilisation), new own resources are needed, preferably linked to the other EU policies. In its latest proposal for a decision (2018), the Commission was also consistent with this premise, proposing a 'basket of new own resources'.[44]

For its part, the European Parliament is the institution that has made the most determined efforts to achieve an increase in the resources available to the EU budget and to link its own resources to genuinely European taxes. Parliament's institutional strategy is understandable: more resources mean more room for European policies, defined in the annual budget session, where Parliament can play a greater role; more tax resources mean less dependence on transfers from the budgets of the Member States.[45]

The Council, however, gave very little follow-up to these impulses. The reports of the meetings on the multiannual budget do not show significant efforts to reach an agreement on new own resources: the reluctance of national governments to negotiate on this issue is quite evident. Faced with this tendency, the European Parliament has tried to assert its position, making the approval of the MFF conditional on some progress also on the revenue side, on which – formally – it would only have the prerogative to be consulted. In 2014, the Parliament has obtained the establishment of the High-Level Group on Own Resources and in 2020, the Parliament's position was instrumental for the inclusion of a 'roadmap towards introducing new own resources' within the Interinstitutional Agreement.

These difficulties, which are specific to the process of approving the EU budget, are compounded by those required for tax legislation. Since the Single European Act 1986, the Union's legislative process has shifted from a predominance of the intergovernmental method to the 'Community' method. The former is characterised by the unanimity rule in the Council and the 'consultative' role of the Parliament. In contrast, the latter provides for qualified majority voting in the Council and a genuine 'co-legislative' role for the Parliament, which acts on an equal footing with the Council. This trend has affected an increasing number of subjects, so much so that we speak of 'ordinary legislative procedure' in the post-Lisbon era. Still, taxation remains one of the most significant exceptions.

In the successive revisions of the Treaties, the unanimity rule for the approval of acts relating to 'provisions on the harmonisation of legislation concerning turnover taxes, excise duties and other forms of indirect taxation' has always been reconfirmed. Similarly, measures in the field of environment and energy must be adopted by unanimity if they are considered to be 'primarily of a fiscal nature' (Articles 192(2)(a) and

[44] European Commission, 'Proposal for a Council decision on the system of Own Resources of the European Union', COM/2018/325 final (2 May 2018).

[45] A D'Alfonso 'Own resources of the European Union. Reforming the EU's financing system' (European Parliament Research Service, October 2020) www.europarl.europa.eu/RegData/etudes/BRIE/2018/630265/EPRS_BRI(2018)630265_EN.pdf; A Vitrey, 'How and Why Did the European Parliament Influence the Reform of the Own Resources System?' in B Laffan and A De Feo, *EU Financing of Next Decade. Beyond the MFF 2021–2027 and the Next Generation EU* (Florence, EUI Repository, 2020) 71 ff.

194(3) TFEU). Finally, other taxes, including direct taxes, are susceptible to harmonisation where they have 'a direct impact on the establishment or functioning of the internal market', but – again, together with regulations on the free movement of persons and labour protection – they are exempt from the general rule of the ordinary legislative procedure of Article 114 TFEU and are expressly subject to unanimity in the Council (Articles 114(2) and 115).

This framework is not without exceptions. Articles 116 and 325 of the Treaty seem to be a potential basis for legislation in the field of taxation, adopted under the ordinary legislative procedure, aiming at eliminating a disparity distorting the conditions of competition in the internal market and preventing and combating fraud affecting the financial interests of the Union. However, these provisions can at most form the basis for specific harmonisation measures (eg in terms of substance, procedure or sanctions) and are therefore not suitable to form the basis for new European taxes.

Numerous authors have pointed out the negative consequences of this arrangement of EU competencies. Indeed, it undermines the fiscal capacity of the Union as a whole and, at the same time, the fiscal capacity of individual states within it. For instance, in the field of digital and environmental taxation, which are of global importance, European states can only be genuinely sovereign 'through' the Union. Moreover, the freedoms of movement of companies and capital, guaranteed by the Treaties 'reduce', de facto, the possibility for individual states to affect these tax bases and lead to a downward tax competition. Using the categories of comparative fiscal federalism, it creates an internal competitive federalism at the EU level that contributes to the crisis of the welfare state model of the European tradition.[46]

To overcome this situation, the Commission has proposed to use some 'passerelle clauses' contained in the Treaties to enable the European institutions to intervene by a qualified majority instead of unanimity.[47] As a general rule, Article 48(7) TEU empowers the European Council to decide, by means of a decision, to switch from unanimity to qualified majority in the Council, where the TFEU provides for unanimity in a given matter. However, the initiative must be forwarded to the national parliaments and – if even one of them opposes it within six months – the decision cannot be adopted.[48]

It is easy to understand how the use of these 'passerelle clauses' actually suffers from the same obstacle as all tax legislation: they could only be activated with the agreement of all Member States. The Treaties grant the Union a power of harmonisation, which is normally exercised through the adoption of a directive. At the same time, the Member States retain the power and the task of establishing the tax through national law.

In a nutshell, both the Union's own resources and taxation are still regulated unanimously by the representatives of the national governments. Although the Treaties have been revised several times, the Member States have so far seemed to be unwilling to give up their sovereignty in extending the scope of the ordinary legislative procedure in

[46] G Esping-Andersen, *The Three Worlds of Welfare Capitalism* (Princeton, Princeton University Press, 1989).

[47] European Commission, 'Towards a more efficient and democratic decision making in EU tax policy', COM (2019) 8 final (15 January 2019).

[48] For the environmental field there are specific 'passerelle clauses', which would enable the Council (and not the European Council) to decide unanimously.

these matters. What seems to emerge is that national governments prefer a Union that continues to be an 'anti-sovereign' rather than a 'sovereign' in fiscal matters.[49]

The reasons for this attitude deserve much wider investigations. The objective interests of some countries in persisting with an aggressive fiscal policy are an important, but perhaps not an exhaustive, aspect. At national level, tax governance is one of the areas in which representative bodies enjoy a broad discretion, and therefore it is a strategic tool for obtaining political consensus. It is indeed well known that the power of national political institutions has been increasingly eroded by supranational institutions and by different actors such as sub-national bodies (devolved powers), constitutional and supreme courts, and the so-called 'technical' bodies (administrative authorities). This process probably contributes to render national political forces opposed to the shift of tax sovereignty 'upwards'.

VI. Conclusions

The evolution of a multilevel tax system consisting of a centralisation of tax sovereignty is a complex process requiring solutions that can satisfy the economic interests of all states involved, which rarely coincide entirely and often radically conflict.[50]

Considering the European Union as a peculiar form of federalising process, the EU cannot be excluded from this historical-constitutional trend. The 'double' unanimity rule contained in the Treaties – which was not even present in the US Constitution – makes it impossible to envisage a 'bloc' of states with homogeneous interests imposing an evolution of the common tax system. Thus, it requires compromises to be accepted by all the Member States.

Against this backdrop, the current context could be the right moment to finally take steps forward. On a strictly fiscal level, the proposed tax measures have an important European dimension since in many cases, these measures would be effective only when adopted at EU level. At the same time, at the financial level, the automatic increase of the GNI-based contribution could represent an incentive to introduce new own resources. In an economic situation in which the consequences of the pandemic already strain states, new resources at EU level could 'lighten' their budgets. Additionally, this path will be attractive insofar as the new European tax proposals will be more burdensome on those economic operators, including non-European ones, who have hitherto been able to benefit from a reduced tax burden.

The reasons making these new instruments appealing in this particular moment in time are not only of a practical nature. In terms of legal and economic analysis, the institutions can benefit from the wide-ranging reflection initiated at the instigation of Parliament following the approval of the 2013–20 MFF and culminating in the Final Report of the High-Level Group on Own Resources, chaired by Mario Monti.

[49] The expression 'anti-sovereign' is used, eg, by P Boria, *L'anti-sovrano. Potere tributario e sovranità nell'ordinamento comunitario* (Torino, Giappichelli, 2004).

[50] In a comparative perspective, see TP Wozniakowski and M Poiares Maduro, 'European Taxes and Fiscal Justice: Citizens' Support and Lesson from the US' (2020) 12(3) *Perspectives on Federalism* 47–58.

Finally, the political and cultural climate should also be considered. The COVID-19 pandemic crisis and the response given to its dramatic economic consequences with the adoption of the Next Generation EU plan have been seen by many as proof that the Union must equip itself with instruments capable of responding to systemic crises symmetrically affecting many Member States. Indeed, this is a historical moment to think about the importance of strengthening the European budget, financed by genuinely supranational EU tax measures. The introduction of EU own resources is a necessary step to coherently support a state building process which has already been initiated.[51] Seen in this light, the COVID-19 crisis becomes an opportunity to acknowledge a fundamental and already existing problem: the necessity for the EU to adopt fiscal instruments to support its current and future level of integration.

[51] See van Ganzen and Vording, ch 2 in this volume.

11

A Case for VAT Treaties: International Tax Cooperation for Sustainable Recovery

YIGE ZU

Abstract

The COVID-19 crisis exacerbated the pre-existing challenges of taxing the digital economy and made it more urgent for governments to respond to the challenges. This chapter considers the challenges created by the rise of the digital economy and further accelerated by COVID-19 for VAT collection on cross-border sales of digital services and low value goods. Drawing on the experience of income tax treaties, this chapter explores the role of international cooperation by way of treaties in offering a long-term solution to the VAT problems, while supporting a sustainable and inclusive COVID-19 recovery.

I. Introduction

COVID-19 has a far-reaching impact on the economy in countries at all levels of development. It also poses significant challenges for tax policy making. Since the outbreak of the pandemic, tax incentives have been used as a valuable tool by governments across the world to mitigate the negative economic consequences faced by individuals and businesses.[1] As the world begins to emerge from the crisis, governments will inevitably explore options for raising taxes to finance the massive national debts resulting from the increased government spending and reduced tax revenue. While the introduction of new taxes is being discussed at both the national and regional levels,[2]

[1] See eg R Krever, 'Tax Responses to A Pandemic: An Australian Case Study' (2020) 1 *Belt and Road Initiative Tax Journal* 52; R Collier, A Pirlot and J Vella, 'COVID-19 and Fiscal Policies: Tax Policy and the COVID-19 Crisis' 48 (2020) *Intertax* 794.

[2] For example, the UK Treasury Committee considered the possibility of introducing windfall and wealth taxes and concluded that introducing such taxes would be either challenging or problematic. See, House of Commons Treasury Committee, *Tax After Coronavirus: Twelfth Report of Session 2019–21* (HC 664, 2021).

the COVID-19 pandemic exacerbated problems of existing tax systems with respect to taxation of the digital economy and makes it more urgent for governments to address these issues. To date, tax measures in response to COVID-19 have primarily been taken at the domestic level. However, the pandemic represents a global challenge and many of the tax issues it brings about have an international dimension. These issues demand a global response and can only be effectively addressed through international cooperation for the benefits of all countries, in particular developing countries that have been disproportionately affected by the pandemic and yet have a much lower tax-to-GDP ratio.[3]

For over a century, international tax cooperation has primarily been pursued in the field of income tax through an extensive network of bilateral treaties that aim to resolve double taxation resulting from overlapping tax claims. However, there is a dearth of international agreements in another key area of taxation, the Value Added Tax (VAT). As the main general consumption tax in about 170 countries, the VAT is a key source of revenue for Organisation for Economic Co-Operation and Development (OECD) countries and its revenue significance is even greater in middle- and low- income countries. The revenue potential of the tax, however, is considerably undermined by the rise of the digital economy, with almost all countries facing significant challenges in collecting VAT from cross-border transactions in recent decades. The tax base has been under further threat during the pandemic that accelerated the shift to the digital economy and e-commerce, following the unprecedented restrictions on movement and economic activity. Addressing the common challenges in this area through international cooperation becomes more pressing in the wake of the COVID-19 pandemic when governments seek revenue-raising opportunities. In addition, there is a particularly strong case for developing international coordinated responses that provide assistance to developing countries where a large proportion of VAT revenue is collected on imports.[4]

This chapter explores the potential role of VAT treaties in addressing the common challenges in taxing cross-border transactions in the digital economy and supporting an inclusive and sustainable post-COVID-19 recovery. The chapter starts with a review of the VAT challenges raised by the digital economy. It then discusses how treaties can be used to address these challenges. Finally, the chapter assesses the distributional consequences of the proposed VAT treaty and its role in providing assistance to developing countries.

II. VAT Challenges in the Digital Economy

A fundamental principle of VAT as a tax on final consumption is that, in cross-border sales, the VAT should operate as a destination-based tax that applies where

[3] The pre-pandemic average tax-to-GDP ratio in developing countries included in the OECD Revenue Statistics database was almost only half of the OECD average. See E Modica, S Laudage and M Harding, 'Domestic Revenue Mobilisation: A New Database on Tax Levels and Structures in 80 Countries' (2018) OECD Taxation Working Paper No. 36, www.oecd-ilibrary.org/taxation/domestic-revenue-mobilisation_a87feae8-en.

[4] L Ebrill et al, *The Modern VAT* (Washington, DC, International Monetary Fund, 2001) 49.

consumption takes place. This is achieved through two separate transactions: first, exports are zero-rated in the exporting country and, second, imports are subject to taxation in the receiving country. Cross-border supplies by foreign businesses to domestic consumers give rise to enforcement difficulties that do not arise in a fully domestic transaction.

Although the VAT is intended as a tax to be borne by final consumers, it is collected through an invoice-credit mechanism in almost all VAT jurisdictions, which places the tax liability on the supplier. This system works well so long as the supplier is present in the country that has the jurisdiction to tax and can be easily susceptible to the country's enforcement mechanisms. It proved problematic in the case of foreign suppliers that are out of reach of local tax administrations, however. Alternative collection mechanisms are therefore needed in these circumstances to overcome the limitations of jurisdictional reach. The initial response of most VAT systems was to shift responsibility for remitting the VAT from the foreign supplier to the local customer. This was done, in the case of tangible goods, by holding the imports at courier depots or post offices until the intended customers paid the VAT due. A parallel response was adopted for importation of intangible supplies through what became known as a 'reverse charge' rule that required the customer to account for the VAT due on imports.

These collection systems proved effective when the customer was a local registered business subject to full audit procedures but became problematic when extended to unregistered final consumers in the internet age. When the VAT systems were adopted between the 1950s and the 1990s in most countries, the volume of cross-border sales of goods and services was relatively small. Cross-border business-to-consumer (B2C) sales of goods of a value below a specified threshold were typically exempt from the VAT in the importing country on the ground that the collection costs would outweigh the revenue yields if these sales were brought into the tax net. The reverse charge mechanism that works well for business-to-business sales of intangibles does not offer an adequate solution for taxing B2C sales, because it would require a large number of unregistered final consumers, who may even not be aware of their tax liabilities, to self-report their tax liabilities.[5] In the absence of an effective collection mechanism, services imported by final consumers remained untaxed in most countries.

However, the advent of internet and globalisation has led to a remarkable surge in online purchase by private consumers of goods and digital services from suppliers located in other jurisdictions in the last two decades.[6] The increasing volume of cross-border digital supplies and low-value goods that are left out of the VAT base gives rise to significant revenue loss.[7] Under-taxation of these imports also causes a number of distortions against domestic businesses. Local retailers of similar goods or services that

[5] OECD, *International VAT/GST Guidelines* (Paris, OECD Publishing, 2017) (3.130).

[6] For data on imported digitally-delivered services in selected countries, see J Brondolo and M Konza, 'Administering the Value-Added Tax on Imported Digital Services and Low-Value Imported Goods' (2021) IMF Technical Notes and Manuals 2021/004.

[7] The VAT foregone as a result of low value imported goods exemption in the EU was estimated to have risen from €118 million in 1999 to €640 million in 2011. See European Commission, 'Assessment of the Application and Impact of the VAT Exemption for Importation of Small Consignments' (Final Report, EY – May 2015).

are subject to full taxation are placed at a competitive disadvantage to their foreign competitors.[8] The exemption threshold for imported goods offers an incentive for offshore suppliers to avoid or evade paying the tax. For example, they may split the order and ship items separately to ensure that each of the items has a value below the threshold. The European Commission also noted that the exemption, known as low value consignment relief, is open to massive fraud and abuse as imported high value goods are 'consistently undervalued or wrongly described' to benefit from the exemption.[9]

The OECD has emphasised the importance of reform in this area in the context of the growing digital economy and has been developing common standards for the effective collection of VAT on cross-border sales of goods and digital services.[10] Some OECD countries adopted unilateral measures to collect the VAT on digital services and low value goods imported by domestic customers, in both cases placing the responsibility for collecting the tax on foreign suppliers. The EU, for example, requires non-EU based businesses supplying services to EU customers to register and collect the VAT in the Member State in which the customer resides. This process is simplified through a one-stop-shop scheme that allows non-EU suppliers to register and account for the VAT in a single Member State on their EU-wide sales (at the rate applicable in the customer's country). The revenue is then allocated through a clearing house mechanism to the customer's country. The one-stop-shop regime was eventually expanded to include all types of intra-Community B2C sales of goods and services in July 2021, effectively removing the exemption for imports of low-value goods.[11]

Many other countries have also implemented measures to collect the VAT on imported goods and services by domestic consumers. Australia, New Zealand, Norway and Switzerland, for example, require foreign suppliers to register and pay the VAT on sales of low value goods into their country.[12] In some countries (for example, Australia and New Zealand), electronic marketplaces such as Amazon and eBay are made liable for VAT on behalf of the underlying suppliers. Although many countries had taken steps to tax digital services under the VAT prior to the pandemic, the economic fallout of COVID-19 has accelerated the trend towards taxing digital services around the globe. In the recent two years, governments, in particular in emerging countries, have been looking to expand the coverage of VAT to include cross-border digital supplies.[13]

The unilateral rules raised a number of concerns. First, compliance with the rules by foreign businesses is largely voluntary because the importing jurisdiction cannot audit, or in the case of non-compliance, suppliers who do not have a physical presence

[8] European Commission, 'Modernising VAT for E-Commerce: Question and Answer' MEMO/16/3746.

[9] ibid.

[10] OECD, *Addressing the Tax Challenges of the Digital Economy, Action 1–2015 Final Report, OECD/G20 Base Erosion and Profit Shifting Project* (Paris, OECD Publishing, 2015).

[11] Council Directive (EU) 2017/2455 of 5 December 2017 amending Directive 2006/112/EC as regards certain value added tax obligations for supplies of services and distance sales of goods.

[12] OECD, *Consumption Tax Trends 2020: VAT/GST and Excise Rates, Trends and Policy Issues* (Paris, OECD Publishing, 2020).

[13] For a list of countries of the Asia-Pacific region that adopted VAT to tax digital services made by foreign suppliers, see R Asquith, 'Indonesia adds to VAT collector list as digital VAT receipts rocket' (VAT Calc, 13 January 2022) www.vatcalc.com/indonesia/indonesia-adds-to-vat-collector-list-as-digital-vat-receipts-rocket/.

in the country.[14] Experience in countries that implemented the measures suggests that high-profile suppliers that take up a considerable market share tend to be more tax-compliant for reputational reasons.[15] There may still be revenue loss, however, if many small non-resident suppliers fail to register in the customer's jurisdiction.[16] This problem could be mitigated by making online marketplaces liable for tax, which would catch a large number of small suppliers. Secondly, the costs for complying with different sets of tax rules are very high, in particular for small businesses that have customers in many countries and have to keep up with changes in tax law in different countries and file foreign tax returns in foreign languages. The high compliance costs may lead to trade barriers for small businesses. Following the UK's exit from the EU, the UK introduced rules that require EU businesses making supplies to UK customers to register for VAT in the UK. As a consequence, many EU exporters, in particular small businesses, ceased to supply to UK customers to avoid the complexities of UK VAT registration.[17]

While Australia was the first country to implement rules to collect the VAT on imports of low value goods,[18] the Australian government acknowledged that the adopted measure 'has limitations and carries significant uncertainty about levels of compliance'.[19] It nevertheless considered the approach to be the 'best available collection model' for adoption at the time.[20] The unilateral measures have achieved some success as stop-gap measures. However, they fall well short of effective long-term solutions to the enforcement difficulties. Addressing these difficulties becomes more pressing in the post-COVID-19 era, with COVID-19 further shifting the tax base from the traditional bricks-and-mortar economy to the digital economy.

III. VAT Treaties

While unilateral measures offer inadequate solutions to the collection of VAT on cross-border online sales of services and goods, an obvious question is whether international cooperation by way of treaties can provide better remedies to the problem? This question is particularly relevant in the wake of a crisis as past experience shows that global crises are often the driving forces of international cooperation.[21] The income tax

[14] OECD (n 10).

[15] ibid 122.

[16] ibid 122. The UK has been considering an alternative method of VAT collection – split payment – that aims to reduce the challenge of enforcing foreign supplier compliance. See, HMRC, 'Alternative method of VAT collection – split payment' (2018) assets.publishing.service.gov.uk/government/uploads/system/uploads/attachment_data/file/687783/Alternative_method_of_VAT_collection___split_payment.pdf.

[17] R Plummer, 'EU Firms Refuse UK Deliveries over Brexit Tax Changes' *BBC News* (4 January 2021) www.bbc.co.uk/news/business-55530721.

[18] The Australian rules took effect in July 2018.

[19] Productivity Commission, Australian Government, *Collection Methods for GST on Low Value Imported Goods: Productivity Commission Inquiry Report* (Commonwealth of Australia, 2017).

[20] ibid.

[21] A similar argument is made by Hernández González-Barreda in the EU context in ch 7 of this volume 'The Role of Crisis in State-Building the European Union through Finance and Taxation: Will COVID-19 and the Russian Attack Trigger Further Union?'.

treaty network, for example, was developed in the context of the spread of income tax systems and the liberalisation of trade and investment following World War I.[22]

In the income tax, treaties have a long history of being used to resolve double taxation.[23] The extensive income tax treaty network now consists of over 3,000 bilateral treaties. Why has the global community not witnessed an equal growth of VAT treaties? The jurisdictional issues in the income tax and VAT are rather different. In the income tax, treaties have been primarily used to resolve double taxation where two or more countries claim taxing rights over the same income.[24] This problem is far less significant in the VAT because the relative uniformity of VAT systems around the globe and the single destination principle underlying the allocation rules largely reduced the possibilities for double taxation.[25] The main problem in the VAT, as discussed earlier, is non-taxation due to the enforcement difficulties that have only arisen in recent decades in the context of the digital economy. With COVID-19 accelerating digital transformation, the necessity of international cooperation will soon be learnt by individual states struggling with the challenges of taxing cross-border online sales.

In the income tax, neither source nor residence countries have significant difficulty with collection of taxes. There may be instances, however, when collection of tax from residents is problematic, particularly if the resident departs for another jurisdiction with all his or her assets. The OECD model treaty includes a provision for mutual obligation of signatories to assist with the collection of each other's tax debts.[26] Mutual assistance in the collection of taxes is only provided on request after the requesting state conducts an audit and assesses the tax debts against a taxpayer. A solution to the VAT problem could be an extension of the scope of mutual assistance in collection in the income tax to cover ordinary VAT liabilities in cross-border sales. In fact, the EU has already adopted this approach through the one-stop-shop scheme to address the problem internally, which can be used as the basis for developing VAT treaties.

A VAT treaty would mirror the one-stop-shop arrangements currently in place in the EU for intra-Community sales of goods and services. The treaty would place the obligations for collecting the VAT on B2C sales of digital services and low value goods on the exporting country. The VAT would be collected at the rate applicable in the customer's jurisdiction by the exporting country as if it were its own tax. The revenue would then be transferred from the exporting country to the importing country via a clearing house mechanism. Between each pair of countries, the revenue inflows and outflows would be netted against each other and only the net balance is transferred.

[22] K Vogel, 'Double Tax Treaties and Their Interpretation' (1986) 4(1) *International Tax and Business Lawyer* 4, 10–11.

[23] See eg S Jogarajan, 'Prelude to the International Tax Treaty Network: 1815–1914 Early Tax Treaties and the Conditions for Action' (2011) 31 *Oxford Journal of Legal Studies* 697.

[24] For the causes of double taxation in income tax, see O Ostaszewska and B Obuoforibo (eds), *Roy Rohatgi on International Taxation – Volume 1: Principles* (The Netherlands, International Bureau of Fiscal Documentation 2018) ch 2.

[25] VAT treaties were considered unnecessary for these reasons by some scholars. See BJ Arnold et al, 'Summary of the Proceedings of An Invitational Seminar on Tax Treaties in 21st Century' (2002) 50 *Canadian Tax Journal* 65.

[26] OECD, Model Tax Convention on Income and Capital (2017) Article 27.

The treaty would address the concerns with the unilateral measures. It has the advantage of reducing compliance costs for exporters because exporters would only deal with their local tax administrations, without having to register and file tax returns in every country where they have customers.[27] This would reduce the tax barriers to cross-border trade, in particular for small businesses, created by the unilateral measures. Removing cross-border tax barriers complements domestic measures governments have been taking to stimulate economic activities in response to the economic downturn resulting from COVID-19 restrictions.

The treaty arrangements would also render more effective collection of VAT on online sales of goods and services. The proposed treaty requires closer cooperation in terms of mutual assistance than in the income tax treaties. The proposed VAT treaty would make it automatically obligatory for states to collect the current tax applied to certain supplies by other countries. An obstacle to the proposed cooperative regime could be that countries, in particular developed countries equipped with strong tax administrations, may be reluctant to rely on foreign tax administrations for the collection of their own taxes due to the disparities in administrative capacities. However, current unilateral measures that rely on voluntary registration by foreign business suppliers for the collection of VAT could be far less effective than the collection by even weak tax administrations.

Although double taxation is less of a problem in the VAT than in the income tax, it may arise in the VAT in two circumstances. First, although nearly all countries agree that the VAT on cross-border transactions should be allocated to the country where consumption takes place,[28] countries may have different views on the place of consumption. When this happens, a transaction may be subject to tax in two countries if they both regard themselves as the place of consumption.[29] Secondly, over-taxation may also arise where foreign registered businesses incur business expenses in a country if the vendor's country does not accept credit claims by foreign registered businesses and the buyer's country does not provide credits for the VAT paid to foreign suppliers.[30]

While these problems have long been identified, responses have not gone any further from general principles and soft law guidelines developed by the OECD.[31] Nevertheless, the OECD is aware that the guidelines and a common understanding of principles are not sufficient in resolving double taxation, given that countries inevitably interpret

[27] The EU estimated that its one-stop-shop regime, known as MOSS, has saved about 95% of the compliance costs for businesses annually compared with the unilateral scheme that requires foreign suppliers to register. See European Commission, 'Commission Staff Working Document Impact Assessment (Accompanying the document: Proposals for a Council Directive, a Council Implementing Regulation and a Council Regulation on Modernising VAT for cross-border B2C e-Commerce' COM(2016) 757 final; SWD(2016) 382 final, eur-lex.europa.eu/legal-content/EN/TXT/PDF/?uri=CELEX:52016SC0379&from=EN.

[28] An exception to the rule is China where exports are not taxed in accordance with the destination principle. See Y Zu, 'China's VAT on Exports: The Glacial Shift from a Heavy hand to the Invisible Hand' (2017) 88 *Tax Notes International* 767.

[29] Hypothetical examples of conflict in cross-border VAT rules can be found in R Millar, 'Cross-Border Services – A Survey of the Issues' in R Krever and D White (eds), *GST in Retrospect and Prospect* (Wellington, Thomson Brookers, 2007).

[30] OECD, 'VAT/GST Relief for Foreign Businesses: The State of Play – A Business and Government Survey' (February 2010), available at www.oecd.org/tax/consumption/44560750.pdf.

[31] See eg A Charlet and S Buydens, 'The OECD International VAT/GST Guidelines: Past and Future Developments' (2012) 1 *World Journal of VAT/GST Law* 175.

concepts differently, and a dispute resolution mechanism would be necessary.[32] A VAT treaty appears to be a rational solution to the over-taxation problems, in addition to the problem of non-collection in the digital economy.[33]

Recent progress made within the EU on its one-stop-shop regime would contribute to the political acceptance of the proposed treaty, given that 27 Member States have already agreed on the treaty terms regarding administrative cooperation and would negotiate with non-EU countries as a single bloc. In recent years, the EU has recognised the necessity of international administrative cooperation in ensuring the effectiveness of its VAT laws. In 2018, it signed an agreement with Norway to strengthen administrative cooperation in preventing VAT fraud and assisting each other in the recovery of VAT claims.[34] The European Commission will propose negotiations of administrative cooperation agreements, similar to the EU's agreement with Norway, with other main EU trade partners to support the COVID-19 recovery strategy.[35] The EU initiatives clearly show the political willingness to enhance international VAT cooperation and will open the door to further cooperation in the form of the treaty model outlined in this chapter.

IV. Distributional Consequences

As in many other areas of cooperation, although it is in the interest of all countries to cooperate, the benefits of international tax cooperation are often not distributed evenly between states. The pandemic highlighted the necessity and urgency of providing assistance through international cooperation to developing countries that are worst affected. Therefore, the distributional consequences should be an important consideration in determining the desirability of cooperation in the post-COVID-19 era.[36] In addition, the distributional consequences have a significant impact on whether treaties take the form of bilateralism or multilateralism. The income tax treaty experience offers important lessons as regards distributional consequences.

A. Income Tax Treaties

The distributional consequences of income tax treaties primarily derive from the functions treaties perform in reducing double taxation. In this respect, income tax

[32] The OECD recognised the need for model-based VAT treaties in OECD, 'The Application of Consumption Taxes to the Trade in International Services and Intangibles: Progress Report and Draft Principles' (2004).

[33] NP Eriksen, 'Should Tax Treaties Play a Role for Consumption Taxes?' (2005) 33 *Intertax* 166. How a VAT treaty would address these problems is discussed in Y Zu, 'Developing VAT Treaties: International Tax Cooperation in Times of Global Recovery' (2022) 42(1) *Legal Studies* 159.

[34] Agreement between the European Union and the Kingdom of Norway on administrative cooperation, combating fraud and recovery of claims in the field of value added tax (2017).

[35] European Commission, 'An action plan for fair and simple taxation supporting the recovery strategy' (Communication) COM (2020) 312 final.

[36] Ozai called for consideration of distributive justice in international tax policymaking in the context of direct taxation. See, I Ozai, 'Two Accounts of International Tax Justice' (2020) 33(2) *Canadian Journal of Law & Jurisprudence* 317.

treaties present two distinct but intertwined features. First, the main function of income tax treaties is to directly allocate the taxing rights. Secondly, income tax treaties are bilaterally negotiated between each pair of countries. However, almost all the bilateral income tax treaties follow the pattern of the OECD model and define the limits of taxing rights in a largely uniform manner.[37]

i. Distributional Consequences

The primary objective of income tax treaties is to eliminate double taxation caused by overlapping tax claims by two countries based on source and residence. This objective is achieved by dividing taxing rights between two countries in treaties to establish exclusive rather than concurrent taxing rights. However, treaties allocate more taxing rights to residence countries than to source countries on a reciprocal basis. The OECD gives the residence country the exclusive right to tax royalties, as well as business income unless the income is earned through a permanent establishment in the source country. In addition, residence countries are given the primary right to tax dividends and interest.

A state can be a source country in one transaction and a residence country in another. If capital flows between two countries are more or less equal in both directions, the two countries have roughly equal chances to be source or residence countries. In this circumstance, the allocation bias towards residence taxation does not have apparent distributional consequences. However, if the capital flows are primarily one way, as is often the case between developed and developing countries, developing countries are almost always the source country.

The unequal distribution of taxing rights in treaties may not be a problem in itself. It only becomes a problem if the distributional effects give rise to unfairness. There seems to be an assumption that a flow of benefits from poor countries to rich countries is unfair. The question of fairness in cooperation, however, cannot be considered separately from the fairness of arrangements without cooperation. There is nevertheless a lack of consensus on the fair division of taxing rights over international income between countries, and developing countries and developed countries will inevitably have different views on fairness.[38] The difficulty has no doubt been compounded by the fact that a state's taxing rights based on both source and residence are accepted as legitimate by other countries. If redistribution is not an objective of the international tax system,[39] the baseline for assessing fairness is that all countries have equal right to impose tax on the basis of source and residence. Evaluated against this baseline, income tax treaties create an allocation bias that leads to unfair distribution of taxing rights in favour of developed countries, more seriously restricting the ability of poorer countries to develop their national tax policy to raise the desired revenue.

[37] F Mann, 'The Doctrine of Jurisdiction in International Law' (1964-I) Hague Recueil, 109.

[38] K Brooks, 'Inter-Nation Equity: The Development of an Important but Underappreciated International Tax Policy Objective' in JG Head and R Krever (eds), *Tax Reform in the 21st Century* (The Netherlands, Kluwer Law International, 2009); and M Devereux et al, *Taxing Profits in a Global Economy* (Oxford, Oxford University Press, 2021).

[39] J Stark, 'Tax Justice Beyond National Borders – International or Interpersonal?' (2021) 42 *Oxford Journal of Legal Studies* 133.

The unfair distribution of taxing rights will likely result in unfair distribution of tax revenue, creating 'anomaly of aid in reverse – from poor to rich countries'.[40] But this is not necessarily the case, because the revenue gain or loss depends not only on the restrictions on taxing rights, but also on the changes of capital flows as a result of the treaty, among other factors.[41]

The necessity of tax treaties has increasingly been questioned because of the distributional bias.[42] Concerns over the distributional consequences have prompted tax scholars and international organisations to advise developing countries to be cautious about entering into treaty negotiations with developed countries.[43] In fact, most developed countries have adopted the unilateral approach in their domestic laws that gives the source country the primary taxing right, leaving the residence country only a residual taxing right where its tax rate is higher than that in the source country. It is often argued that both unilateral and bilateral approaches resolve double taxation by dividing the taxing rights between source and residence countries and the main difference between the two approaches is distributional consequences, with the unilateral approach favouring source countries and the bilateral approach favouring residence countries.[44] From a bargaining perspective, developing countries would lose taxing rights even if tax treaties divide taxing rights equally between source and residence countries. The unfair distributional consequences make it more difficult to justify the desirability of income tax treaties, especially if the main objective of treaties can be achieved unilaterally.

ii. Bilateralism vs Multilateralism

The distributional consequences are a main factor that determines whether tax treaties are bilateral or multilateral. Multilateral agreements in other areas of law are not uncommon, in particular trade policy that is also a key area of a country's economic interest.[45] In the field of taxation, multilateral treaties are often developed in the issue areas concerning tax administration. An example is the Convention on Mutual Assistance in Tax Matters. However, income tax treaties are historically bilateral.

Bilateralism of tax treaties is a result of states jealously guarding their tax sovereignty.[46] Although income tax treaties perform functions in terms of both allocation of taxing rights and administrative cooperation, treaty responses to administrative issues, such as information exchange and assistance in the collection of tax debts, are relatively

[40] CR Irish, 'International Double Taxation Agreements and Income Taxation at Source' (1974) 23 *International and Comparative Law Quarterly* 292.

[41] EM Zolt, 'Tax Treaties and Developing Countries' (2018) 72 *Tax Law Review* 111. Empirical studies show mixed results of the impact of tax treaties on foreign direct investment. See T Dagan, *International Tax Policy: Between Competition and Cooperation* (Cambridge, Cambridge University Press, 2018).

[42] See eg A Eason, 'Do We Still Need Tax Treaties?' (2000) *Tax Treaty Monitor* 619.

[43] See eg International Monetary Fund, 'Spillovers in International Corporate Taxation' (2014) IMF Policy Paper.

[44] K Brooks and R Krever, 'The Troubling Role of Tax Treaties' in V Thurinyi and G Michielse (eds), *Tax Design Issues Worldwide* (The Netherlands, Kluwer Law International, 2015).

[45] An example is the General Agreement on Tariffs and Trade.

[46] BJ Arnold et al (n 25) 94.

distributionally neutral and are consequently less contentious. With respect to allocation of taxing rights, however, the distributional bias in tax treaties can hardly achieve the international consensus necessary for a multilateral treaty. Experience with bilateral income tax treaties and multilateral administrative cooperation treaties suggests that it is the concern over distributional consequences resulting from an allocation of taxing rights that makes a multilateral income tax treaty unachievable.

Another distinct feature of income tax treaties is that almost all the bilateral treaties follow the same principles of allocating taxing rights enshrined in the OECD model. Although the initial purpose of the model was to serve as a manual that reduces the transaction costs that would otherwise incur in bilateral negotiations, the model itself is a product of multilateral negotiation between OECD members. The model is regarded as 'a template for a multilateral web of treaties', with its influence reaching far beyond the OECD countries.[47]

Income tax treaties thus contain elements of both bilateralism and multilateralism.[48] While the key allocation principles were multilaterally negotiated by the OECD members and followed in virtually all treaties, modifications based on these principles suited to specific political and economic circumstances between each pair of treaty partners were negotiated bilaterally. Bilateral treaties are perceived to be a better instrument to preserve tax sovereignty. However, pure bilateral negotiations would inevitably lead to high transactions costs. Bilateral treaties based on a common model are therefore a middle ground that achieves the benefits of cooperation while preserving a degree of flexibility for differentiated negotiations with different treaty partners.

B. VAT Treaties

Two important issues that need to be considered for the adoption of a VAT treaty are its distributional consequences and whether bilateral treaties or a multilateral treaty would be the preferred option. Because the proposed VAT treaty requires closer administrative cooperation than in the income tax treaties, it can be expected that the VAT treaty would not be distributional neutral.

Similar to the distributional problems in bilateral income tax treaties, VAT treaties that assign rights and duties on a reciprocal basis would have unequal distributional consequences once trade flows and administrative capacities are taken into account. If outflows and inflows between two countries were roughly the same, the two treaty partners would have similar incentives to collect the foreign tax. Any significant imbalance inflows between the two parties could lead to uneven distribution of obligations or administrative costs. Moreover, asymmetries in administrative capacities may have a more direct impact on revenue yields, with countries that have strong administrative capacity collecting a larger proportion of foreign VAT due. An important lesson of the income tax treaty experience is that where the distributional consequences of treaties

[47] JFA Jones, 'The David R Tillinghast Lecture: Are Tax Treaties Necessary?' (1999) 53 *Tax Law Review* 1.

[48] T Rixen, 'Bilateralism or Multilateralism? The Political Economy of Avoiding International Double Taxation' (2010) 16 *European Journal of International Relations* 589.

are non-neutral, the international consensus needed for a multilateral treaty is more difficult to achieve. Therefore, a realistic starting point for international VAT cooperation would be the adoption of bilateral treaties.

Although the proposed VAT treaty would also lead to distributional bias, the distributional consequences are nevertheless desirable. Contrary to the direction of flow of benefits in income tax treaties, VAT treaties between developed and developing countries may attribute larger benefits to developing countries. The continued growth of consumer demand for cross-border B2C sales driven by rising incomes in the developing world creates new opportunities for e-commerce market players in developed countries. However, weaker administrative capacity in developing countries places constraints on their ability to capture cross-border sales. VAT treaties would enable developing countries to piggy-back off the administrative capacity of countries selling into their territories while increasing the competitiveness of their domestic exporters.

The benefits that would accrue to developing countries should be seen as a counterbalance to the unfair distributional consequences of income tax treaties. The VAT treaty provisions could be incorporated into the existing income tax treaties to increase the desirability of international tax cooperation, although the VAT treaty may not completely offset the negative distributional consequences of the income tax treaty. Building VAT treaties into income tax treaties would also strengthen developing countries' bargaining positions in negotiating VAT treaties, since they have already made greater compromises in the income tax treaties. The current COVID-19 crisis may provide a unique opportunity for overcoming political hurdles and achieving international agreements, with governments emerging from the pandemic with high levels of debts and looking for new revenue sources.[49]

The income tax treaty experience shows that efficient bilateral negotiations should be accompanied by a model treaty to reduce the transaction costs. The OECD is well-placed to develop the VAT treaty model given its leading role in formulating international tax rules and expertise in developing the income tax treaty model. However, it has been observed that although the existing OECD guidelines in relation to VAT cross-border issues are relevant to developing countries, part of the guidelines may not be achievable in developing countries because of their weaker administrative capacity.[50] The OECD should take into account the administrative constraints in developing countries when developing the VAT model and provide technical support to developing countries to enhance implementation of treaty measures.

The development of VAT treaties could form part of the wider coordinated actions in response to the COVID-19 crisis. The pandemic has exposed inequalities and divisions between countries and the pandemic itself is likely to further increase the disparities. Although almost all countries are severely affected by the pandemic, the economic impact of COVID-19 and the ability to respond to the crisis vary substantially

[49] A similar argument is made by Grisostolo and Scarcella in the context of EU integration in ch 10 of this volume.

[50] K James and T Ecker, 'Relevance of the OECD International VAT/GST Guidelines for Non-OECD Countries' (2017) 32 *Australian Tax Forum* 317.

across social groups and countries at different levels of development. Developing countries facing the challenges with weaker healthcare systems, limited resources and less flexibility for fiscal and monetary policy are being hit the worst and recovery is expected to take longer in these countries. International organisations have emphasised the importance of providing special support to developing countries in light of the interconnectedness and interdependence of territorial states revealed by the pandemic.[51] While direct financial support is no doubt an important instrument to deliver immediate support to developing countries, tax capacity building remains the only long-term solution for sustainable recovery in these economies.[52] The proposed VAT treaty would address the common challenges in the VAT faced by all countries, while providing administrative assistance to support developing countries to grow their tax base.

V. Conclusion

The COVID-19 pandemic poses significant challenges on tax policy development and tax administrations in all countries. But it also opens up a unique opportunity for the international community to address the existing drawbacks in the tax system and fashion a more equitable and efficient international tax system that better serves the interests of all countries.

The pandemic has exacerbated the challenges countries face in taxing cross-border digital supplies and low-value goods under the VAT. Although many countries have adopted unilateral measures to address the issues, international cooperation by way of treaties that requires closer cooperation over mutual assistance in the collection of taxes modelled on the one-stop-shop mechanism currently used in the EU has the potential of providing more effective solutions.

In addition to the need to address common challenges faced by all countries, the pandemic made the case for strengthening international cooperation in areas where assistance to developing countries can be provided. Taxation is a key area for support because of its crucial role in paying off the debts and financing economic recovery. The existing income tax treaties, however, distribute more benefits from cooperation to developed countries than to developing countries. In contrast, the proposed VAT treaties favour developing countries, leading to normatively attractive distributional consequences. These attractive distributional consequences would be worth pursuing in their own right, and *a fortiori* as a corrective to the unappealing distributional consequences that the income tax treaties generate.

The income tax treaty experience shows that where the distributional consequences are non-neutral, bilateral treaties are politically easier to achieve than a multilateral treaty. A model treaty is nevertheless needed to facilitate bilateral negotiations. Therefore, the proposed VAT treaties should follow the path of income tax treaties and

[51] See eg OECD, 'Tax and Fiscal Policy in Response to the Coronavirus Crisis: Strengthening Confidence and Resilience' (19 May 2020).

[52] V Gaspar et al, 'Facing the Crisis: the Role of Tax in Dealing with COVID-19' (Flatform for Collaboration on Tax, 16 June 2020) www.tax-platform.org/news/blogs/facing-crisis-role-tax-dealing-with-covid-19.

take the form of bilateral treaties based on a common model. The potential political resistance from developed countries as a result of the distributional bias may be reduced by incorporating the VAT provisions into the existing income tax treaties. The need to raise revenue in all countries in the wake of the pandemic could provide new impetus for overcoming political hurdles and reaching agreements internationally.

12

In Good Times and in Bad: Global Tax Governance During Economic Downturns

NATALIA PUSHKAREVA

Abstract

This chapter investigates the effects that recent economic crises of 2008 and 2020 had on international tax policymaking in terms of both policy priorities and mechanisms of international tax policymaking in general, and assesses the progress made in the tax policy response to economic downturns over the past two decades.

The author analyses how events of 2007–08 and 2020 affected long-term trends in the architecture of international tax policymaking, and, hence, the policies produced by main international economic policy institutions. Having investigated the reaction of main actors of international tax policymaking to the two main economic downturns of the last 20 years, the author argues that global crises should be seen not only as a call for urgent patching holes in national budgets with quick – and thus temporary – solutions, but also as an opportunity for carrying out more fundamental, structural reforms of international tax policymaking that would lead to a more inclusive design of international policy fora, more equitable and just international tax policies, enhanced sustainable economic development and reduced global economic inequality.

I. Introduction

> After decades of directing global economic policy standards alone, the US and Europe publicly extended leadership power to some developing countries in response to the economic crisis … But an entrenched international architecture of tax policy expertise ensures that a small group of established players continue to shape tax norms and practices throughout the world.[1]

[1] A Christians, 'Taxation in a Time of Crisis: Policy Leadership from the OECD to the G-20' (2010) 5 *Northwestern Journal of Law & Social Policy* 19.

To someone familiar with the international tax agenda of recent years this passage might seem like a recent quote from a business newspaper. However, it was written over a decade ago, in the aftermath of the 2007–08 financial crisis, by Allison Christians, then an Assistant Professor at University of Wisconsin Law School and now an Associate Dean of Research and an H Heward Stikeman Chair in Tax Law at McGill University. In 2009 Professor Christians authored an article entitled 'Taxation in a Time of Crisis: Policy Leadership from the OECD to the G-20' which analysed the changes in international tax agenda and architecture of international economic policy institutions that followed the events of 2007–08.

The study demonstrated how various global policy fora responded to the crisis in terms of tax policy measures, and discussed the shift of leadership from the OECD, then an elite and impervious institution, to a more inclusive G20 which had the potential to voice developing countries'[2] positions. It also discussed the global tax agenda in the years following the crisis being dominated by issues disproportionately benefiting developed economies, such as fighting tax havens, which were not necessarily a priority for lower-income countries.

In the wake of the 2020 pandemic-induced crisis, we have not observed radical changes in tax policy responses of leading international economic policy institutions compared to the crisis of 2007–08. Fighting (non-European) tax havens is still high on the tax policy agenda, institutions are still 'reaching for a low-hanging fruit', ie most politically convenient solutions, and we are still experiencing issues with proper representation of developing economies' interests notwithstanding the progress made in this area. This chapter discusses the changes in tax policy priorities and institutional economic policy leadership during the 2007–08 and 2020 crises, and is structured as follows:

- first, it summarises tax policy responses to the 2007–08 financial crisis and corresponding institutional architecture of tax policymaking;
- second, it summarises tax policy responses to the 2020 economic crisis and related powershifts in economic policy institutions; and
- finally, the chapter assesses the progress made over the past two decades in the way international organisations working on tax respond to economic downturns, as well as the impact the crises have on the dynamics of international tax policymaking.

II. The 2007–08 Crisis

Professor Christian's article provided an excellent coverage of global tax policy responses to the 2007–08 financial crisis as well as corresponding power shifts between international economic policy institutions active in the tax policy field.

[2] Even though the World Bank moved away from using the term 'developing country' some time ago (see blogs.worldbank.org/opendata/should-we-continue-use-term-developing-world for details), it is still widely used by development professionals. While the term is indeed incapable of reflecting the differences between lower-income countries and the variety of the challenges they are facing, for the purposes of this chapter it refers to a group of countries that fare relatively and similarly poorly in social and economic measures.

A. Institutions

The first change brought about by the 2008 crisis and highlighted by Professor Christians is an increasingly important role of the G20 in the international tax debate and policy setting. Unlike the OECD, at that time a union of the world's 30 wealthiest economies, the G20 was positioned as 'an international network of finance ministers and central bankers from eleven developed countries and eight less-developed countries, plus representatives from the European Union, the International Monetary Fund, and the World Bank'.[3] An increasing weight of the G20 in international tax debates as a more inclusive and less traditional and elite institution promised wider inclusion of developing jurisdictions in international tax policy crafting and the OECD sharing its almost exclusive international tax policymaking power with previously discriminated groups. As Professor Christians put it, 'By focusing on the G20 as the appropriate forum for articulating global economic policy, the economic crisis highlighted the importance of inclusion in global tax dialogue for previously marginalised states and peoples'.[4]

However, even though the role of the G20 in the international tax debate did indeed increase in the aftermath of the crisis, it did not really end the US and Europe's dominance over the international tax policy agenda within the OECD 'virtually impervious institutional architecture'.[5] As Professor Christians notes, 'despite the specter of the G20 as a 'new model of multilateral engagement',[6] the US and Europe continue to dominate a virtually impervious institutional architecture of tax policymaking in the form of the Organisation for Economic Cooperation and Development'.[7] And sill, the emergence of the G20 provided an opportunity to use the group's more inclusive and flexible architecture to voice concerns of developing countries more effectively. 'As a result, – prof. Christians concludes, – financial crisis may have elevated developing countries to a more prominent policy leadership position in the G20, but G20 leadership may not provide developing countries with a meaningful voice in global tax policy dialogue … Even so, the rising prominence of the G20 signals that creating opportunities for developing countries to have such a voice is a priority, whether during a time of crisis or beyond'.[8]

B. Tax Policy Response

Just like any other crisis, the financial crisis of 2007–08 resulted in a dramatic increase of public expenditure, as well as a sharp decrease in revenues collected in many countries around the world due to rising unemployment, reduced spending and businesses shutting down. Revenue generation required new ideas.

[3] Christians (n 1).
[4] ibid.
[5] ibid.
[6] The expression is borrowed from President Thabo Mbeki's 2007 Address of the President of South Africa at the G20 Finance Ministerial Conference, Kleinmond, Western Cape.
[7] Christians (n 1).
[8] ibid.

The main focus of the international tax policy community in the aftermath of the 2007–08 financial crisis shifted to addressing the problem of tax havens, an issue with no direct connection to the crisis, no simple or immediate solution and incapable of generating the required amount of revenue even in the most optimistic scenario. The OECD has been working on the issues related to tax havens for a long time, and the economic distress and uncertainty associated with the crisis presented a convenient political momentum for concentrating the attention of the international community on jurisdictions refusing to cooperate (according to OECD standards, at least).

Increasing top rates of personal income tax was another broadly discussed tax policy response to the crisis, with many countries around the world starting to tax the rich more heavily.[9]

III. The 2020 Crisis

A. Institutions

Thirteen years and a major global crisis later, it seems like the OECD only strengthened its position as the market leader in developing tax standards and guidelines. While the G20 seemed to act as the main tax standard-setting body and an agent of inclusivity in tax policymaking after the 2007–08 crisis, in recent years we witnessed the unfolding of a much more widescale initiative, namely the OECD Inclusive Framework.

After receiving significant criticism for lack of inclusivity, in 2016 the OECD launched an Inclusive Framework on BEPS which grew from initial 82 Member States to the impressive 140 members it has today. The Framework gave a seat at the negotiating table not only to developed, but also to developing jurisdictions, positioning itself as representing all its members 'on an equal footing'. But does it really live up to this promise?

Academic articles, policy reports, interviews of tax policy professionals and press publications provide us with convincing proof that the OECD and its Member States are facing difficulties in making the organisation and its BEPS Inclusive Framework truly multilateral. Key problems were brilliantly covered by Rasmus Corlin Christensen, Martin Hearson and Tovony Randriamanalina in their 2020 paper 'At the Table, Off the Menu? Assessing the Participation of Lower-Income Countries in Global Tax Negotiations'.[10] To summarise, participating in OECD meetings is still much more expensive and less convenient for lower-income jurisdictions, as they are facing both financial and operational constrains. Most importantly, Plenary meetings which are mainly attended by developing countries' representatives, mostly approve

[9] J Limberg, '"Tax the rich"? The financial crisis, fiscal fairness, and progressive income taxation' (2019) 11(3) *European Political Science Review* 319–36.

[10] R Corlin Christensen, M Hearson and T Randriamanalina, 'At the Table, Off the Menu? Assessing the Participation of Lower-Income Countries in Global Tax Negotiations' (2020) *ICTD Working Paper* 115, www.ictd.ac/publication/at-table-off-menu-assessing-participation-lower-income-countries-global-tax-negotiations/.

'ready-made' policies designed earlier by Steering Group and Working Parties. Plenary itself rarely presents participants with an opportunity to affect policy design – policies that make it to this stage are effectively already 'pre-approved' and are very likely to be adopted as they are. By contrast, according to the OECD the data attendance rate for Steering Group meetings is 50 per cent for OECD Member States while the corresponding number for lower-income countries is only 12.5 per cent. For Working Parties, where most of the technical work regarding shaping tax policies takes place, such numbers are 77.4 per cent vs 5.4 per cent for developed and lower-income countries respectively.[11] It is hard to imagine equal involvement of OECD Member States and lower-income jurisdictions in a conversation about the global tax standards when in most cases developing countries are not even present.

Thus, a formal – impressive – increase in a number of Inclusive Framework members did not quite translate into their effective inclusion in policymaking and a quality change in policy design mechanisms that would take developing countries' interests into account. The lower-income economies were given a seat at the table, but that did not appear to be enough to effectively include them in agenda-setting and decision-making processes. Doing so will take time and require significant effort as well as organisational – and cultural – changes. Many developing jurisdictions expressed their concerns about OECD inclusiveness as well as their position within the Inclusive Framework, and suggested the UN as a platform whose institutional design is more suitable for leading the international tax debate. However, due to lack of resources and political will from developed countries, such a shift seems unlikely.

Outside of the OECD, the last couple of years also saw an increase in the importance of regional policy for a such as ATAF, African Tax Administration Forum, which plays a vital role in forming and voicing tax policy positions of African countries, and European Parliament's Tax (FISC) Committee, set up to deal with tax-related matters and to discuss the role of the EU in fighting tax fraud, tax evasion and tax avoidance.

Notwithstanding all the efforts to give a voice to developing countries and include them in global tax policymaking, it is often presented in news as if de facto most important decisions are still made by the G7 and communicated 'top-down'. For example, in June 2021 the 'G7 Finance Ministers Agreed Historic Global Tax Agreement'[12] on the global minimal tax of at least 15 per cent and reallocation of taxing rights for the most profitable multinationals towards market jurisdictions. While both the novelty of these ideas and G7's role in making both decisions are somewhat questionable, to the wider audience they are presented as 'historic' and 'global', with the G7 getting all the credit for the work that was in reality done by the G20 and the Inclusive Framework[13] and which still disproportionately benefits developed economies.[14]

[11] ibid.

[12] 'G7 Finance Ministers Agree Historic Global Tax Agreement' (HM Treasury website, 5 June 2021) www.gov.uk/government/news/g7-finance-ministers-agree-historic-global-tax-agreement.

[13] R Corlin Christensen, 'The G7 tax deal: 'historic' and 'global'?' (*International Centre for Tax and Development's blog*, 7 June 2021) www.ictd.ac/blog/g7-tax-deal-historic-global/.

[14] The G20, eg, received criticism for not being active enough in opposing the 'G7 deal' that will disproportionately benefit the rich countries. For details, see: A Cobham, 'G20 could improve on 'one-sided' global tax reform' *Financial Times*, (London, 12 June 2021) www.ft.com/content/2aa756fd-ec1d-4127-891e-b8873da022af.

The institutional shift in tax policymaking towards more inclusive structures, as well as their contribution to policies implemented, remains to be recognised.

B. Tax Policy Response

The multiple crises of 2020, but especially the health crisis associated with the global COVID-19 pandemic, were truly shocking for many, if not all, countries. Even though the economic consequences of the 2020 pandemic ended up being not as catastrophic as expected by some economists initially, it still resulted in significant economic distress for the majority of nations. Tax policy has proven to be one of the most important and effective tools used to support the post-COVID-19 recovery.

Notwithstanding the 13 years between the 2007–08 and the 2020 crises and very different reasons behind them, it is quite surprising how similar policy responses of the international tax community to the two major economic downturns have been. Tax havens and taxing the rich have been high on the global international tax agenda in 2020, just like in 2009. In addition, using the crisis as an opportunity to implement more sustainable, greener fiscal policies has been encouraged. Below I discuss whether these focus areas were the best choice.

IV. What Matters in Times of Crisis?

The two crises considered in this chapter had very different causes: the global financial crises of 2007–08 were associated with undercapitalisation of the banking and insurance systems, while the 2020 crisis was caused by the spread of COVID-19. In 2007–08, a big part of government liability arose as a result of bailing out the financial sector which found itself dangerously undercapitalised, which resulted in a situation where the risks were 'socialised' but the benefits were 'privatised'. As a response to the problem, many governments around the world have been increasing the burden of taxation on the financial sector whilst requiring capital levels to fully take account of risks undertaken by those institutions. It can be argued that the crisis stemmed from the government deciding to socialise risk as opposed to allowing creditors to bear the brunt of their decisions to expose themselves to the risk. The 2020 crisis, however, was induced by a global health emergency and restrictions that followed and significantly changed behaviours of both producers and consumers in most economies around the world. However, when it comes to defining global tax policy priorities in times of economic distress, we seem to mostly stick to a familiar algorithm, and our tax policy response to a crisis hasn't changed that much in the past 13 years.

A. Tax Havens

In 2008 tax havens were a major focus of the international tax policy community, and addressing the issue of non-cooperative jurisdictions lowering their tax rates and refusing to participate in tax information exchange was seen as one of the most important components of the tax policy response to the global financial crisis. In the following years the OECD Global Forum on Transparency and Exchange of Information for Tax Purposes has been working hard on improving tax information exchange between countries, and the OECD implemented the BEPS[15] project aiming to prevent base erosion and profit shifting, including to tax havens. When the pandemic happened in 2020, many suggested 'drying out the tax havens' as a response.[16] However, focusing on tax havens in times of economic recovery might not be the best policy choice for several reasons.

i. Unclear Revenue Potential

The full elimination of tax havens is quite unlikely as some countries receive significant benefits from non-cooperation and currently have no stimulus to change their behaviour. That triggers a collective action problem: the existence of non-cooperating jurisdictions reduces potential gains from cooperation for all other countries, and while the costs of cooperation will still incur, significant value from it will be lost. In any case, addressing such a complex issue will take time and it is unlikely that significant revenues will be generated immediately. The revenue potential of tax havens elimination is unclear, and most likely the developed nations, which are residence jurisdictions for the majority of high-net-worth individuals and home to the headquarters of many multinational corporations, will end up being the net beneficiaries of tax havens elimination. Whether it will be beneficial for all, or at least the majority of, developing economies, is unclear.

It seems like tax haven-related measures were chosen as an anti-crisis tax policy first response not due to their connection to the crises' causes or the potential to generate the revenues required to support the post-crisis recovery, but rather because tax havens are a politically convenient target, and in times of economic distress and rising inequality concealing significant amounts of wealth seems especially unfair. However, given how limited our practical opportunities to tackle the issue are at the moment, how much time and effort spent doing so will require and the uncertain amount of revenue that elimination of tax havens might generate, placing such a strong focus on the issue might be not optimal.

While the desire to protect national tax bases is understandable, making lists of countries not complying with OECD requirements and minimal standards might not be the way to do it. Other measures, such as enhancing the capacity of relevant home institutions, improving compliance with domestic tax legislation or addressing a problem of informality in the case of developing countries might be much more effective and have cumulative, lasting effects helping countries to stabilise their financial systems and achieve fiscal independence.

[15] Base Erosion and Profit Shifting.

[16] D Carden, 'To Pay for the Pandemic, Dry Out the Tax Havens' (*Foreign Policy blog*, 16 July 2020) foreignpolicy.com/2020/07/16/tax-havens-apple-costs-pandemic/.

ii. Tax Havens Lists are Ineffective and Fail to Include EU Tax Havens

EU losses due to tax evasion – ie the illegal reduction of tax bills by both corporations and individuals – are estimated at about EUR 170 bn annually.[17] In 2017, after a formal completion of the OECD BEPS project aiming to stop base erosion and profit shifting, the Council of the European Union introduced its first 'EU list of non-cooperative jurisdictions' which included 17 countries and territories in a hope to change their harmful tax behaviours.[18]

According to the Council's website, the list aims to tackle issues such as:

- tax fraud or evasion: illegal non-payment or under payment of tax;
- tax avoidance: use of legal means to minimise tax liability;
- money laundering: concealment of origins of illegally obtained money.

The European Council claims that the EU 'promotes tax good governance ***worldwide***', but it also admits that the list aims to address ***external*** challenges to *EU countries' tax bases*, and highlights that the list names exclusively ***non-EU jurisdictions*** that 'encourage abusive tax practices which erode ***member states'*** corporate tax revenues'.[19] The main parameters of the tax system that are being assessed to make a decision whether it should be listed as a 'non-cooperative jurisdiction' or not, are:

- transparency of taxation;
- fair taxation; and
- implementation of anti-base erosion and profit shifting measures.

As of February 2021, when the latest version of the list was published, the list included the following 12 countries and territories which were named as non-cooperative on tax matters by the EU:

- American Samoa;
- Anguilla;
- Dominica;
- Fiji;
- Guam;
- Palau;
- Panama;
- Samoa;
- Trinidad and Tobago;

[17] Tax Solidarity, 'How do tax havens work?' (*TaxSolidarityEU*, 10 January 2021) taxsolidarity.eu/how-tax-havens-work, 2.

[18] Website of European Council, Council of the European Union, 'Taxation: EU list of non-cooperative jurisdictions' (*European Council of the European Union* (4 March 2021) www.consilium.europa.eu/en/policies/eu-list-of-non-cooperative-jurisdictions/.

[19] ibid.

- US Virgin Islands;
- Vanuatu;
- Seychelles.

If some jurisdictions on the list like Panama or Seychelles are traditionally associated with tax avoidance, other countries on the list might seem quite surprising. Many would expect it to include countries like Luxembourg, Ireland or Switzerland rather than Anguilla, Samoa or Palau. However, as mentioned above, the purpose of the EU list of non-cooperative jurisdictions is to protect the *European* tax base, and the countries included are those which the EU sees as negatively affecting effective taxation within the Union. But do European countries comply with the tax standards of effective taxation and cooperation on tax matters themselves?

One of the most comprehensive independent tax havens lists is the Corporate Tax Haven Index composed by the Tax Justice Network (TJN).[20] According to TJN, 'The Corporate Tax Haven Index thoroughly evaluates each jurisdiction's tax and financial systems to create a clear picture of the world's greatest enablers of global corporate tax abuse, and to highlight the laws and policies that policymakers can amend to reduce their jurisdiction's enabling of corporate tax abuse'.[21]

The Index assigned every jurisdiction a Corporate Tax Haven Index value, which is a combination of the country's Haven Score, an indicator assessing to what degree the country can be seen as a tax haven and a facilitator of corporate tax avoidance, and a Global Scale Weight which assesses the proportion of all financial activities of multinational corporations that take place in that particular jurisdiction. Thus, 'combining a jurisdiction's Haven Score and Global Scale Weight gives a picture of how much of the world's corporate financial activity is put at risk of corporate tax abuse by the jurisdiction'.[22]

The top ten countries of the 2021 Index which are recognised as enablers of corporate tax avoidance are not small unknown jurisdictions, but rather:

- British Virgin Islands;
- Cayman Islands;
- Bermuda;
- Netherlands;
- Switzerland;
- Luxembourg;
- Hong Kong;
- Jersey;
- Singapore; and
- United Arab Emirates,

[20] Tax Justice Network, 'Corporate Tax Haven Index – 2021 Results' (*Corporate Tax Havens Index*, 9 March 2021) cthi.taxjustice.net/en/.

[21] ibid.

[22] ibid. More information on methodology can be found at cthi.taxjustice.net/en/how-index-works.

which are followed by Ireland which is a close number 11. As can be seen, some European countries were included in the list of top 10 tax havens in the world and are well known for facilitating tax avoidance, while others might come as a surprise, like Belgium, Germany, Hungary, Spain, Sweden and Italy which all made it to the top 30. Being harsh to non-cooperating 'outsiders', the EU seems to fail to take responsibility for harmful behaviour of its own Member States. Even in times of crises, economic policy institutions biased towards protecting the financial interests of large, industrialised economies require other nations to give up the benefits associated with low tax rates and non-cooperation, while not being ready to change their own harmful practices.

iii. Undesirable Effects on Developing Countries

The practical impact of tax havens blacklists is not easy to estimate. While initially the 'naming and shaming' strategy did manage to draw additional attention to the problem – or rather to the part of the problem that is located outside of EU borders as the only list officially discussed and acted upon is the EU one – today its impact is far from clear, after it received massive criticism for lack of objectivity and serving the private interests of EU Member States.[23]

The existing model of listing tax havens can be especially damaging for small, land-locked emerging economies which are especially vulnerable and often prone to additional political and economic problems. The blacklists, especially the tax havens list compiled by the EU, are widely used by different users including, among others, international organisations when they decide if they would like to provide aid, businesses looking to expand overseas, donors who are considering investing in the country and would like to know what to expect, etc. Thus, blacklisting lower-income jurisdictions, especially small and/or land-locked developing states and territories, can lead to harmful, disproportionately harsh consequences. When Tunisia, the smallest country in North Africa, was put on the EU blacklist, for example, many businesses started withdrawing investments from the country[24] as it was not seen as transparent, fair in terms of taxation and, most of all, compliant with the BEPS measures and OECD minimum standards, some of which are quite expensive to implement for a low-income jurisdiction experiencing multiple internal struggles. As the EU list comes from the European Union and is approved by the European Council, EU Member States are not included in the list, while at different periods of time countries like Zimbabwe, Namibia and Tunisia, which can hardly be recognised as significant facilitators of tax avoidance, were blacklisted. Quite often such territories simply do not have the resources to comply with EU/OECD requirements. This imbalance in power between post-industrial countries enjoying control over the main tax havens list while also being responsible for enabling a huge proportion of global tax avoidance

[23] See, for instance, M Collin, 'Did the EU's attempt to name and shame tax havens into behaving better work?' (*Brookings Institution blog*, 25 June 2020) www.brookings.edu/blog/up-front/2020/06/25/did-the-eus-attempt-to-name-and-shame-tax-havens-into-behaving-better-work/.

[24] F Aliriza, 'In Tunisia, many see EU tax haven blacklisting as political move' (*Middle East Eye*, 14 December 2017) www.middleeasteye.net/news/tunisia-many-see-eu-tax-haven-blacklisting-political-move.

and developing jurisdictions having no control over who makes it to the list but being pressured to implement expensive measures that are not even always in their best interest, is deeply concerning.

While some believe tax havens blacklists have some positive impact on countries' willingness to cooperate on tax matters, technically there are no enforceable sanctions for being blacklisted as the undesirable behaviours in question are in fact legal, and the rules involved are standards rather than legal requirements. While in international trade, for example, unacceptable practices can be clearly defined, doing so regarding harmful tax practices presents a real challenge. Tax avoidance and evasion techniques are significantly more complex and technical, information on tax minimisation strategies of corporations and individuals is hard to access, and many such cases require individual consideration. However, more certainty on what tax policies and strategies are seen as harmful is needed, as well as a real commitment from the international community to address the issue, including the part of it caused by developed countries' actions.

iv. A Way Forward

What is clear now is that in their current design blacklists of tax havens are highly arbitrary, and listing developing countries, especially small and land-locked ones, can lead to undesirable consequences and stagnation of economic development. Quite often blacklisting leads to significant financial losses for developing economies, while highly industrialised, European countries are engaging in more harmful tax behaviours at the very same time without facing any consequences. At present, tax havens lists, especially those compiled by political organisations, do little good for the global economy or the international financial system.

Instead of using tax havens lists to navigate the international economic competition in the interests of 'first-world' countries, a deep, paradigm-changing rethinking of the international tax system is needed that will make it more effective, transparent and inclusive, and will not allow those endowed with significant economic resources to artificially detach themselves from their residence jurisdictions and move their funds across the globe instantly without paying an adequate amount of taxes anywhere in the world.

B. Taxing the Rich

Another 'classic anti-crisis move' in global tax policy is making the tax system more progressive by increasing the top personal income tax rate and/or introducing wealth taxes. It was one of tax policy priorities after the 2007–08 financial crisis, and we are observing it being a consensual response to the 2020 pandemic now. Empirical evidence supports the hypothesis that taxing the wealthiest taxpayers more has become an intuitive tax policy response to economic distress in many countries. In 2019 Dr Julian Limberg, now a Lecturer in Public Policy in the Department of Political Economy at King's College London, published an article '"Tax the rich"?

The financial crisis, fiscal fairness, and progressive income taxation' where he illustrated with data on 122 countries that on average the crisis led to an increase of a top personal income tax rate by four percentage points in the middle run (2008–12),[25] given that the common trend for personal income tax rates had been downward. Interestingly, increases in public debt caused by reasons other than economic crises did not lead to similar top PIT rate increases.

A desire to increase the tax burden of the richest members of the society during economic downturns is understandable: governments around the world are searching for ways to collect additional revenues to fund extra expenditures associated with the crisis, and taxing the wealthy presents an opportunity to do so with minimal economic distortions while contributing to decreasing socio-economic inequalities. However, taxing the rich is a controversial topic. First of all, philosophical and moral grounds behind taxing the rich more are less than obvious. In some cases, progressive taxation can be seen as demotivating, if not punishing successful individuals many of whom are contributing to society in various ways, and interfering with property rights. Some other common arguments and challenges being discussed below.

i. Efficiency Concerns

Another classic argument against taxing the very wealthy relates to concerns that if obliged to give a larger proportion of their income away in taxes, they will lose motivation to earn and spend,[26] thus killing jobs[27] and slowing down the economy.[28] In some cases, according to theory, tax hikes for the rich might even lead to decreases in revenues collected. Due to slowing the economy, such increase in tax rates for the top-tier taxpayers can yield diminishing returns.[29]

Latest research, however, questions whether such concerns are valid.[30] For instance, in December 2020 Julian Limberg and David Hope of the LSE International Inequalities Institute published a Working Paper titled 'The Economic Consequences of Major Tax Cuts for the Rich' in which they investigated the effects of recent tax cuts for the wealthiest taxpayers in 18 OECD countries and came to the conclusion that the tax cuts did not lead to significant increases in competitiveness or GDP for the countries concerned. According to Hope and Limberg, the main effect of the tax cuts was an

[25] Limberg (n 9).

[26] W Agbonlahor, 'Punishing the rich is not the answer to inequality, warns top economist' *The Guardian* (23 January 2015) www.theguardian.com/public-leaders-network/2015/jan/23/rich-inequality-economist-christopher-pissarides-davos.

[27] M Hornshaw, 'Why a "Billionaire" Wealth Tax Would Hurt the Working Poor and the Middle Class' (*Foundation for Economic Education*, 4 October) fee.org/articles/why-a-billionaire-wealth-tax-would-hurt-the-working-poor-and-the-middle-class/.

[28] J Daley, 'Taxing the rich might be good politics but it's bad economics' *The Telegraph*, (9 March 2021) www.telegraph.co.uk/news/politics/georgeosborne/9919152/Taxing-the-rich-may-be-good-politics-but-its-bad-economics.html.

[29] A Vitelli, 'Should we raise taxes on the rich?' (*The Perspective*, 1 January 2021) www.theperspective.com/debates/businessandtechnology/raise-taxes-rich/.

[30] 'The case for taxing the rich more' *Financial Times* (21 March) www.ft.com/content/dae03346-581b-4edb-838b-21c90bdb0fc3.

increase in income and wealth concentration as the top one per cent captured nearly all of the gains.[31]

Another problem related to the efficiency of taxing 'the rich' defining who 'the rich' are. There are several policy options for taxing the wealthy more heavily, from making the PIT scale more progressive to introducing a one-off or permanent 'billionaire tax' targeted at the super rich. If a progressive PIT has practical, administrative and strategic advantages and ensures a stable revenue stream for the government due to its broad tax base, a tax aimed at the super wealthy is able to bring in significant additional revenues with a minimal distortion of economic decisions. Triggering the right of taxpayers is crucial for producing the desirable economic outcomes for such taxes, and sloppy design can have negative consequences. For example, in 2020 as a response to the COVID-19 pandemic Russia introduced a higher personal income tax rate (15 per cent versus the general 13 per cent) for the 'wealthy', making the Russian income tax system somewhat progressive for the first time in over 20 years. However, the design of the tax left much to be desired: while it was supposed to be applicable to the wealthiest taxpayers, in its final version the tax triggers only corporate employees making substantial earnings. The limit set is quite high and is significantly higher that an average salary in Russia, but the tax entirely missed out on taxing the really wealthy taxpayers who earn their income in a passive form rather than from employment.[32] Paradoxically, an attempt to tax the rich in Russia failed to tax the Russian oligarchs.

ii. Relocation Risks

Another common argument against taxing the rich more heavily is that in a globalised world with almost perfect mobility, if a country of taxpayers' residency raised the top personal income tax rate significantly or introduced a wealth tax, they can simply move somewhere else, and the residence country will end up losing its tax base to more 'competitive' jurisdictions. However, empirical evidence suggests that the wealthiest taxpayers are not very likely to move when taxes are raised: they are not indifferent to where they live and usually have strong economic, social and personal ties to the country of their residency. This claim is supported with evidence: when the UK briefly raised the top income tax rate to 50 per cent about a decade ago, a small number of affluent persons moved away, but an absolute majority decided to stay.[33] In fact, theory predicts that the level at which marginal tax rates become an overall negative is surprisingly high, for example in their 2011 study 'The Case for a Progressive Tax: From Basic Research to Policy Recommendations' prominent economists Peter Diamond and Emmanuel Saez argued that the ideal top personal income tax rate for society as a whole is 73 per cent,[34] meaning that anything below this rate, which is significantly higher

[31] D Hope and J Limberg, 'The Economic Consequences of Major Tax Cuts for the Rich' [2020] Working Paper (55) Working Paper 55, LSE International Inequalities Institute.

[32] N Pushkareva, 'Politics, Not Economics, Driving Russian Tax Reform' (Tax Notes International, 7 September 2020) 1351.

[33] 'The case for taxing the rich more' (n 30).

[34] P Diamond and E Saez, 'The Case for a Progressive Tax: From Basic Research to Policy Recommendations' [2011] 25(4) *Journal of Economic Perspectives* 165–90.

than top PIT rates of the majority, if not all, countries, will result in increasing, not decreasing, tax revenues.

iii. Effectiveness vs Fairness

The reasons behind the desire to tax the rich are also important to understand. If previously considerations of economic effectiveness prevailed, and taxing the wealthy more heavily was presented as an effective way to quickly generate additional revenues without causing much economic distortions, recently we observed an increase in demand for fairness in tax policymaking.[35] Most of modern literature as well as news stories argue in favour of making income tax systems around the world more progressive, not because it will result in a better economic outcome for the majority of citizens, but because it is 'fair' and 'a right thing to do'.[36]

It is hard to argue with that, especially after watching the wealthiest people of the world enjoying the 'socialism for the rich', as put by Stiglitz,[37] during the 2020 pandemic, and privatising profits while socialising losses. As mentioned earlier, Limberg argues that an increase in public debt results in a higher top PIT rate only when a reason of such an increase is perceived by the society as unfair, ie in case of a global financial crisis. In his 2019 article Limberg examines responses of different countries to the 2007–08 crisis and comes to a conclusion that it resulted in heavier taxation of the rich in a number of jurisdictions because it was perceived as unfair that large corporations received state aid in the form of bailouts financed with ordinary taxpayers' money. With the 2020 pandemic, the unfairness of giant multinationals profiting from the crisis due to sheer luck or monopoly power while the rest of the world struggles is even more obvious, and most 'ordinary' taxpayers are unable to finance the adequate delivery of public services. Thus, progressive taxation of the affluent taxpayers serves a purpose of restoring fairness to the tax system rather than solely generating additional revenues, which is confirmed by the fact that economic crises do not lead to increases in consumption taxes which are considered regressive. Countries do aim to collect additional revenues, but they are also trying to avoid distortions and reduce existing inequalities while doing so.

C. The Green Recovery

While global warming and other climate issues were not really in the focus of international economic policy institutions when reacting to the 2007–08 financial crisis, in 2020 the situation changed dramatically, and ignoring the climate agenda became politically impossible.

The COVID-19-induced crisis caused an unmatched scale of fiscal reforms around the world, and some politicians are trying to catch the momentum for implementing

[35] K Scheve and D Stasavage, *Taxing the Rich: A History of Fiscal Fairness in the United States and Europe* (Princeton, Princeton University Press, 2016).

[36] Emily Stewart, 'Seriously, just tax the rich' (VOX, 18 May 2021) <https://www.vox.com/22432338/joe-biden-tax-plan> accessed 2 May 2022.

[37] J Stiglitz, 'America's Socialism for the Rich' [2009] 6(6) *The Economists' Voice* 1–3.

more sustainable tax and fiscal policies that could help nations to 'build back better' and ensure a 'green recovery' by making more ecological tax policy choices.

The short-term, 'crisis-patching' thinking is clearly not enough to protect our safety or ensure sustainable development anymore. Especially so with regard to ecological crises that develop over time: when we are faced with an ecological disaster, it is already way too late to act, and all we can do is to try to minimise its consequences. We are already well aware that a threat to ecology exists and keeps getting worse even notwithstanding significant reductions in flights and industrial production, and it is vitally important for us to act upon the problem as soon as possible. Fiscal policy can be an important instrument in this fight, if used wisely.

i. *Carbon Tax*

While a consensus among economists is that carbon tax is one of the most effective measures to curb fossil fuel emissions, most voters – and politicians – are often not very keen to support it as 'they (carbon taxes. – *NP*) require consumers to pay higher prices today in return for the promise of a more liveable planet sometime in the future. It is a trade many voters – from France to Canada to Washington State – are rejecting'.[38]

There were indeed several attempts to introduce federal carbon taxes in the US, for example, in Washington state two referenda on the matter were held (in 2016 and 2018[39]), but both of them failed even though the tax was predicted to raise $1 billion by 2023. The proposed carbon tax, which could be the first in the US, unsurprisingly faced strong opposition from the oil industry, and was eventually supported by 44 per cent of voters only. In France, where the national carbon tax was launched in 2014, Emmanuel Macron's attempts to increase the carbon tax already in place and to introduce new motor fuel taxes were met with street riots, which made the President postpone fuel tax changes by six months as well as cut other domestic taxes.

Nevertheless, public and political support of carbon taxation has been growing recently, and richer countries are evidently better positioned to introduce the tax. In fact, the question of whether the carbon tax can – and should – be introduced in lower-income jurisdictions, especially in poor countries in Africa, remains unanswered. The carbon footprint of such territories comes mainly from deforestation, fires and land use rather than burning fossil fuels, and the households meet their energy needs mostly with firewood and charcoal. Local energy markets are very small which will further limit the tax effect, thus, African tax policymakers need to be very careful about how they approach pricing carbon.[40]

[38] H Gleckman, 'Economists Love Carbon Taxes Voters Don't' (*Forbes*, 27 December 2018) www.forbes.com/sites/howardgleckman/2018/12/27/economists-love-carbon-taxes-voters-dont/?sh=23e3a9674338.

[39] H Bernton, 'Washington state voters reject carbon-fee initiative' *The Seattle Times* (6 November 2018) www.seattletimes.com/seattle-news/politics/voters-rejecting-carbon-fee-in-first-day-returns/.

[40] C Lawrie, D Szpotowicz and G Occhiali, 'Pas de « solution verte » – faut-il introduire des taxes sur le carbone en Afrique subsaharienne ?' (*International Centre for Tax and Development Blog*, 30 September 2021) www.ictd.ac/fr/blog/pas-de-solution-verte%E2%80%89-taxes-carbone-afrique-subsaharienne/?fbclid=IwAR3lzAuepbpUKscjJeH60MqeqtvkRh5LB0HDOQGCfw4F8c6sGdEwp64dpdA.

Tax and fiscal policy also offer a variety of measures which have the potential to support a green recovery but require little to no additional spending and which, thus, might be more suitable for lower-income economies. These can be complemented with non-tax measures supporting reducing carbon emission such as providing incentives for increased use of zero-emission transport as well as implementing technologies improving energy efficiency.

ii. Addressing Support to 'Clean', not 'Dirty', Activities and Industries

When deciding which activities to support, preferences should be given to eco-friendly and 'clean' activities where possible. Some examples would be investing in eco-friendly energy sources, improving existing infrastructure and building a new one, modernising electricity and heating systems, etc. Investment in industries/activities damaging the ecology should only be made if necessary, and should be reduced over time.

iii. Conditional Support of 'Dirty' Activities and Industries

Transformation into a greener economy will not happen overnight, and the governments will have to provide some kind of support to 'dirty' activities as well as the 'green' ones. However, this can also be seen as an opportunity for a change by conditioning the government support – whatever form it takes – on the receiver of such aid changing its behaviour and becoming more sustainable. It is advisable that an ambitious yet realistic plan of reducing a negative environmental impact is presented not by eco-friendly receivers of the government support, demonstrating concrete actions they will take to become 'cleaner'. In case such a plan is considered acceptable and the support is transferred, the receiving organisation should be obliged to report regularly on actual steps taken to reduce its negative environmental impact.

iv. Green Budgeting

Even though these are very hard times for many economies, ecological considerations should be taken into account when deciding what support measures will be provided by the government, to whom and on what conditions, and what their net effect on the climate will be. It is important to remember that the results of such measures will stay with us for a long time, and we should therefore design them with careful consideration. Ideally, ecological impact of particular measures should be reflected in the budget, allowing governments to make better-informed policy choices.

v. Green Finance

Climate (green) bonds should be used where possible for raising financing for climate-improving projects, as they are associated with additional tax incentives such as tax exemption and tax credits, which make them a more convenient option compared to taxable bonds. Because this kind of financing is more attractive economically, it stimulates actors to be involved in more environmental-oriented initiatives. Use of other green finance products, such as green-tagged loans, green investment funds and climate risk insurance, should also be encouraged.

While the recent crisis indeed presented an excellent momentum for incorporating climate justice considerations in tax policymaking, such measures need to be designed very carefully to ensure they do not place a disproportional burden on low-income jurisdictions. Attention also needs to be paid to other tax policy measures which are not normally considered eco-related but have the potential to improve the climate in developing countries, such as effective taxation of extractive industries.

V. Conclusions

Comparative analysis of tax policy responses to the two recent yet different major economic crises leads us to conclude that the tax policy aspect of international economic policy institutions' reaction to financial meltdowns remained largely unchanged over the past decade. Like in 2007–08, in 2020 addressing the interconnected problem of tax havens and taxing the rich received a lot of public attention. In the latest crisis, however, climate justice and using tax and fiscal measures to ensure a 'green recovery' were also a priority of global tax policy leaders.

While these issues certainly deserve attention, it is not clear if they are the best ones to focus on in times of post-crisis recovery. Potential benefits for developing economies are in many cases uncertain, and the problematic areas picked by international fora seem to be those most likely to receive political support rather than those more likely to deliver maximum value and to make the global financial system more stable and resistant to economic shocks. Otto von Bismarck used to say that 'politics is the art of the possible' and it is very important to use political opportunities when they arise, but the ability to focus on what matters most is one of the key qualities defining true leadership. More fundamental, complex and long-term solutions are needed for achieving macroeconomic stability, in particular for lower-income jurisdictions. Building more independent, self-sustained, stable and shock-resistant national tax systems is a challenging, but unavoidable task, and the real issues faced by developing jurisdictions are important to address to achieve sustainable development.

Evidently, there is a pressing need for rethinking institutional design of international economic platforms in a way that will facilitate creating truly inclusive policies, effectively voicing and protecting interests of emergent economies while contributing to reducing existing inequalities, as – notwithstanding the significant progress made – the current global tax agenda remains dominated by economically developed countries, and the problems they are focusing on are disproportionally important for large, industrialised economies. Lower-income jurisdictions should be included in all stages of the policymaking process, including OECD Working Parties where the majority of international tax policies are currently designed. Quoting Professor Christians one last time, 'This architecture is based on historical international power relationships and institutional history. For diplomatic restructuring on the world stage to usher in a new age of inclusion for previously marginalised states and peoples, systemic changes must also take place in these entrenched institutions and processes'.[41]

Times of crises make us more dependent on others and show us very lucidly just how fragile our wellbeing is. The problem is that we have a very short memory. We are ready to demand redistribution as long as we are on the receiving side of it, and we can be very critical to harmful tax practices other than our own. But a crisis like this cannot be wasted, and we should use this opportunity to truly commit to building a more inclusive, just and sustainable global tax system.

[41] Christians (n 1).

PART III

Environment and Regulation

13

A Case for Environmental Taxation as a Response to the COVID-19 Economic Crisis

ERIKA SCUDERI, AMEDEO RIZZO AND ARTEMIS LOUCAIDOU

Abstract

The COVID-19 pandemic has had tremendous effects on both human health and the global economy. Lockdown measures, however, led to the unpredicted effect of improving the quality of the environment and lowering daily CO_2 emissions. The disruption of the pre-existing status quo may turn into a unique opportunity to 'lock' these environmental improvements through, inter alia, the alignment of environmental goals with fiscal policies. In the light of this goal, this chapter highlights why unilateral approaches are not sufficient and details the reasons why it is necessary to give a common response. Aware of the challenges and difficulties that may arise in designing and implementing a global solution, the authors propose a potential solution to design a fair and efficient carbon pricing system within and at the EU borders, while taking into account the COVID-19 pandemic's effects on the economy. The research illustrates how suitable measures should be designed to avoid economic distortions, inequality and inefficiency, and which primary purpose they should serve: the improvement of the quality of the environment (irrespective of the revenue produced) or budgetary objectives to provide the EU with adequate resources to support economic recovery.

I. Introduction

The start of the 2020s found the world experiencing two of the direst emergencies: the environmental crisis and the COVID-19 pandemic. The former is slowly – but irreversibly – deteriorating the quality of the environment; the latter has abruptly changed our lives and disrupted the economy. Both force us to rethink the way we conduct business. Supranational organisations and governments are making concerted efforts to support public health systems and economic operators affected by the pandemic with extraordinary social and economic measures.[1] Nevertheless, the disruption of pre-existing habits and the unprecedented circumstances the world is experiencing could offer the opportunity to 'lock' environmental improvements achieved as a side-effect of lockdown measures, align environmental goals with fiscal policies and provide a more sustainable basis for economic recovery measures.

The COP26 outcomes suggest that the goal of the Paris Agreement to limit the rise in global temperature to 1.5°C can be met if countries increase their ambition and deliver their pledges,[2] based on the principle of 'common but differentiated responsibilities' (CBDR)[3] and that the recovery from the pandemic is a 'historic opportunity to tackle climate change at the same time'.[4] Thus, on the one hand, there is the need to raise revenue to support the recovery and relaunch the economy and, on the other hand, it is necessary to introduce effective tools to meet the Paris Agreement goals. In this context, the authors consider whether these circumstances could serve as the cause to introduce environmental taxes.

Although a global response would best tackle global concerns, timely climate global action is highly unlikely. For this reason, the authors considered the EU as the place where environmental taxes could be implemented in the foreseeable future for four reasons. First, the introduction of an environmental tax in the EU will affect 27 countries, which are responsible for 18 per cent of global CO_2 emissions produced since the industrial revolution.[5] Second, the EU has been the pioneer in implementing global tax proposals. Third, the EU recognises the urgency to address the environmental crisis. The European Parliament (EP) declared a global climate emergency, urging the European Commission (EC)

> to fully assess the climate and environmental impact of all relevant legislative and budgetary proposals, and ensure that they are all fully aligned with the objective of limiting global warming to under 1,5°C.[6]

As a result, the EC adopted the European Green Deal (EGD), endorsing the objective of achieving climate neutrality by 2050 and increasing the EU's climate ambition to reduce by 2030 greenhouse gases emissions by 50–55 per cent from 1990 levels (2030 target).[7] Finally, the EU has the legislative framework to take climate action.[8]

However, at the time of writing, Directive 2003/96/EC on taxation of energy products and electricity (ETD) is not in line with EU climate targets; and is inconsistent

[1] See C Garbarino, 'Fiscal Evolution and the Syndemic', ch 9 of this volume.

[2] UN Climate Change Conference UK 2021, 'COP26: The Glasgow Climate Pact', 3, ukcop26.org/wp-content/uploads/2021/11/COP26-Presidency-Outcomes-The-Climate-Pact.pdf.

[3] The Paris Agreement 2015, Article 4(3).

[4] UN Climate Change Conference UK 2021, 'COP26: Explained', 6, ukcop26.org/wp-content/uploads/2021/07/COP26-Explained.pdf.

[5] I Tiseo, 'Emissions in the EU–Statistics and Facts' (*Statista*, 4 August 2021) www.statista.com/topics/4958/emissions-in-the-european-union/#dossierKeyfigures.

[6] European Parliament Resolution 2019/2930(RSP) of 28 November 2019 on the climate and environment emergency (2019) OJ C232/28.

[7] Communication from the Commission to the European Parliament, the European Council, the Council, the European Economic and Social Committee and the Committee of the Regions 'The European Green Deal' COM (2019) 640 final, henceforth 'EGD'.

[8] For a discussion on the justification of introducing an EU tax see K Pantazatou, 'Revising the Justification for an EU Tax in a Post-crisis Context', ch 8 of this volume.

with other climate EU policies (eg renewables Directive, energy efficiency Directive).[9] Moreover, Directive 2003/87/EC establishing a scheme for greenhouse gas emission allowance trading within the Community (EU ETS) does not cover high polluting sectors such as road transports, buildings and the maritime sector. Furthermore, inconsistencies between the ETD and the EU ETS exist, which cause cost efficiency losses and distortion of the internal market.[10] The EGD, recognising discrepancies in the EU legislative framework and acknowledging the crucial role of taxation in the transition towards a more sustainable EU economic growth, announced two initiatives in the tax field: (i) revising the ETD,[11] and (ii) introducing a Carbon Border Adjustment Mechanism (CBAM).[12]

Notwithstanding these proposals, more stringent measures and increased carbon prices are needed to reach the 2030 target. The Organisation for Economic Co-operation and Development (OECD) considered that by pricing all emissions at a minimum of EUR 60 per tonne of CO_2, countries could make significant progress towards the net-zero emissions goal, but 'carbon-neutrality by mid-century very likely requires additional efforts' and that to close the carbon pricing gap entirely, carbon prices would need to increase in non-EU ETS sectors as well.[13]

This research proposes a potential solution to design a fair and efficient carbon pricing system *within* and *at* the EU borders, while taking into account the COVID-19 pandemic's effects on the economy. In section II the authors discuss the possibility of introducing an EU harmonised carbon pricing instrument, as the system *within* the EU. Section III analyses the EU CBAM that can serve as the measure *at* the EU borders. Section IV looks at the effects the pandemic had on the economy, evaluating whether the COVID-19 crisis presents the right 'opportunity' to introduce a more ambitious carbon pricing system in the EU. Research questions related to the double regulation issue[14] or the determination of the tax base and tax rate of the proposed EU CO_2 tax are outside the scope of this chapter.

II. A Common Approach as the Proper Tool to Boost a Green Recovery from the COVID-19 Pandemic in the EU

The interplay between economic crises and fiscal responses is not new. During both the 2008 crisis and the COVID-19 pandemic, governments introduced significant

[9] See A Pirlot, 'Exploring the Impact of EU law on energy and environmental taxation' in CHJI Panayi, W Haslehner and E Traversa (eds), *Research Handbook in European Union Taxation Law* (Cheltenham, Edward Elgar, 2020) 359–88.

[10] See V Solilová and D Nerudová, 'Overall Approach of the EU in the Question of Emissions: EU Emissions Trading System and CO2 Taxation' (2014) 12 *Procedia Economics and Finance*, 616–25.

[11] European Commission, 'Proposal for a Council Directive restructuring the Union framework for the taxation of energy products and electricity' (recast) COM (2021) 563 final, henceforth 'ETD Proposal'.

[12] European Commission, 'Proposal for a Regulation of the European Parliament and of the Council establishing a Carbon Border Adjustment Mechanism' COM (2021 564 final, henceforth 'CBAM Proposal'.

[13] OECD, *Effective Carbon Rates 2021: pricing carbon emissions through taxes and emissions* trading (Paris, OECD Publishing, 2021) 26.

[14] Arising when the same emission is covered by emission trading systems and carbon taxes.

temporary or long-term tax measures to support the recovery. However, in the absence of a global agreement on tackling climate change, and in the light of the difficulties that countries would face in reaching such an agreement in the short term, coordinating tax strategies at the EU level could help with overcoming the crisis while strengthening the fiscal integration among the EU Member States and respecting their 'needs and specificities'.[15]

Combining the needs to fight climate change and raise revenue to cover the costs of the pandemic, the authors analyse the possibility of introducing a carbon tax. Many EU Member States wishing to encourage a shift towards a greener economy have implemented – or are planning to adopt – domestic carbon pricing instruments. National experiences proved that carbon taxes are an effective tool to reduce CO_2 emissions and have a neutral (or slightly positive) impact on the employment level.[16] Notwithstanding the beneficial impact produced by these carbon pricing policies, unilateral approaches are not sufficient to face the environmental crisis. Therefore, the authors analyse whether and why it is necessary to act at the supranational level.

A. Subsidiarity

Under the principle of subsidiarity,[17] in areas which do not fall within the EU's exclusive competence, the EU shall act only if, and to the degree that the objectives of the proposed action cannot be sufficiently achieved by the EU Member States and can be better attained at EU level.

Since the power to tax remains in the hands of the EU Member States, with the EU having only limited competence[18] and considering that the regulation of the internal market and the environmental and energy sectors fall within the area of shared competences, the principle of subsidiarity would apply for the introduction of a new CO_2 tax. In order to verify if an EU measure is compatible with the principle of subsidiarity, it is necessary to assess the existence of two 'components':[19]

- whether the EU is acting 'only if and insofar as the objectives of the proposed action cannot be sufficiently achieved by the Member States' ('negative' component); and
- if these objectives, 'by reason of the scale or effects of the proposed action, be better achieved by the Community' ('positive' component).

[15] G Melis and F Pitrone, 'Coordinating Tax Strategies at the EU Level as a Solution to the Economic and Financial Crisis' (2011) 39(8–9) *Intertax*. See also PA Hernández González-Barreda, 'The Role of Crisis in State-Building the European Union through Finance and Taxation: Will COVID-19 and the Russian Attack Trigger Further Union?', ch 7 of this volume.

[16] For example, the French carbon tax decreased carbon emissions by 5% from 2013 to 2018, while the net effect on employment was smaller in magnitude but slightly positive (+0.8%): see D Dussaux, 'Carbon tax, emissions reduction and employment: some evidence from France' (*OECD Eco Scope Blog*, 4 February 2020) oecdecoscope.blog/2020/02/04/carbon-tax-emissions-reduction-and-employment-some-evidence-from-france/.

[17] Article 5(3) TEU.

[18] See Hernández González-Barreda (n 15) s III.

[19] See G Kofler, 'EU Power to Tax' in CHJI Panayi, W Haslehner and E Traversa (eds), *Research Handbook in European Union Taxation Law* (Cheltenham, Edward Elgar, 2020).

In the authors' opinion, several reasons explain why environmental objectives cannot be sufficiently achieved by the Member States and, therefore could be better attained at the EU level.

i. Spillover Effects

Carbon emissions do not stop at national borders and do not affect only the country where they are emitted. The impact of the greenhouse effect is global in scope and, consequently, countries have an interest in neighbours' environmental policies. As argued earlier, introducing a global CO_2 tax would be ideal.

However, considering the time needed and the difficulties that countries may face in reaching a global agreement, a prompt and concrete initiative to harmonise the efforts towards effectively reducing CO_2 emissions within the EU border could be the second-best solution.[20]

ii. Common Targets Could be Better Achieved with Common Policies and Responsibilities

The need to act at the EU level is also expressed by the impact emissions in one country have on other EU Member States' policies. Indeed, considering that the EU has set a cap on emissions, additional emissions in an EU Member State must be regarded as a negative externality on the other EU Member States forcing them to reduce their emissions or accept that their common objectives will not be met.[21] Uncoordinated approaches within the EU Member States could lead to the failure of the 2030 target.

Therefore, introducing a harmonised measure would be more consistent with the EU mission on the environment. Moreover, the measure could also consider the specific economic situation and technological choices of each country,[22] as the burden imposed on industry and private consumers may vary from region to region.[23] The tax burden could be modulated according to specific needs, differentiating responsibilities within the EU, yet achieving EU goals as a whole.

iii. Preserving the Internal Market and Improving Competitiveness

From an economic perspective, not having an EU CO_2 tax could increase internal market fragmentation. In 1993, in its Opinion on the proposal for an EU CO_2 tax, the Economic

[20] The European Economic and Social Committee has recently expressed its opinion on 'Taxation mechanisms for reducing CO_2 emissions' (2020/C 364/03) and stated that '[a]n ideal outcome should create uniform conditions across the EU single market about the emissions/reductions to be taxed, as well as the specific methods and rates of taxation for an equal impact on the level of CO2 in the atmosphere. Such an outcome may, however, take time, given country-specific needs'.

[21] C Fuest and J Pisani-Ferry, 'Financing the European Union: new context, new responses' (2020) 16 *Policy Contribution*.

[22] P Agostini, M Botteon and C Carraro, 'A carbon tax to reduce CO_2 emissions in Europe' (1992) 14 *Energy Economics* 279.

[23] S Geringer, 'The Future of the EU's Financing in Times of Disruption and Recovery: Normative and Technical Issues of Greening the EU's Own Resources System', ch 14 of this volume.

and Social Committee noticed that 'a Community approach should be given priority over national measures to avoid distortions of competition with the Community'.[24] Indeed, the inhomogeneity stemming from divergences in domestic carbon taxes could alter the level playing field across the involved sectors of the economy.[25]

Moreover, adopting an EU CO_2 tax could influence trading partners to take similar steps, just like the proposal for a CBAM discussed below influenced them to raise their ambitions, thereby limiting the impact on the EU economic operators' competitiveness. Furthermore, achieving an agreement on a joint approach should be easier nowadays compared to 1992. Indeed, as mentioned, many EU Member States have already implemented carbon taxes. As argued in literature (though in favour of a more general environmental tax reform), like-minded countries should cooperate to achieve their common goals and reduce competitiveness risks.[26]

iv. Political Perspective

The introduction of an EU CO_2 tax could help decrease the tax burden on employees and companies as well as the level of unemployment all over the EU (which has also been influenced by the COVID-19 pandemic). Potential benefits from an EU CO_2 tax to contribute to employment objectives could constitute a valid argument and provide a powerful political message to support such coordinated action.

An EU CO_2 tax could be seen as an additional 'political statement' of the EU's commitment to fighting climate change, raising environmental protection's targets worldwide and pushing trading partners to bring their environmental policies in line with EU standards. Attributing to the EU the power to act by introducing such a measure would also achieve a level of consistency as far as 'external' competence (*in foro externo*) and 'internal' competence (*in foro interno*) are concerned.[27] Implementing an EU CO_2 tax may increase transparency, and force tax authorities to better justify and improve the use of their resources. Increased transparency may thus affect the accountability of a government and the overall efficiency.[28] Moreover, it may further

[24] Economic and Social Committee, Opinion on the proposal for a Council Directive introducing a tax on carbon dioxide emissions and energy (93/C 108/06), OJ No 108/20, 19 April 1993.

[25] As an example, higher fuel prices in the Netherlands led to 'tank tourism' to Germany. The same happened on the border between Northern Ireland and the Irish Republic and all over Luxembourg. See K Ussher, 'The spectre of tax harmonisation' (London, Centre for European Reform, 2000) 33–39; P Mastellone and S Dorigo, *La fiscalità per l'ambiente* (Roma, Aracne Editore, 2013) 77.

[26] S Withana and P ten Brink, 'Motivating environmental tax reform through coalitions of like-minded countries' in L Kreiser et al (eds), *Carbon Pricing. Design, Experiences and Issues, Critical Issues* (Cheltenham, Edward Elgar, 2015).

[27] The principle '*in foro interno, in foro externo*', deeply rooted in the structure of the EU, was already applied in Opinion 1/1976 Opinion of the Court of 26 April 1977 – Opinion given pursuant to Article 228(1) of the EEC Treaty ECLI:EU:C:1977:63.

[28] European Commission, 'Tax-based EU own resources: An assessment', Working paper No 1/2004 (available at www.researchgate.net/publication/24134287_Tax-based_EU_own_resources_an_assessment). An EU CO_2 tax could also have a significant impact on the compliance and administrative costs of taxation. Empirical studies showed that a coordinated tax for many countries would lead to substantial cost-savings for taxpayers and tax administrations and would lead to CO_2 emissions reductions at a lower rate and smaller costs. (See K Conrad and T Schmidt, 'Economic impacts of an uncoordinated versus a coordinated carbon dioxide policy in the European Union: An applied general equilibrium analysis' (1998) 10(2) *Economic Systems Research* 161 *ss* and T Barker, 'Achieving a 10% cut in Europe's CO_2 emissions using additional excise duties: coordinated,

support the EU in meeting the goal of the 'Enhanced Transparency Framework' under the COP26.[29]

B. How the EU CO_2 Tax Purpose Shapes its Design and Implementation Procedure

History demonstrates that the introduction of carbon taxes at the EU level faced numerous difficulties. In 1992, the EC proposed the introduction of a harmonised CO_2 tax noting that 'the greenhouse effect is a problem that should be resolved in an efficient and coherent manner', that 'a number of Member States have already introduced, or are planning to introduce, taxes on carbon dioxide emissions and the use of energy' and, therefore, that 'a harmonised approach is needed to ensure the functioning of the internal market'.[30] This, and all the subsequent attempts the EC made, have failed; since then, almost 30 years have passed and the arguments the EC used to explain the urgent need to adopt such a tax are more valid than ever.

Understanding the problem that a measure needs to solve and, consequently, its main purpose is key to determining the appropriate legal basis and the legislative procedure to be applied. Environmental taxes are generally designed to pursue environmental goals. Of course, defining a measure's primary purpose does not prevent it from achieving other – incidental or intended – goals.[31] Although the revenue-raising function clearly comes into play in crisis, tax systems may perform redistributive and regulatory functions.[32] In the case at hand, the proposed EU CO_2 tax could aim at: (i) protecting the environment; (ii) protecting the competitiveness of the European economic operators and the functioning of the internal market; or (iii) raising revenue.

i. Protecting the Environment

To achieve the 2030 targets, carbon pricing signals must be strengthened to boost the CO_2 emissions decrease. An EU CO_2 tax would raise the level of environmental protection all over the EU and encourage non-EU countries to align their efforts to European ones. This type of measure would aim at protecting the environment by changing consumers' and producers' behaviour and could be adopted based on Article 192(2)(a) TFEU, if considered a measure 'primarily of a fiscal nature', or based on Article 192(1) TFEU if not considered as having *primarily* such a fiscal nature according to its primary environmental objectives.[33]

uncoordinated and unilateral action using the econometric model E3ME' (1999) 11(4) *Economic Systems Research* 401.).

[29] UN Climate Change Conference UK 2021 (n 2) 3.

[30] European Commission, Proposal for a Council directive introducing a tax on carbon dioxide emissions and energy (92/C 196/ 01) COM (1992) 226 final.

[31] On 'the five dividends of environmental taxes' see JP Barde and O Godard, 'Economic principles of environmental fiscal reform', in JE Milne and M Skou Andersen (eds), *Handbook of Research on Environmental Taxation* (Cheltenham, Edward Elgar, 2012).

[32] See RS Avi-Yonah, 'The Three Goals of Taxation' (2006) 60(1) *Tax Law Review* 1–28; Pantazatou (n 8).

[33] See E Scuderi, 'Provisions primarily of a fiscal nature: time to dispel doubts' (2022) 5 *EC Tax Review*; in literature, the concept of 'provisions primarily of a fiscal nature' is debated. For a detailed analysis see

ii. Protecting the Competitiveness of the European Economic Operators and the Functioning of the Internal Market

Many divergent domestic carbon pricing instruments risk distorting the internal market. An EU CO_2 tax would help to ensure a level playing field within the EU borders and protect the competitiveness of all the EU economic operators, irrespective of where they operate within the EU. Therefore, this type of measure would aim at protecting the internal market and the appropriate legal basis would be Article 113 TFEU.

iii. Raising Revenue

Because of the economic crisis, EU Member States need adequate resources to support the economic recovery. The EU CO_2 tax would raise the revenue needed to cover the short-term costs incurred during the pandemic and support future expenses necessary to boost the recovery. This type of measure would be subsumed under the category of 'provisions primarily of a fiscal nature' and adopted according to Article 192(2)(a) TFEU.

iv. Interim Conclusion

In this context, the authors assume that the proposed measure's primary goal is to protect the environment. For this reason, this measure could be adopted based on Article 192(2)(a) TFEU, which requires unanimity at the Council for the adoption of provisions primarily of a fiscal nature. However, if one considers that the *primary* purpose of this measure is not raising revenue but reducing emissions, there could be room to argue that it could be adopted based on Article 192(1) TFEU, since it should not be considered a measure 'primarily of a fiscal nature'.[34]

III. How Could the Proposed EU CO_2 Tax Fit Into the Framework of Existing EGD'S Initiatives?

The EGD's proposals in the tax field relate to the revision of the ETD[35] and the adoption of a CBAM.[36] Whereas the revision of the ETD addresses the taxation of fuels and energy products based on their energy content and environmental performance, it does not put a price on carbon emissions. Carbon emissions are however priced under the EU ETS system.

SE Weishaar, 'Fault lines between fees and taxes: legal obstacles for linking', in L Kreiser et al (eds), *Carbon Pricing – Design, Experience and Issues* (Cheltenham, Edward Elgar, 2015) 40; SE Weishaar, 'Carbon Taxes at the EU Level. Introduction Issues and Barriers' (2018) *WIFO. Working Papers*, 4; R Ismer and M Haussner, 'Inclusion of consumption into the EU ETS: The legal basis under European Union law' (2016) 25(1) *Review of European, Comparative & International Environmental Law* 69–80; Geringer (n 23).

[34] See Scuderi (n 33).

[35] ETD Proposal (n 11).

[36] CBAM Proposal (n 12).

Scholars note that a carbon tax and a cap-and-trade system with full sectoral coverage would be broadly equivalent in terms of setting carbon prices and the amount of revenue they can raise.[37] Therefore, expanding the EU ETS to all major emitting sectors could be an easy carbon pricing solution to implement, through the ordinary legislative procedure in Article 192(1) TFEU. However, under the current proposal for revising the EU ETS, the limited scope and the continuation of the free allocation of allowances in the sectors covered suggests that domestic carbon pricing instruments would still be necessary for non-ETS sectors.

Scholars affirmed that correctly designed CO_2 taxes could guarantee greater reliability in anticipating energy prices because they can be more predictable than ever-fluctuating prices in a cap-and-trade system, they can reduce emissions in a cheaper and more effective way while help planning investment decisions.[38] They could also contribute to economic growth by generating, inter alia, productive investments in new technologies. Therefore, a harmonised EU CO_2 tax would present a well-suited approach in fighting climate change and raising revenue. A border mechanism must exist to ensure the effectiveness of an EU CO_2 tax. The EU has already proposed a CBAM to serve as 'commensurate with the internal EU carbon price',[39] provided under the EU ETS.

A. The EU CBAM Proposal

Border carbon adjustments are controversial instruments. They have been discussed and proposed but never implemented.[40] They are measures introduced at the border, in the form of monetary contributions which aim to level the playing field between domestic producers, subject to a carbon price, and foreign producers subject to no or minimal carbon pricing.[41] Their design is challenging as it involves decisions over the type of instrument to be used, the scope of emissions, product, geographical and trade coverage and addressing circumvention issues.[42]

A number of instruments including an import carbon tax, an excise duty and import certificates at average EU emissions or actual emissions with the possibility for a transition period and the inclusion of more products were assessed.[43] Options like a customs

[37] LH Goulder and AR Schein, 'Carbon Taxes Versus Cap and Trade: A Critical Review' (2013) 4(3) *Climate Change Economics* 1–28.

[38] I Bilbao Estrada and P Pistone, 'Global CO_2 Taxes' (2013) 41(1) *Intertax*; R Cooper, 'Towards a Real Global Warming Treaty (The Case for a Carbon Tax)' (1998) 77 *Foreign Affairs* 66–79; R Cooper, 'International Approaches to Global Climate Change' (2000) 15 *World Bank Research Observer* 145 et seq; WD Nordhaus, 'To Tax or Not to Tax: Alternative Approaches to Slowing Global Warming' (2007) 1 *Review of Environmental Economics and Policy* 26–99.

[39] European Commission, 'Inception Impact Assessment on CBAM' Ares (2020)1350037 2.

[40] M Mehling et al, 'Designing Border Carbon Adjustments for Enhanced Climate Action' (2019) 113(3) *AJIL* 433, 435.

[41] Whether the measure is considered a tax, an excise duty, or just a monetary contribution depends on the choice of the instrument and the domestic carbon pricing instrument it accompanies.

[42] For example, resource shuffling and substitution of materials under the scope of the instrument with materials that are not covered or substitution of products.

[43] European Commission, 'Impact Assessment Report Accompanying the document: Proposal for a Regulation of the European Parliament and of the Council establishing a Carbon Border Adjustment Mechanism' SWD (2021) 643 final 31–36, (henceforth 'CBAM Impact Assessment').

duty, extending the EU ETS to imports, export rebates and a Carbon Added Tax were discarded because of incompatibility with the objectives of the mechanism and World Trade Organisation (WTO) rules.[44]

The instrument chosen is a system of CBAM certificates for importers, with the possibility of proving actual emissions, with parallel continuation of free EU ETS allowances for a transitional period, for aluminium, fertilisers, cement, iron, steel and electricity sectors.[45] The CBAM certificates were chosen as the most effective instrument in meeting the objectives of the EU, complying with WTO rules, and not imposing unnecessary burdens on administrations, industries and consumers. These factors are analysed below.

B. Objectives

The CBAM is necessary to meet the objective of carbon neutrality by 2050. The EU is increasing its climate ambitions in line with the commitments made under the Paris Agreement. However, under the principle of CBDR, the nationally determined contributions (NDC) are not ambitious enough to meet the objective of the Paris Agreement.[46] Therefore, as the EU increases its climate ambitions, the risk of carbon leakage arises.[47] Carbon leakage occurs when 'production is transferred from the EU to other countries with lower ambition for emission reduction, or EU products are replaced by more carbon-intensive imports'.[48] If this risk materialises, the climate efforts of the EU will be frustrated as carbon emissions will decrease in the EU, but increase elsewhere.[49]

The risk of carbon leakage is a real concern. Although *ex post* studies show minimal carbon leakage and studies assessing the EU ETS find no evidence of carbon leakage,[50] *ex ante* studies show a possibility of carbon leakage rate up to 40 per cent, suggesting that the higher the ambition level the higher the risk.[51] As carbon emissions embedded in imports to the EU increase[52] and free allocation under the EU ETS is phased-out,[53] the issue is whether the CBAM can effectively address this risk. *Ex ante* studies suggest that the CBAM can limit carbon leakage,[54] which makes addressing the risk of carbon leakage the overarching objective of the CBAM.[55]

[44] ibid 41–42.
[45] ibid 86, CBAM Proposal (n 12).
[46] OECD, *Climate Policy Leadership in an Interconnected World: What Role for Border Carbon Adjustments?* (Paris, OECD Publishing 2020) paras 2 and 12.
[47] CBAM Proposal (n 12).
[48] EGD (n 7).
[49] ibid.
[50] OECD (n 46) paras 21–23, 25–26 and 29–30. These findings suggest that the current mechanism of addressing carbon leakage, free allocation of allowances, is effective, not that the risk of carbon leakage is minimal.
[51] ibid paras 19 and 30.
[52] European Parliament (EP), Resolution of 10 March 2021 towards a WTO-compatible EU carbon border adjustment mechanism 2020/2043(INI) para 6 (henceforth 'EP Resolution').
[53] CBAM Impact Assessment (n 43) 11.
[54] OECD (n 46) paras 34–35; M Pyrka et al, 'The Effects of the Implementation of the Border Tax Adjustment in the Context of more Stringent EU Climate Policy until 2030' (2020) *Institute of Environmental Protection – National Research Institute* para 65.
[55] CBAM Proposal (n 12) 2; CBAM Impact Assessment (n 43) 14.

Other specific objectives include providing a framework for investments in low-carbon technologies, ensuring domestic production and imports are subject to a similar level of carbon pricing, encouraging producers in third countries to adopt low-carbon technologies and minimising the risk of the measure being circumvented.[56] It is also suggested that the EU through the CBAM exerts political pressure on other countries to raise their ambitions.[57] The EC suggests this is an ancillary effect of the CBAM.[58] The commitments made by China, Japan, South Korea and the US to reach climate neutrality by 2050s–2060s suggests that the CBAM is an effective measure to encourage third countries to reconsider their NDCs, and could eventually lead to a global agreement on carbon pricing.

Lastly, another ancillary effect of the CBAM is raising revenue.[59] Whereas Milne explains that environmental tax theory gives discretion to policymakers on what purpose to use the revenue for,[60] Mehling argues that less political and legal challenges arise if the revenue is used to further environmental objectives and benefit developing countries affected by the measure.[61] Recognising the need to raise revenue to cover the costs of the pandemic, the Council concluded in July 2020, that revenue from CBAM will be an own resource used for 'early repayment of NGEU borrowing'.[62] However, highlighting that raising revenue is an ancillary effect of the CBAM and not a central objective is important to make the CBAM acceptable to the international community.

C. Compatibility with the WTO Framework

Designing a CBAM compatible with WTO rules is feasible.[63] The proposed CBAM does not seem to violate any provision of the General Agreement on Tariffs and Trade (GATT), and when it does it can be justified under Article XX if it falls within one of the provisions and complies with the chapeau.[64] It is likely that the environmental objectives of the CBAM will satisfy either Article XX(b), as necessary to protect human animal or plant life or health, or XX(g), relating to the conservation of exhaustible natural resources, given the adverse consequences of climate change.

The most-favoured nation principle (MFN) under Article I could be violated with country of origin exemptions, like those in Annex II of the Proposal, to account for a

[56] CBAM Impact Assessment (n 43) 14–15.

[57] Mehling et al (n 40) 441.

[58] CBAM Impact Assessment (n 43) 15.

[59] ibid.

[60] JE Milne, 'VIII.12 Environmental taxes' in M Faure (ed), *Elgar Encyclopedia of Environmental Law* (Cheltenham, Edward Elgar, 2020) 176.

[61] Mehling et al (n 40) 478.

[62] European Council, 'Conclusions of the European Council of 21 July 2020' (EUCO 10/20 CO EUR 8 CONCL 4) para A29, hereinafter 'European Council Conclusions', www.consilium.europa.eu/media/45109/210720-euco-final-conclusions-en.pdf. For a discussion on how the EU will use revenue from an EU tax see Pantazatou (n 8).

[63] J Trachtman, 'WTO Law Constraints on Border Tax Adjustment and Tax Credit Mechanisms to Reduce the Competitive Effects of Carbon Taxes' (2016) *RFF Discussion Paper* 16-03, 1.

[64] The chapeau provides that the application of the measure 'should not constitute a means of arbitrary or unjustifiable discrimination between countries where the same conditions prevail, or a disguised restriction on international trade'.

national carbon pricing system. The OECD suggests that violation of Article I could be avoided if the exemptions arise from objective emissions-related criteria or if they target developing countries.[65] As Annex II includes countries participating in the EU ETS, the violation could be justified. Moreover, Article 9 which provides the possibility to claim a reduction where a carbon price has been paid in the country of origin[66] is a way for importers from countries where carbon pricing applies to ensure that no double taxation arises without violating the MFN clause. Trachtman also argues that where states enter into mutual recognition agreements for their carbon pricing regimes then a violation of the MFN could be defended under Article XX.[67] Therefore, the conclusion of a global agreement on carbon pricing would further dissolve any concerns on the incompatibility of the CBAM with the WTO framework.

Moreover, the CBAM is not enacted as an import tax or a customs duty, which could exceed the tariff schedule, violating Article II(1)(a) of the GATT.[68] Furthermore, as it treats imports and domestic products consistently, it complies with Article XI(2)(a) and the national treatment principle in Article III(2).[69] In addition, as there is no export rebate there are no issues under Articles I and XX, and the Agreement on Subsidies and Countervailing Measures.[70] Given that instruments which could violate the GATT were discarded early,[71] it is apparent that the need to comply with WTO rules played a major role in the design of the instrument.

D. The Impacts of the CBAM on the Economy, Businesses and Consumers

The EC recognises the need to provide predictability for investors.[72] Establishing a CBAM which meets its environmental objectives and does not impose unjustified burdens on European and foreign businesses and consumers is a great balancing exercise. Several studies and the Impact Assessment, based on different models and options, were undertaken to determine the possible effects of the CBAM.

The CBAM will primarily impact foreign businesses, who will face additional costs and could choose not to export in the EU, or to direct in the EU their 'cleaner' products.[73] Several studies estimate a small decrease in the volume and value of imports in the sectors affected by the CBAM and growth in imports of other sectors and an increase in the price of imported products.[74]

[65] OECD (n 46) paras 49–50; Mehling et al (n 40) 463.
[66] CBAM Proposal (n 12) Article 9.
[67] Trachtman (n 63) 17.
[68] OECD (n 46) para 38; Trachtman (n 63) 4.
[69] OECD (n 46) paras 38–41.
[70] OECD (n 46) paras 43–46; Trachtman (n 63) 27 and 39.
[71] CBAM Impact Assessment (n 43) 41–42.
[72] EGD (n 7) 4.
[73] This leads to the problem of resource shuffling.
[74] This could indicate substitution of materials with finished, manufactured goods. Pyrka et al (n 54) paras 47–49; AFEP, 'Trade & Climate Change: Final Report' (AFEP, 2020) 53, afep.com/en/publications-en/trade-climate-friends-or-foes-making-the-case-for-cbam-and-green-trade-rules/; CBAM Impact Assessment (n 43) 64–67.

Moreover, as the CBAM will be imposed on products facing a carbon price within the EU, European businesses will also face increased costs.[75] Yet, no double taxation is expected to arise and there are low negative output effects on the sectors under scope.[76] However, where the costs of moving to low-carbon technologies are high, European businesses may choose to relocate outside the EU, thus affecting the European economy and increasing unemployment, suggesting that carbon leakage materialises. However, as the CBAM will address carbon leakage, minimal impacts are expected on employment.[77]

Furthermore, whereas consumer prices might increase for both imported and domestic products, these will be immaterial for final consumers.[78] Moreover, the EP expects that citizens and consumers will support the energy transition,[79] through behavioural changes towards more sustainable products. In addition, GDP and household consumption will only be affected slightly and AFEP suggests a positive long-term impact if revenues are recycled back to the economy.[80]

Compliance costs for businesses and administrative costs for the authorities will increase because of documentation, collection, monitoring, verification and certification procedures.[81] Where the importers choose to prove actual emissions higher costs are expected, but there will be lower or no CBAM charge.

Thus, the CBAM entails increased administrative and compliance costs, certain negative effects with respect to imports and exports and increased prices. However, given the limited coverage of the EU ETS and the CBAM, these effects will not be material.[82] In addition, these costs should be measured against the positive effects of CBAM on climate, as there will be prevention of carbon leakage and a reduction in carbon emissions in the EU and abroad, including partner states like Ukraine, Moldova and Belarus.[83]

E. Overall Assessment

Thus, the CBAM is essential to ensure the effectiveness of the EU's climate objectives and is a promising instrument as it can also raise revenue,[84] which can be used to cover the costs of the pandemic in the short term. In the long term, being a pigouvian tax, its revenue raising nature will subside as its environmental purpose is being achieved.

Since the coverage of carbon pricing within the EU under the ETD and the ETS is limited, the authors believe that it would be more effective if the proposed CBAM is

[75] Especially since free allocation is phased out. The EP stresses the importance of CBAM not providing double protection to European businesses, to comply with WTO rules (EP Resolution (n 52) para 14).
[76] CBAM Impact Assessment (n 43) 62.
[77] ibid 69.
[78] ibid 71–72.
[79] EP Resolution (n 52) para 4.
[80] Pyrka et al (n 54) paras 5–6, 58, 61; AFEP (n 74) 53.
[81] EP Resolution (n 52) para 18; CBAM Impact Assessment (n 43) 74–80.
[82] CBAM Impact Assessment (n 43) 57.
[83] Pyrka et al (n 54) paras 5 and 67; AFEP (n 74) 53; CBAM Impact Assessment (n 43) 46–52.
[84] The revenue generation from the CBAM certificates is lower than the revenue raised from the EU ETS. The amount of revenue depends on the carbon price and will be higher where there is no free allocation under the EU ETS. CBAM Impact Assessment (n 43) 81.

paired with a CO_2 tax applicable within the EU that covers carbon emissions currently not included within the EU ETS. However, in proposing and implementing such a tax it is important to take into account the effects of the COVID-19 pandemic on environmental tax design.

IV. The Effects of the COVID-19 Pandemic on Environmental Tax Design

The COVID-19 pandemic has had a double effect on the environmental debate. On the one hand, the increasing importance that climate change had been gaining, both in political and scientific debates, was hindered by the health emergency. On the other hand, it produced a surprising temporarily drop in air pollution,[85] related to the restrictive measures adopted by governments to counter the pandemic.[86]

These factors must be considered when designing an environmental tax in the post-pandemic era. Even some of the schemes, already in place and calibrated to pre-pandemic conditions for contrasting the contamination of the environment, may need to be revisited.[87] In this section, the main ways that COVID-19 might have affected the optimal design of environmental taxes will be analysed, considering the consequences that national lockdowns and restrictive measures are having on the population.

A. The Use of Taxes as Corrective Measures

When choosing a tax over other measures for correcting an externality or influencing people's behaviour, several factors should be considered. Primarily, whether other more direct measures, such as restrictive regulations, might be more effective in achieving the objective. Indeed, as clear as the need for a corrective measure might seem, its correct design is often problematic. Some of the effects of a specific measure might be unpredictable and act as a disturbing factor in the application of the policy.

Using tax as a corrective measure is generally recognised to have two main advantages *vis à vis* the use of restrictive regulations, which compensate for the reduced effectiveness.[88] First, environmental taxes can limit the damages on the specific industry or sector hit by the corrective measure. Indeed, after the economic shutdown of

[85] C Le Quéré and A Peregon, 'Carbon dioxide emissions continue to grow amidst slowly emerging climate policies' (2020) 10 *Nature and Climate Change* 3–6.

[86] It acted as a reset button on several aspects of people's lives and of governments' approaches to politics. Many aspects of the world's economy, societal framework and technological reliance have been completely disrupted by the pandemic and the majority of them seem not to be returning to what used to be considered 'normal'. The concept of reset in economic, societal, geopolitical, environmental and technological aspects of the world is widely presented in K Schwab and T Malleret, 'COVID-19: The Great Reset' (Cologne/Geneva, Forum Publishing, 2020).

[87] A Rowell, 'COVID-19 & Environmental Law' (2020) *University of Illinois College of Law Legal Studies Research Paper* No. 20–19.

[88] J Mirrlees et al (eds), *Dimensions of Tax Design: The Mirrlees Review* (Oxford, Oxford University Press, 2010) 136.

numerous industries due to COVID-19, too stringent regulatory limitations to pollution might be considered vexatious to some businesses and push them out of the market. Second, there is a political favour to environmental taxes. Differently from regulations, proposals for a tax, especially if starting at a low rate, are less likely to be stopped at an early stage due to strong lobbying activities or to political discontent.

All in all, although regulations might result in being more effective in reducing the targeted polluting activity, taxation can be the first step toward a broader environmental policy. Furthermore, taxes have the interesting additional benefit of collecting revenue, useful in the post-pandemic scenario.

i. Identifying the Objectives of Environmental Taxation

The main two purposes of environmental taxation are the idea of making polluters pay the social cost they impose on society through pollution and, contemporarily, the actual reduction in the production or consumption of the polluting factor. These two objectives are oddly intertwined, as the reduction of the socially damaging activity is a consequence of the increase of the social cost of pollution. Nonetheless, this connection is not as straightforward as it seems because it depends on many factors, such as the elasticity of the demand for the targeted polluting factor and the design of the tax.

Achieving only the first objective of making polluters pay is still a desirable outcome but probably not optimal. In principle, governments might want to increase environmental taxation until the marginal cost for polluters to produce or consume polluting goods is equal to the marginal environmental benefit of the additional abatement the tax induces.[89] Therefore, the most desirable outcome is reaching an equilibrium between the polluting behaviour and the benefit for the environment induced by the tax. This is the basic principle of Pigouvian taxes, as opposed to the so-defined 'environmentally-related taxes', which have the main goal of raising revenue.[90]

Pigouvian taxes have the distortion of the socially harmful behaviour they target as a main objective. They also raise revenue, as they collect money from entities that adopt that behaviour. This implies a double positive effect of these taxes, referred to as a 'double dividend':[91] raising revenue and improving the environment, reducing the targeted polluting factor.[92] Nevertheless, as appealing as this intuition might be, especially after the pandemic, some counterintuitive effects need to be considered.[93] Generally, increasing the price of polluting goods makes consumers relatively poorer and less keen on consuming. Disincentivising the use of these polluting goods reduces the revenue collected through environmental taxes. Pigouvian taxes can therefore be considered 'self-destructive' as their long-term objective is to annihilate their own

[89] J Mirrlees et al, *Tax by Design: The Mirrlees Review* (Oxford, Oxford University Press, 2011).

[90] See MP Herrera Molina, 'Design options and their rationales' (2014) in JE Milne and M Skou Andersen (eds), *Handbook of Research on Environmental Taxation* (Cheltenham, Edward Elgar, 2014).

[91] D Pearce, 'The Role of Carbon Taxes in Adjusting to Global Warming' (1991) 101(407) *Economic Journal*, 938–48. However, see also WK Jaeger, 'The double dividend debate' in JE Milne and M Skou Andersen (eds), *Handbook of Research on Environmental Taxation* (Cheltenham, Edward Elgar, 2014).

[92] Mirrlees et al (n 88).

[93] Mirrlees et al (n 88); Mirrlees et al (n 89).

taxable base. As a consequence, when adopting a Pigouvian tax, the main objective of creating a disincentive to a specific behaviour must be kept in mind.

Conversely, when an environmental tax is imposed as a levy on a polluting activity with the main objective of raising revenue and positive environmental side effects, which might still be a possible idea, especially in the post-pandemic scenario, further considerations are needed. In particular, the debate would exit the framework of environmental protection and enter the framework of revenue-raising taxes, which is far more delicate and could even trigger constitutional issues, especially if proposed at a supranational level.[94] For the purpose of this analysis, the authors will consider environmental taxes that are primarily aimed at addressing, directly or indirectly, environmental problems (ie Pigouvian taxes).

B. Criteria of Good Environmental Tax Design

The criteria of good tax design must be shaped according to the objective of the tax, re-adapting the principles of the Smithian nature of equity, neutrality, simplicity and stability.[95] As environmental taxes are generally designed to change people's behaviour and consequently self-erode, neutrality and stability must be interpreted differently. It is rather worth considering the coherence of the environmental tax with its objectives, and its economic efficiency as compared to other instruments.

Table 1 Criteria of good environmental tax design

Criteria of good tax design	Description	Pandemic effects
Economic Efficiency	Coherence with the objective of the tax without unwilled distortions	Potentially improved due to the increase in elasticity to prices
Fairness	Equity foundations of the tax	Controversial, potentially improved
Ease of Administration	Resources used to administer and collect the tax	Unaffected
Practicability	Actual possibility to introduce the tax	Controversial

i. Economic Efficiency

Environmental taxes here analysed are meant to be distortive, as they aim to change the behaviour of individuals and firms to reduce their negative externalities. The more

[94] Molina (n 90) 89.

[95] Mirrlees et al (n 88); Mirrlees et al (n 89). See also the criteria used by AJ Auerbach, MP. Devereux, M Keen and J Vella, 'Destination-Based Cash Flow Taxation' (2017) *Oxford University Centre for Business Taxation WP* 17/01; a different set of good design criteria is selected in J Pavel and L Vìtek, 'Transaction costs of environmental taxation: the administrative burden' in JE Milne and M Skou Andersen (eds), *Handbook of Research on Environmental Taxation* (Cheltenham, Edward Elgar, 2014).

they change people's behaviour towards their desired goal, the more effective they are. However, one must acknowledge that they might also have unwilled distortions, which should be predicted and avoided.

a. The Role of Elasticity in Environmental Taxes

Considering the existence of a 'green' (non-polluting) alternative to the activity hit by a generic environmental tax, it is possible to hypothesise that the green and non-green activities are less than perfect substitutes, as for equal prices, the green activity would be preferred. This is because the green activity would incorporate the 'environmental protection' good and, under the standard assumption of non-satiation of individuals, it is at least weakly preferred.

Assuming that there are externalities in the system, the first fundamental theorem of welfare economics is not valid. Therefore, a market-based solution is used to attempt the correction of the market failure.

Figure 1 Partial equilibrium analysis on the introduction of a corrective tax

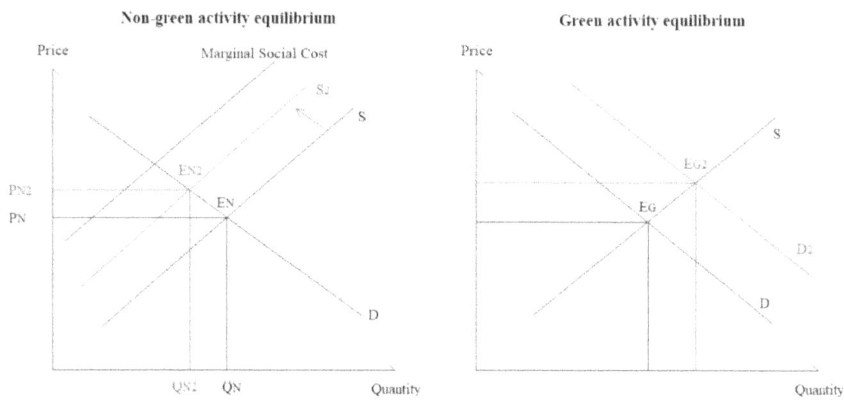

After the introduction of the corrective tax in the system, the supply of the non-green activity is shifted upwards, the price of the polluting activity will increase, and the quantity traded will decrease in the new equilibrium (EN2). As the green activity is a substitute for the non-green activity, its demand will increase, reaching a new equilibrium (EG2). However, as price increases, a wealth consideration that arises is that people are relatively poorer and they will be more inclined to buy the cheaper good, which is still the non-green activity. Overall, we can say that there are contrasting effects: if the final price of the non-green activity is still significantly lower than the green activity price, individuals will tend to still opt for the polluting activity; if the final prices are close to each other, then the effect is uncertain, but individuals may start opting for the green activity.

Up to this point, we have focused on a partial equilibrium analysis, taking some relevant factors as exogenous. However, it would be interesting for further research to structure a general equilibrium analysis of a specific tax. Another effect that could be taken into account might be the incentive for firms to stop providing polluting activities and start providing green activities instead.

Elasticity plays a fundamental role in this equilibrium.[96] The switch to a green activity after the introduction of the environmental tax heavily depends on the actual substitutivity of the activities and the price elasticity of the tax base.

The effect is even stronger in the long term rather than in the short term because in the long term individuals have more time to adjust their behaviours according to new prices.[97]

b. Specific Considerations on CBAM

At the international level, environmental taxes might be damaging to the firms operating in the country of adoption.[98] In the absence of international cooperation, the implementation of environmental taxes can result in weaker national firms or relatively poorer consumers, without any true environmental impact, as polluting neighbour countries might not change their behaviour. This would disincentivise the nation from introducing an environmental tax at all and from increasing its rate once adopted. Therefore, in case a pan-European carbon tax was to be adopted, a CBAM as discussed in section III would be necessary to address these distortions.[99]

c. Effects of the Pandemic

In this context, the constrictions related to COVID-19 created a situation that might incentivise individuals to alter their behaviour in response to an environmental tax. The effects of the lockdown on people can be summarised as follows:

- Collapse of the short-run–long-run dimension.
- Eradication of individuals' habits, making them more responsive to changes.
- Pauperisation of households, making them more price elastic.

These three factors can strategically be used to introduce effective environmental taxes. Indeed, individuals have become more responsive to changes and more price elastic, due to their pauperisation and the disruption in their routines.

Imposing an environmental tax on a polluting activity that has an available green alternative would be an effective measure for reducing future emissions. Thus, the pandemic has potentially positively impacted the efficiency dimension of a well-designed environmental tax. Consequently, this might be considered a good moment for introducing such a tax, as the effect would be more in line with the desired outcome because people are generally more prone to change their habits based on changes in prices.

[96] Mirrlees et al (n 88) 544.
[97] Mirrlees et al (n 89).
[98] This is generally the case. However, see the thorough analysis conducted in P Ekins and S Speck, 'Impacts on competitiveness: what do we know from modeling?' in JE Milne and M Skou Andersen (eds), *Handbook of Research on Environmental Taxation* (Cheltenham, Edward Elgar, 2014).
[99] C Garbarino, 'How countervailing measures could be used to limit strategic tax competition. An international overview' (2020) 48(4) *Intertax*, 416–31. For a broader discussion on EU tax coordination, see also C Garbarino, 'Harmonization and Coordination of Corporate Taxes in the European Union' (2016) 5–6 *EC Tax Review* 277–95.

ii. Fairness

Fairness and equity are very difficult dimensions to evaluate in a tax system, because of the multitude of factors involved and because of the subjectivity involved in the evaluation. Nonetheless, it is worth making some considerations related to fairness in environmental taxes and how COVID-19 might have affected them.

a. Polluters Pay Principle

The 'polluters pay' principle can be seen as a Pigouvian version of the benefit principle. It is fair to tax polluters as they are the ones damaging the environment: environmental taxes make them pay the price for the negative externalities. Environmental taxes appear to be in line with this principle and the CBAM too.

However, the logic might not be as straightforward as it seems. Green taxes are generally levied on polluting companies or final consumers of the polluting activity. The problem, though, is detecting who actually bears the burden of the tax.

For example, when environmental taxes are levied on polluting companies, they are very likely to be rebated on individuals, as companies are artificial entities and cannot be the ultimate bearer of a tax.[100] The bearer could be the shareholders of the company, who might also be held responsible for owning a polluting company. Or else, through an increase of prices, the tax could be rebated on the final consumers, who are the ones consuming the polluting activity. These would probably be two desirable scenarios, although we could not tell which one would be fairer. Nonetheless, the tax could also impact labour instead. Individuals working for the companies hit by the tax might see their wages lowered. This scenario might be considered a little less fair, or, at least, it would not be coherent with the polluters pay principle. It could be argued that the employees can consequently change their employer, not working for polluting firms, but this seems too optimistic of an assumption and often infeasible.

Therefore, it is difficult to link the adoption of an environmental tax to the 'fair' idea that polluters are the ultimate bearer of the tax. It can be said, however, that the individuals that are hit by the tax are somewhat related to the polluting activity.

b. Ability to Pay Principle

The ability to pay principle is the Smithian assumption according to which individuals should contribute to public expenditures in proportion to their wealth. This principle is fundamental in income taxes and determines the degree of progressivity of tax systems. However, being levied on externalities, Pigouvian taxes do not usually take into account the taxpayers' ability to pay.

Because they often result in an increase in prices of the targeted polluting goods, environmental taxes might rather have the same regressivity features witnessed in

[100] For a thorough collection of analyses, see K Kosonen, 'Regressivity of environmental taxation: myth or reality?' in JE Milne and M Skou Andersen (eds), *Handbook of Research on Environmental Taxation* (Cheltenham, Edward Elgar, 2012) 162.

consumption taxes.[101] As they do not consider the level of wealth of the individuals on which they are levied, environmental taxes can be more burdensome for poorer households.

Although progressivity in a tax system should be looked at as an overall concept, one must make sure that the introduction of an environmental tax does not become vexatious for individuals that live in conditions of poverty, especially if other cheap solutions are not provided. This can happen when taxes are imposed on bare necessities, such as energy, which is used for basic needs (eg, hot water).

c. Effects of the Pandemic

Confinement measures and restrictions to certain activities put in place by various governments have forcefully changed the habits of many individuals, often working from home and reducing their presence in public spaces. Additionally, travel restrictions, due to forced fiduciary quarantine on arrival or travel bans, are heavily discouraging people to travel internationally. This altered the demand for certain types of goods, such as air and land transport. In consequence, the substitutivity of these goods has changed, most likely increased as they are, in some cases, no more fundamental to carrying out ordinary activities.

The pandemic resulted in a reset of habits, values, and international relations. While the restrictions applied, individuals seemed, and in many cases still seem, more receptive to changes in their routines. Additionally, poorer households have become more elastic to prices and, therefore, more likely to switch to the non-polluting alternative to the good hit by the environmental tax.

The existence and availability of an affordable 'green' alternative might be fundamental to the fairness dimension, under an equity perspective. The risk is to have a mere increase in prices for all individuals indistinctly, aggravating some already dreadful situations. Under the polluters pay principle, a more efficient tax, due to more elastic reactions to the levy, can also be considered a fairer tax as it is more in line with its own objectives and more successful. Considering both variables, the effect of COVID-19 on this dimension is rather controversial. However, after the pandemic, a well-designed environmental tax in the presence of a green alternative could be more effective and fairer, due to the increased elasticity and a possible post-lockdown inclination to engage in different habits.

iii. Ease of Administration

Environmental taxes tend to be quite hard to administer because they target variables that are generally difficult to measure. Therefore, it is often suggested to administer them through tax and environmental experts.[102]

Moreover, the revenue collected is generally small and might not even cover administrative expenses. However, some proxies of pollution can be identified and used as tax

[101] However, this obviously depends on the design of the tax. See ibid 172.
[102] Molina (n 90) 95.

bases, making taxation easier to administer and more effective. Therefore, the dimension concerning the cost of administration heavily depends on the design of the tax. The pandemic does not seem to have affected this dimension, concerning environmental taxes.

One factor that might be worth mentioning is that governments will tend to prefer environmental taxes that are easy to administer, for the budget constraints consequent to the pandemic. Therefore, too specific Pigouvian taxes might not be the ideal choice, whereas taxes based on approximations, which can work even with the resources already at disposal of tax administrations, might be preferred.

iv. Practicability

Together with sustainability, which is less important in Pigouvian taxes because of their 'self-destructing' feature, practicability is a relevant factor that measures the actual possibility to introduce the new tax. Some taxes that are technically sound might encounter difficulties in their adoption as they might harm the interests of some political groups or be proposed at the wrong time.

Environmental taxes are generally considered more acceptable than other policy instruments for environmental regulation. However, the psychological order of the population is a relevant factor. Taking into account that all losses from the status quo are generally perceived as painful,[103] it is fundamental to understand whether this dimension is significantly affected by the pandemic or not.

a. Effects of the Pandemic

Measuring the effects of the pandemic on people's mindsets and behaviours is quite hard. Lockdowns seem to have had contrasting effects on populations. The overall outcome of the pandemic is likely to depend upon what people perceive as the status quo.

The environmental effects of the pandemic (eg, cleaner air, often cleaner water, exploding animal populations, reduced GHG emissions) might be seen as the new normal or as a temporary positive effect of the pandemic.[104] If this improvement is seen as a new equilibrium, then a loss from this new status quo would be perceived negatively by the population. This would imply an inclination towards the adoption of a corrective tax that helps to avoid the degradation of the environment. If the pre-pandemic is perceived as normalcy, then environmental degradation would simply constitute a return to the status quo.

From an economic perspective, national lockdowns and shutdown of industrial sectors made populations poorer and less willing to accept further burdens. Therefore, society will be more inclined to accept the introduction of an environmental tax if the willingness to maintain the current environmental benefits is stronger than the perceived burden of the tax.

[103] Rowell (n 87).
[104] ibid.

For further research, it would be interesting to analyse how the pandemic affected people's perception of the environmental crisis or the population's attention to global issues.

C. The Use of Revenue

When designing a new tax measure, the destination of the revenue could play a key role for several reasons. First and foremost, environmental taxation could grant a handful of resources that could be earmarked for being dedicated to achieving environmental goals.[105] The process of earmarking taxes has been highly criticised in optimal tax design.[106] It is argued that there are no reasons for spending on particular items and that in the absence of a binding constraint on spending, earmarking becomes an 'empty rhetoric' that misleads taxpayers. However, earmarking can have a strong political impact for advertising the adoption of a tax, especially at the EU level. Additionally, if well regulated, it can grant commitment to the solution of the environmental problem.[107]

In the context of the EU recovery, the resources coming from environmental taxation could act as a 'motivator', both for the EU Member States and taxpayers. Specifically, the need to collect revenue to cover the huge costs incurred for COVID-19, and to finance the economic recovery after the pandemic, could constitute an incentive for the EU Member States to support the adoption of a new EU CO_2 tax.

Designing an EU CO_2 tax as a new EU own resource would prevent the effect of turning environmental taxation into an important part of countries' public revenues, which could lead to an undesirable effect of not providing incentives for less polluting behaviour so as not to erode the tax base and thus the revenue.[108] However, it is believed that such a solution would bring many practical criticalities against the need to provide a solution in the short term (eg unanimity required by Article 311 TFEU). Moreover, the EU Member States could lose the aforementioned interest in supporting the adoption of the proposed measure, as the revenue would no longer flow into national funds but EU 'funds'.

In light of the above, a harmonised solution to be implemented at the national level by the EU Member States should be preferred. On the contrary, revenues from CBAM should become a new EU own resource that could be used to pay for NGEU as stated by the European Council.[109] Alternatively, they could be used for environmental purposes – for example, to provide finance under the third goal of COP26, which adheres better with the environmental purpose behind such a measure and international expectations.

It should also be considered that post-pandemic corrective taxes ought to be levied on the use or consumption of polluting goods and activities that have an affordable

[105] On earmarking, see JM Buchanan, 'The Economics of Earmarked Taxes' (1963) 71(5) *Journal of Political Economy* 457–69. See also A Kotha, 'Earmarking of Taxes for Disruption and Recovery' ch 5 of this volume.

[106] See Mirrlees et al (n 89) 471.

[107] See M Marsilian and TI Renstrom, 'Time Inconsistency in Environmental Policy: Tax Earmarking as a Commitment Solution' (2000) 110(3) *The Economic Journal*, C123–38.

[108] Geringer (n 23).

[109] European Council Conclusions (n 62) para A29.

green substitute, to avoid excessive burdens on poorer households. The revenue raised from the EU CO_2 tax could be used to provide affected households with lump-sum refunds[110] or to reduce other charges, particularly those on labour.[111] This would help increase the level of employment all over the EU. Indeed, as showed above, potential benefits from an EU CO_2 tax to contribute to employment objectives could provide a powerful political message to support the introduction of this measure.

Governments could also decide to earmark revenue raised from the proposed EU CO_2 tax to promote green initiatives and protect the environment, as a more sustainable basis for economic recovery measures.[112] Another solution could consist of channelling the revenue into funds specifically set up to finance regional policy measures. Moreover, in the long term, revenues will decrease as the environmental objectives of the tax are achieved.

According to the authors, the post-pandemic era is the perfect timing to introduce such a tax not only from environmental and economic perspectives[113] but also from a psychological point of view. Many changes have been triggered by COVID-19: changes in social values, changes in people's approach to the environment, economic and investment decisions' changes. Research showed[114] that considering the impact each of them may have on the way environmental law operates can help us to develop thoughtful and effective strategies. Such planning is particularly important in times when society is psychologically ready for an extended period of physical, emotional, economic and environmental recovery.

V. Conclusions

The COVID-19 pandemic has significantly shaped the environmental tax debate. The relevant reduction in pollution witnessed at the global level might constitute a step forward when seen as a new normal. In this chapter, the authors underlined that, building on the experience gained from the 2008 economic crisis, a well-designed corrective tax can be even more effective after the pandemic. Using the EU as a case study, they propose a potential solution to design a fair and efficient carbon pricing system 'within' and 'at' the EU borders while taking into account the COVID-19 pandemic's effects on the economy.

This research highlights the main arguments to reopen discussions on the introduction of an EU CO_2 tax, commensurate with the CBAM, as a tool to boost EU efforts to protect the environment while supporting the recovery from the COVID-19 pandemic.

[110] On the potential regressive effect of environmental taxes see Kosonen (n 100).

[111] See C Dias Soares, 'Earmarking Revenues from Environmentally Related Taxes' in JE Milne and M Skou Andersen (eds), *Handbook of Research on Environmental Taxation* (Cheltenham, Edward Elgar, 2014); H Ashiabor, 'Financing Environmental Expenditures through the earmarking of taxes and charges' in *Tax Expenditures and Environmental Policy* (Cheltenham, Edward Elgar, 2020) 148.

[112] Kotha (n 105).

[113] For a discussion on how COVID-19 led to a 'unitary moment of the EU fiscal evolution' see Garbarino (n 1).

[114] Rowell (n 87).

14

The Future of the EU's Financing in Times of Disruption and Recovery: Normative and Technical Issues of Greening the EU's Own Resources System

STEFANIE GERINGER

Abstract

The recent developments in EU fiscal policies indicate the existence of a current zeitgeist to break new ground and reassess earlier positions which might have been thought unwavering prior to the COVID-19 pandemic. It hence appears to be the right moment to discuss the cornerstones of the EU's financing, such as the composition of EU revenues. Green own resources could prove particularly favourable, as they can stimulate the green transition within the EU and mitigate the next – probably more destructive – crisis. However, whether these effects materialise, depends crucially on their legal structure. This chapter elucidates the normative and technical issues permeating the introduction of environment-related own resources. The author argues that all green own resources should be paired with an obligation to introduce corresponding national taxes in the Member States via an EU directive. The revenues collected by the Member States should then be broadly passed on to the European Commission. By introducing new green own resources in the form of tax-based contributions, both the fiscal and environmental goals could be achieved. However, notwithstanding these benefits, potential challenges and obstacles related to the introduction of tax-based contributions should also be taken into account.

I. Introduction

The EU's financing has hardly ever enjoyed comprehensive media coverage or the attention of a broader public.[1] This might stem from the fact that for many years the focus in EU fiscal policies was put on sustaining the status quo. Similarly, the lack of future-oriented spending was at the centre of criticism in academic scholarship.[2] It was held that any evolvement would require a commitment to a higher level of fiscal federalism. A real switch in time towards a more tightly-knit European community however appeared rather doubtful.[3]

Similar to developments at the national level,[4] the COVID-19 pandemic and its devastating socio-economic effects[5] initiated an unexpected, tremendous shift at the EU level both on the revenue and the expenditure sides.[6] It was decided that the means combined in the multi-annual framework (MFF) 2021–27[7] and the recovery programme 'NextGenerationEU' (NGEU) should be used at least to the extent of 30 per cent to achieve the EU's climate goals (ie reduction of carbon emissions to at least 55 per cent compared with 1990 levels and carbon neutrality by 2050).[8] To achieve their ambitious aims, the Member States agreed on a joint borrowing of money from the international markets for the first time in the EU's history.[9] These loans should be re-financed by a set of new own resources, among them three green own resources.[10] One of them, a new own resource based on the amount of non-recycled plastic packaging waste (plastic waste-based contribution),[11] was already introduced and has been applied as

[1] H Enderlein, O Funke and J Lindner, 'The EU budget: Which fiscal capacity at the European level?' in J Richardson and S Mazey (eds), *European Union: Power and policy-making*, 4th edn (London, Routledge, 2015) 212.

[2] M Nettesheim, '§ 8. Finanzordnung' in T Oppermann, CD Classen and M Nettesheim (eds), *Europarecht*, 8th edn (Munich, CH Beck, 2018) para 4.

[3] Enderlein, Funke and Lindner (n 1) 213; LP Feld, 'Zum zukünftigen Finanzrahmen der EU' in KA Konrad and T Lohse (eds), *Einnahmen- und Steuerpolitik in Europa: Herausforderungen und Chancen* (Frankfurt am Main, Peter Lang, 2009) 147 (who also strongly advises against the idea of working towards fiscal federalism at the EU level).

[4] B de Witte, 'The European Union's COVID-19 recovery plan: The legal engineering of an economic policy shift' (2021) 58(3) *Common Market Law Review* 635–36.

[5] For a discussion of the COVID-19 pandemic's impact through the lens of socio-economic (tax) justice, see Y Lind in ch 17 of this volume.

[6] For a general overview, see FE Grisostolo and L Scarcella in ch 10 of this volume.

[7] The EU budget consists of the multi-annual framework which determines the pillars of the EU budgets for the following seven years as well as the yearly budgets. The fundamental legal framework is described in Articles 312–316 of the Consolidated Version of the Treaty of the Functioning of the European Union [2012] OJ C326 (hereafter TFEU). With regard to the aim of this chapter, issues concerning the budgetary procedure are not assessed in the following.

[8] Special meeting of the European Council (17, 18, 19, 20 and 21 July 2020) – Conclusions [2020] EUCO 10/20 CO EUR 8 CONCL 4, 7 and 14 (at paras A21 and 18) (hereafter Council Conclusions). For an overview of the EU's ambitions to mitigate the effects of climate change, see, eg, H Kogels, 'Good Intentions and a Call for Higher Speed on the Bumpy Road to Carbon Neutrality' (2022) 31(1) *EC Tax Review* 2–3.

[9] See in detail Grisostolo and Scarcella (n 6).

[10] Council Conclusions (n 8) paras A7 and 145–150; Interinstitutional Agreement between the European Parliament, the Council of the European Union and the European Commission on budgetary discipline, on cooperation in budgetary matters and on sound financial management, as well as on new own resources, including a roadmap towards the introduction of new own resources [2020] OJ L443I/28 (hereafter IIA). See in detail Grisostolo and Scarcella (n 6).

[11] The European Commission uses the term 'plastics own resource' to refer to this new revenue source; ec.europa.eu/info/strategy/eu-budget/long-term-eu-budget/2021-2027/revenue/own-resources/plastic-own-resource_en. The author however prefers to refer to it as the plastic waste-based contribution for purposes of

of 2021. These amendments were made in order to respond to the critiques related to the outdatedness and lack of coherence between the EU's own resources system and the EU's budgeting as highlighted above.

The recent developments in EU fiscal policies indicate the existence of a current zeitgeist to break new ground and reassess earlier positions which might have been thought unwavering prior to the COVID-19 pandemic. Seen in this light, it appears to be the right moment to evaluate the cornerstones of the EU's financing such as the composition of EU revenues and how these revenues ought to be accrued. Discussing these inquiries ought not be left to fiscal experts, as they address fundamental issues beyond the obvious financial aspects. After all, questions related to the structures of the EU own resources system are inextricably linked to the basic conception and function of the EU as the institution that brackets our economies and societies. This assertion holds particularly true for purposes of the green new own resources which are meant to stimulate the green transition within the EU territory. Their introduction should also be understood in the broader context of tax and crises, considering that climate change, in contrast to the COVID-19 pandemic, is a crisis that can be expected to affect our lives also in the mid and long term.[12] The effective use of green new own resources could hence be understood as an instrument to alleviate the next – likely more destructive – crisis. Additionally, our decisions regarding the design of the new own resources crucially determines the EU's future reliance on or independence of the Member States' national politics.

The aim of this chapter is not to replicate other research efforts in academic scholarship dedicated to discussing the future of EU financing in light of the COVID-19 pandemic in a general manner[13] or performing an environmental analysis of the green new own resources.[14] Instead, this chapter elucidates the normative and technical issues permeating the introduction of environment-related new own resources.[15] This assessment is grounded on a depiction of the EU own resources system until 2021 (legal background, core elements and criticism), which forms the necessary basis for a profound discussion of the more recent developments. An overview of the introduced and proposed green new own resources is then followed by an analysis of the implications of the legal design of the plastic waste-based contribution, the only green new own resource already adopted. In particular, its suitability for achieving the desired fiscal and environmental objectives is to be assessed. Highlighting the critical flaw in its current design – the lack of commitment to put the financial burden on businesses and consumers who use single-use plastics effectively – the author argues that the plastic waste-based contribution and all other green new own resources should be paired with an obligation to introduce corresponding national taxes in the Member States via an EU directive. The revenues collected by the Member States should then be broadly passed on to the European Commission. Hence, the author advocates the introduction or corresponding adjustment of new green own resources in the form of tax-based

this chapter as a matter of coherence (if we consider the existing VAT-based and GNI-based contributions; see s II below).

[12] R Collier, A Pirlot and J Vella, 'Tax Policy and the COVID-19 Crisis' (2020) 48(8/9) *Intertax* 800.

[13] See Grisostolo and Scarcella (n 6).

[14] See E Scuderi, A Rizzo and A Loucaidou in ch 13 of this volume.

[15] Questions related to the fundamental justification of EU taxes are hence not covered by the aim of this chapter. See K Pantazatou in ch 8 of this volume.

contributions to achieve both fiscal and environmental goals. The benefits as well as potential challenges and obstacles related to the adoption of tax-based contributions are discussed in detail in the following. The chapter concludes with a summary of the key findings and an outlook to future research.

II. The Pillars of the EU's Financing System Until 2021

The status of the EU as a supranational organisation is also reflected in its financing system. Accordingly, the Union 'shall provide itself with the means necessary to attain its objectives and carry through its policies', hence the EU budget 'shall be financed wholly from own resources' (Article 311 TFEU[16]). The means to finance the EU's budgets predominantly derive from EU own resources.[17] Until 2021, these consisted of the traditional own resources (custom duties, as of writing), a Value Added Tax (VAT)-based own resource and a Gross National Income (GNI)-based own resource.[18] Their legal design diverges significantly:

- The revenues accrued from the collection of custom duties are broadly transferred to the European Commission (less collection costs[19]). These structures reflect some features of what could be regarded as an EU tax.[20]
- The other two 'own' resources are effectively contributions from the Member States' budgets.[21] These contributions can further be differentiated by considering their existing or absent correlation with the EU citizens' behaviour. The VAT-based own resource arguably shares an indirect relationship with the taxpayers although it does not translate into a direct transfer of a share of VAT revenues.[22] By contrast, the GNI-based own resource is fully uncoupled from the individual taxpayer's tax burden.[23]

[16] Consolidated Version of the Treaty of the Functioning of the European Union [2012] OJ C326 (hereafter TFEU).

[17] See in detail Grisostolo and Scarcella (n 6).

[18] Article 2(1) of the Council Decision 2014/335/EU on the system of own resources of the European Union [2014] OJ L168/105 (hereafter Own Resources Decision 2014). The wording is borrowed from E Traversa and G Bizioli, 'Solidarity in the European Union in the Time of COVID-19: Paving the Way for a Genuine EU Tax?' (2020) 48(4/9) *Intertax* 744.

[19] 20% until 2020 (Article 2(3) of the Own Resources Decision 2014 (n 18)) and 25% as of 2021 (Article 9(2) of the Council Decision (EU, Euratom) 2020/2053 on the system of own resources of the European Union and repealing Decision 2014/335/EU, Euratom [2020] OJ L424/1 (hereafter Own Resources Decision)).

[20] Traversa and Bizioli (n 18) 744. See moreover PA Hernández González-Barreda in ch 7 of this volume.

[21] The EU treaties are hence shaped by a formal, not a material understanding of the term 'own resources'; eg, B Meermagen, 'Beitrags- und Eigenmittelsystem: Die Finanzierung inter- und supranationaler Organisationen, insbesondere der Europäischen Gemeinschaften', Münchner Universitätsschriften Vol 169 (Munich, CH Beck, 2002) 218–25.

[22] ie the VAT revenues only form the starting point of the calculation basis; Article 2 of the Council Regulation (EEC, EURATOM) No 1553/89 of 29 May 1989 on the definitive uniform arrangements for the collection of own resources accruing from value added tax [1989] OJ L155/9, as amended by Council Regulation (EU, Euratom) 2021/769 of 30 April 2021 amending Regulation (EEC, Euratom) No 1553/89 on the definitive uniform arrangements for the collection of own resources accruing from value added tax [2021] OJ L165/9.

[23] Meermagen (n 21) 190.

The EU own resources system has long been described as outdated, opaque and complex.[24] The European Commission, among others,[25] has moreover pointed to the missing link between the EU's policy agenda and the VAT- and GNI-based own resources:

> New own resources could fully replace the existing VAT-based own resource as well as reducing the scale of the GNI-based resource, taken directly from national treasuries. The introduction of new own resources would mirror the progressive shift of the budget structure towards policies closer to EU citizens and aiming at delivering European public goods and a higher EU added value. It could support – and be closely linked to – the achievement of important EU or international policy objectives, for instance in relation to development, climate change or the financial markets.[26]

However, until 2020, the Commission's proposals on new own resources that would have met these criteria failed to reach unanimous consent among the Member States.[27]

III. Environment-Related Own Resources in the EU's COVID-19 Recovery Strategy

Each of the six new own resources outlined in the Commission's recovery plan is linked to specific EU objectives. Three of them should contribute to achieving the EU's goals related to environmental protection as well as to the combat against climate change:

- a new own resource based on the amount of non-recycled plastic packaging waste;
- a new own resource linked to the recently agreed[28] carbon border adjustment mechanism (CBAM); and
- a new own resource funded by the to be extended EU Emissions Trading System (ETS).

As mentioned above, the new own resource related to non-recycled plastic packaging waste (plastic waste-based contribution) was already introduced and has been applied as of 2021. Technically, it was adopted as (another) contribution from the Member

[24] See eg Proposal for a COUNCIL DECISION on the system of own resources of the European Union [2011] COM(2011) 510 final (hereafter Commission Proposal 2011) (at s 1.1).

[25] See eg High Level Group on Own Resources, 'Future Financing of the EU: Final report and recommendations of the High Level Group on Own Resources' (December 2016), ec.europa.eu/info/sites/default/files/about_the_european_commission/eu_budget/future-financing-hlgor-final-report_2016_en.pdf (hereafter Monti Report).

[26] Communication from the Commission to the European Parliament, the Council, the European Economic and Social Committee, the Committee of the Regions and the National Parliaments: The EU Budget Review [2010] COM(2010) 700 final (hereafter EU Budget Review 2010) 26. These considerations are further reflected, inter alia, in the Commission Proposal 2011 (n 24), the Own Resources Decision 2014 (n 18) and the recent Own Resources Decision (n 19).

[27] For an overview of earlier reform proposals see eg Policy Department for Budgetary Affairs, 'Reform of the EU own resources' (March 2021), www.europarl.europa.eu/RegData/etudes/IDAN/2021/690963/IPOL_IDA(2021)690963_EN.pdf (hereafter Own Resources Report) 7–8 (with further references). See moreover Grisostolo and Scarcella (n 6).

[28] See www.consilium.europa.eu/en/press/press-releases/2022/03/15/carbon-border-adjustment-mechanism-cbam-council-agrees-its-negotiating-mandate.

States' budgets.[29] These contributions are calculated on the weight of non-recycled plastic packaging waste[30] at a rate of 0.80 euros per kilogram.[31] Similar to earlier contributions, the plastic waste-based contribution entails a correction mechanism in the form of an annual lump sum reduction for less prosperous Member States[32] to avoid an excessively regressive impact.[33] The plastic waste-based contribution is intended to encourage the reduction of use of single-use plastics, increase recycling efforts and foster the circular economy.[34] To achieve these purposes, 'Member States will be free to take the most suitable measures […], in line with the principle of subsidiarity.'[35] According to the wording, the Member States might thus freely decide either to pass the financial burden on to the producers, importers or consumers[36] of single-use waste by way of introducing a correlating tax, or to come up with these payments from their treasuries.[37]

As of writing, the two other green new own resources have not yet been adopted.[38] A critical assessment of the plastic waste-based contribution's legal design can thus prove revealing and valuable in the sense that, as we shall see below, potential learnings from the identification of normative and technical flaws accompanying the plastic waste-based contribution can be translated into recommendations for future EU fiscal policies. This process particularly allows us to describe ways of adoption through which the new green own resources' common objective to contribute to the EU's environmental goals could be best achieved.[39] These issues are addressed in the following section.

IV. Assessment of the Plastic Waste-Based Contribution's Legal Design in Light of the Objectives Pursued

The plastic waste-based contribution, like all of the green new own resources, is aimed at serving both fiscal and ecological objectives. From an environmental protection

[29] Which accordingly reduces the share of the GNI-based own resource.

[30] See on the relevant definitions as well as the calculation method in detail Article 2(2) of the Own Resources Decision (n 19). See also Grisostolo and Scarcella (n 6).

[31] Article 2(1)(c) of the Own Resources Decision (n 19).

[32] ie with GNIs per capita below the EU average. See in detail Article 2(2) of the Own Resources Decision (n 19).

[33] This lump sum amounts to 3.8 kilograms multiplied with the respective Member States' population in 2017; Recital 7 of the Own Resources Decision (n 19). The exact sums for each of the entitled Member States can be found in Article 2(2) of the Own Resources Decision (n 19).

[34] Recital 7 of the Own Resources Decision (n 19).

[35] ibid.

[36] From the experience with other forms of indirect taxes it can be assumed that a tax on non-recyclable plastic packaging waste would be passed on to the consumers. In a similar vein, see Scuderi, Rizzo and Loucaidou (n 14).

[37] In this sense, eg, A Cordewener, 'EU Budgetary Reform and Tax Harmonization: Becoming Brothers in Arms' (2022) 31(2) *EC Tax Review* 65–66. However, there are some hints that the European Commission expected the Member States to introduce corresponding national taxes to make citizens pay for the consumption of single-use waste (see s IV below).

[38] For an analysis of the latest developments, see Grisostolo and Scarcella (n 6).

[39] Council Conclusions (n 8) para 18; Annex II, Preamble Point H. of the IIA (n 10). With regard to the aim of this chapter, a discussion of possible models for an extended EU ETS and/or a CBAM is not included in the following assessment. See therefore Scuderi, Rizzo and Loucaidou (n 14).

perspective, it should lead to a reduction of use of single-use plastics, an increase of recycling efforts as well as a boost of the circular economy. From a fiscal perspective, it should contribute to financing the EU's expenditures and particularly repaying the borrowings related to the NGEU recovery programme as discussed above.

The plastic waste-based contribution's design might lead us to assume that Member States would be keen to introduce a corresponding national tax in an effort to minimise the contribution's effects on their national budgets. Passing the respective financial burden on to the producers, importers or consumers of single-use plastics would indeed prove capable of killing two birds with one stone. On one hand, a Member State's payment obligation would not have to be financed from the general budget. On the other, introducing a related tax might set an incentive to change ways of production as well as consumption behaviour. Hence, it might appear as the intuitionally logical outcome.

However, this result is not set in stone. Competition for foreign investment has likely become even more fierce during the course of the COVID-19 pandemic, as each country has been grappling with tremendous losses in revenues. In their recovery strategy, heads of state will have to walk a thin line between raising taxes and creating favourable environments for new businesses and economic growth.[40] Hence, Member States could likewise prefer to pay the plastic waste-based contribution from their general budgets to gain a competitive advantage over other Member States than pass this financial burden on to businesses and consumers.[41]

These observations are not of purely theoretical relevance, as can be demonstrated using the example of Austria.[42] When the plastic waste-based contribution was adopted, the Austrian minister for climate action, Leonore Gewessler, planned to introduce a corresponding domestic tax in accordance with the polluter pays principle.[43] However, the then-Austrian minister of finance, Gernot Blümel, intended to come up with the estimated 142 million euros per year from the federal budget.[44] His plans were harshly criticised by environmental organisations and opposition parties alike. They pointed

[40] P Baker, 'International Tax in the Time of COVID-19' (2020) 48(8/9) *Intertax* 806. This might be further exacerbated by the devastating effects stemming from the current war in Ukraine.

[41] See in this regard Own Resources Report (n 27) 12: 'The advantage of introducing such a levy at the EU rather than national level is that it could prevent the displacement among Member States of plastic waste for treatment.' See also Feld (n 3) 142 (who generally points to the advantages resulting from a transfer of competences to a higher level from a political-economic perspective against the background that national decision-makers tend to protect their local and domestic economies).

[42] Note that similar discussions have also been held in other Member States. For an overview of the diverse ways of adoption in the Member States, see E Scuderi, 'Towards A Plastic-Free Economy: The Italian Plastic Tax' (2021) *Rivista di Diritto Tributario* (supplemento online), www.rivistadirittotributario.it/2021/04/07/towards-a-plastic-free-economy-the-italian-plastic-tax, s 3.

[43] Austrian Federal Ministry of Climate Action, Environment, Energy, Mobility, Innovation and Technology, '3-Punkte-Plan gegen Plastik in Österreich' (7 September 2020) www.bmk.gv.at/service/presse/gewessler/20200907_3punkteplan.html.

[44] Note that the plastic waste-based contribution has cost the Austrian taxpayers approximately 220 million euros in the period between 1 January 2021 and 14 April 2022 according to a calculation by the not-for-profit organisation *Greenpeace*; 'Plastikmüll kostet SteuerzahlerInnen bisher schon 220 Mio. Euro' (*Greenpeace*, April 2022) plastik.greenpeace.at/plastikmuell-kostet-steuerzahlerinnen-bisher-schon-220-mio.-euro/?_ga=2.236506889.94428924.1650095801-292393818.1650095801.

to the insufficient nudging effect and additionally denounced the fact that all taxpayers would thereby have to carry the burden instead of those who produce, import or consume single-use plastics.[45] Nevertheless, as of writing, a domestic tax on non-recycled plastic packaging waste has not yet been introduced in Austria.[46]

This example is prone to illustrate a critical flaw in the plastic waste-based contribution's current design. Undisputedly, the fiscal objectives can be achieved no matter whether the contribution is paid from the general budget or financed through a corresponding national tax. Because the contribution is not paired with an obligation to introduce such a domestic tax, it might, however, not produce the intended steering effect related to its ecological objectives. Indeed, its aptitude to foster the EU's environmental goals depends crucially on the willingness of the Member States' governments to align their national tax policies with the EU's agenda. Due to divergent political, economic, social and cultural environments, this might yet prove unpopular in some Member States so that a voluntary introduction of a related plastics tax in all Member States appears rather illusory. The overall nudging effect of the plastic waste-based contribution in its current form can hence be called into question.

V. Proposal for a (Re-)design of Green New Own Resources as Tax-Based Contributions

It was discussed in the last section that the current legal design of the plastic waste-based contribution correlates with the underlying ecological goals only insufficiently. Provided that both the European Commission and the Member States are determined to green the EU's financing and thereby parallel the environmental protection efforts taken on the expenditure side, it should hence be considered adjusting the plastic waste-based contribution's structure.

In the author's opinion, a similarly effective steering effect in all Member States can only be realised by way of obliging national lawmakers to introduce a domestic tax at least at the same level as the existing own resource (ie 0.80 euros per kilogram). This could be achieved by adopting an EU directive that would set a minimum standard. For procedural purposes, the established mechanisms for traditional own resources (ie custom duties) could be broadly mimicked. Hence, the revenues related to the minimum tax should be passed through to the European Commission, while a certain percentage of these revenues could be left to the Member States as compensation for collection costs. The plastic waste-based contribution would thereby be transformed into a plastic waste tax-based contribution.[47] These structures could then be analogously

[45] See eg A Gabriel, 'Kritik an ÖVP-Plänen zu Plastiksteuer' (*Die Presse*, 31 July 2020) www.diepresse.com/5847173/kritik-an-ovp-planen-zu-plastiksteuer.

[46] See also M Lohmeyer, 'Österreich bei "Plastiksteuer" unter den Spitzenreitern' (*Die Presse*, 14 April 2022) www.diepresse.com/6125401/oesterreich-bei-plastiksteuer-unter-den-spitzenreitern.

[47] The idea of tax-based own resources is also supported by F Vanistendael, 'Will the Coronavirus Pandemic Cure the EU Budget?' (*Tax Notes International*, 19 June 2020) www.taxnotes.com/featured-analysis/will-coronavirus-pandemic-cure-eu-budget/2020/06/19/2cm4w?highlight=vanistendael%20eu%20taxes and Traversa and Bizioli (n 18) 751.

introduced for purposes of further green own resources, hence the proposed own resources linked to the extended EU ETS and the CBAM.[48]

The (re-)designing of the green new own resources as tax-based contributions entails several advantages beyond a safeguarding of their capability to serve both fiscal and environmental objectives.

The introduction of tax-based contributions (instead of 'real' EU taxes) would allow for an effective greening of the EU's fiscal system within the boundaries of the existing legal framework. Hence, identical results can be achieved without having to interfere with the delicate balance of competences between the EU and the Member States. This would also serve the EU principle of subsidiarity stipulated in Article 5(2) TEU.[49] For the time being, a further transfer of tax competences to the EU level does not seem preferable anyway, due to the lack of key democratic features and core elements of a financial constitution.[50]

Implementing a minimum standard at the EU level would still leave a certain degree of leeway to national lawmakers. Hence, they would be empowered to introduce a tax that goes beyond the minimum standard and assign the exceeding amount (ie, in the case of the plastic waste tax-based contribution, the revenues beyond the obligatory 0.80 euros per kilogram) to be used to finance the national budgets. The possibility to collect extra revenues solely in the national interest might additionally set a meaningful (fiscal) incentive for the Member States to diligently comply with their collection obligations.[51] Conversely, the introduction of a minimum tax does not mean that the Member States lose out on revenues. This assertion stems from the fact that the Member States would otherwise have to pay their contributions from the general budget. Replacing traditional contributions with tax-based contributions could thus be seen as a fiscal zero-sum game.

The (re-)designing of green new own resources as tax-based contributions would also allow for an analogous application of established procedures used for purposes of the traditional own resources (ie custom duties). No new collection mechanisms would hence have to be invented and tested, which would foster both simplicity and administrability.[52]

Another advantage[53] in (re-)designing green new own resources as tax-based contributions could moreover be seen in its effects on the political dimension of EU

[48] Reproducing the structures already in use for the collection of custom duties appears particularly appropriate for purposes of the CBAM if we keep in mind that the CBAM would fulfil a similar function. Their different foci (ie the CBAM's aim to correct diverging cost levels particularly stemming from different environment protection standards) can be identified as the main difference.

[49] Consolidated version of the Treaty on European Union [2012] OJ C326 (hereafter TEU).

[50] J Hey, 'Das Einnahmesystem der Europäischen Union: neue Steuern als neue Eigenmittel?' (2021) 32(7) *Europäische Zeitschrift für Wirtschaftsrecht* 285.

[51] Similarly (though in the context of a new own resource related to the Global Anti-Base Erosion (GloBE) proposal), J Englisch, 'Designing a Harmonized EU-GloBE in Compliance with Fundamental Freedoms' (2021) 30(3) *EC Tax Review* 141.

[52] See also Annex II, Preamble Point J. of the IIA (n 10): 'The calculation, transfer and control of the new own resources should not lead to an excessive administrative burden for Union institutions and national administrations.' For an elucidation of the criteria of 'good' environmental tax design, see Scuderi, Rizzo and Loucaidou (n 14). For a discussion of the eight features of 'good' law (among others, practicability) according to Lon Fuller, see H Filipczyk in ch 18 of this volume.

[53] Depending on individual preferences regarding the degree of European integration.

financing. The implementation of tax-based contributions that would use similar structures as traditional own resources[54] would lead to a simultaneous decrease of the share of GNI-based contributions in EU revenues.[55] Thereby, the EU's budgets would become increasingly independent from the Member States' national budgets, which would basically reduce the possibility of using contributions as a bargaining chip.[56] The EU own resources system's recalibration would then moreover be prone to diffuse political tensions between so-called 'net payers' and 'net receivers' in budget negotiations.[57]

Lastly, financing EU budgets to an increasing extent through tax-based contributions rather than through contributions from the Member States' general budgets helps realise intergenerational justice. This assertion stems from the fact that Member States might have to take on new borrowings to finance their expenses. Depending on the exact repayment conditions, these borrowings might have to be repaid by future generations. Contributions based on taxes however are financed by citizens now that are also likely to benefit from related investments.[58]

VI. Challenges and Obstacles to a (Re-)design of Green New Own Resources as Tax-Based Contributions

There are several arguments which speak in favour of a (re-)design of green new own resources as tax-based contributions. Nevertheless, this approach is likewise confronted with numerous impediments.

A competence base that would allow for the introduction of an EU-wide minimum plastics tax paralleling the existing plastic waste-based contribution can be found in Article 192(2)(a) TFEU.[59] This provision however demands for unanimous consent among the Member States' representatives in the Council of the European Union. Accordingly, adopting a related EU directive can be considered rather a political than a legal issue.[60] It must be pointed out that the adoption of such an EU directive would

[54] Indeed, the CBAM-related own resource can be expected to work as a traditional own resource, if we bear in mind the CBAM's broad comparability with existing custom duties; see (n 48).

[55] Such an automatism is indicated due to the current ceiling for own resources; see also, eg, de Witte (n 4) 666; Monti Report (n 25) 7.

[56] Nevertheless, it cannot be completely ruled out that some Member States would likewise withhold their tax-based contributions for political reasons.

[57] In the same vein, eg, Own Resources Report (n 27) 8; A Krenek, M Sommer and M Schratzenstaller, 'A WTO-compatible Border Tax Adjustment for the ETS to Finance the EU Budget' (2020) 596 *WIFO Working Papers*, www.wifo.ac.at/jart/prj3/wifo/resources/person_dokument/person_dokument.jart?publikationsid=65841&mime_type=application/pdf, 6–7. See also Grisostolo and Scarcella (n 6) and Pantazatou (n 15).

[58] Indeed, the postponement of proposals for corresponding own resources was the reason why Johannes Hahn, the EU budget commissioner, voted against the legislative proposals delivering on the European Green Deal's objectives in July 2021. He further justified his vote by arguing that he did not want future generations to carry the financial burden stemming from the COVID-19 recovery measures. T Mayer, 'Warum EU-Kommissar Hahn gegen das EU-Klimapaket stimmte' (*Der Standard*, 17/18 July 2021) www.derstandard.at/story/2000128245867/warum-eu-kommissar-hahn-gegen-das-eu-klimapaket-stimmte. For similar observations in the context of national measures, see A Brassey in ch 15 of this volume.

[59] It is widely held that Article 311 TFEU does not imply a general power of taxation for the EU bodies. A substantive provision in the TFEU is thus needed to legitimise the introduction of tax measures at the EU level (eg, Article 192(2) TFEU in relation to environmental taxes).

[60] See also Traversa and Bizioli (n 18) 751–52. In the same vein, see Grisostolo and Scarcella (n 6).

naturally lead to further limitations to the Member States' tax sovereignty. The latter, in conjunction with the related loss of bargaining power in budget negotiations discussed above, might indeed prove to be the greatest obstacle to the implementation of tax-based contributions.[61] Notwithstanding, an agreement on the introduction of a minimum plastics tax at the EU level could yet appear preferable to some of the Member States' governments particularly in the age of rising populism and nationalism. The funding of green new own resources through taxes which were imposed by 'the EU'[62] would take away the strain from national budgets.[63] At the same time, it would allow national lawmakers to introduce these taxes in a face-saving way (ie without being held primarily responsible for it).[64]

Both the introduction of a CBAM and the extension of the EU ETS would not encounter political issues to the same extent. The CBAM, as a specific type of custom duties, falls under the exclusive competence of the EU,[65] whereas directives related to the EU ETS only require a qualified majority.[66]

As soon as the Member States agree on the adoption of EU directives setting a minimum standard for taxes related to green new own resources, the issue of deficient democratic representation in the EU legislative procedure would also come to the forefront. Corresponding reforms would become an increasingly pressing issue as more tax-based contributions would be introduced.[67] A thorough assessment of this matter goes beyond the scope of this chapter.[68] Notwithstanding, it should be stressed that a higher degree of democratic representation in the legislative procedure could likely contribute to an increase in interest in EU politics among its citizens and their identification with the EU project.[69] It might also secure the public support regarding the introduction of green new own resources that, as we shall see below, is key to a successful implementation of the EU's environmental agenda. Setting standards for minimum taxation at the EU level in a process which upholds democratic representation would also help mitigate the effects of the phenomenon that an increasing number of EU citizens is not able to cast their vote in the EU country in which they live and/or work. Their voices would accordingly be heard via their representatives in the European

[61] See on the political dynamics in detail Grisostolo and Scarcella (n 6).

[62] No EU legal act can be adopted without the consent of the representatives of the Member States' governments (ie the Council of the European Union) and/or directly voted representatives (ie the European Parliament). Nevertheless, it can be observed that national politicians might successfully blame 'the EU' in order to boost their own agenda in domestic politics.

[63] Due to the EU budget's overwhelming reliance on the contributions paid from the Member States' budgets, 'the budget of the EU is considered by most member states to be a burden on their national budgets and their only interest is to get as much return from the EU budget as they can' (Vanistendael (n 47)).

[64] In the same vein, ibid: 'Because there is strong support for a European green deal while many national governments are reluctant to impose new environmental taxes, it would be convenient if the EU did the tax job and took the blame in public opinion for implementing these taxes.'

[65] de Witte (n 4) 666.

[66] See eg R Ismer, K Neuhoff and A Pirlot, 'Border Carbon Adjustments and Alternative Measures for the EU ETS' (2020) 1855 *DIW Discussion Papers*, www.diw.de/de/diw_01.c.743700.de/publikationen/diskussionspapiere/2020_1855/border_carbon_adjustments_and_alternative_measures_for_the_eu_ets__an_evaluation.html, 2.

[67] In a similar vein, Hey (n 50) 285–86.

[68] On the significance of democratic representation, see in more detail Pantazatou (n 15).

[69] In a similar vein, Meermagen (n 21) 105–06.

Parliament who should then be involved in the decision-making process on the core elements of tax-based contributions.

Another important factor which should not be overlooked in this context is the corresponding increase in the overall tax burden of EU residents. The introduction of taxes related to green new own resources should hence be carefully monitored and balanced out so that the overall tax burden remains at a manageable and acceptable level for taxpayers within the EU (eg, by reducing taxes on labour).[70] This assertion holds particularly true for vulnerable groups, such as poor and socially disadvantaged people.[71]

Living up to these principles also requires that structural differences in the Member States' economies are taken into account.[72] The significance of this matter might not be evident at first sight. After all, the total sum of contributions per Member State will not be affected through the introduction of tax-based contributions due to the balancing character of the GNI-based own resource.[73] However, it ought to be borne in mind that residents across the EU are likely to experience divergent levels of EU-induced tax burdens depending not only on the individual consumption behaviour, but particularly on the Member States' characteristics.[74] Such an effect would also run counter to the basic idea of the European Green Deal to 'leave no one behind'.[75]

Finding a good balance is thus particularly crucial to ensure that the introduction of tax-based contributions is supported by a critical mass of EU citizens. The green transition can only become successful if the EU's policy goals are broadly shared by the people in the Member States.[76] This requires public participation and information campaigning initiatives.[77]

[70] Indeed, a fundamental reform of national tax systems and hence a shift in tax burden from labour to environmentally harmful practices has long been advocated by the OECD; eg, OECD, *Towards Green Growth? Tracking Progress* (Paris, OECD Publishing, 2015) 34–35. For general considerations on the necessity to adapt the mix of revenue sources for national budgets in light of current economic and societal changes, see B van Ganzen and H Vording in ch 2 of this volume.

The necessity to protect citizens against overburdening might also be derived from the requirements of national financial constitutional laws; Hey (n 50) 281.

[71] Meermagen (n 21) 109; CB Blankart and GB Koester, 'Stillstand trotz Reform – die politische Ökonomie des EU-Haushalts von Rom bis Lissabon' in KA Konrad and T Lohse (eds), *Einnahmen- und Steuerpolitik in Europa: Herausforderungen und Chancen* (Frankfurt am Main, Peter Lang, 2009) 16.

[72] Own Resources Report (n 27) 9.

[73] See eg Meermagen (n 21) 157 and 159.

[74] Indeed, the first proposal for an EU ETS-related own resource was not adopted, among other things, because 'the economic impact of the ETS varies significantly from one Member State to the other due to the fact that the national economic structures and energy mixes are different' (Monti Report (n 25) 44).

[75] In the communication on the European Green Deal (Communication from the Commission to the European Parliament, the European Council, the Council, the European Economic and Social Committee and the Committee of the Regions – The European Green Deal [2019] COM(2019)640 final (hereafter European Green Deal Communication)) also referred to as 'just transition'. This effect could materialise whenever EU citizens are not in a position to opt for eco-friendlier alternatives (for example, due to a lack of supply or financial means).

[76] See in detail European Green Deal Communication (n 75) s 4.

[77] The importance of such initiatives can be illustrated using the data from a survey that was conducted in Austria in August 2020. This survey included 810 people that were representative of the Austrian population entitled to vote. Nearly half of the respondents agreed that carbon emissions should be higher taxed. The levels of consent yet varied significantly depending on the focus set in the follow-up questions. If the question specifically referred to higher taxes on fossil fuels, respondents opposed the idea to a larger extent. Increases in taxes linked to the use of vehicles were met with utmost disagreement. C Seidl, 'Für Corona sollen

The necessity to both monitor the overall tax burden and safeguard public support should also be valued through the lens of state competition. Countries might take on more aggressive policies, such as tax cuts, to attract increasingly mobile and financially potent taxpayers in the aftermath of the COVID-19 pandemic in an effort to secure the revenues needed for the repayment of state debts. Conversely, changed work environments – particularly the increased acceptance of hybrid work models as a result of COVID-19-induced lockdowns – allow taxpayers to resettle to avoid an excessive tax burden in the EU.[78]

In the mid and long term, additional issues are likely to become increasingly relevant. Most importantly, it ought to be borne in mind that the EU own resources system should provide for stable and sufficient revenues.[79] It is questionable to what extent and for how long the green new own resources are capable of living up to these standards. The plastic waste-based contribution was expected to bring in revenues at the level of approximately 4 per cent of the EU's budget (ie, 7 billion euros).[80] Figures from the past years show that the revenues derived from the EU ETS are rather volatile.[81] It will highly depend on the CBAM's concrete design to what extent these effects will be paralleled.[82] Estimates regarding the revenues accrued from these green new own resources have been remarkably incoherent.[83] The latest figures presented by the European Commission imply that the CBAM- and the ETS-based own resources could contribute to the EU budget with approximately 9.5 billion euros per year for the period of 2023–30.[84] If the green new own resources' steering effect – combined with green investments in accordance with the MFF and the NGEU – prove successful, a significant decrease in the revenues accrued therefrom will naturally emerge over time.[85] Under these circumstances, the relevant stakeholders will have to recalibrate the EU own resources system and define other sources of revenues which will be capable of making up for the losses to the EU's financing in due course.[86]

bitte andere zahlen – aber daraus wird wohl nichts' (*Der Standard*, 28 September 2020) www.derstandard.at/story/2000120293637/fuer-corona-sollen-bitte-andere-zahlen-aber-daraus-wird-wohl. For similar observations in the US and France, see N Pushkareva in ch 12 of this volume.

[78] R de la Feria and G Maffini, 'The Impact of Digitalisation on Personal Income Taxes' (2021) 68(2) *British Tax Review* 154–68; E Traversa, 'EU and International Income Tax Coordination After the Pandemics: It Is Time to Take It Personal' (2021) 49(5) *Intertax* 390–92. For an assessment against the background of Schumpeter's theories, see van Ganzen and Vording (n 70). For an analysis from a global tax governance perspective, see Pushkareva (n 77).

[79] See eg Traversa and Bizioli (n 18) 752; Own Resources Report (n 27) 8.

[80] Own Resources Report (n 27) 12.

[81] ibid 13.

[82] A CBAM will yet have to impose a tax or tariff equivalent to the burden imposed on intra-EU products (ie through the use of the product-based benchmarks of the EU ETS) in order to be considered compatible with world trade law; Own Resources Report (n 27) 14; Krenek, Sommer and Schratzenstaller (n 57) 11.

[83] See in detail Cordewener (n 37) 68 (particularly fns 43 and 44).

[84] Communication from the Commission to the European Parliament, the Council, the European Economic and Social Committee and the Committee of the Regions: The next generation of own resources for the EU budget [2021] COM(2021) 566 final, 3.

[85] In the same vein (in the specific context of the plastic waste-based contribution), Own Resources Report (n 27) 12.

[86] Provided that the Member States would then not prefer to return to a system which would again rely on GNI-based contributions to a greater extent.

VII. Conclusion and Implications for Future Research

The COVID-19 pandemic's disruptive effects have led to remarkable shifts in EU fiscal policies. A minimum of 30 per cent of the EU budget has been earmarked for projects which shall contribute to reaching the EU's ambitious environmental goals. Additionally, the EU lawmakers agreed on pairing their future-oriented spending strategy with a reform of the EU's financing. The own resources system should hence be made consistent with EU policy objectives such as the European Green Deal. This includes the introduction of three green new own resources. A new own resource based on the amount of non-recycled plastic packaging waste (plastic waste-based contribution) has been in effect as of 2021. The other two green own resources related to a CBAM and an extended EU ETS are scheduled to be implemented as of 2023.

This contribution centred on a critical assessment of the plastic waste-based contribution's design. This analysis allowed for the identification of deficiencies which run counter to the green new own resources' environmental objectives. These findings formed the basis for a proposal on how to (re-)design the green new own resources to meet these criteria, using the plastic waste-based contribution as an example. Although it was found that the recommended structures would bring about noticeable benefits, related challenges and obstacles were also addressed.

The plastic waste-based contribution could principally materialise a steering effect. However, its proneness to accordingly contribute to the EU's environmental agenda depends critically on the introduction of a related tax that passes the financial burden on to the producers, importers and consumers of single-use plastics. In the author's opinion, the plastic waste-based contribution's structures should hence be amended by way of combining it with an obligation to implement a corresponding national tax and thereby transforming it into the plastic waste tax-based contribution. An EU directive would then define a minimum taxation standard at the level of the plastic waste-based contribution (ie 0.80 euros per kilogram). The revenues allocated to the minimum standard should be passed through to the European Commission (less a fixed percentage which serves as a compensation for collection costs). These basic structures could be used analogously for purposes of the other proposed green new own resources.

The proposed (re-)designing of the green new own resources would entail several advantages, among them:

- ensuring an effective greening of the EU's fiscal system within the boundaries of the existing legal framework;
- leaving a certain degree of leeway to national lawmakers (by way of introducing higher national taxes as to accrue additional revenues for the national budgets), thereby simultaneously setting an incentive to diligently comply with collection obligations;
- fostering both simplicity and administrability through the use of procedures established in the context of traditional own resources;
- rendering the EU's budget independent from the Member States' national budgets;
- realising intergenerational justice.

However, there are also some impediments which would have to be likewise taken into account:

- the requirement of unanimous consent in the Council of the European Union for purposes of introducing an EU directive on a minimum plastics tax;
- deficiencies in the democratic representation of EU citizens in the legislative procedure;
- related increases in the overall tax burden of EU residents;
- divergent levels of EU-induced tax burdens due to differing economic structures in the Member States;
- the relevance of public support;
- issues of state competition;
- the safeguarding of stable and sufficient revenues.

The findings in this chapter notwithstanding, it should be borne in mind that the significance of environmental protection as well as the combat against climate change do not stop at the EU's external borders.[87] A fundamental reform of the EU own resources system by way of introducing a set of green new own resources should thus be paralleled by initiatives for international cooperation. The EU and its Member States could particularly take on a leading role in initiating a dialogue at the international level (for example, in the UN committees or in the context of the OECD Inclusive Framework). The work in these bodies should be aimed at formulating binding minimum standards for all parties involved as well as ensuring that developing countries receive sufficient financial support to enable them to meet these obligations.

Moreover, it needs to be stressed that green new own resources can only form one component in a multi-faceted strategy to fight the climate crisis. This should include, among other things, the safeguarding of an efficient and purposeful use of the earmarked financial means in the EU budgets as well as broad information campaigning to win over EU citizens for the purpose of the green transition. Considering the enormous sums that will be needed to achieve the EU's ambitious environmental goals, it will also be indispensable to create an attractive environment for private investments in climate and environmental action.[88]

In the author's opinion, deficiencies in the democratic representation of EU citizens in the legislative procedure are likely to become one of the most pressing issues in context with the envisaged transformation of the EU own resources system. In addition to analyses of the basic structures of the new EU own resources system and specific types of new own resources, this issue should hence be put at the centre of future research in this field.

[87] See eg Feld (n 3) 143; Ismer, Neuhoff and Pirlot (n 66) 15.

[88] In the same vein, European Green Deal Communication (n 75) (at s 2.2.1, where it is expected that investments worth 260 billion euros per year ought to be taken to achieve the EU's environmental goals up to 2030).

PART IV

Justice, Distribution and Society

15

The Implications of Intergenerational Issues on Tax Policy in a Post-COVID World: An Examination of Age Discrimination

ALEXIS BRASSEY

Abstract

This chapter considers the principal factors that have led to large inequalities that have developed between generations in the UK. It explores the difficulties younger people will experience trying to get on to the housing ladder as well as the challenges of saving for a pension. The chapter examines the way in which the tax system has exacerbated these growing inequalities whilst acknowledging the macro-economic picture that has led to the decline in interest rates, the main casual factor. The chapter then considers a number of policy responses that seek to address the problem in the context of a post-pandemic world. These policy responses weigh up the challenge of tax policy directed towards wealth as opposed to labour as well as considering the taxation of housing more generally.

I. Introduction

This chapter explores tax law and policy issues arising from government responses to the COVID-19 pandemic in so far as they impact on intergenerational groups. The chapter focusses on possible changes in the law relating to capital gains tax (CGT) and proposals to introduce wealth taxes.

The Office for Budget Responsibility (OBR) initially estimated government borrowing resulting from COVID-19 would be ~£394 billion although this was revised lower in the March 2021 Economic and Fiscal Outlook at around £344 billion.[1]

[1] OBR, *Economic and Fiscal Outlook* (OBR, 2020) obr.uk/efo/economic-and-fiscal-outlook-november-2020/; OBR, *Economic and Fiscal Outlook* (OBR, 2021) obr.uk/efo/economic-and-fiscal-outlook-march-2021/.

The sectors most affected included hospitality, given the government's response, which involved restrictions and lockdowns of that sector. What is not so clear from the analysis, is whether the economic impact is disproportionately falling on the young given the damage done to education, the prevalence of youth employment in the hospitality industry and the long-term effects of extensive government borrowing which will require financing over many decades.

In light of the crisis effects, this chapter examines possible government responses in changes to tax law with respect to their intergenerational impact. This chapter explores how those potential changes, particularly those proposed by the Office of Tax Simplification (OTS) pre-COVID-19 recommendations on CGT,[2] are likely to influence redistribution from an intergenerational perspective. The chapter also considers the findings of the Wealth Tax Commission (WTC) which proposes a one-off wealth tax,[3] and the House of Lords (HL) pre-COVID-19 report on tackling intergenerational unfairness.[4]

The chapter is divided into sections. Section II explores the current data on intergenerational income and wealth inequality. This section examines the challenges faced by young people as compared with previous generations. The empirical analysis considers the substantial government debt that has accrued resulting from the COVID-19 pandemic, but also considers the impact of declining interest rates and attendant effects on asset prices. These increases in asset prices have created inequalities now faced by the younger generation when it comes to housing and pensions. Tax law and policy, if it is to operate fairly, needs to factor in these multi-faceted aspects on intergenerational equity as multi-year planning takes place to stabilise post-COVID-19 finances.

Section III draws on the background data in section II, highlighting the areas of greatest inequality, namely housing and pensions wealth to explore how potential changes to tax law might be altered in light of these inequalities. The challenges faced by government finances mean that generous reliefs or low tax rates are likely to be reviewed. Intergenerational unfairness is likely to be exacerbated in circumstances where, for example, capital gains are left at current rates whilst consumption or labour taxes are increased, given capital and wealth are predominately owned by the older generations. Exploring proposals for change, the section is subdivided into three parts, consideration of: (i) the OTS report,[5] (ii) the WTC report,[6] and (iii) the HL report into tackling intergenerational unfairness.[7] The reports' recommendations are evaluated in so far as they impact on intergenerational tax issues.

Section IV draws on the three reports considered in section III to propose an alternative framework for assessing intergenerational unfairness. The COVID-19 pandemic

[2] OTS, *Capital Gains Tax Review: Simplifying by Design* (OTS, 2020) assets.publishing.service.gov.uk/government/uploads/system/uploads/attachment_data/file/935073/Capital_Gains_Tax_stage_1_report_-_Nov_2020_-_web_copy.pdf.

[3] Wealth Tax Commission, *A wealth tax for the UK* (Wealth Tax Commission, 2020) www.wealthandpolicy.com/wp/WealthTaxFinalReport.pdf.

[4] House of Lords, *Tackling intergenerational unfairness* (House of Lords, 2019) publications.parliament.uk/pa/ld201719/ldselect/ldintfair/329/329.pdf.

[5] OTS (n 2).

[6] WTC (n 3).

[7] HL (n 4).

is the greatest fiscal shock to the UK and for the world since World War II. The way in which the deficit is managed will have long-term consequences and affect different generations in different ways. The proposals in this section, on the one hand, recognise the need to make changes to tax law that address intergeneration unfairness, but on the other hand recognise the challenges that arise when taxing long-term accumulated wealth. The chapter proposes a 'tax rule of recognition' overseen by a Fiscal Policy Committee (FPC) which operates as a meta rule designed to encourage policymakers to balance immediate political needs with respect for future generations when creating policy.

Along with a number of other chapters in this volume, this chapter concludes that crisis planning presents opportunities for policymakers but emphasises that decisions will inevitably affect different generations in different ways. Tax law and policy changes are also likely to create long-term effects which have, in the past, exacerbated inequalities by paying insufficient attention to the ways in which those inequalities have emerged. The proposals engage in attempting to address these problems by positing the re-introduction of fiscal rules that can act as a mechanism to mitigate the effects of unfairness.

II. Intergenerational Inequality, the Numbers

This section is designed to highlight the financial hurdles faced by young people considering the need for post-pandemic fiscal tightening. Once that picture is made clear, the way in which tax law and policy has contributed to the problem might be better understood. The chapter is based on the UK experience although the chapter will pick out London given the substantial differentials that arise in both wages and house prices.

This section considers prospects for the younger generation with a focus on employment, income, housing, interest rates and pensions with the pandemic effect as a backdrop. The data suggests that there are no significant intergenerational disadvantages to younger people from an employment and income perspective. There are, however, serious differences in the cost of housing and pensions which have been exacerbated by tax law which provides for generous exemptions as discussed in section III.

A. Employment and Income

At the start of 2021, the youth unemployment rate rose to 14.2 per cent compared with an adult unemployment rate of around 5.9 per cent.[8] Youth unemployed had more than doubled from the start of the pandemic in March 2020.[9] The young were hit harder by the pandemic as 47 per cent of eligible youth jobs were furloughed as compared

[8] ONS, *Unemployment rate (aged 16 and over, seasonally adjusted)* (ONS, 2021) www.ons.gov.uk/employmentandlabourmarket/peoplenotinwork/unemployment/timeseries/mgsx/lms.

[9] House of Commons Library Briefing Paper, *Youth Unemployment Statistics*, Number 5871 (2019).

with 29 per cent for those over 25.[10] Whilst the numbers demonstrate the younger generation were more adversely affected by the pandemic, 14.2 per cent youth unemployment remained far from previous crisis levels. Since 2004, youth unemployment has ranged between 11–22 per cent, peaking in the period following the global financial crisis around 2011.[11] As restrictions were lifted the rate reduced down to 11.3 per cent between August–October 2021, those furloughed were also offered generous support relative to unemployment benefit.[12]

Younger people are likely to suffer from a more insecure working life compared with previous generations. For example, they are more likely to work in the gig economy without the security of an employment contract, holiday and sick pay among other statutory protections.[13]

What can a young person expect to earn relative to previous generations? The data suggests that whilst average household income rises steadily from 20 to mid-50s, followed by a shallower decline into old age, these intergenerational differences change depending on the generation being measured.[14] For those born during 1930–1950 average income rose from ~£19,000 to ~£30,400.[15] This pattern was not repeated for later generations. Those born in the 1970s may have started out with higher earnings at the beginning of their working lives but would have experienced lower annual average income growth, giving them parity with those born in the 1960s. More recent generations have fared worse than the previous generation as wages and salaries fell by around 0.1 per cent on average from 2004.[16]

The data suggests on average people pay in more to the tax and benefits system than they receive with the net transfer being greatest in their 50s where households have fewer children using educational services. People then tend to become beneficiaries as they draw pensions and reduce working time. Over time the tax burden has increased but is offset with greater benefits.[17]

In summary, a young person in 2021/2 faces some difficulties with finding a job but this is abating as COVID-19 restrictions are lifted. That job, however, is likely to be more insecure than previous generations. They may have a slightly less advantageous future from an income perspective albeit with wide variations but these intergenerational differences are not meaningfully different from the sort of income differentials faced by previous generations. A young person today can expect to pay more tax than

[10] HMRC, *Job Retention Scheme Statistics: August 2020*, www.gov.uk/government/statistics/coronavirus-job-retention-scheme-statistics-august-2020.

[11] House of Commons (n 9) 3.

[12] HMRC, *COVID-19 financial support for businesses* (2020) www.gov.uk/government/collections/financial-support-for-businesses-during-coronavirus-covid-19.

[13] HL (n 4) paras 162–173; this trend may reverse given the case of *Uber BV v Aslam* [2021] UKSC 5 which has clarified Uber drivers were not independent contracts but in fact worked for Uber and were entitled to certain employment rights. The case revolved around Employment Rights Act 1996, s 230 which defines 'employment status'.

[14] ONS, *Generational income: The effects of taxes and benefits* (2019) para 4, www.ons.gov.uk/peoplepopulationandcommunity/personalandhouseholdfinances/incomeandwealth/articles/generationalincometheeffectsoftaxesandbenefits/2019-08-21.

[15] ONS data is inflation adjusted.

[16] ONS (n 14).

[17] ibid.

previous generations, but they can also expect to receive higher benefits. The impact of COVID-19 measures on education may also play a role, those effects are likely to be unevenly distributed but it is too early to measure those effects.

B. Housing

Housing, along with pensions, represent the greatest difference in costs faced by this generation compared with previous generations. For most people, the two most expensive lifetime costs, aside from the cost of their own children, are their house and their pension. The data sets below show they pose a particular challenge for intergenerational fairness and tie into a discussion on how tax policy treats property gains and pension contributions.

Since 1997 housing affordability issues have become worse, with London prices affected more than elsewhere. In 2019 the earnings to house price multiple ranged between 2x–40x with significant regional variations.[18] How do these numbers compare with previous generations? In 1997 house prices worked out at around 3.6x worker's annual gross full-time earnings. House prices across the UK increased by around 360 per cent between 1997 and 2016.[19]

The literature on house prices is extensive, for example, the case for government action on providing cheaper housing stock,[20] how London prices affect the national housing market,[21] and why prices tend to rise in large vibrant cities which attract talent from elsewhere.[22] What flows from this analysis is that over many years, those who have put money into housing have experienced a significant increase in their wealth. Much of the increase in value remains untaxed with IHT reliefs extended to preserve this benefit. The average cost of a semi-detached property in Zone 2, London exceeded £1m in 2020.[23] With average London wages of around £38,000 pre-tax and post-tax earnings of circa £29,500 the capacity of the average Londoner being able to buy a semi-detached house is no longer viable over a lifetime of work.[24] A young person starting out

[18] Earnings multiples: 2–11x (North West, West, East Midlands, Wales, Yorkshire, North East), 6.3–17.7x (South West. South East, East), 10.6–40x (London). See ONS, *Housing affordability in England and Wales: 2019* (2019) para 4, Fig 3, www.ons.gov.uk/peoplepopulationandcommunity/housing/bulletins/housingaffordabilityinenglandandwales/2019#:~:text=Housing%20affordability%20improves%20in%20England,when%20the%20ratio%20was%208.0.

[19] The increase was not uniform, eg, Wales increased by 60% compared with Kensington and Chelsea showing increases of 2500%, ibid fig 3. Note, there are many ways to calculate the cost of housing, the point to bear in mind is the extent to which housing costs have risen relative to salaries and particularly in London/South East UK.

[20] LSE, 'The case for investing in London's affordable housing' (2011) www.lse.ac.uk/geography-and-environment/research/lse-london/documents/Archive/HEIF-4-2010-11-Series/Report-The-Case-for-Investing-in-Londons-Affordable-Housing-1.pdf.

[21] G Meen, 'Regional house prices and the ripple effect: a new interpretation' (1999) 14(6) *Housing Studies* 733–53.

[22] H de Groot, G Marlet, C Teulings and W Vermeulen, *Cities and the Urban Land Premium* (Cheltenham, Edward Elgar, 2015).

[23] House Prices, Zone 2, London: £1,015,983 (Rightmove) www.rightmove.co.uk/house-prices/zone-2-93814.html.

[24] Assuming a cost of £1m, take home pay of £29,500 – even if repayments on the mortgage were 40% of take home pay it would take around 85 years to pay off the mortgage, ie, beyond any working lifetime.

in London today has little chance of being able to afford a modest semi-detached house in Zone 2 without support. This last point is becoming a major issue that will inevitably increase inequalities throughout society. Foreign buyers have also reduced available housing supply and increased prices, although this demand may have stimulated building in high demand areas such as London.

The next section sets out the way in which property is taxed and discusses proposed changes which might alleviate house price affordability for the younger generation. What is clear, however, is that the exemption to tax on main residence is a contributory factor in driving prices beyond affordability in parts of the UK. The differences are also likely to create intra as well as intergenerational inequalities.

C. Interest Rates and Pensions

Apart from housing, pensions are the other long-term major expense that people in the UK need to make provision for. Pensions, like housing are heavily influenced by the tax system. The following section discusses the generous exemptions afforded to pensions along with policy suggestions. What is often missed in the analysis of both housing and pensions is the importance of interest rates. For the purposes of this chapter, it is important to understand some basic rules.

Interest rates determine the cost of borrowing and influence investment returns.[25] The significance for housing is that as interest rates fall, the cost of mortgage borrowing falls and affordability increases.[26] Interest rates in the UK have been consistently falling since the early 1990s and, as a result, house prices have become higher.[27] While interest rates have been falling, other asset prices, including bonds and equities have been rising.[28] Lower interest rates also mean more money is required to generate the same returns as in previous generations.[29] Evidence suggests this lower interest rate environment is likely to persist, given the increase in government borrowing and the pressures on international economies.[30] By way of example, consider the change in the return of an annuity for a male of 65 years old in 1990. A £100,000 annuity would have produced ~£13,000 of income;[31] by 2018, £100,000 would only produce £4,808. Taking into account inflation, these figures are even more challenging.[32] For younger people,

[25] F Mishkin, 'Symposium on the Monetary Transmission Mechanism' (1995) 9(4) *Journal of Economic Perspectives* 3–10.

[26] BIS, *House Prices, Mortgage Interest Rates and the Rising Share of Capital income in the United States* (2016) BIS Working Paper, Number 572, para 5.1.

[27] Other factors are important, eg housing supply, however the cost of borrowing significantly affects house prices. Average house prices have risen from around £55,000 to £250,000, see: 'UK House Prices since 1952', www.nationwidehousepriceindex.co.uk/resources/8djon-9earo-60y36-skf61-wbx2i.

[28] The FTSE 100 has risen from around 2100 pts in 1990 to around 6800 in 2021 during a period in which rates fell from around 10% in 1990 to 0.1% in 2021.

[29] P Johnson, 'Ultra-low interest rates have huge consequences for the country and its citizens' *The Times* (London, 9 November 2020).

[30] C Macchiarelli, 'Government bond term premia during the pandemic' (2020) 254 *National Institute Economic Review*.

[31] OECD, *Annuity Margins in the UK* (2000) Fig 1, www.oecd.org/unitedkingdom/2402277.pdf.

[32] The change in annuity rates means to maintain nominal returns a person would need to save around 2.7x the amount. Factoring in inflation, which increases to around 5.4x. See Hargreaves Landsdown, 'Retirement data' www.hl.co.uk/retirement/annuities/best-buy-rates.

the shift in long-term rates has therefore had the double effect of influencing a growth in both house prices and the long-term cost of pensions provision.[33]

Pensions, along with real property, constitute most of UK wealth.[34] In the public sector, final salary pension liabilities amount to around £1.9 trillion.[35] That liability is unfunded, meaning it will need to be paid by future taxpayers. These outstanding liabilities, combined with COVID-19 costs are going to remain a long-term burden for future taxpayers, ie, the younger generation.

Pensions in the private sector are largely funded using money-purchase schemes, meaning there has to be a pot of capital sufficient to pay out claimants; adjustments are made to contributions to ensure that the assets of the fund can meet the future liabilities.[36] Final salary pensions, however, have fixed outgoings and with no corresponding adjustment mechanism. In the case of public sector workers, the adjustment mechanism is the amount of tax that will need to be raised to fund the pensions liabilities.

Tax law and policy in the UK has provided that contributions into pensions have been largely exempt from income tax, which along with Private Residence Relief (PRR) represent the most generous and expensive reliefs.[37] The discussion below considers the potential intergenerational unfairness which arises from these reliefs. It is notable that the introduction of a Health and Social Care Levy (now repealed), charged through NICs, will create further intergenerational inequality given it is a tax on labour as opposed to capital, with the burden falling on the young. The extent to which HMG have chosen to tax labour as opposed to capital may be a function of the growing political divide given support for the Conservative Party is heavily weighted towards the older generation.

In concluding this section, it is also worth noting that the move to defined contribution pensions may lead to future pension provision becoming unsustainable. Whilst interest rates have remained low and capital gains have lessened the burden for current retirees, it remains to be seen how future pensioners would cope in a rising interest rate/capital declining market.

III. Tax Law and Policy

Section II has shown that growth in property prices and pensions affordability are significant sources of intergenerational unfairness. Property and pensions are expenses that are paid for over decades, and for this reason, policy proposals ought to take into account this duration when considering fairness and changes to law.

[33] Most private sector firms now operate using defined contribution schemes, or money purchase schemes. The cost of final salary/defined benefit schemes became prohibitively expensive and have been largely phased out.

[34] ONS survey data indicate around 70%, See Resolution Foundation, *The UK's wealth distribution and characteristics of high-wealth households* (2020) Resolution Foundation Briefing, Fig 4.

[35] HM Treasury, *Whole of Government Accounts: Year ended 31st March 2019* (2020) 32.

[36] Pensions Advisory Service, Defined Contribution, Money purchase scheme (2021) www.pensionsadvisoryservice.org.uk/about-pensions/pensions-basics/workplace-pension-schemes/dc-money-purchase-schemes#:~:text=Money%20purchase%20schemes%20provide%20benefits%20on%20retirement%20based, over%20this%20period.%20How%20money%20purchase%20schemes%20work.

[37] HMRC, Estimated Costs of Tax Reliefs (2019) 10, assets.publishing.service.gov.uk/government/uploads/system/uploads/attachment_data/file/930728/Oct20_tax_reliefs_bulletin_v7_-_Accessible_Final.pdf.

This section is divided into two parts. Part A investigates how property and pensions are taxed which, it is argued, exacerbates existing intergenerational unfairness. Part B of this section explores three proposals which may address the way in which the tax system creates these problems. The OTS report shows how CGT might be changed in light of the differences between how capital and income are taxed. The second report is from the WTC. This report proposes a one-off wealth tax which it claims, would redress, among other things, intergenerational inequality as part of the post-COVID-19 settlement. The final report is the HL Committee Report on intergenerational unfairness which also makes recommendations on changing the tax system to address aspects of intergenerational issues.

A. The Taxation of Property and Pensions

i. Property Taxation on Residential Property

Given the accumulation of wealth that has taken place in residential property as discussed above, how is residential property taxed in the UK? There are two taxes relating to the purchase and sale of residential property in the UK;[38] Stamp Duty Land Tax (SDLT) and CGT.[39] SDLT is levied against the purchase price of the property and ranges from 0 per cent < £250,000 up to 12 per cent > £1.5m. There is a 3 per cent rate applied on purchases of an additional property regardless of value as well as non-natural purchasers, ie, companies. Residential property can be purchased by buying the shares of a company that owns property. In this case the shares of the company are subject to a 0.5 per cent rate. To avoid SDLT avoidance there is an annual tax on enveloped dwellings (ATED) which charges a tax on property above £500,000 ranging from £3,700 to £237,400 for property > £20 million.[40] Save for ATED, SDLT is a one off charge and evidence suggests it is an inefficient tax which, although it raises around £12 billion in revenue,[41] tends to prevent movement in the housing market and leaves people reticent to move.[42] SDLT is progressive given the step up in rates; although this only occurs when the property is sold. The tax has been described as inefficient relative to, for example, a mansion tax or more progressive council tax given these latter taxes would be unavoidable whereas SDLT can be deferred.[43] As property prices rise, the cost is paid by the buyer, albeit influencing the sale price, causing an even greater burden on the younger generation.[44]

[38] Council tax, which is applied on property is considered below.

[39] See Stamp Duty Land Tax Act 2015; Taxation of Chargeable Gains Act (TCGA) 1992, ss 222–226.

[40] Finance Act (FA) 2013, ss 94–174.

[41] HM Revenue & Customs, *UK Stamp Tax statistics* Chart 2B, www.gov.uk/government/statistics/uk-stamp-tax-statistics/uk-stamp-tax-statistics-2019-to-2020-commentary.

[42] LSE, *A Sustainable Increase in London's Housing Supply?* (2018) 12, www.lse.ac.uk/geography-and-environment/research/lse-london/documents/Reports/REPORT-LSE-KEI-digital.pdf.

[43] House of Commons (n 9). The 'inefficiency' arises because whilst an annual tax is continual, the SDLT can stop people from moving for many years. The deferral does not necessarily make up for the loss of annual tax given it is only paid as a one-off. At the same time the householder may end up living in inappropriate accommodation to avoid the charge preventing, eg, a family from moving into a family home which may be occupied by an elderly couple or a single person.

[44] ibid 28. SDLT costs are part of the price negotiations.

CGT is payable by the vendor on gains arising from a disposal of residential property.[45] The CGT rate is 18 per cent or 28 per cent depending on other UK sourced income and gains in the year of disposal. Disposals of private residences are exempt from CGT,[46] where they are the main residence of the owner. This relief originates from the 1955 Royal Commission on Income and Gains. The Commission were concerned about taxing inflation on property that might lead to discouraging homeowners from moving.[47] Their objection was given statutory force when CGT tax was introduced in 1965 and meant that any gains on a main residence were untaxed.[48] This relief remains but is only available to vendors for 18 months from disposal or after it ceases to be your residence.[49] HM Revenue and Customs (HMRC) have litigated against a widening of the scope of the meaning of residence.[50] HMRC cost estimates for PRR are ~£26.5 billion and although one must be cautious with the methodology, it is fair to assume the cost is substantial.[51] As with all changes to the tax system any changes to PRR are likely to affect behaviour.

How does the PRR exacerbate intergenerational unfairness? If the relief applies to both generation A and B, why is that unfair? The answer is complex given the interplay of house prices, interest rates and accelerating effects of taxation. Falling interest rates mean cheaper mortgages and attract investment into housing and away from stocks and bonds as yield opportunities reduce.[52] This is because property yields can remain high as rents tend to be stickier, ie slow to respond to changes.[53] House prices have an inverse relationship with interest rates, hence the generation that enters the market at a point of lower interest rates will be disadvantaged relative to those who enter the market at a time of higher interest rates. The tax exemption creates an accelerating effect given gains on property are untaxed, encouraging buyers to spend more on property relative to assets that might otherwise be taxed. Although timing is largely a matter of luck, it does not mitigate the impact of tax-free gains that accrue during a period of reducing interest rates. For a generation entering the property market at a time of low rates, their property costs, relative to previous generation, are pregnant with untaxed gains making purchases and subsequent financing onerous, or in the case of London, unaffordable. The magnitude of price movements is made worse by the operation of SDLT as they become more unaffordable, given the progressive nature of that tax causing a 'property fiscal drag'. In times of falling prices, no relief would be available on losses.

Property wealth in the UK is estimated to be ~£4.1 trillion.[54] The influence of the tax exemption on this figure can only be guessed at, however, the notion that many in the

[45] Including non-residents.
[46] TCGA 1992, s 222(1).
[47] United Kingdom, Royal Commission on the taxation of profits and income, Cmd. 9474 (1955) para 92.
[48] FA 1965, s 29(1)(a)(b), which is replicated in TCGA 1992, s 222(1).
[49] FA 2014, s 58.
[50] Cases include: de Goodwin v Curtis [1998] STC 475 (CA); Favell v HMRC [2010] UKFTT 360 (TC); Eghbal-Omidi v HMRC [2013] UKFTT 449 (TC); Dickenson v HMRC [2013] UKFTT 653 (TC).
[51] HMRC (n 37).
[52] BIS, 'Search for Yield Sustains Buoyant Markets' *BIS Quarterly Review* (December 2020).
[53] J Gallin and RJ Verbrugge, 'A theory of sticky rents: Search and bargaining with incomplete information' (2019) 183(C) *Journal of Economic Theory* 478–519.
[54] ONS, *The UK national balance sheet estimates: 2018* (2018) para 5, www.ons.gov.uk/economy/nationalaccounts/uksectoraccounts/bulletins/nationalbalancesheet/2018.

older generation view their house as their 'pension' is unsurprising.[55] With interest rates at 0.1 per cent, the same is unlikely to be true for their children unless we are entering into a period of long-term negative rates, something which commentators in the City believe is unlikely, even in the context of a global pandemic.[56]

This analysis suggests the PRR, along with the lower rates of CGT, have helped create a problem for the younger generation. Tax law and policy are not the only reason for heightened property prices and there is compelling research which suggests housing supply is the main culprit.[57] Nevertheless, tax law and policy are undoubtedly an aggravating factor causing considerable intergenerational unfairness. The discussion of the reports below makes suggestions as to how changes to the taxation of CGT and wealth more generally might mitigate these effects which might mitigate the additional costs faced by the young in a post-crisis world.

ii. Pensions in the UK

The income tax free amount that can be paid annually to a pension is £40,000.[58] Growth of funds within a pension is tax exempt. Withdrawals are taxed as income although 25 per cent of the value can be withdrawn tax-free once the beneficiary reaches 55.[59] Pension funds typically invest in a variety of equities and bonds. As with property these assets tend to be inversely correlated with interest rates and over the last 30 years have performed well.[60]

Total pensions wealth in the UK is estimated to be ~£6.1 trillion.[61] As discussed above, it requires ~2.7x the amount for a retiree today to match the annuity cost of a retiree in 1990 or ~5.4x in real terms. Someone starting their pension in 2021 will need to pay substantially more into their pension to achieve the same standard of living in retirement. Recent sharp rises in interest rates will impact on these numbers.

The tax reliefs have reduced as higher earners could have paid in as much as £255,000 of their taxable salary each year.[62] In previous generations, typical pensions operated as final salary schemes which paid out a percentage of someone's final salary. Those schemes had to be discontinued to new entrants because of cost, as interest rates fell, and the schemes became unaffordable.

[55] N Green, 'Your home as retirement fund – the pros and cons' (*Unbiased*, 3 December 2020) www.unbiased.co.uk/news/retirement/your-home-as-retirement-fund-the-pros-and-cons.

[56] O Williams-Grut, 'Negative rates seen as all talk despite Bank of England prep work' (*Yahoo Finance UK*, 5 February 2021) uk.finance.yahoo.com/news/bank-of-england-negative-interest-rates-how-likely-112123378.html.

[57] House of Commons Library, *Tackling the under-supply of housing in England*, Briefing Paper Number 07671, (2021) 7; although it should also be noted whether increasing housing supply would improve affordability is contested, see p 11.

[58] The amount tapers down to £4,000 for incomes > £240,000. £160,000 can be carried forward and there is a lifetime limit of £1,073,100, see HMRC, *Tax on your private pensions contributions* (2021) www.gov.uk/tax-on-your-private-pension/annual-allowance.

[59] ibid.

[60] Mishkin (n 25).

[61] ONS, *Pension wealth in Great Britain: April 2016 to March 2018* (2019) para 3, www.ons.gov.uk/peoplepopulationandcommunity/personalandhouseholdfinances/incomeandwealth/bulletins/pensionwealthingreatbritain/april2016tomarch2018.

[62] HMRC, *Pensions Tax Manual* (2015) PTM054200, www.gov.uk/hmrc-internal-manuals/pensions-tax-manual/ptm054200.

The above data show that the younger generation entering the workforce in 2021 face a series of additional financial burdens not faced by previous generations. Although incomes have remained relatively stable the cost of pensions and house prices is likely to have a significant impact on lifestyles, particularly for those wanting to live and work in London.

The tax system in the UK has acted to exacerbate the situation by granting relief on increases in house prices. The impact of tax-free contributions and growth within pensions has also had the effect of creating differences in the capacity of the younger generation meeting their future needs as compared with previous generations. COVID-19 has served to make matters worse, driving down long-term interest rates and causing an increase in asset prices, including property. Deficit spending will also need to be financed, but tax revenues derived from pensions and property are subject to generous reliefs meaning the funding will need to come from elsewhere, more likely to be labour, hence affecting younger generations.

The second part of this section looks at three policy responses which could have an effect on redressing the balance between the intergenerational gap.

B. Policy Responses

This part considers proposals to address inequality concerns from three reports. Although the OTS and WTC do not expressly consider intergenerational fairness, their proposals are relevant to the issue. Both reports seek to tax the capital value of property which is a source of intergenerational unfairness and relevant to potential government responses in light of COVID-19. The HL report directly addresses the issue. To contextualise the reports this part considers the latest data which show that government revenues are largely derived from income and consumption, not housing or wealth. The extent to which revenue might be derived from capital is explored below.

Of £825 billion of government revenue in 2019/20 ~£525 billion is raised from income tax/national insurance contributions (NICs), VAT, and corporation tax. Capital taxes raised ~£31 billion.[63] In 2020/21, the OBR estimate of government borrowing in response to COVID-19 was ~£344 billion.[64]

Government borrowing is likely to increase in the near term meaning future fiscal tightening, as signalled by a series of proposed tax increases such as the Health and Social Care Levy as well as increases in Corporation Tax. Although the impact of deficit spending on growth is contentious,[65] government spending may become problematic if it indefinitely accelerates at a faster rate than government revenue. How will the government respond to financing the deficit created by COVID-19 and how will this response impact different age groups?

[63] ONS, *Public sector current receipts, Appendix D* (2021) www.ons.gov.uk/economy/governmentpublicsectorandtaxes/publicsectorfinance/datasets/appendixdpublicsectorcurrentreceipts.

[64] OBR (n 1).

[65] C Checherita and P Rother, 'The Impact of High and Growing Government Debt on Economic Growth, An Empirical Investigation for the Euro Area' ECB Working Paper No. 1237.

Although Rishi Sunak's Budget kept to the Conservative Party manifesto not to raise income tax, VAT or NICs this was subsequently reversed with the introduction of the Health and Social Care Levy (now repealed).[66] The following assessment looks at the specific policy recommendations with a view to assessing its impact on intergenerational fairness in the context of the fiscal demands posed by COVID-19.

i. The OTS Report on CGT

The OTS report's terms were to 'identify opportunities relating to administrative and technical issues as well as areas where the present rules can distort behaviour or do not meet their policy intent'.[67] This chapter focuses on the proposals in the design that may impact on intergenerational unfairness.

ii. Background on CGT

CGT is applied on the disposal of an asset which has increased in value from the time of purchase. Most CGT is collected from the sale of businesses, investors and second homeowners. There has been much debate over the political aims of the tax since its inception in 1965.[68] Broadly speaking disagreements have revolved around whether gains in capital values equate to earnings. For those policymakers who believe they do such as James Callaghan and Nigel Lawson,[69] their policies have tended to align CGT rates with incomes taxes. For those policymakers who believe risk-taking, and enterprise need to receive additional rewards, such as Alistair Darling, and George Osborne,[70] they have tended to provide generous allowances, for example, Entrepreneurs' Relief which only taxed gains at 10 per cent.[71]

CGT is not a large contributor to government revenues. In 2017–18 the total amount paid came to ~£8.3 billion, ~1 per cent of revenue. Only ~265,000 people pay CGT compared with 31.2 million income taxpayers.[72] CGT has a series of rates ranging from 10 per cent for Business Asset Disposal Relief to 28 per cent applied on residential property.[73]

iii. OTS Recommendations

The OTS recommends aligning CGT with income tax rates whilst providing for inflation relief.[74] It also suggests that loss reliefs are given more flexibility.[75] Its concerns are

[66] The Conservative and Unionist Party Manifesto (2019) 15, assets-global.website-files.com/5da42e2cae7ebd3f8bde353c/5dda924905da587992a064ba_Conservative%202019%20Manifesto.pdf. The 2021 Budget did, however, freeze basic and higher rate allowances, www.gov.uk/government/speeches/budget-speech-2021.
[67] OTS (n 2) 2.
[68] House of Commons Library, 'Capital gains tax: background history' (2010) SN860.
[69] ibid 4–7.
[70] HC Deb 22/6/2010 cc178–179.
[71] FA 2008, s 9 and Sch 3.
[72] HMRC, *Capital Gains Tax Statistical Tables* (2020) www.gov.uk/government/statistics/capital-gains-tax-statistical-tables.
[73] Entrepreneurs' Relief was renamed Business Asset Disposal Relief in the FA 2020.
[74] OTS (n 2) 46.
[75] ibid.

that as long as rates are sufficiently different, owner managers will be incentivised to characterise their rewards as capital rather than labour.[76] The OTS does consider PRR; however, it does not suggest any changes.[77] It has concerns about distorting behaviour arising out of capital transfers on death. On death, the beneficiary is entitled to assets which are uprated at market value, hence eliminating the CGT. Although the beneficiary will have to pay inheritance tax (IHT), if the asset value falls within the IHT exempt allowance then no further tax is payable. This does create a tax gap, albeit with some policy justification. The OTS recommendation is to remove the CGT uplift on death.[78]

iv. Analysis on OTS Report

The OTS report does not directly tackle intergenerational unfairness. The cost of PRR, however, is significant and distorting, costing around £26.5 billion each year between 2015–20,[79] and contributes to intergenerational unfairness as discussed above. Given this cost it is surprising to see the OTS fail to raise the possibility of taxing the main home beyond the IHT band. Ultimately, the costs of this relief need to be funded from elsewhere and that slack is largely made up out of employment and consumption taxes which disproportionately affect those who are likely to miss out on significant tax-free property gains going forward, ie, the younger generation.

It could be argued that different generations are bound to suffer from the vagaries of the interest rate cycle, given its influence on property and that the last generation just got lucky.[80] However, it is argued that *ad valorem* taxes such as CGT are fair as they mean tax raised is in proportion to the gain, ie, those best placed to pay more, pay more.[81]

The OTS proposal to increase CGT in line with income tax is problematic, although it does deal with the most common objection, namely an allowance for inflationary gain.[82] The main objection relates to the nature of a capital gain as distinct from taxation of labour, ie in the latter case there is no capital risk to the employee, whereas for an investor, losses can accrue.[83] Although the OTS suggest more flexible offsetting reliefs, it is argued this still leaves investors and entrepreneurs' exposed to rates of tax incommensurate with the risk they take.[84] The extent to which increases in the rate will lead to reductions in tax take, ie on a Laffer curve analysis are also highly debated and without consensus.[85]

It seems reasonable to assume that increases in CGT are likely to lead to greater intergenerational fairness, given most of the gains are held by the older generation.

[76] ibid.
[77] ibid 74.
[78] ibid 84.
[79] HMRC (n 37). By way of comparison to other reliefs over the same period; Entrepreneurs' Relief costs c £2.5 billion, Patent Box c £1 billion, R&D tax relief for large businesses, c £2.2 billion, Enterprise Investment Schemes c £590 million, exemption income to Charities c £2 billion.
[80] S Adam and H Miller, 'The Economics of a Wealth Tax' (2020) Wealth Tax Commission Evidence Paper 3.
[81] M Keen, 'The balance between specific and ad valorem taxation' (1998) 19 *Fiscal Studies* 1–37, 21.
[82] OTS (n 2) 38–41.
[83] House of Commons Library, 'Capital gains tax: recent developments' (2020) Briefing Paper No. 5572, s 3.
[84] ibid.
[85] Strulik, Holger & Trimborn, Timo, 'Laffer Strikes Again: Dynamic Scoring of Capital Taxes' (2010) *Hannover Economic Papers*, dp-454, Leibniz Universität Hannover; House of Commons (n 83) 32.

Whether it remains good policy, however, depends on the empirical question as to whether it is likely to produce more tax overall and it is far from clear whether it would achieve that objective.

v. WTC Report

The WTC report recommends a one-off tax, lasting five years, which they believe would raise around £260 billion.[86] The report considers intergenerational inequality by recognising wealth is disproportionately held by older generations.[87] They state:

> … a one-off wealth tax would tend to offset the increases in intergenerational inequality that are likely to arise from concurrent monetary policy responses to the crisis.[88]

They point to the existence of inequality as being a justification for their proposals and cite survey evidence which demonstrates there is support for a wealth tax.[89] They suggest this is not a call for a radical redistribution, rather it is 'reflecting ideas about who could fairly be asked to contribute more'.[90] The report points to the different tax rates applied to income and capital and suggest the wealth tax is a way to redress that imbalance.[91] The report addresses the issue about why taxing the stock of wealth is fairer than the flow:

> … unlike past income, profits or other flows, which might not be a good guide to the economic resources that a person will receive in the future, their stock of wealth provides a better indication of their current 'ability to pay', despite being determined by reference to an assessment date that is in the past.[92]

The report acknowledges the tax may be regarded as retrospective. Their justification for taxing wealth is based on grounds of practicality; there is an urgent need for government funding, therefore we must see who has the ability to pay.[93] The bond markets, which were trading at record low long-term yields, indicated this latter argument had little merit at the time it was written. Evidence at the time suggested there were few constraints on long-term government borrowing, although recent events after the Kwarteng mini-budget provide reasons to be cautious.[94]

The WTC report considers whether their proposal is unfair on three grounds, whether it is designed to 'punish the wealthy', whether it is 'confiscatory' and whether is it 'retrospective'.[95] They dismiss the first claim as the tax does not target any particular group, it is focused on an individual's ability to pay. The second argument is dismissed on grounds that all taxation might be regarded as confiscatory. Finally, the retrospective argument is dismissed for several reasons. They argue retrospectivity is not black

[86] WTC (n 3) 8.
[87] ibid Fig 4, 36 sets out the distribution of wealth on an age basis.
[88] ibid 36.
[89] ibid Fig 1, 22.
[90] ibid 21.
[91] ibid para 5.1.
[92] ibid 30.
[93] ibid 31.
[94] R Lee, 'The UK can avoid the Boom/ Bust Recovery' (*Briefings for Britain*, 14 March 2021) briefingsforbritain.co.uk/the-uk-can-avoid-the-boom-bust-recovery/.
[95] WTC (n 3) 36.

and white and many tax policies have the effect of unsettling expectations. They suggest because other reforms disrupt plans the wealth tax is no different,[96] eg, the application of NICs to pension withdrawals.

The attractiveness of a wealth tax to proponents of the idea is straightforward. It assists with funding government pandemic spending and does so using money from those best able to afford it. The tax also assists in reducing inequalities within society and between generations.

vi. WTC Report Analysis

A tax on wealth may address intergenerational equality, given much of the wealth held in the UK is held by older generations. The wealth tax is designed to create greater equality between groups within society rather than being targeted at intergenerational inequality, for example, a 60-year-old with a pension of £60,000 pa and an unmortgaged home of £500,000 would be exempt but could hardly be described as poorly off.[97] A 30-year-old living in a small London terraced property would, however, be subject to the charge.[98] This is hardly the stuff of intergenerational redistribution.

Are wealth taxes viable and how have they fared internationally? There is a great deal of adverse evidence on wealth taxes and in the light of this it is understandable they were rejected by the Mirless Review and Treasury Select Committee (TSC).[99] Some object to the wealth tax because of their controversial claim it is retroactive.[100]

Although a one-off wealth tax might help in the short term to repair government finances, the spectre of a one-off tax has the capacity to damage future receipts and hence cause further damage to intergenerational fairness. Wealth taxes have been tried and failed in a number of countries over a long period of time.[101] The reasons revolve around how wealthy people react to the tax, ie the elasticity is high at the top of the distribution,[102] they are costly to administer, in particular in the area of valuation,[103] fail to raise meaningful revenue,[104] and do little for wealth distribution.[105] For those

[96] ibid 36.
[97] ibid para 6.1.
[98] See London average house prices at time of access was £644,631. Zoopla available at www.zoopla.co.uk/house-prices/london/.
[99] R Boadway, E Chamberlain and C Emmerson, 'Taxation of Wealth and Wealth Transfers' in *Dimensions of Tax Design* (Oxford, Oxford University Press, 2010) Section 8; Treasury Select Committee, 'Tax after coronavirus', House of Commons paras 85–88, publications.parliament.uk/pa/cm5801/cmselect/cmtreasy/664/66407.htm#4.5.
[100] T Worstall, 'On the subject of a wealth tax' (*Adam Smith Institute*, 2021) www.adamsmith.org/blog/on-the-subject-of-a-wealth-tax.
[101] Wealth taxes were repealed in 10 out of 13 European Countries. See C Edwards, 'Taxing Wealth and Capital Income' (2019) 85 *Tax and Budget Bulletin*, Cato Institute, Table 1.
[102] K Jakobsen, J Jakobsen, H Kleven and G Zucman, 'Wealth taxation and Wealth Accumulation: Theory and Evidence from Denmark' (2020) 135(1) *The Quarterly Journal of Economics* 329–88; M Rose, 'Macron Fights 'President of the Rich' Tag after Ending Wealth Tax' (*Reuters*, 3 October 2017); H Agnew, 'French Government Opens Door to Wealth Tax Concession' *Financial Times* (5 December 2018). The wealth tax was replaced by a tax on high-end real estate.
[103] M Drometer et al, 'Wealth and Inheritance Taxation: An Overview and Country Comparison' IfO DICE Report 16, no 2 (June 2018) 49.
[104] OECD, 'The Role and Design of Net Wealth Taxes in the OECD' OECD Tax Policy Series, p 20.
[105] ibid 101, p 787.

countries that have managed to maintain a wealth tax, this tends to operate in lieu of IHT or other capital taxes.[106] Although one-off taxes have worked in the past, these sorts of taxes face a bigger challenge in the context of a globalised world.

As the concluding section of this chapter argues, if intergeneration fairness is to be resolved, the best approach is to adopt a long-term, gradual pathway to refine rules to achieve equity.

vii. HL: Tackling Intergenerational Unfairness

The HL report is important for the analysis in this chapter given the pandemic is likely to cause further hardship to the younger generation as government finances are strained. For this reason, a long-term and balanced approach to tax and spending as encouraged by the report is to be welcomed. The report suggests the government adopt:

> a broad equivalence, and sense of equivalence and fairness, about what is contributed over a lifetime and what is received by successive generations.[107]

In terms of primary causes of inequality, the report notes younger people struggle to find affordable housing as a consequence of insufficient supply, and that this is coupled with problems of security and stability in the private rented sector.[108] On the jobs front, they note insecurity arising out of greater flexibility in working patterns.[109] In respect to tax, the report notes successive government failure to deal with intergenerational unfairness:

> Successive governments have failed to make proper provision for the costs of social care in old age for the large post war cohort who are now entering a lengthy retirement and who will rely on smaller, younger generations to pay for them.[110]

The report criticises the way in which social security spending for older people has been prioritised, claiming this may have been originally justified but is no longer reasonable given retired people have higher average incomes than younger groups.[111] This criticism is more potent, given the effects of the pandemic on the young. Even before the crisis those households over the pension age had a higher income than those below the state pension age with children.[112] Policy had consistently favoured the old rather than the young as reductions in social security spending for those under the pension age were to be cut by around £37 billion in 2021,[113] at the same time as the triple lock meant the state pension would be increased by the highest of inflation, wages or 2.5 per cent per

[106] M Brülhart, J Gruber, M Krapf and K Schmidheiny, 'Taxing Wealth: Evidence from Switzerland' (2016) National Bureau of Economic Research Working Paper no 22376; ibid 105.
[107] HL (n 4) 5.
[108] ibid 8.
[109] ibid 12
[110] ibid 4.
[111] ibid 4.
[112] ibid para 220, 71.
[113] The figures in the report did not take account of changes in expenditure which resulted from COVID-19.

annum. This uprating of pensions compared with the period between 1980 and 2010 when pensions were increased with inflation, not earnings.[114]

Benefits provided to the older generation are wider than pensions, such as the Winter Fuel Payment paid out on the basis of age, not need. Sir John Hills noted that 26 per cent of single parents were likely to experience fuel poverty as compared with less than 10 per cent for households over 60.[115] Other age-related benefits noted included transportation passes and TV licences, neither of which were means tested.[116] Similar concerns were raised with respect to NICs, given that employees over the state pension age were not subject to the charge. Paul Johnson[117] described this as 'hard to justify on any normal grounds'.[118] John Glen MP[119] explained the cessation of the NIC charge related to the idea that on retirement, a person was considered to have made a sufficient contribution to their expected benefit. He acknowledged, however, that this no longer held true.[120]

The report highlighted a feature of the tax system which necessarily impacted on intergenerational equity, namely that individuals paying tax today are not paying into a fund for their own benefit, rather they are paying for the current expenditure of the older generation.[121] The implications of this are that the difference between the contributions individuals make and the benefits they receive are likely to change over time. Factors such as increased life expectancy, population bulges, improvements in healthcare systems etc will all play a role in determining resource availability. For those born between 1945–60, the benefits have been great, given the population dynamics since that time.[122]

The report's assessment of property taxes acknowledged regional differences,[123] and recognised the impact of government interventions such as Help-to-Buy or Lifetime ISAs which can assist those buying property. Consideration is given to the way in property is taxed, mainly via SDLT and council tax, although Paul Johnson notes that whilst council tax might be viewed as a tax on the consumption of housing, it is regressive given the upper values are capped.[124] The report does not consider the PRR which is surprising given the cost of the relief.[125]

The report's recommendations about intergenerational tax issues included suggesting the pensions triple lock should be removed, free TV licences should be phased out, and a focus ought to ensure support is targeted toward those outside the workforce with age thresholds increased.[126] Recommendations specifically on tax include treating

[114] HL (n 4) para 232.
[115] ibid para 234.
[116] TV licences became means tested during from August 2020.
[117] Director, IFS.
[118] HL (n 4) para 243.
[119] Economic Secretary to the Treasury and City Minister.
[120] HL (n 4) para 244.
[121] ibid para 39.
[122] ibid para 244.
[123] ibid para 252.
[124] ibid para 255.
[125] HMRC (n 37).
[126] HL (n 4) 84.

benefits as taxable income for those above the threshold, and that NICs should be paid by pensioners still working in higher income groups. Additionally, the report encouraged the government to change regulation to encourage housing supply,[127] as well as to improve tenancy security.[128] On property taxation, they suggest changing council tax to better reflect property values whilst allowing low income, high asset value households to delay payment until the sale of the property. They also argue in favour of full local tax for second homes. There is a call for the reform of SDLT to better improve housing choices for young families. Finally, there is a call for wholesale reform of IHT which they describe as 'capricious and not currently fit for purpose'.[129] The suggestions for reform include taxing the transfer of gifts as they are transferred or allowing exemptions to tax sums left for the purposes of being used for a deposit on a house.[130] Since the publication of the report, free TV licences based only on age have been removed. It seems likely we will see more of their proposals being carried out in upcoming budgets.

viii. HL Analysis

The HL report recognises the long-term aspects of intergenerational issues on fairness in tax law and policy. Factors such as changes in population growth, advances in technology and housing supply all need to be taken into account when designing the fairest approach. The report avoids making suggestions that might disturb the equilibrium of tax-raising by seeking a redistributive objective, rather it seeks ways in which tax might be better designed to reflect affordability, such as the recommendations on council tax.

A number of the suggestions made by the HL were reflected in the TSC report on post-pandemic planning, in particular the universal support that changes ought to be made with a view to the long term.[131] The HL report also acknowledges the issue of housing is only likely to be resolved by a supply-side approach.[132]

IV. A Long-term Approach

The data above has shown us there are serious financial challenges for the younger generation, particularly in housing and pensions. The problem has arisen largely because of changes in asset prices and interest rates. Successive governments have failed to recalibrate tax law and policy to respond to the growing problem which is likely to become worse as the government becomes ever more reliant on revenue derived from labour.

The OTS recommendations, in the absence of the removal of PRR, are unlikely to make too much difference to the price of houses, although it might alleviate some of the tax burden on labour. As with any significant cliff edge change in the tax regime, it is also problematic that changes to CGT would have the unfortunate consequence of

[127] ibid 84, paras 6, 9–12.
[128] ibid 85, para 7.
[129] ibid 83, para 272.
[130] ibid paras 270–271.
[131] Treasury Select Committee, 'Tax after coronavirus' s 2, Edwards (n 101).
[132] HL (n 4) eg paras 72, 73, 92, 94, 100, 257–258.

impacting on long-term capital planning. Decisions made decades ago, for example, might leave someone with 90 per cent of their capital value as opposed to 55 per cent of the value depending on whether Business Asset Disposal Relief is abolished in favour of the additional income tax rate level of 45 per cent. This level of uncertainty has caused many businesses to sell up before changes are made to CGT.[133]

The WTC report argues that given the large amount of wealth available, a one-off tax is a reasonable approach to tackle the pandemic circumstances. As discussed above, this approach is unlikely to be seen by taxpayers as a one-off given the ability of government to simply change its mind at the next point it deems a raid necessary. The undermining of the importance for property rights are likely to influence future conduct given high levels of elasticity been shown to persist.[134]

A. Fiscal Rules

This chapter proposes that to protect against intergenerational unfairness fiscal rules ought to be introduced. Taxation needs to be raised in order to ensure the proper functioning of government; however, governments are always under pressure from short term demands to increase spending and reduce taxation by each generation who plead a special case. Similarly, public sector spending in the form of higher wages, better pensions and greater job security will always be promoted by trade unions.

There is, of course, nothing wrong with these demands and society has gradually improved conditions both in the public and private sector tremendously since the passing of the Reform Act 1832. There is, however, a limit to increases in government spending and reductions in taxation which is usually set by the global bond and FX markets. Recent examples of countries setting a profligate agenda have seen their currencies collapse, inflation increase, and bond yields climb to unsustainable levels.[135] The greatest effect of those consequences tends to fall on the young, who then suffer from periods of great austerity relative to previous generations.

In 1997 Gordon Brown proposed a series of fiscal rules.[136] Political pressure prevented the Treasury from keeping to those rules which were abandoned in the wake of the global financial crisis of 2008. The idea, however, contains within it a map through which future generations might find equity. Although the size of government expenditure relative to GDP is a function of political consensus, the cyclical element of the deficit is a matter of technicality. The rule that would protect generations going forward might then be formulated as creating balance around a politically acceptable level of debt relative to GDP, albeit that this might be characterised as itself a politically motivated rule.[137]

[133] D Prosser, 'Why Britain's entrepreneurs are rushing to sell their businesses' (*Forbes*, 8 January 2021).
[134] OECD (n 104).
[135] R Nelson, 'Argentina's Economic Crisis and Default' (15 June 2020), Congressional Research Service available at fas.org/sgp/crs/row/IF10991.pdf (accessed 10 March 2021); C Carletti, P Colla, M Gulati and S Ongena, 'Pricing contract terms in a crisis: Venezuelan bonds in 2016' (2016) 11(4) *Capital Markets Law Journal* 540–55.
[136] HC Deb 02 July 1997 vol 297 cc 303–16
[137] See R Hughes, J Leslie and C Pacitti, 'Britannia waives the rules?' (2019).

This idea would need to become a matter of convention as opposed to law given Parliamentary supremacy. The rules, however, would need to be articulated out of a sense of regard to future generations, notwithstanding the political debate surrounding what level of government spending should be set relative to GDP. Empirical evidence suggests that economies can be run well with both higher and lower levels of government involvement depending on political taste.[138] Once the rule had been established by convention, proposals about tax and spend would then operate within the framework of the rule, although the rule would remain open to revision given Parliamentary sovereignty.

The evaluation of tax law and policy surrounding, for example, capital, income or tax relief would then take place in the context of an overarching 'tax rule of recognition'. Changes to tax law and policy would then be made within the confines of the tax rule of recognition and overseen by an FPC,[139] that would engage in scrutinising changes. The FPC would act as the advisory committee to HM Treasury (HMT) in ensuring compliance with rule of law issues as well as providing independent guidance on the effectiveness and consequence of fiscal proposals.

Intergenerational unfairness arises largely because short-term electoral concerns can often trump long term equity. It can lead to harmful policy proposals that only make sense in a static as opposed to dynamic perspective such as proposals for a one-off wealth tax.

V. Conclusions

This chapter has shown that the UK has a problem with intergenerational unfairness. The sorts of issues raised here might also or alternatively give rise to intra as much as intergenerational inequalities as the unconsumed increases in wealth, in particular property and pensions wealth, are passed on to the next generation. The data shows that whilst the younger generation are likely to be able to find work at a wage commensurate with previous generations, the cost of housing and pensions has become prohibitive. The cost of housing and pensions have increased largely as a result of interest rates; however, generous government tax reliefs have exacerbated the problem and continue to do so.

Proposals to redress the intergeneration problem have been put forward by the OTS in respect to CGT and the WTC. The government have yet to respond to the OTS recommendations and it is unlikely a Conservative administration would introduce a wealth tax. The differential taxation of capital over income is a perennial subject and is likely

Resolution Foundation Briefing. IEA, 'Binding the hands of government – a credible fiscal rule for the UK' (2012) IEA Current Controversies Paper No 36. Rishi Sunak's 'Charter for Budget Responsibility' has moved HMT towards these goals, see questions-statements.parliament.uk/written-statements/detail/2022-01-05/hcws513.

[138] E Sheehey, 'The effect of government size on economic growth' (1993) 19(3) *Eastern Economic Journal* 321–28; S Nyasha and N Odhiambo, 'Government size and economic growth: A review of international literature' (2019) 9(3) *Sage Open*.

[139] A Brassey, 'Tax Gaar and the Rule of Law' (PhD thesis, University of Cambridge, 2017) ch 4.

to continue to be debated into the future. Wealth taxes, on the other hand appear to be declining in popularity given the myriad of reasons relating to design and the problems of taxing the stock as opposed to the flow of wealth. The most promising proposals to deal with intergenerational tax matters came from the HL report which made a series of sensible recommendations that, in time, are more likely to be translated into policy.

This chapter concludes that if government policy is going to create intergenerational fairness for the future, it ought to consider introducing a tax rule of recognition where convention persuades policymakers towards long-term thinking. The proposal here is the creation of a FPC to act as an independent body to advise HMT and Parliament on new policy proposals with a view to protecting future generations. COVID-19 has presented great challenges for the government but there will be more crises in the future that also need to be dealt with and the proposals here are made with regard to creating equity between us and future generations as those crisis hit the economy.

16

Flexible Work within Employment Relationships: A Conceptual Scheme for Fiscal Policies

WEI CUI

Abstract

Across the world, public finance instruments have been deployed at unprecedented scales to support labour markets during the COVID-19 pandemic. This chapter argues that it would be unwise for tax scholars to treat governments' labour market interventions during the pandemic as lying outside the purview of tax law and policy, and analyses two commonly-adopted types of interventions: (1) income support delivered directly to workers, and (2) support delivered indirectly through employers via various forms of wage subsidies. Two observations guide the analysis. First, despite the gig economy's increasing prominence, in many industrialised countries, the proportion of self-employed individuals in the total working population has not been rising. In contrast, the growth of 'flexible work' is more notable within the formal employment sector. Second, the workplace itself has long been a vital site of substantial economic redistribution, independent of redistributive policies carried out by the state. The increasing prevalence of 'flexible employees' will make the workplace's redistributive role even more prominent. The chapter advances these arguments by reference to the Canadian federal government's fiscal response to COVID-19 in 2020–21, which bears much resemblance to policies adopted in other major economies. Building on an assessment of Canada's initial pandemic fiscal response, the chapter argues for the long-term policy relevance of targeted work subsidies.

I. Introduction

Across the world, a key priority in government responses to the COVID-19 pandemic has been supporting labour markets in crisis. Such support has often involved public finance instruments – for example, income assistance to the unemployed, and tax reliefs and subsidies offered to employers to retain or hire workers – deployed at unprecedented scales. Yet tax policy commentators and tax scholars have contributed relatively little to the analysis of these vital policies. Indeed, a prevailing assumption seems to be that tax policy intersects with the economic upheaval brought about by the pandemic at a later stage – *after* economies have sufficiently stabilised and recovered, and when governments try to raise taxes to pay for their massive spending in 2020 and 2021.[1] One might even say that from this perspective, the topics of taxes and crises do not really intersect.

But there are at least three reasons why it is unwise to treat governments' labour market interventions during the pandemic as lying outside the purview of tax law and policy. First, such a stance relies on arbitrary intellectual divisions. For instance, payroll taxes and income taxes on wage income are very similar taxes on labour income. Targeted reductions of the two types of taxes are in many economic respects equivalent to each other, and both are equivalent to targeted wage subsidies. The fact that tax legal scholars specialising in the income tax have paid relatively little attention to payroll taxes in the past might *explain* why they have contributed little to the analysis of pandemic fiscal policies targeted at the labour market. It would be clearly wrong to *justify* this lack of contribution by insisting that such policies are not 'tax' policies.

Second and relatedly, choices about pandemic fiscal policies aimed at the labour market should not be viewed as independent of choices about how to finance such policies. Instead, at least when one adopts a welfarist framework, the efficiency and distributional trade-offs implied by these policies should be considered together.[2]

Third, and perhaps most importantly, pandemic fiscal policies have inevitably generated substantial redistributions, raising significant normative questions about whether those most in need have been reasonably identified and properly assisted. Tax experts have traditionally regarded the normative evaluation of large-scale redistributive policies as their core specialty. Failing to engage with the rich moral intuitions implicated by governments' initial responses to COVID-19 would be a significant missed opportunity.

In this chapter, I explore two types of labour market interventions commonly adopted by governments during the first, crisis year of the pandemic: (1) income support delivered directly to workers who suffered income loss (as a result of either losing their jobs or facing reduced work hours), and (2) similar support delivered indirectly through employers via various forms of wage subsidies. My explorations are guided by two observations. First, even before the pandemic, the increasing prominence of the 'gig economy' and 'alternative work arrangements' led to frequent claims that individuals in self-employment should be given greater policy attention. Such claims have shaped government pandemic response in countries such as Canada. However, in many industrialised countries, the proportion of self-employed individuals in the total population of workers has not been rising. In contrast, the growth of 'flexible work' is more notable

[1] See, eg R de Mooij et al, 'Tax Policy for Inclusive Growth after the Pandemic' (Special Series on COVID-19, IMF Fiscal Affairs, 2020); OECD, 'Tax and Fiscal Policies after the COVID-19 Crisis' (OECD Policy Responses to Coronavirus (COVID-19), 2021).

[2] As noted in ch 15 in this volume by Brassey 'The Implications of Intergenerational Issues on Tax Policy in a Post-COVID World. An Examination of Age Discrimination', the pandemic's unprecedented fiscal shock may add to existing intergenerational inequalities. New tax policies and fiscal rules that mitigate these effects are needed to deal with the burdens of the current system.

within the formal employment sector. Therefore, I argue, labour-related redistributive policies should not focus only or primarily on the self-employment sector in identifying individuals in need of government support: instead, greater policy attention should be given to what one might call 'flexible employees.'

Second, the workplace itself has long been a vital site of substantial economic redistribution, independent of redistributive policies carried out by the state. The increasing prevalence of 'flexible employees' will make the workplace's redistributive role even more prominent. Therefore, while the 'self-employed v formally-employed' distinction is not necessarily useful in identifying individuals in need, it is significant because redistributive policies must carefully consider the interaction between state and non-state institutions for redistribution.

I develop my arguments mainly with reference to the Canadian federal government's fiscal response to COVID-19 in 2020–21, although the relevant Canadian policies bear much resemblance to policies adopted in other major economies.[3] I argue that in justifying these policies, the Canadian government erred in over-emphasising assistance to self-employed workers, and in not acknowledging the redistributive functions of firms. But Canada's pandemic fiscal responses have been inadvertently successful, precisely because they delivered substantial benefits to 'flexible employees' – especially part-time and temporary workers – and tapped into the workplace's redistributive potential. Building on this assessment of Canada's initial pandemic fiscal response, I argue for the long-term policy relevance of targeted work subsidies in rich countries like Canada.

Section II of this chapter shows that in many advanced economies (such as Canada and the US), flexible work in the formal employment sector has risen faster than self-employment in recent decades. This means that the association between 'precarious work' with self-employment, and the prevalence and policy significance of misclassifying employees as independent contractors, may have been exaggerated. Instead of hoping that the staid 'employee v independent contractor' legal distinction will gain new life from the ascendance of the gig economy, legal scholars should directly evaluate the normative issues raised by self-employment and flexible employment.

Section III of the chapter illustrates these issues with Canada's pandemic fiscal response, emphasising the government's misdiagnosis of policy problems. In section IV, I discuss the normative controversies surrounding pandemic wage subsidies, and outline a preliminary framework for comparing income support delivered directly to precarious workers with those delivered indirectly through employers. The Conclusion summarises the chapter's arguments and considers directions for further research.

II. The Rise of Flexible Work in the Workplace

In recent years, the novelty of services available for hire on digital platforms and the 'gig economy's' transformation of daily lives have led many to expect increases in the self-employed worker population. Such widely-shared expectations also shaped

[3] Ch 17 in this volume by Lind 'How to Award Financial Aid Amidst a Pandemic Through the Lens of a Tax Scholar', for instance, discusses similar programmes in Australia and Sweden.

formulations of policy priorities. For example, Canada's federal government repeatedly declared an intention to potentially extend unemployment insurance to the self-employed and gig workers.[4] Political momentum for such proposals is likely to grow in response to reports of actions taken in other countries, such as the recent European Commission proposal to treat gig workers as employees entitled to a minimum wage and legal protections.[5]

However, labour market statistics suggest that the underlying expectations may not always be sound. Data from Canada's Labour Force Survey (LFS), for example, shows that the portion of unincorporated self-employed workers (ie not including those who work for corporations that they themselves own) among all workers in Canada (ie the sum of employees and the self-employed) has experienced a long-term decline. This proportion was 9 per cent in 1990, peaked at 11.3 per cent in 1998, but has stayed below 9 per cent since 2011.[6] In other words, whatever misclassification of employees as independent contractors is practiced, the proportion of 'independent contractors' in the Canadian labour force has been dwindling. In the first part of 2020, the COVID-19 shock pushed some workers into self-employment. But un-incorporated self-employment still represented only 8.5 per cent of all Canadian workers, just slightly above the average (8.4 per cent) since 2011. Remarkably, recent LFS statistics show that between September 2020 and September 2021, the number of Canadians in un-incorporated self-employment *shrank* by 9 per cent,[7] leading the press to ask, 'Where did all the self-employed workers go?'[8]

Researchers have shown that in the US, the share of self-employed individuals in the labour force has also stayed stagnant in recent years. A recent survey of the empirical literature concludes that 'there have not been substantial changes in the rate of nonstandard work arrangements in terms of independent contracting, self-employment, or electronically mediated gig work'.[9] In the US Bureau of Labour Statistics Contingent Workers Supplement, the rate of independent contractors has remained at approximately 7 per cent.[10] Similarly, the share of self-employed workers has been declining in Germany and Italy, and increasing only slightly in France.[11] Even in the UK,

[4] Canada's 2021 Budget, released on 19 April 2021, indicated the intent to conduct 'targeted consultations' in the next two years regarding 'future, long-term reforms' to Employment Insurance with self-employed and gig workers in mind. See also The Canadian Press, 'EI Should Cover Gig Workers, Self-employed, Says Commons Committee' *The Globe and Mail* (17 June 2021) www.theglobeandmail.com/politics/article-ei-should-cover-gig-workers-self-employed-says-commons-committee/; J Gray, 'Gig economy the next target in Ontario labour-law changes' *The Globe and Mail* (25 October 2021) www.theglobeandmail.com/canada/article-gig-economy-the-next-target-in-ontario-labour-law-changes/.

[5] A Satariano and E Peltier, 'Europe Pushes New Rules Turning Gig Workers into Employees' *The New York Times* (9 December 2021) www.nytimes.com/2021/12/09/technology/european-commission-gig-workers-uber.html.

[6] W Cui, 'Non-Standard Employment and Canada's Initial Pandemic Response' (2021) 69 *Can Tax J* 475, 476.

[7] P Brethour, 'What is Driving the Decline in Self-Employed Workers?' *The Globe and Mail* (12 October 2021) www.theglobeandmail.com/investing/personal-finance/taxes/article-what-is-driving-the-decline-in-self-employed-workers/.

[8] M Lundy and C Hannay, 'Where Did All the Self-Employed Workers Go?' *The Globe and Mail* (2 December 2021) www.theglobeandmail.com/business/article-where-did-all-the-self-employed-workers-go/.

[9] A Mas and A Pallais, 'Alternative Work Arrangements' (2020) 12 *Annual Rev of Economics* 631, 639.

[10] ibid.

[11] A Teichgräber and J Van Reenen, 'Have Productivity and Pay Decoupled in the UK?' (Discussion Paper No.1812, Centre for Economic Performance, 2021) 28.

where the self-employment share of the workforce has steadily risen since 2001, this share is no higher than in an earlier era of high self-employment between 1987 and 1994.[12]

There are some simple reasons why gig work enabled by digital platforms may not be reflected in labour force surveys. Such surveys tend to classify respondents according to their main or only job position. If most individuals undertaking gig work do so in addition to their main jobs, such supplementary labour activities would not lead to a greater share of self-employment among those surveyed. This hypothesis is supported by empirical evidence from Canada and the US. For example, a Canadian government analysis based on confidential tax returns shows that the median net gig income of a gig worker was only $4,303 in 2016. Moreover, for most, gig work is only a temporary activity: 'Roughly one-half of those who entered gig work in a given year had no gig income the next year'.[13] Only about one quarter of gig work entrants remain gig workers for three or more years. Researchers in the US similarly found that gig jobs rarely provide a substantial amount of income: the main benefit of gig work appears to reside in 'occasional moonlighting and income smoothing'.[14] Indeed, workers taking on gig jobs are those who 'have falling income, declining assets, and increasing debt': they are individuals whose labour market status is in transition.[15]

In other words, even in countries with deep 'gig economy' penetration, the proportion of individuals whose main job status is 'individual contractor' need not rise. In sharp contrast to this pattern, the proportion of the labour force engaged in temporary employment *has* been rising in some countries. For example, the proportion of temporary workers (full- or part-time) in Canada reached a peak of 11.7 per cent in 2017. Even after suffering the most severe contractions in 2020 due to COVID-19, that figure – at 9.8 per cent of all workers – stood higher than unincorporated self-employment. If we define 'non-standard workers' as comprising the categories of the unincorporated self-employed, temporary employees, and permanent part-time employees, then the most notable change in non-standard work in Canada has not been an overall expansion: the proportion of non-standard workers to total workers has remained at around 30 per cent since 1997. Instead, it is the increasing share of *employees* among non-standard workers, which rose from 64.8 per cent in 1998 to 73.4 per cent in 2017.[16]

Analogous patterns have been found in the US: the population of contract workers that are formally employed has grown faster than the population of independent contractors.[17] The reasons for the rising share of contract employment are not

[12] ibid 17.

[13] S-H Jeon, H Liu and Y Ostrovsky, 'Measuring the Gig Economy in Canada Using Administrative Data' (Analytical Studies Branch Research Paper, Statistics Canada, 2019).

[14] Mas and Pallais (n 9) 643. The authors argue that as 'a safety net, electronically mediated gig jobs allow workers to quickly adjust their labor supply in response to the loss of other income or increased demand for consumption'. Consequently, there is 'a high degree of turnover in participants of online labour platforms': 643–44.

[15] ibid. See also DK Koustas, 'What Do Big Data Tell Us about Why People Take Gig Economy Jobs?' (2019) 109 *AEA Papers and Proceedings* 367 (entry into gig work in the US is generally preceded by a decline in non-gig income).

[16] Cui (n 6) 476.

[17] LF Katz and AB Krueger, 'The Rise and Nature of Alternative Work Arrangements in the United States, 1995–2015' (2018) 72 *Industrial and Labor Relations Rev* 382.

well-understood. In Canada, for instance, older workers (aged 55 and over) represent a rising share of temporary employment, which points to demographic factors as an explanation.[18] On the other hand, the growth in temporary employment in Canada is most pronounced in the health and education sectors, suggesting that sector-specific factors may be at play.[19] Whether such sector-specific factors involve country-specific institutions is unknown.

In the US, a potential explanation of the rise of temporary employment may be the rise of 'domestic outsourcing' – contracting with other firms for the performance of non-core jobs such as janitorial and security services. Empirical evidence for domestic outsourcing has been produced through measures of 'occupation concentration' among employers: high occupation concentration is found in firms whose workers belong to few occupations, and outsourced jobs are likely to be in firms that offer a single service, such as cleaning. In the US, from 1999 to 2015, there appears to have been a large increase in concentration in the lowest-paid occupations.[20] Similar to the growth in Canada's temporary employment in select sectors, this US trend points to changes in the organisation of production rather than demographic shifts.

Whatever the explanation may be for the rise of temporary employment, it is instructive to compare policy issues potentially raised by gig workers who are independent contractors and by temporary employees. The latter group is, by definition, not victimised by employer misclassification. Temporary employees benefit from whatever workplace regulations that apply to employees in general. Yet are temporary employees generally better off than independent contractors? The answer is likely to be *no*. For one, in terms of wages, temporary employees tend to face a substantial wage discount relative to permanent employees.[21] Independent contractors, by contrast, do not in general show lower labour income than employees.

Whether gig workers specifically earn lower (hourly) wages is also unclear. If (as discussed above) most gig workers hold a main job, or if they pursue gig work mainly while transitioning among jobs, then many will likely manage their gig work to maintain a certain wage level that is comparable to their regular (permanent) job.[22] Furthermore, while temporary employees enjoy some legal protection associated with the workplace, gig workers benefit significantly from the flexibility of their work.[23]

The overall level of personal wellbeing of these two types of workers may be reflected by whether their work status is voluntary. In Canada, only 5 per cent of self-employed individuals surveyed in 2018 reported 'Could not find suitable paid employment' as their reason for being self-employed. By contrast, 21.8 per cent of part-time employees (who also face a wage discount relative to full-time employees) were involuntary

[18] C Busby and R Muthukumaran, 'Precarious Positions: Policy Options to Mitigate Risks in Non-Standard Employment' (2016) 462 *CD Howe Institute Commentary* 1, 8.

[19] ibid 6–7 (the authors also note that the rise of temporary employment in Canada is not attributable to seasonal and casual work).

[20] Mas and Pallais (n 9) 640.

[21] This discount was on average 23% in 2015 in Canada: Busby and Muthukumaran (n 18) 8.

[22] Mas and Pallais (n 9) 644 (suggesting that it will be difficult either to raise or to lower the hourly wage of gig workers because they select the quantity of hours worked by anchoring to a reservation wage).

[23] MK Chen et al, 'The Value of Flexible Work: Evidence From Uber Drivers' (2019) 127 *Journal of Political Economy* 2735.

part-timers. Researchers have also found that temporary employees in the US generally earn lower wages and are more likely to be taking nonstandard jobs involuntarily than independent contractors.[24]

In summary, the 'independent contractor v employee' distinction (or even the 'gig worker v employee' distinction) is unlikely to reliably identify vulnerable populations in today's changing workforce. Fundamentally, this is because the labour market (even before the pandemic) has been transformed by deep forces including demographic change, trade, and technological change in general; many manifestations of such transformations are found in the workplace, rather than outside of it. In some ways, digital platforms facilitating gig work merely offer responses to such changes in the employment experience (ie a temporarily unemployed worker can use gig work to smooth consumption.)

This is a critical point to remember because in many common law countries like Canada, the UK, and the US, the 'independent contractor v employee' distinction is sustained by common law: the application of the distinction based on 'facts and circumstances' is left to the courts. Judicial decisions are closely followed by the legal profession (and legal scholars) and tend to attract press attention. The association between the distinction and judicial decisions, however, should not be taken to necessarily signify the distinction's policy importance. Classifying more independent contractors as employees will not solve a social problem if the policies applicable to employees engaged in non-standard work are inadequate to begin with.

If 'independent contractor v employee' distinction is a poor heuristic for identifying individuals in need, what policy issues arising from the labour force today should tax law scholars pay attention to? To answer this question, one must adopt a less stylised approach and look at the specifics of the labour market. Yet this is a challenging task. The reason is that there are substantial variations within common worker classifications. For example, 'independent contractors' come in all types, ranging from successful entrepreneurs and highly-paid professionals who opt out of employment by others, to those who struggle to find any employment. Because of this heterogeneity, any redistributive policies aimed generically at the 'self-employed' is likely to be ill-targeted.

The same can be said about non-standard workers in the formal employment sector. For example, it is well-known that women are both more likely to pursue part-time employment than men and value part-time employment more.[25] Yet women and men are equally likely to be found among temporary employees,[26] even though women are likely to have a stronger preference against the unpredictable schedules and earnings that might come with temporary employment.[27] In other words, *part-time* workers who are men are more likely to hold such positions involuntarily,[28] while *temporary* workers who are women are more likely to hold such positions involuntarily. What types of

[24] LF Katz and AB Krueger, 'Understanding Trends in Alternative Work Arrangements in the United States' (2019) NBER Working Paper No 25425, www.nber.org/papers/w25425.

[25] Mas and Pallais (n 9) 644; M Wiswall and B Zafar, 'Preference for the Workplace, Investment in Human Capital, and Gender' (2017) 133 *The Quarterly Journal of Economics* 457; Busby and Muthukumaran (n 18) 5.

[26] As of August 2021, for example, the ratio of men to women holding temporary employment in Canada is roughly 1:1.

[27] Mas and Pallais (n 9) 635–36.

[28] Busby and Muthukumaran (n 18) 5.

workers are vulnerable, therefore, may depend on complex interactions between job characteristics and individual traits.

In the next part of this chapter, I will show how misconceptions about the labour market have led to significant discrepancies between the design and outcomes of Canada's fiscal response to the pandemic. Yet studying these discrepancies may lead to a new appreciation of the redistributive function of the workplace.

III. Canada's Pandemic Fiscal Response: Inadvertent Success

The largest components (in terms of dollar amounts) of Canada's fiscal response to the pandemic all focused on the labour market. Table 1 summarises the particularly broad range of labour market interventions (LMI) they represent and identifies some comparable programmes in other OECD countries.

Table 1 Classification of Pandemic LMI Measures[29]

	Canadian versions	Non-Canadian examples
Income assistance to participants in unemployment insurance	Enhanced Employment Insurance benefits and relaxed eligibility conditions (≈$60 billion)	Enhanced unemployment insurance benefits in US (CARES Act) and Australia
Income assistance regardless of participation in unemployment insurance	Canada Emergency Response Benefits ($74.08 billion) Canada Recovery Benefits ($28.34 billion)	US 'Pandemic Unemployment Assistance'
Income support to employees with reduced hours	Work-sharing ($1.711 billion approved)	UK Job Support Scheme 'Short-Time Work' schemes in Germany, France, Italy and other European countries
Wage subsidies for distressed businesses	Canada Emergency Wage Subsidy ($98.6 billion)	US Paycheck Protection Program (forgivable loans) Australia JobKeeper programme Payroll tax cuts in Scandinavia

Two notable aspects of Canada's pandemic LMI portfolio emerge from Table 1. First, unlike some other countries, Canada did not make an exclusive choice between 'insuring workers' and 'insuring jobs'.[30] In many European countries, for example, it is reported that the expansion of unemployment insurance during the pandemic was

[29] Amounts in Canadian dollars refer to aggregate government spending for a particular programme during the pandemic period either up to early December 2021 or programme expiration (if a programme was terminated before December 2021).

[30] G Giupponi et al, 'Should We Insure Workers or Jobs During Recessions?' forthcoming in the *Journal of Economic Perspectives*.

limited, but participation in job retention programmes in the form of short-time work schemes 'skyrocketed'.[31] In the US, on the other hand, greater emphasis was given to the rapid activation of the unemployment insurance system.[32] In contrast to these two types of responses, massive income assistance was concurrently delivered in Canada to workers both directly and, through job retention schemes, indirectly. Second, not only did Canada's federal government attempt simultaneously to insure workers and insure jobs, but for each of these two objectives, it also adopted multiple instruments to do so.

In particular, in providing direct income assistance to individuals, Canada made temporary enhancements to Employment Insurance (for one year) both to provide higher levels of benefits and to allow more workers to access benefits.[33] Key changes included reduced 'insurable employment' hour requirements (the number of hours a worker must have worked in a year to be eligible for Employment Insurance was reduced to 120 hours); a floor to the benefit rate set at $500 per week; and at least 50 weeks of benefits. At the same time, a separate, larger, and unprecedented income assistance scheme was implemented first as the Canada Emergency Response Benefits (CERB) and then as the Canada Recovery Benefits (CRB).[34] CERB/CRB claimants need not have participated in Employment Insurance at all: they only need to have earned at least $5,000 in 2019 or 2020, and to have not returned to work due to COVID-19 or have seen an income drop by at least 50 per cent. CERB/CRB thus allowed even self-employed individuals who have not contributed Employment Insurance premia to receive income assistance – which some viewed as receiving free unemployment insurance.[35]

In terms of income assistance delivered through employers, Canada also combined the enhancement of existing programmes with unprecedented policies. Since the Great Recession, Canada has implemented a federal 'work-sharing' programme, which is analogous to other countries' short-term work programmes in supporting job retention during business downturns by subsidising hours not worked. In response to COVID-19, Canada extended the permissible duration of 'work-sharing agreements' between employers and the government, and adjusted benefits payable under the programme to be comparable to the enhanced Employment Insurance benefits discussed above. But Canada also enacted the massive and unprecedented Canada Emergency Wage Subsidy (CEWS), which provided payroll subsidies to employers depending on their revenue loss levels. This combination of a large wage subsidy and short-term work programme

[31] ibid. One might say that in these countries, workers were insured by keeping them at their current jobs.

[32] ibid. The fraction of the working age population on unemployment insurance benefits surged from about 2% to 12% in April 2020. See also HJ Holzer et al, 'Did Pandemic Unemployment Benefits Reduce Employment? Evidence from Early State-Level Expirations in June 2021' (2021) NBER Working Paper No 29575, www.nber.org/papers/w29575.

[33] Department of Finance Canada, 'Fall Economic Statement 2020: Supporting Canadians and Fighting COVID-19' (2020) www.budget.gc.ca/fes-eea/2020/report-rapport/toc-tdm-en.html, 25. The government claimed that the Employment Insurance programme was 'supporting an additional 400,000 people' as a result of these changes (ibid).

[34] CRB replaced CERB in September 2020.

[35] R Boadway, 'The Canada Recovery Benefit: Employment Insurance or Basic Income Guarantee?' (*Finances of the Nation*, 3 November 2020) financesofthenation.ca/staging/6309/2020/10/09/crb-ei-or-basic-income-guarantee/.

is uncommon internationally: countries tend to choose between these two types of programmes instead of activating both simultaneously.[36]

Why did Canada invest in such an expansive portfolio of policies? Since both Employment Insurance and work-sharing are existing programmes, the enactments of CERB/CRB and CEWS require the most explanation. In terms of CERB/CRB, one rationale was simply that the existing Employment Insurance programme could not handle a very sudden and massive wave of layoffs, and a parallel emergency programme was needed. From this perspective, if the Employment Insurance system had been ready to cope with massive labour market shocks, CERB/CRB would not have been necessary.[37] However, the government may also have expected CERB/CRB to receive popular support because they experimented with new policies, such as a universal basic income or new social insurance for gig workers.[38] From this perspective, CERB/CRB represent policy designs that possess long-term political currency.

The situation for CEWS was different. Its enactment may partially have been motivated by doubts about whether the existing job retention programme could rise to the pandemic's challenge: work-sharing never had the high level of use in Canada as short-term work programmes had in Europe;[39] relying on it exclusively to incentivise job retention during the pandemic would have been risky. However, few Canadian commentators have seen long-term policy relevance for CEWS (as some did for CERB/CRB). Many claimed that CEWS was poorly targeted, contributed little to job retention, and instead perversely filled corporate coffers and enabled profitable companies to pay high compensations to their executives.[40] Political support for CEWS was chalked up to business and union lobbying.[41] Even Canadian political leaders expressed interest in European-style short-term work programmes as demonstrating potentially superior design than CEWS.[42] Overall, in evaluating and rationalising the federal government's pandemic fiscal response, Canadian commentators tend to favour refining the existing Employment Insurance and work-sharing programmes to support the labour market. While some insist on the need for universal basic income or social insurance for the self-employed, and therefore refrained from criticising the generosity of CERB/CRB, almost no one favours wage subsidies of the kind introduced by CEWS.

[36] See S Scarpetta et al, 'Job Retention Schemes During the COVID-19 Lockdown and Beyond' (OECD Policy Responses to Coronavirus (COVID-19) 2020).

[37] See M Corak, 'An Employment Insurance System for the 21st Century: Lesson 2, The Future of Work Calls for Better Income Insurance' (*Finances of the Nation*, 1 February 2021) financesofthenation.ca/2021/02/01/an-employment-insurance-system-for-the-21st-century-lesson-2-the-future-of-work-calls-for-better-income-insurance/.

[38] Boadway (n 35).

[39] Scarpetta (n 36).

[40] T Cardoso, 'CEWS: A Massive Subsidy Shrouded in Secrecy' *The Globe and Mail* (11 May 2021) www.theglobeandmail.com/business/article-cews-a-massive-subsidy-shrouded-in-secrecy/.

[41] J Robson and M Smart, 'Canada's New Wage Subsidies: Better Targeted, Or Just Better Hidden?' (*Finances of the Nation*, 4 November 2021) financesofthenation.ca/2021/11/04/canadas-new-wage-subsidies-better-targeted-or-just-better-hidden/.

[42] K Bolongaro, 'Trudeau's Finance Minister Praises Germany's Short-Work Program' (*Bloomberg*, 12 November 2020) www.bloomberg.com/news/articles/2020-11-12/trudeau-s-finance-minister-praises-germany-s-short-work-program.

Figure 1 COVID-19 Impact on Non-Standard Work Positions[43]

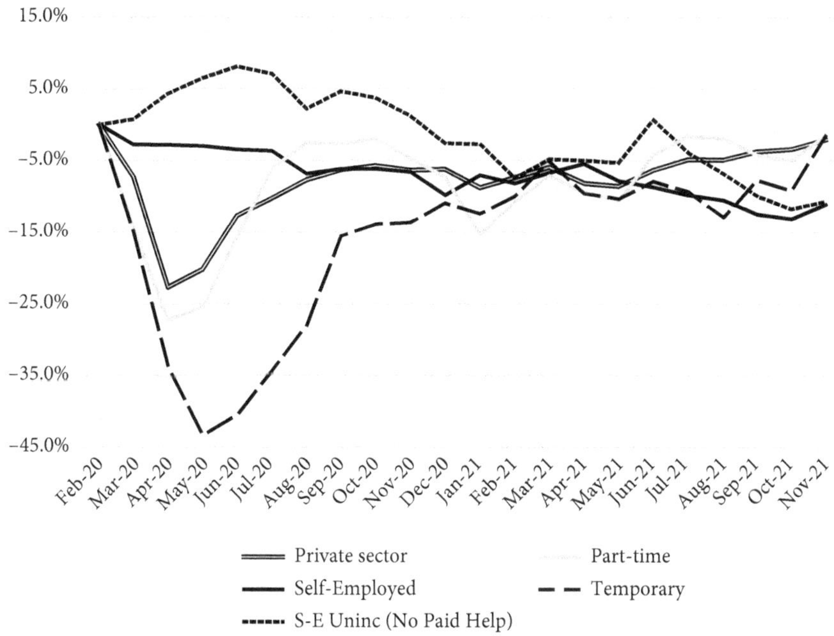

This outlook, however, arguably misses some of the most important lessons taught by the pandemic. Figure 1 illustrates the pandemic's impact on the total number of job positions in Canada for three types of work: temporary employment, part-time work, and self-employment.[44] The graph shows that, in 2020, temporary employment was by far the most negatively affected portion of the workforce. By May 2020, close to 45 per cent of temporary jobs had been lost, compared to about 20 per cent for all private sector employees. Recovery of temporary jobs also lagged behind the recovery of private sector employment in general. In addition, during the early months of the pandemic, the job loss for part-time positions was also worse than the average for all private sector employment. By contrast, unincorporated self-employment rose relative to February for most of 2020, and dominated the recovery of other types of work until July 2021.

While Figure 1 examines the number of positions in the labour market, Figure 2 reveals the pandemic's impact on aggregate hours worked by the same three types of work. For all types of work, COVID-19's impact on hours worked is more severe than on the number of positions. Notably, during most months, the private employment sector as a whole suffered smaller losses than the self-employed sector – the reverse of the pattern observed for the number of positions. But the greater losses for flexible

[43] The measurements of work loss in Figure 1 and 2 are both seasonably adjusted, in the sense that differences in a particular month (in 2020 or 2021) from the initial condition in February 2020 are reported after netting out differences between that month and February in 2018.

[44] The type of self-employment that is most important in terms of the number of individuals involved – unincorporated self-employment – is separately displayed for clarity.

employees are the same. The greatest loss again accrued to temporary employment – aggregate work reduction reached close to 60 per cent in May 2020. The recovery of hours among part-time employees followed a largely similar path as the unincorporated self-employed until June 2021, generally below private sector average. Together, Figures 1 and 2 indicate that part-time and temporary employees were more vulnerable to the pandemic's adverse effects than both self-employed and permanent full-time workers.

Figure 2 COVID-19 Impact on Aggregate Hours Worked by Non-Standard Workers

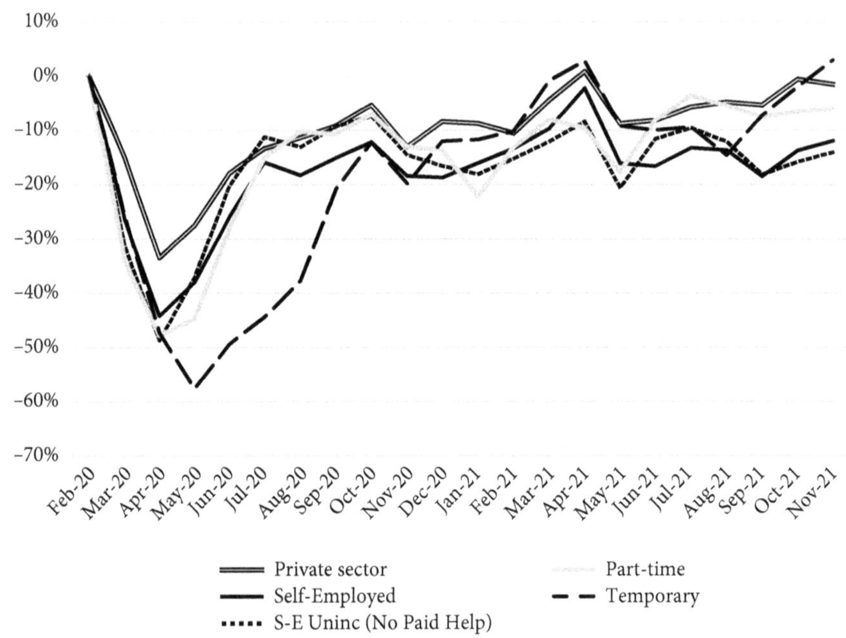

A further set of notable facts concerns the type of workers who were helped by Canada's COVID-19 fiscal policies. Government statistics report that the cumulative number of unique applicants under the CRB, as of 4 April 2021, was 1.84 million individuals. By the time of the CRB's inception in October 2020, the aggregate reduction in hours worked relative to February 2020 for self-employed Canadians was 10 per cent. Because eligibility for CRB requires a worker to have experienced at least a 50 per cent income reduction, it is reasonable to infer that no more than 20 per cent of all self-employed individuals in Canada made CRB claims. Because there were 2.843 million self-employed Canadians at the end of 2019, it follows that no more than 570,000 CRB claimants could have been self-employed workers. Therefore, the majority of CRB claims were made by employees – which is ironic, in light of the CRB being heralded as unemployment insurance for the self-employed.[45]

[45] It is even clearer that the large majority of applicants for CERB benefits were dependent employees, rather than the self-employed. Government statistics indicate that as of October 2020, there were fewer than 1.4 million active Employment Insurance beneficiaries. Yet the cumulative number of unique applicants

These facts point to two significant conclusions. First (and confirming the arguments in the first part of this chapter), the status of self-employment, even on average, does not capture the most vulnerable workers. Not only may temporary and part-time employees be more vulnerable in normal labour markets, but this vulnerability was also clearly manifest during the pandemic.[46] Even for income assistance delivered directly to individual workers, formal employees represent the largest group – it would thus clearly be wrong to continue assuming that the primary policy effect of CERB/CRB would be on the self-employed. Second, traditional Employment Insurance and short-term work programmes serve flexible employees poorly. Their flaws thus lie not only in whether they can be scaled up quickly when facing an economic shock, but in whether they are even designed to deliver the right kind of assistance to the right people.

To understand this second conclusion, consider first how Employment Insurance applies to flexible employees. The basic condition for a worker to claim Employment Insurance benefits is that she must have lost employment, been temporarily laid off, or be on leave without pay (unless she participates in a work-sharing agreement, as discussed below). That is, the insurance benefits of Employment Insurance are available only when there is a loss in the number of jobs – work stops entirely – and not just reduced hours or pay. Moreover, under Canadian rules, if an Employment Insurance claimant receives benefits but works part-time while 'on claim', benefits are clawed back 50 cents for each dollar earned. This very high tax rate on earnings is evidence that Employment Insurance is primarily designed as insurance for full-time workers: laid off workers are encouraged to search for full-time jobs, while part-time work during claim periods is expected to be only a transitional, and not the normal, state.

Canada's work-sharing system is even more strongly biased against flexible employees.[47] For example, an explicit restriction of the programme is that only permanent, year-round, Employment Insurance-eligible 'core staff' are eligible to participate. Moreover, equal and proportional hour reductions must be made for all employees within a work unit described in a work-sharing agreement between an employer and the government, making it less likely for employers to include employees with different wage rates and work statuses in the same work-sharing agreement. Work-sharing also limits the hours reduced to no more than 60 per cent of normal hours. Given that part-time workers have reduced hours to begin with, proportional reduction requirements may also make it less likely for part-timers to participate in work-sharing. Finally, many of the procedural costs of work-sharing – including the need for employers and all participating employees to enter an agreement with the government – imply that it is only when the cost of layoff is high that work-sharing is sufficiently attractive to employers. Again, this suggests that short-term work programmes in general, and Canada's work-sharing in particular, may never have been intended to help flexible employees.

for CERB and Employment Insurance benefits during the COVID-19 pandemic was 8.9 million individuals. Thus, the vast majority of the 8.9 million individuals accounted for received CERB as opposed to regular Employment Insurance payments. It follows that even if all of Canada's 2.8 million self-employed workers claimed CERB benefits, an even greater number of CERB claimants were employees.

[46] Immigrant workers are also more likely to be part-time or temporary employees than residents. The vulnerability of immigrant workers during the pandemic is touched on in ch 17 of this volume by Lind.

[47] See Cui (n 6) for more detailed discussion.

Fortunately for Canada's most vulnerable workers, the government did not rely mainly on Employment Insurance or work-sharing to deliver pandemic assistance. Instead, flexible employees benefitted from CERB/CRB and CEWS.[48] CERB/CRB did not require a claimant to have completely stopped work, and offered income assistance to the large population of workers who suffered loss on hours worked.[49] Moreover, for these workers, whatever pay they continued to receive from their employers may have been subsidised by CEWS. The irony, though, is that these much-needed benefits materialised inadvertently – direct assistance provided to individuals is portrayed as mostly relevant for the unemployed and self-employed – while assistance to employers is generally discussed in connection with the goal of pre-empting changes on the number of workers retained.

When one takes seriously the need to protect flexible employees (even if they still form a very heterogeneous group), however, a question arises for them that is unlikely to arise for either the unemployed or the permanent full-time workers: is the simultaneous delivery of both direct and indirect income assistance to flexible employees too generous?[50] This is certainly a possibility. In the next part of the chapter, I turn to the question of how to choose between these two modes of government assistance.

IV. Redistribution via the Workplace

Though they are far from being the most widely adopted policies,[51] and despite the controversies that surround their adoption, the case for using wage subsidies to mitigate the pandemic's economic shock is rather compelling. Lockdowns and other public health measures posed severe challenges to business operations, and in the absence of government intervention, many businesses losing revenue and liquidity would have had no choice but to lay off workers. Not only would the workers lose income as a result, but the job losses would also destroy the valuable matches between employers and employees. By preventing many of these job losses, wage subsidies both provide income support to workers (whom the government would have had to support anyway during their unemployment), and preserve the valuable job matches.[52]

Moreover, if the wage subsidy rate is set at no higher than the replacement rate of any unemployment insurance, the income support delivered by wage subsidies to a

[48] Young adults, which represent a significant portion of the flexible employee populations, are among the beneficiaries. As the Brassey chapter argues, young workers, such as students, face significant economic challenges in the COVID-19-era job market.

[49] The claw-back of CERB/CRB benefits is also triggered by an annual income measure ($38,000) rather than at 50% for the first hour of work.

[50] Canadian commentators have mainly focused on whether CERB and CEWS were each too generous. For the former, see, eg J Lester, 'Overcompensation of Income Losses: A Major Flaw in Canada's Pandemic Response' (*Finances of the Nation*, 2020) financesofthenation.ca/2020/12/08/overcompensation-of-income-losses-a-major-flaw-in-canadas-pandemic-response/. For the latter, see Robson and Smart (n 41).

[51] Scarpetta (n 36).

[52] Abbott and Phan model this dual function of wage subsidies and argue that the longer the duration of the pandemic shock and the lower the average profitability of affected firms, the greater is the welfare enhancement brought about by wage subsidies: see B Abbott and N Van Pham, 'Should Wages be Subsidized in a Pandemic?' (2021) Working Paper, drive.google.com/file/d/18TsfnrmZRYetLqNCwrbqA0-Ms_8yJOw5/view.

particular worker is no costlier than income support that would be delivered to that worker through unemployment insurance. But the worker generally would have higher income if she stayed employed (by being paid at least some additional amount by the employer). Finally, wage subsidies not only preserve jobs, but can also facilitate the reallocation of jobs during an economic shock by subsidising the hiring of new workers.[53]

These basic attractive properties of wage subsidies are separable from other inessential features in the designs of particular wage subsidies. For example, the US chose to deliver pandemic wage subsidies in the form of forgivable loans originated by banks. This reliance on financial intermediaries significantly impeded subsidy delivery,[54] but it is clearly not a problem with wage subsidies per se. Similarly, because wage subsidies can be tied to particular measures of revenue loss or work hour reduction as much as short-term work schemes can, there is no reason, in principle, why they cannot be as well targeted as short-term work schemes are.[55]

The most basic objection to wage subsidies is that it is difficult to avoid subsidising the payroll of workers who would have been kept on the same jobs (and wage levels) even in the absence of the subsidies. Such subsidies strike many commentators as wasteful.[56] Yet there are two important replies to this objection. First, insofar as wage subsidies can be designed to be (almost) as targeted as short-term work schemes, subsidies to employees with secure jobs can be minimised.[57] Second, and perhaps more importantly, the workers improperly being subsidised are likely to be high-wage earners.[58] Because work subsidies are typically capped, their benefits to high-wage earners should represent a smaller portion of their wages: wage subsidies are in this sense progressive. Further, wage subsidies will ultimately need to be financed through higher taxes. Insofar as the subsequent tax instruments used to pay for pandemic spending bear more heavily on high-wage earners,[59] whatever subsidies such earners initially receive

[53] While work subsidies and short-term work schemes are similar in serving the income support and job retention functions, short-term work schemes, unlike work subsidies, may impede job reallocations.

[54] J Granja et al, 'Did the Paycheck Protection Program Hit the Target?' (2021) NBER Working Paper No 27095, www.nber.org/papers/w27095. In contrast, Scandinavian countries and China enacted the equivalent of wage subsidies by reducing payroll tax rates, which arguably represent the most effective mechanism of benefit delivery. See W Cui et al, 'How Well-Targeted Are Payroll Tax Cuts as a Response to COVID-19? Evidence from China' (2021) SSRN Working Paper, papers.ssrn.com/sol3/papers.cfm?abstract_id=3686345.

[55] For example, eligibility for CEWS in Canada was initially determined on the basis of revenue loss in particular monthly periods, but many businesses that suffered revenue loss in the first half of 2020 ended up being profitable at the end of the year. Clearly, CEWS could have been designed to include a claw-back of benefits from profitable businesses.

[56] See, eg Robson and Smart (n 41). This criticism implicitly assumes that workers who would have kept their jobs in the absence of wage subsidies would have also kept the same wage level. If this is not the case, wage subsidies could deliver income support even when they have no effect on job retention. The assumption of wage levels being maintained in the absence of subsidies may be justified by assuming wage rigidity. But note that wage rigidity is already partially violated by short-term work schemes: workers participating in such schemes clearly have agreed to lower overall wages through bargaining.

[57] Giupponi et al report that the reductions in value added per worker in firms participating in the Italian short-term work scheme closely correspond to reduced hours claimed, which indicates success in targeting benefits at marginal workers. See Giupponi (n 30).

[58] Abbott and Phan (n 52) 31–32.

[59] In contrast, under common unemployment insurance systems, both contributions and benefits are capped, which means that for high-income earners, much of their wage income simply falls outside the insurance range. Since pandemic wage subsidies are not financed by the collection of individual insurance premia, there will likely be no similar cap on high-income earners' tax liabilities.

are more likely to be clawed back. Wage subsidies thus accomplish redistribution in the right direction.[60]

Work subsidies, of course, cannot stop all layoffs nor provide income support to the unemployed, and therefore cannot entirely supplant unemployment insurance. But since they do provide income support to those who continue to be employed, they largely obviate the need for CERB/CRB-type income support for employees (including flexible employees). In other words, Canada could have restricted eligibility for CERB/CRB benefits to non-employees (ie the unemployed and self-employed). This conclusion is at odds with the restrained criticisms of CERB/CRB and the more vocal objections to CEWS in Canada.

What can one say about the choice between providing income support directly to workers and providing such income indirectly through employers in normal, non-pandemic times? Arguably, the most important policy goal associated with 'precarious workers' – whether they are self-employed, flexible employees, or full-time workers suffering from low wages and poor work conditions – is redistribution, not the provision of social insurance in the face of likely insurance market failures. Consider first individuals whose pursuit of precarious work is transitory. If an individual does gig work during a temporary period of unemployment, for example, the gig work itself represents that worker's act of self-insurance: this act itself need not be insured against.[61]

Consider next workers who voluntarily choose non-transitory flexible employment for age-specific reasons (eg young students or workers near retirement) or because of compatibility with family burdens (eg women). Such choices involve trade-offs of benefits (eg of flexibility) against the disadvantages of lower wages and impediments to career progress. But having to face such trade-offs does not represent a bad condition that workers generally can insure against. Finally, for both individuals who are self-employed because they cannot find formal employment and full-time workers who suffer from low earnings and low amenities, the public's concern – at least in wealthy countries like Canada – is how to improve their best outcomes (eg through job training or income redistribution), not to hedge against even worse outcomes.

The question, then, is how redistribution to precarious workers should be carried out. For the self-employed, state-sponsored redistribution tends to involve direct interactions between individuals and government agencies. But for flexible employees, redistribution can also occur indirectly through employers. This is critical because the workplace very often functions as a self-standing institution of redistribution. Because labour markets are characterised by all kinds of imperfections, firms can often exercise substantial monopsony power – the number of local employers to whom workers can supply their labour is relatively small.[62] Just as the state's monopoly power fundamentally undergirds its capacity for redistribution, firms that exercise various degrees of monopsony power over workers can implement redistributions.

[60] See n 59 above. This is just one illustration of how, as mentioned in the Introduction, separating the analysis of a government's pandemic fiscal response from the analysis of post-pandemic tax policy could lead to unreliable conclusions.

[61] The same can be said about individuals who pursue part-time or temporary employment during a period of high unemployment.

[62] A Manning, 'Monopsony in Labor Markets: A Review' (2021) 74 *Industrial and Labor Relations Rev* 3.

The types of workplace redistributions that have been most extensively studied are various forms of cross-subsidies that result from mandated benefits: by virtue of employer mandates, for example, the government can secure substantial workplace redistribution to employees who are disabled, who raise children, or who are more prone to fall ill.[63] But redistribution frequently occurs at the workplace even in the absence of government mandates, as illustrated by widely-observed pay equity norms.[64]

Unlike the self-employed, therefore, flexible employees can potentially benefit from intra-firm redistributions. A meaningful policy objective may thus be to give more workers access to such redistributive mechanisms, and to sustain the mechanisms' robustness. After all, the significance of intra-firm redistribution is also supported by evidence of its erosion: the main reason why 'domestic outsourcing'[65] has been viewed as problematic, for example, is that when low-wage occupations and tasks are separated into specialised firms, workers performing such tasks are found to earn lower wages than they would when performing the same tasks in firms with a greater variety of occupations.[66]

Wage subsidies, especially when designed to target low-wage workers, can potentially advance this objective of activating and expanding workplace redistributions. An important recent study of a Swedish employer payroll tax cut aimed at encouraging employment of young workers – equivalent to a wage subsidy for such workers – offered several relevant findings.[67] First, the tax cut did not result in a market-wide increase in wages for young workers. This meant that the firms hiring young workers enjoyed substantial reductions in labour costs, which led firms to expand both capital investment and employment. Second, firms that employed many young workers – and therefore especially benefited from the payroll tax cut – also raised the average wage of all employees, young and old. The windfall from the tax cut thus not only financed business expansions, but also led to rent-sharing with workers. Moreover, workers with lower earnings in such firms tended to benefit more from the wage increase induced by the tax cut.

Whether wage subsidies can enhance and expand workplace redistributions is likely to be highly contingent on both their design and the institutional environment. The authors of the Swedish payroll tax cut study attribute the remarkable results to workplace pay equity norms, union power in Sweden, and the likelihood that the employers enjoyed monopsony power due to technological differentiation – such conditions may not always be present elsewhere. But the study at least confirms the real-world possibility of beneficial effects. Two additional nuances about workplace redistribution are worth noting. First, firms often offer amenities valued by employees that are not reflected in wages.

[63] For a recent review of cross-subsidies among employees brought about by nondiscrimination legislations (such as the American Disability Act) and employer mandates such as paid family leave and employer-based group health insurance, see JR Brooks et al, 'Cross-Subsidies: Government's Hidden Pocketbook' (2018) 106 *Georgetown LJ* 1229.

[64] E Saez et al, 'Payroll Taxes, Firm Behavior, and Rent Sharing: Evidence from a Young Workers' Tax Cut in Sweden' (2019) 109 *American Economic Rev* 1717, 1718 (n 3).

[65] See text accompanying n 20 above.

[66] A Dube and E Kaplan, 'Does Outsourcing Reduce Wages in the Low-Wage Service Occupations? Evidence From Janitors and Guards' (2010) 63 *Industrial and Labor Relations Rev* 287.

[67] Saez (n 64).

Therefore, an employee earning the same wage as a self-employed individual is likely to value the position of employment significantly more.[68] Second, firms can offer different unique packages of amenities, insurance, and/or redistribution. This variety of choices is something that the government is not able to provide directly to each citizen.

Contrast these features of workplace redistributions with redistribution made directly from the government to individual workers. Such latter policies have well-known illustrations in refundable tax credits to workers with low earnings and are also envisioned in universal basic income (UBI) proposals. Three points of contrast stand out. First, transfers received by workers directly from the state tend to be in cash rather than in-kind. This is perhaps necessary for any scheme of transfers to a broad population of working individuals, but it represents an immediate limitation. On the one hand, at least in rich countries like Canada, much of the targeted government assistance to low-income households are in-kind (eg through housing, health, family, and training services), and these government services are highly valued by individual recipients.[69] On the other hand, workplace redistribution also allows combinations of cash and in-kind benefits, as well as the possibility of choice among different types of in-kind benefits offered by different employers. The limited options under the state's centralised and cash-based redistribution schemes thus already dampen their welfare-enhancing potential.

Second, a longstanding challenge in the design of direct transfers to individuals is that if they are strongly means-tested, they create strong work disincentives when benefits are phased out at higher levels of earning. This, however, is less of a concern for wage subsidies for low-wage workers. Such subsidies are generally conditional on the type of workers hired and need not put constraints on the size and profitability of business operations. Even when they do impose such constraints, the disincentives are likely to be smaller than the effect of claw-backs of government benefits for individual labour supplies.

Third, an advantage of direct transfers to individuals is that there is little risk that such transfers are captured by parties other than the intended recipients of the transfers. For example, a strong objection to work subsidies is that the employer – especially shareholders – may capture a significant portion of the subsidies' benefits. However, this advantage of direct transfers likely depends on an implicit assumption that the transfer is targeted, and, in particular, means-tested. If transfers are not means-tested – as would be the case in UBI proposals – then there will be many recipients of government benefits who do not need such benefits, which is also why such proposals are very expensive. It would not, however, be consistent for anyone who can tolerate a high level for 'leakage' under UBI programmes to voice qualms about leakage in wage subsidies.

[68] A recent study suggests that American workers are on average willing to pay 13% of their annual earnings to stay in their current jobs, and even workers with the lowest quality jobs may still value their amenities at somewhat less than 10% of their pay. See T Lamadon et al, 'Imperfect Competition, Compensating Differentials, and Rent Sharing in the US Labor Market' (2022) 112 *American Economic Rev* 169, 202–04.

[69] For a comprehensive review of existing forms of government assistance to the poor in a representative Canadian province, and the comparison of such assistance to UBI proposals, see 'Covering All the Basics: Reforms for a More Just Society' (Final Report of the Expert Panel on Basic Income, 2020) bcbasicincomepanel.ca/wp-content/uploads/2021/01/Final_Report_BC_Basic_Income_Panel.pdf.

These reflections lead to the following conclusion: for the policy goal of redistribution in normal economic circumstances as well as the goal of social insurance against economic shocks, the strengths of work subsidies hold against the alternative of direct transfers to individuals. Clearly, work subsidies cannot shoulder the responsibility of redistribution to the unemployed, and therefore direct transfers to the latter are an indispensable policy tool. But for those who are employed (or who may become employed as a result of work subsidies), the attraction of these subsidies as a redistributive tool is arguably stronger than has been generally recognised.

V. Conclusion

This chapter has argued that even before the onset of the COVID-19 labour market crisis, a significant population of workers classified as employees, especially part-time and temporary employees, are likely to have been as vulnerable (on average) as workers classified as independent contractors or gig workers. Evidence in Canada suggests that these flexible employees were also harder hit by the COVID-19 crisis than the self-employed on average, and therefore are at least as deserving of policy attention as the latter. Yet flexible employees have suffered considerable policy neglect: the design of traditional unemployment insurance systems tends to work better for full-time permanent employees. Flexible employees also fall into the blind spot of those who advocate for expanding the social insurance system to independent contractors. When policymakers hold such a stubborn misconception of today's labour market, they may fail to recognise even the benefits of the policies they actually adopt – as illustrated by conventional wisdom about Canada's fiscal response to the pandemic so far.

I have also analysed the strengths of work subsidy programmes for both the goals of social insurance and redistribution. Work subsidies lie at the intersection of two ideas: they allow the government: (1) to intervene at the intensive margin of employment (ie not just whether individuals are employed, but how much they work and get paid), and (2) to tap into the unique redistributive potentials of the workplace. The majority of flexible work takes place precisely at this intersection: unlike the traditional, permanent, and full-time employee, the well-being of flexible employees is observable mainly on the intensive margin, and unlike independent contractors, flexible employees stand adjacent to a rich layer of *social, but non-governmental*, redistribution. To adequately respond to the changing nature of work, I suggest that tax policymakers must start with an appreciation of these two critical ideas.

Much recent tax scholarship, especially in countries influenced by discourse emanating from the US, has focused on how to 'tax the rich', which tends to demand intuitions about who is 'rich' and about how high a tax on the rich is morally appealing. Arguably, however, our moral intuitions about these issues are less robust than our intuitions about who among our fellow citizens deserve our support and compassion.[70] Both the

[70] This arguably is reflected in John Rawls' Difference Principle, the main moral principle regarding the distribution of economic outcomes in Rawls' theory of justice.

fiscal responses to the pandemic adopted in advanced economies and the extensive experimentations with LMI that took place before the pandemic in these economies (which will no doubt continue in the future) are richly informed by these latter intuitions. Tax scholars can contribute much by reflecting on these intuitions and bringing them to bear on policy design, if they could leave behind arbitrary distinctions about what constitutes tax as opposed to spending policies.

17

How to Award Financial Aid Amidst a Pandemic through the Lens of a Tax Scholar

YVETTE LIND

Abstract

This chapter describes and analyses the necessary considerations, both of a practical and theoretical nature, when attempting to design a legal framework for how to award financial aid in connection to an epidemic, pandemic, or crisis. Consequently, the chapter provides an in-depth commentary on the what may be considered as a best-practice design and implementation of such financial aid measures through the inclusion of legal, economic and political considerations. These considerations are drawn from both legal and economic scholarship and are supported by empirical material gathered from a variety of jurisdictions across the globe.

I. Introduction and Research Approach

The pandemic and subsequent state actions have greatly impeded the economy through various lockdown measures, such as working from home and most notably the closure of borders. Consequently, large parts of society have been closed for stretches of time. States have supported business life and individuals through various financial aid packages. A majority of EU Member States followed the guidance issued by the EU Commission, through its temporary financial aid frameworks, when issuing these financial aid measures.[1] This guidance has expedited the implementation

[1] Since its adoption, the Temporary Framework has been amended six times and the current framework is extended until 30 June 2022. European Commission, 'Sixth Amendment to the Temporary Framework for State aid measures to support the economy in the current COVID-19 outbreak and amendment to the Annex to the Communication from the Commission to the Member States on the application of Articles 107 and 108 of the Treaty on the Functioning of the European Union to short-term export-credit insurance' (2021/C 473/01).

of financial aid measures and assisted Member States to deviate, through temporary exemptions, from the otherwise strict regulation of the functioning of the internal market through EU competition law and accompanying state aid rules.[2] Other financial aid packages, such as the American Rescue Plan have taken a significantly differing approach than the EU framework, due to, for instance, the inclusion of social policy goals rather than merely awarding financial aid on seemingly neutral criteria.[3]

One of the most debated approaches among the various financial package frameworks has been the introduction of exclusion criteria based upon, for instance, taxpayment, the financial status of the receiver, formal citizenship for individuals and tax residence for companies. The exclusion of companies located/registered in tax havens has been widely debated among scholars, politicians and the public. Other financial aid measures targeting individuals, such as stimulus checks and reimbursement of lost income, followed similar justifications.[4] In other words, to be eligible for publicly funded financial aid the receiver, whether it be a physical person or a business, needed to prove a concrete previous taxpayment or alternatively satisfy an economic substance test. These requirements could, and possibly should, were one to adhere to the political argumentation, be considered as an analogy to the unspoken contractual relationship between state and taxpayer. Some states openly supported their exclusion criteria on such argumentation.

From a public finance perspective, this may be considered sensible as it efficiently limits the number of eligible recipients and subsequently minimises the financial aid payments. Thus, state funds can be preserved in harsh financial situations that are expected to deteriorate further as tax revenues decline in the aftermath of the pandemic and the inevitable financial crisis follows. However, from the perspective of the potential recipient other considerations may be necessary to consider when ensuring rule of law and competition neutrality within the market.

This chapter describes and analyses the necessary considerations, both of a practical and theoretical nature, when attempting to design a legal framework for how to award financial aid in connection to an epidemic, pandemic or crisis. Consequently, the chapter provides an in-depth commentary on what may be considered as a best-practice design and implementation of such financial aid measures through the inclusion of legal, economic and political considerations. These considerations are drawn from legal scholarship in addition to the author's own experience as a legal expert involved in the awarding of financial aid measures in Denmark.[5] The latter experience enables an inclusion of several legislative reports provided by economists which are of great value when attempting to understand the differing considerations that need to be taken into

[2] European Commission, 'Factsheet: List of Member State Measures approved under Articles 107(2)b, 107(3)b and 107(3)c TFEU and under the State Aid Temporary Framework' (7 June 2022).

[3] American Rescue Plan Act of 2021 117-2 (03/11/2021).

[4] The basic idea of awarding COVID-19 aid through a stimulus check is to stimulate the economy by providing consumers with spending money.

[5] Appointed by the Danish government as the legal expert in the working group drafting the principles for awarding financial aid attached to the Danish Epidemic Act (epidemiloven) June–December 2021. The work was led by the Ministry of Business, Industry and Financial affairs and included the Ministry of Finance, and Ministry of Taxation. See M Ditmer et al, *Rapport fra arbejdsgruppen: Principper for hjælpepakker ved nye epidemier*, (Copenhagen, Erhvervsministeriet, 2021).

account when legally awarding financial aid. Therefore, the ambition is to provide a more common knowledge foundation emphasising both the income and expenditure sides ('tax and spend') when designing future financial aid in the case of future epidemics, pandemics or crises of a comparable nature.[6] The author welcomes additional studies within this field as this chapter is merely an initial guide to how financial aid packages may, or may not, be designed on a best-practice basis.

Furthermore, there is an emphasis on the underpinning principles that have determined the allocation of financial aid in connection to the COVID-19 pandemic. As a result, this chapter introduces and discusses examples of how individual states have allocated financial aid through some comparative examples gathered from primarily EU Member States, but also from other jurisdictions such as Australia and the US. It should be underlined that this is not a comprehensive comparative study. Instead, these comparative examples are included to assist in the identification, description and analysis of the underpinning principles that have influenced the financial aid measures that were awarded in connection to the COVID-19 pandemic. The reader should consider that highly individual circumstances within each jurisdiction will have had a natural impact on the design of the included financial aid examples and this is considered in the chapter when these are included.

The findings of this chapter are analysed through the application of Adam Smith's four characteristics of a good tax.[7] These four characteristics, or principles as they are occasionally spoken of, comprise: fairness, certainty, convenience and efficiency. As a supplement to these characteristics, there is also an attempt to consider the descriptive and analytical parts from two differing lenses. The first lens is that of public finance and consequently that of the state, and the second is that of the recipient (both physical persons and corporations). The latter lens encompasses rule of law considerations in which the rights of the individual are emphasised through discussions on legality, equality, transparency and foreseeability.

Lastly, some clarification of the employed terminology should be made. This chapter often employs pandemic, epidemic and crisis in an intertwined fashion. According to the Center for Disease Control and Prevention,[8] the difference between an epidemic and a pandemic is that an epidemic is a sudden outbreak of a disease in a certain geographical area. A pandemic on the other hand is an outbreak of a disease that has spread across several countries or continents. However, as the aim of this chapter is to provide the reader with the fundamentals of how to design financial aid measures it is of less importance to separate between epidemic, pandemic or crisis as they will generally apply similar underpinning principles and considerations when designing financial aid measures.

This chapter is structured as follows:

Section II of this chapter offers the reader an introduction to the differing phases which needs to be considered and addressed when designing financial aid measures. Section III offers the reader an introduction to public finance considerations

[6] See ch 5 in this volume by A Kotha and ch 6 by L Panadès-Estruch.

[7] A Smith, *The wealth of nations* (Ware, Wordsworth Editions Ltd, 2012).

[8] CDC, *Principles of epidemiology in public health practice*, 3rd edn (U.S. Department of Health and Human Services Centers for Disease Control and Prevention (CDC), 2020).

in connection to awarding financial aid. The Danish case is used as a concrete example of such considerations. Section IV introduces how financial aid may be awarded in accordance with a principle of taxpayment, a principle of employment, a principle of residence and a principle of the financial situation (finances) of the recipient. These differing categories were identified in the initial stage of the comparative study of financial aid measures. The final section of the chapter provides a concluding summary of the discussions in addition to some policy recommendations that may be of use to legislators when designing future financial aid measures. The theoretical framework based on Adam Smith's four characteristics of a good tax is applied to these discussions.

II. The Importance of Acknowledging Differing Phases of a Pandemic, Epidemic, or Crisis

When designing financial aid measures, it is of great importance to understand the differing phases of a pandemic, an epidemic, or any other crisis for that matter. We may divide these phases into four main events:[9]

1. *Restrictions* as a result of the pandemic or crisis at hand. Such restrictions could encompass instructions to limit the number of customers at a store, the number of guests at a restaurant and the need to enforce proof of negative tests or vaccine certificates when attempting to participate in certain activities.
2. *Closures* follow these restrictions. Such measures may, for instance, include lockdown measures at differing levels (local, regional, and national) and the extent of these restrictions will have great impact on what financial aid measures should be implemented. These closures could be restricted to closures of certain industries or alternatively closures of the society. During the COVID-19 pandemic we witnessed varying closure measures between countries.
3. *Openings* will at some point be possible once the epidemic, or crisis, has been mitigated or overcome. Once again, differing countries will choose to implement opening measures at various stages depending on the financial and social needs of their unique situation.
4. *Phasing out* of financial aid measures. This signifies the ending of the epidemic or crisis and is of great importance for many reasons. Initially, the public finances cannot take an endless supply of financial aid measures. Moreover, the companies and sectors that have been supported need to find a way back to economic independence. The longer or more generously a country awards financial aid, the greater is the challenge for the recipients to adjust to managing without the aid. And finally, it is likely that the financial aid measures have been targeting specific sectors and therefore it is of the essence to phase out these aid schemes if competition neutrality is to be upheld in the long term.

[9] TM Andersen, M Svarer and P Schröder, *Rapport fra den økonomiske ekspertgruppe vedrørende udfasning af hjælpepakker II*, (Copenhagen, Finansministeriet, 2021).

Besides these phases it is also important to distinguish between the effects of the pandemic, epidemic or crisis at hand. For instance, there is a difference if restaurants are forced to close due to local/regional/national regulations or if individuals choose to not go out and eat due to the ongoing situation. In the latter case, it is often assumed that these restaurants will adapt to the situation and the changed terms of the market and subsequently not be entitled to financial aid to the same extent as in the former situation. In connection to the COVID-19 pandemic, several restaurants adapted to take-out and food delivery as a response to the situation. Generally, only the former situation will be taken into consideration by governments when choosing how to award financial support. However, this is merely the general rule and there are naturally exemptions and factors each individual country will need to take into consideration. This conundrum underlines situations where problems arise when individuals and/or businesses are not eligible for support because restrictions *have not* been imposed.

III. Public Finance Considerations When Awarding Financial Aid in Connection with a Pandemic, Epidemic or Crisis

In a scenario where there is no crisis or ongoing epidemic, there is a general assumption that companies should be capable of supporting themselves as they are subject to market competition. In a simplified version this entails that companies will be subject to a natural dynamic in which some companies will be able to thrive while others will fail.

This assumption does no longer hold true during a crisis, hence the need for the state to issue financial aid measures. The state will attempt to 'freeze time' or to uphold the status quo when intervening and assuming financial responsibility for some businesses and sectors due to the nature and circumstances of the crisis in question. Companies that would have otherwise failed as a result of market competition may instead be supported during this hiatus, and as a result (artificially) prolong their survival. The hiatus will naturally affect all businesses, albeit differently. Depending on the length of the hiatus and the extent of financial aid companies may grow dependent on the state intervention regardless of their situation before the crisis. This is why it may be encouraged, for several reasons, that states not implement extensive financial aid measures. Not only from a public funds' perspective but also for the companies to be able to remain competitive and financially independent once the crisis has passed.

One may argue that state intervention through financial aid measures is done with reference to *fairness*. In other words, instead of leaving affected businesses or sectors to carry the costs of a crisis that is affecting the society to a larger extent, the society resumes responsibility for these costs through the state's intervention. These losses are then distributed over several generations and society when they are recovered through, for instance, tax increases or new taxes.[10] From a business perspective it could be

[10] See ch 15 in this volume by A Brassey.

reasonable to assume that financial losses stemming from governmental restrictions and/or closures are mitigated with public funds.

From an economic lens there are three general considerations that need to be made:

1. *Efficiency and allocation* are assured through, for instance, measures aimed at saving jobs in addition to preventing bankruptcy and insolvency. However, measures such as these may at the same time act as a disincentive for adapting your business model to the current crisis. Long-term, measures such as these also risk hindering the natural growth and dynamic development of a business.[11]
2. *Reallocation and insurance* concerns the redistribution of the financial responsibility from the affected businesses to the state, or society as a whole, as public funds mitigate the impact and the emerging costs. The state acts as an insurance party as it mitigates the financial shock of unexpected restrictions. In this respect, a state may justify it not compensating 100 per cent of the losses on the argument that the uncovered losses are considered the premium payment for this insurance. Financial aid measures based upon this logic should be considered as a short-term solution as the aid is legitimised on the existence of state restrictions and closures. Once these have been removed there is no legitimate reason to continue with this reallocation of the financial burden. The implementation of long-term aid, or generous aid, could lead to financial dependency and subsequently a moral hazard.[12]
3. *Economic stabilisation from a macro perspective* is achieved when the financial aid measures prevent incomes losses and ensures a safety net for the businesses to not only survive but to also recover long term. However, as discussed it is vital to ensure that business do not become dependent on the aid measures.[13]

Therefore, it is essential to implement concrete details concerning the period and extent of planned financial aid measures. By implementing these details in the design of the aid measures the state may reduce the risk of dependency in addition to upholding legal *certainty* through foreseeability. Through some common tax principles, we may find a best practice for the legislative design of these measures.

IV. Principles that have been, Directly or Indirectly, Integrated in the Design of Financial Aid Measures in Connection to the COVID-19 Pandemic

A. Introduction to the General Design of Financial Aid Measures Among the EU Member States

Many financial aid measures have, explicitly or inexplicitly, been allocated on the premise of past or ongoing tax liability/taxpayment. The EU temporary framework[14]

[11] Andersen, Svarer and Schröder (n 9) ch 2.
[12] ibid.
[13] ibid.
[14] See n 2.

comprises some clear examples of it and constituted the basis for most financial aid packages awarded by EU Member States in connection to the COVID-19 pandemic. The framework was initially structured on five aid categories that, for a limited period, the EU Commission deemed compatible with EU state aid rules and the functioning of the internal market:

1. Advance payments, selective tax advantages, and direct grants from Member States to taxpayers.
2. Member State guarantees of loans that banks provide to companies.
3. Subsidised public loans for companies.
4. Safeguards to help banks channel state aid to businesses in the real economy.
5. Short-term credit insurance for Member States.

The figure below illustrates EU Member State financial aid measures in connection to the COVID-19 pandemic:

Figure 1 Overview of pandemic financial aid measures issued by EU Member States[15]

Country	**Wage compensation**	**Compensation to the self-employed**	**Compensation for fixed costs**	**Compensation to organisers of cancelled events**	**Access to liquidity measures**
Countries with extensive support measures					
Denmark	x	x	x	x	x
Belgium	x	x			x
France	x	x	x		x
Netherlands	x	x	x	x	x
Norway	x	x	x	x	x
Switzerland	x	x	x	x	x
UK	x	x	x	x	x
Sweden	x	x	x	x	x
Germany	x	x	x	x	x
Austria	x	x	x	x	x
Countries with less extensive support measures					
Estonia	x	x	x	x	x
Finland	x	x	x	x	x
Ireland	x	x			x
Iceland	x	x	x	x	x
Czech Republic	x	x	x	x	x
Hungary	x	x	x		x

(continued)

[15] Ditmer et al (n 5) 48.

Figure 1 ***(Continued)***

Country	Wage compensation	Compensation to the self-employed	Compensation for fixed costs	Compensation to organisers of cancelled events	Access to liquidity measures
Countries with least extensive support measures					
Bulgaria	x	x			x
Greece	x	x	x		x
Italy	x	x	x	x	x
Latvia	x				x
Lithuania	x	x	x		x
Malta	x		x		x
Poland	x	x	x	x	x
Portugal	x	x	x	x	x
Romania		x	x		x
Spain	x	x			x
Croatia	x	x	x		x

The first group of countries comprises Denmark, Belgium, France, the Netherlands, Norway, Switzerland, the UK, Sweden, Germany and Austria. These are countries that share common features when comparing tax systems and welfare systems. Due to their generally extensive welfare systems, it is not surprising to find that they all applied a wide range of financial aid. Consequently, the financial aid packages in these countries had a relatively high coverage and aid intensity.

In many jurisdictions there was a general hesitation to issue aid measures towards specific sectors or businesses, for instance the cultural sector or aviation sector. This reasoning is often grounded in a belief that broader and more general frameworks provide an equal basis for support. Additionally, in many jurisdictions it is common for the legislator to provide more overarching legal frameworks and for the details to be determined and implemented by executing governmental agencies. This provides a more flexible framework that may be updated with greater ease, compared to the more rigid legislative process. Additionally, if a framework targets specific sectors with more narrow conditions it may unintentionally exclude some receivers or actors. However, as the pandemic progressed many countries eventually introduced financial aid measures targeting specific sectors and businesses such as culture, sports and aviation. Such aid is naturally justified on the basis that these sectors are considered to be vital to society as they provide infrastructure and cultural values. These sectors are generally prioritised by states as they often receive state aid even in times stability and prosperity.

The second grouping is Estonia, Finland, Ireland, Iceland, the Czech Republic and Hungary. These countries can be referred to as a middle group and differ from the first group by having fewer and/or less comprehensive aid schemes than those described above. Despite these countries' aid schemes being considered less comprehensive, they still contained a wide range of aid measures with comprehensive conditions.

The third group of countries are Bulgaria, Greece, Italy, Latvia, Lithuania, Malta, Poland, Portugal, Romania, Croatia and Spain. These countries have relied on a smaller supply of aid packages, most likely an outcome of them having weaker economies pre-pandemic and consequently less resources to grant during the pandemic.

In general, the countries in groups one and two relied more heavily on financial support through payments and direct grants while the third group showed a preference for subsidised loan schemes and short-term credit insurances.[16] A design pattern that is logical given that the latter group had a more restricted cash-flow.

B. Awarding Financial Aid in Accordance with a Principle of Taxpayment

In connection with EU Member States designing their own financial aid measures (to a large extent based on the EU framework) some states added exclusion criteria to preserve state funds and ensure that aid assisted businesses which were within their jurisdiction.[17] Denmark led this development by, rather controversially, announcing that companies registered in tax havens would be excluded from pandemic financial aid programmes.

> The parties to the agreement agree that companies seeking compensation in accordance with the schemes should follow the UN human rights guidelines, and that companies pay the tax to which they are liable to in accordance with international agreements and national rules. This means that companies based on tax havens in accordance with EU guidelines cannot receive compensation to the extent that they can be cut under EU law and any other international obligations that Denmark or the EU has undertaken.[18]

This inspired international debate and instigated other states – including France, the Netherlands, Poland, and Sweden – to follow suit. The EU Commission promptly confirmed that this action was to be considered to comply with EU state aid rules since Member States have the right to design state aid measures that uphold existing EU rules and advance established policy objectives, including combating tax fraud and preventing tax evasion. More specifically, the EU Commission stated:

> Member States are free to design national measures in line with additional policy objectives, such as further enabling the green and digital transformation of their economies or preventing fraud, tax evasion or aggressive tax avoidance.[19]

The above stated exclusion of taxpayers concerns corporate taxpayers, and not specifically individuals. Yet it conveys a discourse in which taxpayment plays a central role

[16] Andersen, Svarer and Schröder (n 9) ch 6.

[17] See ch 6 in this volume by L Panadès-Estruch.

[18] The author's translation of Appendix 13, Danish government, *Aftale om hjælpepakker til lønmodtagere og virksomheder mv. i forbindelse med gradvis genåbning af Danmark 18 April 2020* (Copenhagen, Danish government, 2020).

[19] European Commission, 'State Aid: Commission Expands Temporary Framework to Recapitalisation and Subordinated Debt Measures to Further Support the Economy in the Context of the Coronavirus Outbreak' IP/20/838.

when distributing financial aid in connection to the crisis. From a state perspective this makes financial sense as it efficiently limits the number of eligible recipients and subsequently minimises the aid which needs to be provided, thus saving state funds in harsh financial times which are only expected to worsen.

In a Nordic welfare context like that of Denmark, there is an implied awareness of a fiscal contract in which the state may utilise its taxing ability while in return offering the taxpayer access to the welfare system.[20] Despite the lack of a clearly expressed contract between state and taxpayer there is a general acceptance of such a contractual relationship as these welfare systems are legitimised upon a fair application of the ability to pay principle (progressive taxation that matches the taxpayer's income) as an outcome of vertical equity.[21] For instance, payroll taxes in Sweden are levied in order to finance social security, yet these contributions are not earmarked for the individual taxpayer and as such the link between potential benefits and taxes paid is weak, yet commonly accepted. In the Danish case we see a similar application through the labour market contribution (AM-bidrag).

However, it should be emphasised that recent discussions concerning the implied social contract and taxpaying have commonly dealt with international tax avoidance and tax evasion at a corporate level. The principal aim with such reasoning is to reform existing tax regimes to ensure that multinational enterprises pay their 'fair share' of taxes, thus support the functioning of our welfare systems, the enforcement of human rights and the operation of state governance.[22] It is therefore of importance to scrutinise any requirements of taxpaying when considering financial aid, especially as this contradicts the underpinning principle of redistribution within a welfare state which becomes evident when looking at the Danish case.

From the perspective of the potential recipient other considerations may be necessary to consider when ensuring rule of law and competition neutrality within the market. Businesses excluded from financial aid measures due to failing to either prove previous taxpayment or satisfy the economic substance test have often argued that their presence within the jurisdiction still justified financial support. This argumentation includes claims grounded in the creation of jobs, providing essential services and goods to society, the generation of tax revenues linked to consumption of the goods and services provided by the business in question in addition to employment taxes and payroll taxes linked to the salaries of their employees.

Moreover, it could be argued, with reference to the economic considerations that were described in section III, that there is a general assumption of the state acting as an insurance provider during a crisis. In other words, public funds mitigate the unexpected

[20] Y Lind, 'Voting rights compared to income taxation and welfare benefits through the Swedish lens' [2020] *Florida Tax Review* 713.

[21] This link is discussed in Swedish scholarship, see for instance: Å Gunnarsson, *Fördelningen av familjens skatter och sociala* förmåner, (Uppsala, Iustus, 2003); M Tjernberg, 'Frågan om kongruens mellan rätten att erhålla vissa sociala förmåner och skyldigheten att betala skatt' [2009] *Skattenytt* 214.

[22] This line of argumentation has often been employed by the EU Commission in connection to state aid investigations and many countries, such as Denmark, appear to have adapted it to their own domestic contexts.

economic losses that have occurred, and the recipient provides a premium payment either through previous taxpayment and/or taking on partial responsibility for the losses as the state does not cover the complete loss.

Finally, one may also consider the intergenerational dimension.[23] By using public funds the state can spread the risks in a different manner to a corporation. The state may recover the losses over time through tax revenues and, if necessary, public debt. Moreover, the state can expand the recovery phase over several generations and thereby access a different time frame than that of a private actor.[24]

C. Awarding Financial Aid in Accordance with a Principle of Formal Citizenship

The Australian case comprises several aspects of how formal citizenship is linked to financial aid measures in connection to the COVID-19 pandemic. One such example would be New Zealanders residing in Australia as this group has traditionally experienced problems linked to the lack of having Australian citizenship. To fully understand their situation some background is needed. Under the initial Trans-Tasman Travel Arrangement introduced in 1973, both Australian and New Zealand citizens were able to enter each other's country to visit, live and work without any restrictions or time-limited conditions.[25] It is a unique relationship when considering that Australia has no similar arrangement with any other state or jurisdiction. Since 1973, some restrictions have been applied to New Zealanders crossing the Tasman over to Australia. Political discussions in the 1980s and 1990s resulted in New Zealanders having to reside in Australia for a minimum of six months to qualify for social security benefits. Later, access to social security was restricted further. From 1986, New Zealanders have been required to reside in Australia for a minimum of two years to qualify for social security.[26] Furthermore, as of 1994, all non-citizens in Australia are required to hold a valid visa. New Zealanders are subject to possessing a so-called Special Category Visa (SCV).[27] This visa facilitates New Zealanders staying in Australia without any time constraints. However, it is still classified as a temporary visa and consequently its holders do not have the same rights and benefits as Australian citizens or permanent Australian residents.

Prior to 2001, New Zealanders with SCVs could access social security and obtain Australian citizenship without initially being permanent residents in Australia.

[23] See ch 15 in this volume by A Brassey.

[24] Andersen, Svarer and Schröder (n 9).

[25] For a more extensive description of the background on the Trans-Tasman Travel Arrangement and the Closer Economic Relations agenda, see the joint Australian and New Zealand productivity commissions report from 2012: Australian Productivity Commission and New Zealand Productivity Commission, *Research report – Strengthening Economic Relations between Australia and New Zealand Productivity Commission*, (Melbourne, Australian Government Producitivity Commission, 2012).

[26] Australian Government Services Australia, *New Zealand citizens claiming payments in Australia* (2022) www.servicesaustralia.gov.au/new-zealand-citizens-claiming-payments-australia.

[27] Australian Government Department for Home Affairs, *Subclass 444 Special Category visa (SCV)* (2022) immi.homeaffairs.gov.au/visas/getting-a-visa/visa-listing/special-category-visa-subclass-444.

However, after 26 February 2001, this only applies to those entering Australia before 2001. Those who had already entered Australia had begun being referred to as protected SCV holders and retained their previous privileges. Those who entered after this date were instead required to apply for the permanent residence programme to access social security and be eligible to apply for Australian citizenship.[28] As a result of the changes introduced by the Howard government, the nonprotected SCV holders (those entering after 2001) are liable for full taxation similar to Australian citizens and protected SCV holders, yet without the same access to social security. For instance, to qualify for Australian pensions, including the Age Pension and Disability Support Pension, persons must have been Australian residents for 10 years or more (including at least five of those years in one continuous period) before they become eligible.[29]

As a result, the pandemic had a compound effect on the nonprotected SCV holders. Many unprotected SCV workers were only able to access limited parts of the pandemic financial aid schemes in place due to them being temporary visa holders alternatively not having resided in Australia for a long enough period. One exemption to this exclusion would the JobSeeker subsidy that was decided on at the federal level in March 2021.[30]

However, unprotected SCV holders were excluded from some pandemic aid schemes. In Australia three main categories of aid schemes were applied:

1. COVID-19 disaster payment (described above in connection to the employment eligibility criterion);
2. JobKeeper payment; and
3. Coronavirus supplement which was paid to recipients of JobSeeker payments, Youth Allowance, Farm Household Allowance and Special benefit.[31]

Unprotected SCV holders were eligible to receive support from the COVID-19 disaster payment scheme and, after the changes in March 2021, the JobSeeker scheme. However, they had limited access to the JobKeeper scheme and some Coronavirus supplement schemes due to them not meeting the social security residence criteria.[32]

Consequently, New Zealanders remain a vulnerable group in Australia due to few of them having permanent residency and many being unprotected SCV holders. Rigid migration rules in Australia appear to enable an exclusion of low-income migrants and, alternatively, migrants subject to precarious employment, eg within the healthcare or service sectors. Subsequently, many migrant workers from New Zealand risk being excluded from accessing social security and only being eligible to access limited support dependent on their residential situation.

[28] S Love and M Klapdor, *New Zealanders in Australia: a quick guide* (Canberra, Parliament of Australia Research Paper Series 2019–20, 2019).

[29] Australian Social Security Act 1991, s 2(43).

[30] B Worthington, 'Federal Government offers $130b in coronavirus wage subsidies for businesses to pay workers' *ABC News Daily* (30 March 2020).

[31] M Klapdor and A Lotric, *Australian Government COVID-19 disaster payments: a quick guide* (21 January 2022).

[32] ibid.

D. Awarding Financial Aid in Accordance with a Principle of Employment

Most of the financial aid measures that have been awarded so far have targeted the business sector with the intention to provide immediate assistance to: (1) sustain businesses, (2) preserve jobs, and to (3) stimulate the labour market. Less consideration has been given to social expenditures supporting individuals although countries like Sweden, Denmark, the US and Australia have taken a differing approach and provided, to a varying extent, financial aid directly to individuals through differing instruments.

One of the most important aid measures issued by Sweden was the short-time lay-off (korttidsarbete) scheme. The scheme allowed employers to have their employees sent home with salary. The Swedish state compensated up to 80 per cent of the salary of such a worker through a direct payment to the employer. A measure such as this could be considered a hybrid measure as it is be paid out to the employer/business, yet it mainly assists the individual employee as they may retain their employment despite being temporarily laid-off.[33] The business is naturally also assisted as they can retain the workforce they have invested in through time and training without having to pay salaries during the challenging period. Consequently, this saves the employer from the practical efforts of having to lay-off employees and in a later stage find and hire new staff who may need additional training. Some countries paid out direct cash benefits to individuals based upon their employment relationship. For instance, Denmark paid out a cash transfer on two occasions. This cash transfer has the same function as a stimulus check (a check sent to a taxpayer by the state) as it is intended to stimulate the economy by providing consumers with some spending money. The underpinning principle of stimulus checks would be that when taxpayers spend their checks, it will boost consumption and drive revenues at retailer and manufacturer level and subsequently boost the economy.

To understand the background and function of this stimulus check some historical context is needed. On 25 January 2018, a new Danish Holiday Act was adopted in order for Denmark to adapt to how other EU Member States awarded paid holidays.[34] The Act introduced the practice of concurrent holiday, which allows employees to take paid holiday in the same year as that in which the holiday entitlement is accrued, instead of the past practice of having the employee having to work for at least for a year in order to collect their paid vacation days. The Act therefore facilitates the transition from staggered holiday to concurrent holiday and adapts the Danish system to that already existing within the EU. In connection with the transition to concurrent holiday, a transitional arrangement was adopted. This transitional arrangement resulted in holiday entitlement accrued under the existing Holiday Act in the period from 1 September 2019 to 31 August 2020 being frozen and could neither be taken out as leave nor paid in lieu. Instead, a separate fund, Employees' Fund for Residual Holiday

[33] Lag (2013:948) om stöd vid korttidsarbete.
[34] LOV nr 60 af 30/01/2018 Lov om Ferie.

Funds (Lønmodtagernes Fond for Tilgodehavende Feriemidler), was set up to administer these frozen funds. The employees would as a result receive these funds as a part of their future pension payments instead of them being paid out in the summer of 2020 which would have been the case with the former Holiday Act.

In June 2020, the Danish government issued a fast-track legislation due to a citizen initiative where it was requested that these frozen funds would be released and paid out as COVID-19 stimulus checks. Initially, it was decided that taxpayers that have been earning vacation days between September 2019 and August 2020 were to be granted a check corresponding to three weeks out of their entitled five weeks of holiday pay. The political decision was revised during the autumn and the two remaining weeks were subsequently paid out during the winter/spring. Besides paying out parts of the frozen holiday pay, the stimulus check programme also comprised a small sum corresponding to DKK 1,000 to individuals without employment, such as pensioners and those on unemployment benefits or social welfare benefits (overførselsindkomst). Unlike the holiday pay this sum was exempt from taxation.

This stimulus check was criticised by Danish high-income earners as they were unsatisfied with the prospect of having to pay the higher federal/state tax on their stimulus check (as a result of their total income for the year exceeding the threshold for state taxation) compared to low-income earners.[35] One could assume this positioning was influenced by high-income earners having experienced less financial hardship than other groups such as the unemployed or those with employment in more vulnerable sectors that often pay lower salaries, such as the service sector. As a result of the complaints of high-income earners, this group of taxpayers was offered to either be exempted from the state tax on these funds, or alternatively abstain from the stimulus check and instead have the funds frozen in their retirement fund as was originally planned. From this debate one may deduce that several of those employees eligible for the stimulus check were in no dire need of the COVID-19 aid. Additionally, as the stimulus check was based upon earned holiday pay the aid measure automatically favoured high-income earners compared to low-income earners as they will have earned a higher holiday pay covering their normal salary.

This links into a previous legislative proposal from Enhedslisten, a Danish political party, which suggested a summer-stimulus check in which low-income/average-income earners (those earning less than 32,000 DKK/month) would receive a cash transfer of 10,000 DKK.[36] This aid would instead have, based upon the proposed income threshold, benefited 3 million Danes (out of a population of 5.8 million). The legislative proposal was not successful and shortly after the abovementioned stimulus check was instead implemented. A measure such as the summer-stimulus check had the potential to assist impoverished and low-income earners to a greater extent than the stimulus checks that were issued by the Danish government in 2021. This approach was similar to the one embedded in the American Rescue Plan.

[35] 55% instead of the average 24% municipal tax applicable to incomes under a certain threshold.

[36] Enhedslisten, 'Enhedslisten vil sparke gang i økonomien med sommercheck på 10.000,- til alle med lave og almindelige indkomster' (*Enhedslisten*) enhedslisten.dk/2020/06/06/enhedslisten-vil-sparke-gang-i-oekonomien-med-sommercheck-paa-10-000-til-alle-med-lave-og-almindelige-indkomster.

When considering the preservation of state funds, alternatively efficient ways of allocating public funds, the Danish stimulus check provides a good example as there were, factually, no additional funds being paid out. From a state perspective this is a beneficial solution as it enables the preservation of public funds. Instead of freezing the already set aside funds and having them paid out with future pension payments, parts of them were paid out directly as would otherwise have been the case had it not been for the new Holiday Act. It was simply a matter of paying out the funds earlier than expected, which may, of course, also be an issue for a state in financially harsh times. In this specific case Danish employees were simply receiving funds they were already entitled to, and it was merely a matter of the individual deciding whether they have best use of the funds now or in the future when retiring.

Moreover, allocating financial aid in accordance with taxpayment results in the general exclusion of individuals who are working cash-in-hand/unreported employment, unemployed, students or are retired. The impact that COVID-19 has had on income-generating activities is especially harsh for unprotected workers and the most vulnerable groups in the informal economy. Impoverished and vulnerable groups are not only at risk of losing their sources of income due to the pandemic's economic effects, but they are also excluded from receiving crucial financial aid.[37] This illustrates that there is great need for a revision of national COVID-19 policies and budget allocations to ensure a more equitable protection of individuals as was discussed in the previous section of the chapter when dealing with the case of New Zealanders in Australia.

Some countries, such as the US and Australia, have taken some of these vulnerable groups into consideration when designing their financial aid measures. For instance, in the absence of federal intervention, some Australian states such as Tasmania, South Australia, the ACT, Queensland and Victoria implemented support schemes to assist temporary visa holders, including international students, asylum seekers and working visa holders.[38] This opens up a discussion whether financial aid measures in connection to future epidemics should address social policy goals. This is a question too comprehensive to answer in this context, but nonetheless an important one which deserves further thought. The US introduced a wide range of social expenditures supporting individuals through the American Rescue Plan as is elaborated in the following section.

E. Awarding Financial Aid in Accordance with a Principle of Residence

Awarding financial aid in accordance with a principle of residence, rather than other principles such as taxpayment or citizenship, would directly benefit the receivers in

[37] Y Lind, 'Ekonomiska stödåtgärder i samband med COVID-19 och Danmarks markering gentemot skatteflykt' [2020] *Svensk Skattetidning* 186; Y Lind, 'Sweden and Denmark Incorporate Anti-Tax-Avoidance Rules into Very Different COVID-19 Responses' [2020] *Tax Notes International* 1127; Y Lind, 'Allocating COVID-19 State Aid Equitably – The Case of Denmark, [2020] *Europarättslig tidskrift* 551; Y Lind and Å Gunnarsson, 'Gender equality, Taxation and, the COVID-19 Recovery: A Study of Sweden and Denmark' [2021] *Tax Notes International* 581.

[38] M Pakula, 'Emergency Support For Victoria's International Students' (Victoria State Government, 29 April 2020).

addition to indirectly benefiting businesses and economies. This would be a result of it being more likely that those with less to begin with will spend their awarded cash funds compared to high-income earners who, in accordance with the ongoing debate within behavioural economics, are more inclined to save or invest rather than to spend. The content of this section of the chapter naturally relates to previous discussions concerning tax residence found in section IV(B). Therefore, discussions concerning taxpayment and tax residence are excluded from this part of the chapter, yet the author should be aware of the interlinking between the two.

The American Rescue plan realised, somewhat controversially, the idea of awarding financial aid amidst the pandemic in accordance with residence, employment and need rather than other justifications commonly applied, eg taxpayment, tax residence and formal citizenship. It emphasises the need to assist families which may be considered as an extension of already implemented pandemic measures assisting families, eg the Families First Coronavirus Response Act.[39] The American Rescue Plan is comprehensive, but below is an outline of the main features linked to financial aid measures.

The American Rescue Plan devoted nearly $1 trillion towards building a bridge to economic recovery for working families[40] in particular. Initially these families were awarded a $1,400 per-person stimulus check which supplements the stimulus checks previously issued in connection to the CARES Act.[41] The American Rescue Plan extended eligibility for the checks and included, for instance, adult dependents. As a result, a lower or middle-income family of four was awarded an additional $5,600.[42]

Furthermore, it extended pre-existing unemployment insurance benefits and the eligibility to receive these by providing a $300 per week cash supplement. The Child Tax Credit was increased from $2,000 per child to $3,000 per child ($3,600 for children under age 6) in addition to including 17-year-olds in 2021. Families were additionally awarded an additional tax credit with the aim to lower their costs for childcare.[43]

The American Rescue Plan has been one of the most noticed financial aid schemes introduced in connection with the COVID-19 pandemic. One of the most prominent features of it is the underpinning motivation to provide social change to the American society through its historical anti-poverty measures. While it has provided great relief it has also underlined pre-existing problems within the US system, mainly that of how undocumented workers are left out of social expenditures and essential assistance despite contributing to the US economy and social security.

In conclusion, awarding financial aid on other criteria than taxpayment or citizenship does not result in complete equity as, for instance, undocumented workers may still be at risk of being excluded from such aid. Yet awarding financial aid with a principle of residence does result in a greater inclusion of impoverished and vulnerable groups than would otherwise be the case.

[39] Families First Coronavirus Response Act 116-127 (03/18/2020).
[40] Working families are commonly defined as families with a non-elderly, non-disabled head of household whose income is reported.
[41] CARES Act 116-136 (03/27/2020).
[42] American Rescue Plan Act of 2021 117-2 (03/11/2021).
[43] ibid.

F. Awarding Financial Aid in Accordance with a Principle of Finances[44]

In connection with the exclusion of financial aid to corporations registered in tax havens, most countries additionally excluded financial aid to businesses if they decided to pay out dividends or alternatively required shares within the same calendar year as receiving pandemic financial support.[45] Sweden acted no differently and applied these exclusions to their financial aid packages.[46] The Swedish government further added in the political rhetoric attached to the introduction of financial aid:

> … respite will not be granted to companies that mismanage their finances or are in some other way considered unethical. Nor will any relief be granted to companies that have large tax debts.[47]

In April 2020, the Swedish government introduced COVID-19 financial aid schemes targeting businesses.[48] The size of financial aid was calculated on the extent of the turnover loss a business had experienced and varied between 22.5 and 75 per cent of the business's fixed costs excluding wage costs for March and April 2020. To be eligible for the support, the business applying for the aid scheme needed to provide proof of a turnover of at least SEK 250,000 during the past financial year and a loss of turnover of at least 30 per cent. The loss of turnover was calculated based on financial results from March and April 2020 compared with the same months last year.

In practice, this requirement caused several problems concerning legal certainty and legality, such as:

- Was there a need for a certified accountant to provide the proof of turnover losses? There were several Swedish legal frameworks involved in this question, yet the general rule was that all aid above SEK 100,000 needed a certificate from an authorised accountant.[49]
- There was general confusion as there were several governmental agencies involved (primarily the Swedish Tax Agency and then Swedish Agency for Regional and Economic Growth) when applying for aid schemes.
- The appeal process for decisions linked to pandemic financial aid was infamously slow and involved additional actors such as the County Administrative Board.

Furthermore, the Swedish aid scheme stated that for a business to be entitled to financial aid the business was, during the period of March 2020–June 2021, not allowed to execute a decision on certain value transfers. Such value transfers primarily comprised

[44] In this context 'finances' concerns the management of money within a business and includes activities such as investing, borrowing, lending, budgeting, saving, and forecasting.

[45] Lind (n 20).

[46] 3§ Lag (2020:548) om omställningsstöd.

[47] Ministry of Finance, *Crisis package for Swedish businesses and jobs* (The Government of Sweden, 16 March 2020).

[48] Ministry of Finance, *Businesses to receive support based on loss of turnover* (The Government of Sweden, 30 April 2020).

[49] 5§ para 5 Lag (2020:548) om omställningsstöd.

the transactions regulated in Chapters 18–20 of the Swedish Companies Act[50] and Chapters 13–15 of the Swedish Economic Associations Act.[51] For instance, profit distribution, acquisition of own shares and reduction of the share capital and/or the reserve funds of which the two former are the most central to this discussion.

The prohibition against transfers of value included decisions made by the company's annual general meeting (AGM), board or equivalent body during this period. If a company executed or decided on such a value transfer during the relevant period, it was considered deficient in the conditions for the aid and subsequently the company was to be considered ineligible for adjustment aid. If such aid has already been awarded to the recipient, it should be repaid.[52]

Swedish authorities have actively investigated potential financial aid fraud in connection with the financial aid packages, in particular the requirement of no value transfers. They have in a large number of cases either requested previously awarded financial aid to be repaid via a claw-back clause and/or prosecuted individual businesses. During 2021, several cases were dealt with by the Swedish Administrative Court of Appeal as a result of this work. Notably, the Swedish Tax Agency has proven rigid in its judgments of these value transfers and shown less leniency towards individuals or businesses in the case of COVID-19 financial aid. For instance, it posted the following assessment in the updated administrative case law:

> A company has made a formally correct decision to pay a dividend at the annual general meeting in March 2020. In April 2020, an extraordinary general meeting will be held where it is decided not to pay a dividend. In this case, the AGM has made such a decision on a dividend in March that the company is not entitled to adjustment support. In the opinion of the Swedish Tax Agency, the fact that the AGM later makes a new decision not to pay a dividend does not affect this assessment. The company is therefore not entitled to adjustment support.[53]

The statistics from the Swedish Agency for Regional and Economic Growth imply that as much as one out of four of the short-term support awards that had been granted failed to fulfill the requirements for financial aid. Consequently, Swedish agencies have clawed back SEK 2,3 billion and decided to prosecute 170 cases so far.[54] In some parts of Sweden, as much as half of the awarded aid has been reclaimed.[55] This is an ongoing process and there are surely more cases to follow as the agencies are working through the backlog stemming from the pandemic.

The problems discussed in this section are of a general nature and most jurisdictions have faced similar problems when implementing aid schemes issued with short notice as has often been the case in connection with the COVID-19 pandemic. Consequently,

[50] Aktiebolagslag (2005:551).

[51] Lag (2018:672) om ekonomiska föreningar.

[52] *KRNJ 2020-11-26, mål nr 3236-20* Kammarrätten *KRNS 2020-10-21, mål nr 5944-20* Kammarrätten *KRNS 2021-06-04, mål nr 7724-20* Kammarrätten.

[53] Swedish Tax Agency, 'Skatteverket Rättslig Vägledning: Särskilt om vinstutdelning och andra värdeöverföringar 2022', www4.skatteverket.se/rattsligvagledning/edition/2022.3/392535.html.

[54] J Ahmadi, 'Var fjärde har fått återkrav på coronastöd – "vi har varit tydliga"' *Dagens Industri* (16 August 2021).

[55] P Kalmar, 'Hälften av företagen har fått återkrav på sitt korttidsstöd' (21 October 2021).

problems such as these should be taken into consideration when designing future aid schemes in connection with crises such as a pandemic. The strengthening of legal certainty through the upholding of rule of law is essential from the perspective of individuals and businesses that are in need of financial aid.

V. Concluding Summary and Policy Recommendations

As initially promised in this chapter, this final discussion integrates Smith's four characteristics of fairness, certainty, convenience and efficiency.

Fairness has been repeatedly used in the political rhetoric linked to financial aid packages. Most notably when introducing, and justifying, the exclusion of businesses registered in tax havens. In this context, there is a tangible argument reviving the idea of a contractual relationship between the state and the taxpayer and subsequent fairness between those who comply with this relationship versus those who are considered not to do so. In the view of the author, and as has been illustrated throughout this chapter, the reasoning behind this argument may be of a more pragmatical nature as it efficiently reduces the public funds that need to be dispensed to aid receivers.

Throughout this chapter it has become evident that most aid measures, regardless of the jurisdiction that issues them, have caused uncertainty. To provide *certainty* it is essential for the legislator to provide a robust legal framework based upon clear legal provisions. The legal design should encompass the following:

- When and on what terms is an individual/business eligible to receive aid? The requirements should be objective and clear to all parties.
- When fulfilling the requirements asked for how is this to be done in practice (remember discussion of authentication of losses from certified accountants for instance) and to what governmental agency/agencies should these be presented to receive financial aid in a timely and efficient manner? A coordination of differing governmental agencies and pre-existing case law and administrative case law may be necessary.
- When is the aid planned to be phased out alt. prolonged dependent on the ongoing situation and unforeseen developments? This may naturally be difficult to predict in a state of crisis or a pandemic. However, it would be sensible to attach limited time periods to each measure and have these prolonged over time depending on the need rather than having measures without a clear time limitation.

Efficiency and *convenience* can, and have been in many countries, achieved through the utilisation of pre-existing civic ID numbers or identification/organisation numbers for companies. The Nordic countries have for years regulated all interactions between state and individual through civic ID numbers. The feature was historically introduced as a way of ensuring tax compliance,[56] yet it now also benefits the individual as it

[56] S Steinmo, *Taxation and Democracy: Swedish, British and American Approaches to Financing the Modern State* (New Haven, Yale University Press, 1996).

allows them to receive social welfare benefits in a more efficient, timely and predictable manner when interacting with governmental agencies. The utilisation of civic numbers and the high degree of digitalisation has been credited as one of the key reasons for the successful Danish handling of the economic consequences amidst the COVID-19 pandemic. This action can be compared to that of, for instance, the US who experienced hardship to provide financial relief as it initially sent out physical debit cards with the funds instead of simply transferring to registered accounts digitally via civic ID numbers.

18

Law and Beyond: Legislation in Times of Pandemic and the Rule of Law

HANNA FILIPCZYK

Abstract

Taking the example of the Polish COVID-19 emergency legislation, this chapter investigates how it is possible that 'bad law' – ie falling short of Fuller's postulates of the inner morality of law – can nonetheless be followed, and discusses implications of this possibility for the formal concept of the rule of law.

I. Introduction

In his 1964 seminal book *The Morality of Law* Lon Fuller formulated canons of 'inner morality of law'. Legislation adopted in Poland in 2020 with a view to alleviating multiple adverse implications of the COVID-19 pandemic falls short of Fuller's postulates. This provokes a question: how to reconcile such 'bad law' with the rule of law?

The analysis unfolds as follows. I recall basic tenets of Lon Fuller's account and relate them to the rule of law. Against this background, I briefly present the anti-COVID-19 tax legislation adopted in Poland. Then I address the question of how law so bad can still be law. The analysis pinpoints several elements in the law functioning which the traditional outlook on the rule of law neglects.

The example of the Polish anti-COVID legislative shield is in my view illustrative. It opens discussion to wider, and unspecific to any given normative order or any given country, issues of interpretation and application of legal rules. Still, it is important to note that Poland is a civil law country, with a written (codified) Constitution. The Constitution of the Republic of Poland of 2 April 1997 states that the Republic of Poland shall be a democratic state ruled by law and implementing the principles of social justice. This core provision declares the standard of the rule of law. While I believe that the rule of law, as presented in this chapter, is a universal standard, I admit that – despite my efforts to keep the discussion general – some remarks here formulated may prove specific to civil law countries. Readers will judge for themselves if, and to what extent, these remarks remain relevant for common law countries.

II. Fuller's Inner Morality of Law

Lon Fuller propounded the concept of the so-called inner morality of law. In the function of thought experiment, he developed the allegory of the unfortunate legislator, King Rex, who tried to give laws to his citizens. Famously, King Rex failed in his numerous attempts to legislate, and failed both on a spectacular scale and in a characteristic manner. Fuller uses this allegory to indicate 'eight ways to fail to make law':

> The first and most obvious lies in a failure to achieve rules at all, so that every issue must be decided on an ad hoc basis. The other routes are: (2) a failure to publicize, or at least to make available to the affected party, the rules he is expected to observe; (3) the abuse of retroactive legislation, which not only cannot itself guide action, but undercuts the integrity of rules prospective in effect, since it puts them under the threat of retrospective change; (4) a failure to make rules understandable; (5) the enactment of contradictory rules or (6) rules that require conduct beyond the powers of the affected party; (7) introducing such frequent changes in the rules that the subject cannot orient his action by them; and, finally, (8) a failure of congruence between the rules as announced and their actual administration.[1]

The counterparts of these failures are demands or desiderata addressed to a legal system: the failures correspond, by contrast, to desirable features of legislative process and the resulting laws. These features are 'eight kinds of legal excellences towards which a system of rules may strive' and 'standards by which excellence in legality may be tested'.[2] 'All of them are means toward a single end (…)',[3] this end being the ideal of perfect inner (internal) morality of law.

As observed by Fuller,

> [a] total failure in anyone of these eight directions does not simply result in a bad system of law; it results in something that is not properly called a legal system at all, except perhaps in the Pickwickian sense in which a void contract can still be said to be one kind of contract.[4]

Therefore, according to Fuller, these requirements are essential to law – ie such that the failure to meet them brings about the lack of law. The features the thought experiment pinpoints are constitutive of law.

Looking closer into the desiderata put forward by Fuller – demands of law's generality, publicity, prospectivity, intelligibility, consistency, practicability, stability and congruence (between formulation of the law and its application)[5] – we can detect their

[1] L Fuller, *The Morality of Law* (New Haven, Yale University Press, 1964) 39.
[2] Fuller (n 1) 41.
[3] ibid 104.
[4] ibid 39.
[5] *cf* J Waldron, 'The rule of law' in EN Zalta (ed), *The Stanford Encyclopedia of Philosophy* (Summer 2020 Edition), available at plato.stanford.edu/archives/sum2020/entries/rule-of-law/.

common denominator. They demand that there be rules which are 'obeyable' – ie such that they can be obeyed (followed). The gist of these demands is that law should be such that it can be followed by its addressees. The essence of law is that it consists of rules made for human agents to follow. Rules (or pseudo-rules) which are not publicised are retroactive, contradictory, etc, are inapt to be followed.

The recurring theme of Fuller's book is that law should be understood as 'the enterprise of subjecting human conduct to the governance of rules'.[6] Features of law corresponding (by opposition) to the failures of unfortunate King Rex are analytic for law.

Such nature of law has a dignitarian aspect. It entails

> a commitment to the view that man is, or can become, a responsible agent, capable of understanding and following rules, and answerable for his defaults. Every departure from the principles of the law's inner morality is an affront to man's dignity as a responsible agent.[7]

Human beings – law-addressees – are free agents having a capacity of self-determination. They can and should be guided rather than terrorised or manipulated – and this is what law is designed for.

This theme is vividly present in the thoughts of Joseph Raz and Jeremy Waldon. Waldron – in a similar vein to Fuller – links generality of law with the human capacity to follow rules and with dignity of such agency. He observes the 'self-application' of law as the manner of law functioning, and considers that people are by nature rule-followers, able and willing to understand norms, to follow and apply them.[8] Every system of law is premised upon voluntary application of legal norms by addressees.

> I believe this pervasive emphasis on self-application is definitive of law and that law is therefore sharply distinct from a system of rule that works primarily by manipulating, terrorizing or galvanizing behavior. Lon Fuller has argued that this embodies law's respect for human agency (…).[9]

Also Raz points out that '[r]especting human dignity entails treating humans as persons capable of planning and plotting their future'.[10]

III. The Rule of Law (Formal Concept)

Let us see how the above viewpoint on human agency and the nature of law relate to the rule of law. The simplest answer could be that if there is to be the rule of law, there has to be law – and Fuller's postulates determine what is needed for a given undertaking to be law. Yet there is something more to it, as the rule of law is interesting and rich in content as a concept in its own right.

[6] Fuller (n 1) 74 and *passim*.
[7] Fuller (n 1) 162.
[8] J Waldron, 'The Concept and the Rule of Law' (2008) 43(1) *Georgia Law Review* 26–27.
[9] ibid 27.
[10] J Raz, 'The Rule of Law and its Virtue' in J Raz, *The Authority of Law. Essays on Law and Morality* (Oxford, Oxford University Press, 1979) 210–26, 221. See also HLA Hart, *The Concept of Law* (Oxford, Clarendon, 1961): 'the rules must satisfy certain conditions: they must be intelligible and within the capacity of most to obey (…)'.

The rule of law is both an ideal of political morality and a fundamental virtue of law. It is venerable in these two roles – discernible and in need of disambiguation, and in multiple conceptual incarnations. Its concepts vary, ranging between formal, procedural and substantive. The accounts of the rule of law vastly differ in 'how much' is inscribed into the concept (and usually, as a consequence, how 'neat', rigorous and precise the concept is). Moreover, the popular understanding of the rule of law tends to be even richer in content than most theoretical accounts – the ideal is often loaded (and overloaded) with all possible positives the legal system can exhibit.[11] Certain variations in understanding of the concept may stem also from legal tradition, which is different for common law countries (such as the UK) and civil law countries (such as Poland).

Following Raz,[12] I espouse here the formal concept of the rule of law. This concept is based on formal properties of law, ie such that they characterise law irrespective of any substantive content. As a consequence, it is the rule of law *simpliciter*, and not (necessarily) the rule of good law. Importantly, there being a law is prerequisite for law to be good: in Fuller's words, 'law is a precondition for good law'.[13]

In the account of Raz, the rule of law has two main dimensions: '(1) that people should be ruled by the law and obey it, and (2) that the law should be such that people will be able to be guided by it. [...] [T]he law must be capable of being obeyed'.[14] There are, therefore, two fundamental features law should display for the rule of law to be observed, and in fact, for law to be law:

- legitimacy (legality): legal rules should satisfy the 'criterion of identity', ie come from legislative authority and be adopted in the proper procedure (be compliant with the 'rules of recognition'[15] which dictate what valid law is); and
- certainty: legal rules must be such that they can be obeyed, because 'if the law is to be obeyed it must be capable of guiding the behaviour of its subjects. It must be such that they can find out what it is and act on it';[16] therefore law should be understandable and predictable.[17]

This formulation makes it clear that the fulfilment of Fuller's desiderata of the inner morality of law is a prerequisite for the rule of law – namely, it corresponds with the dimension of certainty. Fuller himself recognised that *law* and *the rule of law* are related concepts. Therefore – despite fundamental differences in positions of these thinkers[18] – Waldron rightly sees Fuller as a proponent of formal, 'Razian' or 'thin' concept of the rule of law.[19]

[11] For panorama of the rule of law accounts see Waldron (n 5).
[12] Raz (n 10) 210–26.
[13] Fuller (n 1) 157.
[14] Raz (n 10) 213.
[15] Hart (n 10) 97–107.
[16] Raz (n 10) 214.
[17] *cf* H Filipczyk, *Tax avoidance and rationality of law* (Warsaw, Wolters Kluwer, 2017) ch IV.
[18] Raz disagrees with associating the rule of law with morality, which is the gist of Fuller's thought. 'Fuller's attempt to establish a necessary connection between law and morality fails' (Raz (n 10) 224). Curiously enough, Raz subsequently proposes that 'the rule of law is the specific excellence of the law', ie its inherent virtue (ibid 225). In the ancient Greek tradition it is exactly moral virtue, though Raz sees it differently.
[19] Waldron (n 8) 7.

From all eight Fuller's postulates predictability can be distilled as their essence. If operation of (legal) rules is to be predictable, they should be general, publicised, prospective, intelligible, consistent, stable and the practice of their application has to be congruent with their sense. Legal certainty is a feature of law which consists in the subjects of law (law addressees) being able to predict legal consequences of facts (states of affairs), including acts and omissions of the same subject and other subjects of law. As a consequence, predictability with regard to law is legal certainty.

The underpinning of Fuller's inner morality of law, and also of the rule of law as virtue, is freedom. Because a human being is a free actor, legal rules can be addressed to him/her. And when they are (and when they *really* are, ie they are rules which have a form appropriate to be followed by an agent), a human being can arrange his/her affairs.

Within the context of the common law Constitution Allan observed that '[t]o govern through law is, at a minimum, to respect human agency, allowing everyone to take responsibility for their own efforts to conform to published and practicable standards (…) Rule by terror is not rule by law'.[20]

For centuries legal certainty has been considered important in the domain of taxation. It is, however, noteworthy that it is not only desirable as a feature of law but constitutive of law. Law deprived of legal certainty is no longer law – this is the fundamental tenet of Fuller. His basic claim is that a citizen is under no obligation to obey such non-existent law; in fact rule-following may not even be possible.

In what follows, let us bear in mind that there are two dimensions of the rule of law: legality and certainty – and not certainty alone.

IV. Anti-COVID Legal Shield in Poland (An Overview)

I move now to a short presentation of the anti-COVID legal shield in Poland – legislation adopted with a view to alleviating multiple adverse implications of the COVID-19 pandemic.

The most important element of the legislation is the Act of 2 March 2020 on special arrangements related to preventing, counteracting and combatting COVID-19, other infectious diseases and resulting crisis situations (as amended; furthermore: the Act). It is a horizontal Act: it spans over a number of domains, belonging in both public and private law, and both substantive and procedural (including labour law, civil law, tax law, etc). While it is generally of episodic nature – its provisions are to be binding only in the period of pandemic or in the period of pandemic and in the predefined period afterwards, it also contains provisions of general application. They have been included in the Act for convenience – the Act was fast tracked in Parliament, and was processed swiftly and without much reflection (the entire legislative process from the day the bill entered the lower chamber of Parliament to the day it was signed by the President of the Republic of Poland took five days). Immediate action was necessary to provide legal basis for various measures urgently needed during the pandemic.

[20] TRS Allan, *The Sovereignty of Law* (Oxford, Oxford University Press, 2013) 46.

Since its adoption this basic Act has been amended (revised) 93 times by 46 amending Acts. Two amendments were substantial: they revised large portions of the Act. Currently, ie as of 23 April 2022, it counts over 117,000 words and over 817,000 characters. It has a complex structure and contains provisions with rather appalling indications, such as 'Article 15zzzzzxa'.

Its tax part contains provisions – scattered in the Act – which provide exemptions from taxes, defer payment of tax or fulfilment of administrative tax-related duties (such as filing duties, TP documentation, validity of certificates of residence, etc) or intervene in the tax proceedings (eg, by postponing or suspending procedural deadlines). They are imperative or (which is more common) facultative; in the latter case they authorise the minister of finance or a tax authority to grant various reliefs without obliging them to do so.

It is not in the length of the Act or frequency of changes it undergoes where the real problem lies, but rather in its qualitative characteristics. The Act is badly written. One could say – after Fuller – that it is a 'masterpiece of obscurity'.[21]

The negative evaluation of this legislation can be illustrated by the following three examples pertaining to procedure in tax matters. The first problem arises with respect to the suspension of deadlines in tax and court proceedings. The period of pandemic has been officially announced in Poland on 14 March 2020. The provisions of the Act, as amended on 31 March 2020, stated that deadlines in tax and administrative court procedures are suspended in the period of pandemic (the provisions were repealed as of 16 May 2020). The Act did not contain, however, the provision expressly stating that the Act in this respect is retroactive. This omission gave rise to the controversy of whether deadlines were suspended as of 14 March or starting 31 March 2020.

The second issue arises with regard to the suspension of periods of limitation. The law read that the elapse of periods of limitation 'regulated/provided for in the administrative law' are suspended in the period of pandemic. It is unclear whether the expression covers also the period of limitation for tax liabilities: whether in this particular context 'tax law' be considered part of 'administrative law'.

Yet another problem arose with respect to the management of cases in administrative courts. Starting from 16 May 2020, the Act provided for the possibility to hear court cases in closed session – without the public hearing and without the presence of parties (a taxpayer and a tax authority or their proxies). Formally, the application of the provision was premised upon the joint fulfilment of three conditions. These conditions were phrased in open-ended formulae giving no clear indication of their meaning (the president of the court division 'considers that the recognition of the case is necessary'; 'organization of the public hearing, as mandated by the act, could bring about the excessive threat to the health of the participation'; 'the hearing cannot be organised remotely with the direct transmission of picture and sound'). As a result, public hearings were superseded by closed sessions, also where taxpayers expressly demanded to be heard by the court. Such practice was problematic in light of the taxpayer's right to fair trial.

[21] Fuller (n 1) 36.

Three problems outlined above vary in several respects. What they have in common, however, is the detriment to legal certainty. Additionally, the Polish lawmaker decided to execute in 2020, effective 2021, and in 2021, effective 2022, major changes in tax law (in the income tax and VAT areas). Several new taxes and public fees have been introduced. The newly adopted legislation is complex and again, badly drafted.

The resulting situation of growing complexity has implications going beyond its immediate impact on tax settlements of Polish taxpayers. It inspires reflection on how the current state of play in the tax law measures against the standard rules of law.

Admittedly, the pandemic outburst called for immediate legislative action and resulting shortcomings in the drafting of the Act were attributable to difficulties of the state of emergency (and as such, arguably, excusable). What is understandable in March 2020 – when the Act was first adopted in the time of pressing legislative needs, is less so in 2021 or 2022 – when the Act has been repeatedly amended in a much calmer social environment. Above all, however, my goal is not to criticise the low quality of the Act (whether finally judged as excusable or not) but rather to understand how despite its low quality it can still be law. In this endeavour the 'pandemic' legislation is not treated here as a problem in its own right but rather as a flagrant manifestation of a wider phenomenon.

V. The Rule of (Bad) Law?

The low quality legislative output of the pandemic exacerbated the problem of low quality tax law and brought it to the fore. The banal observation is that tax law is badly written and falls foul of Fuller's desiderata. Going beyond this observation, it is worth asking the question (transcendental – Kantian in its structure): how is it possible that bad law is followed (by law addressees) and applied (by law applying agencies, including tax authorities and courts)?[22]

The remaining part of this chapter is devoted to answering this very query. This analysis aims to offer several insights into the nature of law and the rule of law principle.

A. Grades of the Rule of Law

A part of the answer is furnished by the observation that the rule of law is a virtue which can be 'present' or 'fulfilled' by any given legal system (law in books and law in action) to varying degrees. It is not an 'all-or-nothing' or binary quality, such that either it obtains or does not obtain. Therefore, the case may be that the anti-COVID shield does not infringe the rule of law, or infringes it but only to a degree.

Fuller's inner morality of law is composed of characteristics which, individually and collectively, admit of degrees. It is therefore an ideal which can be realised to a greater or (as in the case at hand) lesser extent. The same is true about the rule of law.

[22] I put aside the possibility that the rule of law standard is not applicable to rules enacted in the state of emergency (see Waldron (n 5) point 8.4 for discussion).

Fuller explains that referring to the distinction between morality of duty and morality of aspiration.[23] He observes that while inner morality of law has aspects of each of these moralities, the latter by far prevails: 'the inner morality of law is condemned to remain largely a morality of aspiration and not of duty'.[24] Such morality, and its eight distinctive components, is an aspirational ideal, an ideal which lawmakers should strive to realise to the maximum attainable extent. And what is achieved does not reach maximum in absolute terms.

The picture is even more complicated than that. As observed by Fuller, '[a]t the height of the ascent we are tempted to imagine a utopia of legality in which all rules are perfectly clear, consistent with one another, known to every citizen, and never retroactive', etc – yet 'the goal of perfection is much more complex'.[25] There are tensions between components of the inner morality of law, antinomies and trade-offs between desiderata.[26] There can also be compensations between building-blocks of this morality, such that the shortage in 'supply' in one of them can be compensated by fuller realisation of the other.[27]

Fuller embraces the somewhat paradoxical consequence of this doctrine: that human enterprise called 'law' can in fact be law only to an extent – that the very existence of law is a matter of degree. Fuller himself formulates this view explicitly. In discussion of possible objections to his theory he asserts that both the rule of law and legal system can enjoy 'varying degrees of success' and 'can and do half exist'.[28]

The same is claimed about the rule of law by Raz and Waldron.[29] Raz adds the new insight: that the rule of law is neither the only nor absolute virtue of law, and that consequently, in real life cases it may be desirable to compromise the rule of law to allow for realisation of other objectives – it should be 'balanced against competing claims of other values'.[30]

This position, as intellectually appealing as it is, can have some adverse implications. Fuller is adamant in claiming that total failure results in there being no law at all. This standpoint leaves open the question how little there can be such morality – ie how spectacular can the failure to legislate be – for there still be law. It is uncertain if this question is valid. The aspirational standard is not very strict, perhaps not strict enough to provide a benchmark able to disqualify any given set of rules as law. It serves to evaluate law but not to the point of disqualifying it – or rarely does.

At first glance, on this point Fuller and Raz seem to disagree. According to Raz, the rule of law is 'a standard to which the law ought to conform but which it can and sometimes does violate most radically and systematically'.[31] Therefore – as I understand – for Raz even legislation tainted with gross violations of certainty remains law.

[23] Fuller (n 1) 5 ff.

[24] Fuller makes an exception for the requirement of formal promulgation – postulating that it be treated as requirement of duty.

[25] Fuller (n 1) 41.

[26] ibid 45.

[27] ibid 104.

[28] ibid 122.

[29] Waldron (n 8) 47 ff.

[30] Raz (n 10) 228.

[31] ibid 223.

Even Raz admits, however, that some minimal degree of generality, etc, is necessary for a legal system to subsist. The difference between Fuller and Raz – on this particular point – may eventually come down to where the quality bar is placed.

Be that as it may, surely the anti-COVID shield in Poland (evaluated as a whole) is not *sufficiently* bad, in terms of legislative excellence, to claim that the legislator totally failed as Fuller's Rex did. As a result, it can be claimed that the legislation is deficient in the rule of law aspect (or, if we dissect the ideal into the eight postulates – aspects, it is deficient with regard to selected or all such aspects) but not that it infringes the rule of law. For the latter claim the standard should be categorical, whereas it is not.

All this discussion helps to understand the anatomy of the rule of law but does not answer the crucial question of: how it is possible that bad law functions as law, ie effectively guides human behaviour?

B. (Rules of) Interpretation as the Source of Law

This is where legal interpretation comes into play. Despite all conceptual and technical flaws of the legislation, the majority of legal questions it gives rise to can be resolved with the aid of legal interpretation.

Law is not 'pure' legislation but the mixture, 'fusion' of legislation (legal text) and interpretation – it is constructed out of both. The gist of legal interpretation is rationalisation: an interpreter strives to rationalise legal text, that is to make it understandable (intelligible) to the maximum possible extent. In a way legal interpretation compensates for deficiencies of legislation. Legislator and interpreter go hand in hand in a concerted effort to construct law.

Going back to three examples given above – the first problem (one of retroactivity) can be resolved with the aid of interpretation. Even in the absence of intertemporal regulation it can be concluded that the legislator in a sufficiently lucid manner expressed his will that the procedural deadlines be suspended retroactively, ie starting from 14 March 2020.

Fuller is more than conscious of the existence of the interpretation (legal construction) as a social practice. In the famous jurisprudential debate with Hart he supported teleological construal of legal text, purposive interpretation seeking 'the intention of the statute' (rather than any empirical legislator).[32] In *The Morality of Law* he expressed, though casually, the view that '[w]ith all its subtleties, the problem of interpretation occupies a sensitive, central position in the internal morality of the law. It reveals, as no other problem can, the cooperative nature of the task of maintaining legality'.[33] For Fuller law as a 'human enterprise' is a purposive activity – and this should be acknowledged and reflected in the interpretative activity.

[32] Fuller (n 1) 87. For the debate see: HLA Hart, 'Positivism and the Separation of Law and Morals' (1958) 71(4) *Harvard Law Review* 593; L Fuller, 'Positivism and Fidelity to Law – A Reply to Professor Hart' (1958) 71(4) *Harvard Law Review* 630.

[33] Fuller (n 1) 91.

Still, in the thought experiment employing King Rex, Fuller seems to have underplayed the role of interpretation. In fact there is *almost* no case of doubt that cannot be remedied with legal interpretation. There is *almost* no law so bad it cannot be ameliorated with the aid of legal interpretation. Fuller is right when he posits that '(…) if this obscurity [of law] exceeds a certain crucial point, then no virtuosity in draftsmanship or skill in interpretation can make a meaningful thing of a statute afflicted with it' – 'fundamental defects in design'[34] do exist. Yet such irreparable defects are strikingly rare.

'An Act of Parliament is what the best interpretation indicates'.[35] The ability of legal interpretation (or – we should rather say – of interpretative community) to overcome even gross imperfections of legal text testifies to the human power of rationalisation. Human beings are by nature rationalisers. Such an idea of human nature can be traced back to the classic Greek philosophy, to Socrates, Plato and Aristotle, or even further back to the times where the *arche* has been sought as the rational principium of being.[36]

The activity of rationalisation is fuelled by the will to understand. 'Rational' means 'intelligible', ie, accessible to reason. The impulse to understand is inherently human, and it is realised in many forms and manifestations. One of them is the urge to understand law as a type of communication (law is communicated by a legislator to subjects).

This is not to say that legislator is free from qualitative obligations, because even faulty law at the end of the day will be understood. For various reasons a legislator is under such an obligation. Yet whatever is a legal rule which ultimately can be understood, belongs in law.[37]

Taking into account two dimensions of the rule of law: certainty and legality, the position of legal interpretation is potentially controversial in light of each of them. The problem with legal certainty is surmountable if we add provisos concerning the characteristics of legal interpretation. Interpretation has the potential to provide certainty, but on condition that its rules are themselves sufficiently 'certain', ie predictable (which can be evaluated by applying to them Fuller's conditions).[38] Rules of interpretation are – trivially – rules, they are therefore normative, just as rules of positive law are. Thus, generally, norms – either norms of positive law or norms of interpretation – should satisfy the conditions jointly amounting to predictability. If this is so, predictable rules of interpretation can compensate for rules of positive law lacking in predictability.

More serious, however, is the challenge posed to the position of legal interpretation by the legality postulate – in civil law countries. Rules of legal interpretation

[34] ibid 88.

[35] Allan (n 20) 46.

[36] See G Reale, *A History of Ancient Philosophy, Vol. I and II* (New York, State University of New York, 1987).

[37] Waldron accentuates 'the law's susceptibility to rational analysis' – '[i]n this way, the law pays respect to the persons who live under it, conceiving them now as bearers of individual reason and intelligence' (Waldron (n 8) 37). Waldron puts forwards the procedural account of the rule of law ('thicker' than the formal account of Fuller and Raz) within which the deliberation, exchange of arguments, etc, has a prominent place.

[38] Rules of interpretation do not in fact satisfy these conditions in full; eg as observed by many authors, they are often contradictory (there are pairs of opposing canons of interpretation).

are usually not decreed or codified in law – if they are 'in books', they are books of jurisprudence,[39] and typically not legal acts where (as it seems under the requirement of legality in any civil law country) they should be placed.[40] As mentioned, rules of interpretation are normative, but it is difficult to say where this normativity comes from.

This objection cannot be discarded easily. Rules of interpretation, treated as normative, are a tacit component of law, part and parcel of the 'enterprise' of law. They are indispensable. The mechanical jurisprudence of Montesquieu – under which judges should be 'no more than the mouth that pronounces the words of the law, mere passive beings, incapable of moderating either its force or rigour'[41] – is unattainable. Yet, in a sense, there is no positivistic 'pedigree test' one can apply to rules of interpretation, and as a result, their 'legality' component is missing or obscure.

In my view given the pervasiveness and indispensability of interpretation and its being rooted in the communicative nature of law, we should accept its role despite the challenge of legality it faces in any civil law country. It is a shadow to a legal text. Yet it is still worthwhile to consider whether it is the case that the more interpretation is needed to construct law, the less rule of law there is in the law in the strict sense (legislation) – or rather no such diminishment in the rule of law takes place – provided that rules of interpretation satisfy Fuller's conditions of predictability.

If the way out of this conundrum is to reject the rigorous positivist position, with its focus on the rule of recognition, and accept that law is constituted by 'black letter' legal text combined with rules of interpretation, the legality problem is solved. It is important, however, to appreciate fully the contribution of interpretation – not to downplay it as 'interstitial' to the law but place it on par with legal text. The fact that Poland is a civil law country and that textual interpretation of tax law is commonly advocated by the Polish jurisprudence does not make a substantial difference: legal interpretation remains a constitutive force of law, which in fact testifies to the inevitability of it in this role irrespective of legal tradition.

C. Resolving Doubts in Favour of a Taxpayer

As far as interpretation-as-rationalisation can lead us through difficulty in establishing the substance of law, it cannot do the job completely. Sometimes, if rarely, it is helpless. This is, in my view, the case with the second problem of the anti-COVID shield indicated above – one concerning the period of limitation. With arguments pulling the interpreter in opposite directions, it cannot be decided which interpretative option is correct.

In such a case one can use the argument that interpretative doubts should be resolved in favour of a taxpayer, as the last resort reason. The argument demands that faced with

[39] See eg W Baude and SE Sachs, 'The Law of Interpretation' (2017) 130(4) *Harvard Law Review* 1082 ff.

[40] Exceptions aside – I am aware that rules of interpretation are sometimes regulated directly in law (eg in several common law countries or in Vienna Convention on the Law of Treaties). Even there, their regulation is not exhaustive.

[41] C De Secondat, Baron De Montesquieu, *Spirit Of The Laws* Book XI, ch VI (New York, MacMillan, 1949).

major, unsurmountable difficulty in understanding legal text, an interpreter should construe and apply it in a way favourable to the taxpayer. This argument is raised in the case of two or more equally plausible readings of legal text. It is instrumental in cases where other devices in the interpreter's toolbox prove insufficient, and a legal puzzle has no solution.

The argument works in two ways: abstract and concrete. The former application takes place when an abstract legal rule can be constructed – out of two or more possible readings of legal text, the one that is the most favourable to taxpayers should be adopted and considered valid. This can be done in cases where such abstract legal rule in all its possible applications consistently renders results favourable to taxpayers. In some cases, however, no such abstract rule can be proposed – as all candidates for it render inconsistent results in terms of taxpayer's interest. For such situations the concrete application of the argument is proposed. In short it can be encapsulated in the formula addressed to a taxpayer: 'whatever you do, it is ok'.

As provocative as it is, the formula is legitimate. One could even submit that it is a Fullerian theme.[42] The responsibility of the legislator is to make good laws. Before we decide there is no law, we should make vigorous attempts to interpret legal text and establish the content of law. Yet if such attempts fail, the 'sanction' for the legislator for failing to make minimally good laws will be that the substance of law will be determined exclusively in the function of addressees' interest. This way the legislator will be denied its legislative power. The argument invites unrepairable flaws in lawmaking against the legislator.

In the Polish tax law the argument is elevated to the rank of legal principle. Previously derived from general standards of the Constitution, it has been written down in the tax law in 2016. The Tax Ordinance reads that '[d]oubts as to the substance of the tax law provisions that cannot be removed are resolved to the benefit of a taxpayer'. In the concrete form or application the principle can be understood boldly, and in a Fullerian vein: if law is not understandable, there is no law at all, and within the area of extreme uncertainty taxpayers can act as they please.

D. Administrative Guidance

Possibly the most important factor in dealing with bad law is administrative guidance, in the form of both individual and general advice. In practice, flaws of legislation are often compensated by official guidance provided by tax administration. The collection of instruments at one's disposal in Poland comprise in particular private tax rulings (issued upon application for individual taxpayers), public tax rulings (issued for indeterminate group of taxpayers and concerning a specific tax problem), and tax explanations (issued for indeterminate group of taxpayers and concerning a larger piece of legislation).

[42] Indeed, Fuller himself suggests a similar rule regarding criminal law (Fuller (n 1) 58). Consider also his imaginary example of conflicting rules and plates installed on 1 January and way out of the conundrum through allowing both actions in Fuller (n 1) 67.

Rulings and explanations do not have binding force. Still, a taxpayer who has followed such official guidance cannot suffer adverse tax consequences of trust invested in tax administration. Based on written-law provisions embodying the doctrine of legitimate expectations,[43] such a taxpayer may even be exonerated from the obligation to pay tax.

There is a formal legal basis for the issuance of rulings and explanations.[44] In theory, they are to interpret or explain the law, and not to create it. Under the Polish Constitution, administrative guidance is not listed among sources of law. What is more, the Constitution demands explicitly that elements of tax (including object and subject of taxation) be determined by a statute.[45]

Practice differs from theory, however. Particularly worrying is the case of tax explanations. In recent years the Minister of Finance has been prolific in publishing them (between 1 January 2019 and 23 April 2022 30 tax explanations have been issued; several of these documents count more than 100 pages). As suggested by the name of the institution, they are put in place to 'explain' the law, with the noble intention of increasing its accessibility to laymen. In reality, the explanations do not 'explain' or 'clarify' the law but also 'determine' it. Importantly, and in contrast to individual tax rulings, tax explanations are not subject to scrutiny by administrative courts (they cannot be appealed against to the court). As a result, they are not objectivised and tend to be systematically skewed for the benefit of tax administration, biased or prejudiced in the interest of the state budget.

The trend, observable even before, to substitute official guidance for legislation, has only been reinforced by the necessities of the pandemic. Tax explanations have been issued also to 'explain' anti-COVID shield and new tax legislation adopted in 2020, and to make up for its deficits. Confronted with the deficient law taxpayers seek guidance and are willing to accept it. As instrumental as they are in providing guidance and ensuring compliance (or, more precisely, what is perceived as compliance by tax authorities), instruments of administrative guidance are problematic from the rule of law perspective. If we take two components of the rule of law in the sense proposed by Raz: legality and certainty, the instruments enhance certainty but often at the cost of legality.

It can justifiably be claimed that official guidance is legitimate to the extent the substance of law it explicates could be extracted from the law itself (legislation, legal text) even without it. The benchmark is therefore whether the impartial competent reader would be able to derive legal norms of the text in the absence of the guidance. In many cases this would not be possible.

[43] My understanding is that the possibility for a UK taxpayer to rely on administrative guidance and/or practice discordant with the Act of Parliament is based also on the ideal of legitimate expectations, and that the conditions for such reliance are stringent; eg the practice must be 'so unambiguous, so widespread, so well-established and so well-recognised as to carry within it a commitment to a group of taxpayers (…) of treatment in accordance with it' (*R (Davies) v HMRC and R (Gaines-Cooper) v HMRC* [2011] UKSC 47, para 49).

[44] Contrary to certain forms of guidance in the UK, as per S Daly, *Tax Authority Advice and the Public* (Oxford, Hart Publishing, 2020).

[45] Compare to *Vestey v Inland Revenue Commissioners* [1980] AC 1148, 1171 as discussed in J Freedman and J Vella, 'HMRC's Management of the UK Tax System: The Boundaries of Legitimate Discretion' in C Evans, J Freedman and R Krever (eds), *The Delicate Balance – Tax, Discretion and the Rule of Law* (Amsterdam, IBFD, 2011) 95–96.

From the rule of law perspective, administrative guidance should be 'correct' in the sense of conforming to the underlying legislation. The problem is that if legislation is badly written, it cannot serve as a yardstick or standard by which correctness can be evaluated. Alluding to the famous Hart's metaphor – where there is no core and penumbra of concepts used in legal text but such text is composed only of penumbra, the core is solidified only in the administrative guidance. In such a situation there is in fact no criterion of correctness. The problem is therefore even more fundamental than one of *satisfaction* of criterion of correctness, it is the problem of the very *existence* of such criterion.

On the one hand, 'patching' legislation by what, strictly speaking, is not the source of law, manifestly runs counter to the legality component of the rule of law principle. On the other hand, in practical terms, administrative guidance provides valuable assistance to citizens, and taxpayers among them – hence the reluctance to ignore or contest it, as it probably deserves on constitutional, rule-of-law grounds. Yet it has to be stated openly: the Emperor's new clothes are non-existent. Administrative guidance is deemed to be the source of legal rules while it should not be so.

Instruments of administrative guidance provide certainty but – in the strict sense, linked to the condition of legality within the rule of law standard – it quite often is not *legal* certainty.

E. Understandability of Law

Finally, the new, fast changing and prolific legislation exacerbates the complexity of tax law.[46] This trend negatively impacts clarity, and as a result, intelligibility of law (legal text).

Fuller obviously demands in his postulates that law be understandable for addressees, ie such-that-it-can-be-understood by them. He does not, however, specify for whom law should be understandable. Understandability of an object (here: legal text) is a quality to be assessed relative to the subject – person – who is to understand. Fuller hesitates between laymen and lawyers and considers that bad law is inaccessible to both laymen and lawyers: '[l]egal experts who studied it [ie the code of King Rex] declared that there was not a single sentence in it that could be understood by an ordinary citizen or by a trained lawyer'.[47] Elsewhere, in the context of promulgation, he concedes: '[i]t would in fact be foolish to try to educate every citizen into the full meaning of every law that might conceivably be applied to him, though Bentham was willing to go a long way in that direction'[48] – but laws must be published (promulgated) because of the entitlement for everyone to have access to them. 'The requirement that laws be published

[46] Sources of complexity of tax law are numerous, both universal and specific to this branch of law. Amongst the latter one should place the exploitation of grey areas of tax law by tax avoiders, often leading to further complication of a legal text (amended in order to 'close' the gap).

[47] Fuller (n 1) 36.

[48] ibid 49.

does not rest on any such absurdity as an expectation that the dutiful citizen will sit down and read them all'.[49] A similar position is presented in his claim that

> [t]he norms should be public knowledge in the sense of being available to anyone who is sufficiently interested, and available in particular to those who make a profession of being public norm-detectors – lawyers as we call them – and who make that expertise available to anyone who is willing to pay for it.[50]

Thus Fuller suggests that the minimum requirement is that his postulates are fulfilled in the eyes of lawyers. For laymen legislation should be formally accessible but – it seems – just for the sake of it, or for them to be potentially able to acquaint themselves with it, which they will never really do.

Waldron observes that law should be not only formally but 'epistemically accessible':

> [l]aws must be public not only in the sense of actual promulgation but also in the sense of accessibility and intelligibility. True, much modern law is necessarily technical (…) and the lay-person will often require professional advice as to what the law requires of him. It is also an important part of the Rule of Law that there be a competent profession available to offer such advice and that the law must be such as to make it possible for professionals at least to get a reliable picture of what the law at any given time requires.[51]

Again, we can see in this passage reluctance to admit openly that it is sufficient for law to be 'epistemically accessible' to lawyers, moderated by the concession that laymen can and should make use of professional advice.

These observations, though generally true, are in my view not straightforward enough. First, they blur the distinction between the readings of law by professionals on one hand and by laymen on the other. Fuller, for example, seems to suggest that an unprofessional reader is or should be able to read and grasp legal rules if only they cared to give it a try and were (in his own words) 'sufficiently interested'. In reality, lawyers read legal text using competences unavailable to others. It is after many years of training and experience that their exegetic abilities are developed and excelled. It is only adequate to consider that these two groups do not form a uniform interpretative community. In Wittgensteinian terms, laymen and lawyers do not play the same 'language game'. As a consequence, comprehension by professionals and by laymen are two distinct standards. One cannot be equated with the other – they are disparate, and if a legal text fulfils both it is only by accident.

It goes beyond the scope of this text to explore the differences between these two standards. To be minimally specific, however, let me mention one of such differences. When reading a legal text, lawyers pay heed to systematicity of law. They typically relate a provision to its context, or rather multiple contexts. To do that, a reader needs to know what such contexts can be, ie, know other parts of law (synchronically and diachronically, ie in evolution of the law). In a perhaps characteristic way, Fuller's Rex is a bold reformer – he considered the legal system is in need of a profound reform and strived to 'make his name in history as a great lawgiver',[52] and he began the reform by the

[49] ibid 51.
[50] ibid 26–27.
[51] Waldron (n 5).
[52] Fuller (n 1) 34.

immediate repeal of all existing law. Contrary to what is assumed in the Fuller's thought experiment, there is never the 'clean slate' of law. There is never only the unrealised potential of boundless receptivity – because, to use the words of Waldron, 'law grows by accretion'.[53] Lawyers have wide horizons in seeing the law in its multiple layers – which laymen typically do not.

Second, it can plausibly be claimed that no legislator strives to give legal text understandability for laymen. The one and only standard that is in fact (though maybe not in declarations) used is comprehension for professionals. Realistically speaking, a high level of complication makes it improbable that tax law will ever be intellectually accessible to laymen. Understanding law not only *can* but in real life *must* be mediated by lawyers. Any project of tax law simplification should aim not to render legislation simple enough to be grasped by laymen (this is un unrealisable objective) but to give it (to the extent attainable given all contexts) internal logic – ensure satisfaction of Fuller's postulates as much as possible – so that legislation can in any standard circumstances be understood by lawyers.

Importantly, in everyday activities taxpayers typically are not confronted with tax laws in a manner demanding their intellectual involvement (customers pay VAT in the price of goods and services, employees have income tax remitted within PAYE schemes, etc).

In practical terms, in the pandemic subjects of law, in particular business operators have profusely used and benefitted from information in the content of the anti-COVID shield provided through channels such as webinars, podcasts, brochures, etc, organised and issued by professional bodies of tax advisers, consultancy firms, newspapers, etc.

Fuller himself notices that:

> (…) in many activities men observe the law, not because they know it directly, but because they follow the pattern set by others whom they know to be better informed than themselves. In this way the knowledge of the law by a few often influences indirectly the actions of many.[54]

The role of lawyers thus observed is but a manifestation of a wider social phenomenon: the distribution of work in society and specialisation of function. Since we do not expect everyone to be able to perform a surgical intervention or to build a house, we should not realistically expect that everyone is able to understand law.

The possible rebuttal can go in two directions. First, it can be claimed that the limitation for builders and surgeons stems from the laws of nature – these laws cannot be simpler, whereas tax law can be made simple if only we try hard enough. This is, however, an improbable possibility.[55] Second, it can be argued that although it is a brute social fact, such status does not legitimise the discussed phenomenon from the rule of law perspective. As long as legal rules apply to all subjects (and not only those dealing with law professionally) they should be intellectually accessible to all of them.

[53] Waldron (n 8) 33.

[54] Fuller (n 1) 51.

[55] I am aware of multiple simplification projects. To the best of my knowledge, they were not conducive to laws being accessible to laymen.

It is difficult to see how it can otherwise be considered that – as wished by Fuller and Raz – legal rule guides human behaviour, ie that subjects of law willingly act upon the law based on their knowledge of it.

A threat posed by this fact to the rule of law – or a challenge to its concept – is real. Whatever we decide to do with this threat or challenge, the worst idea would be to chase chimeras and demand something which will never be attained (and which, possibly some attempts of tax simplification aside, no one even tries to attain), that is intellectual accessibility of law to all. Hypocrisy, even if noble, is never a solution.

VI. Conclusion: Fuller's Thought Experiment Revisited

Fuller's postulates are at first sight convincing. They express quite natural expectations we all address to law. However, in reality we can observe our ability to deal even with 'bad law' – such as the Polish law adopted in the time of pandemic – falling short of Fuller's desiderata. Investigating how this is possible, we have to revisit Fuller's position.

Part of the answer to the transcendental question about the possibility mentioned above is provided by the gradual nature of the internal morality of law (and more generally, of the rule of law), as a non-binary feature (or collection of features). Such a characteristic of the rule of law was fully recognised and espoused by, among others, Fuller and Raz. The last resort argument of statutory construction, demanding that doubts be resolved in favour of a taxpayer, despite its somewhat desperate and paradoxical appearance, can also be accommodated in the Fuller-Raz account, in particular when (as it is now the case in Poland) it has a statutory basis. However, other elements discussed – the unwritten code of rules of interpretation, administrative guidance, understandability of law limited only to lawyers – do not fit into the framework of Fuller and Raz equally well. These elements, on one hand, explicate how in practice subjects of the law can deal with it, and in particular, how (ie, with what instruments or aids) they are able to orientate their behaviour towards compliance with it. On the other hand, they restrict the traditional outlook on the rule of law, by diminishing rigidity of requirements this standard or ideal entails. And this diminishment goes to the heart of the standard – the tension can no longer be done away with or dismissed by pointing to the graduality of the rule of law.

Perhaps the best we can do is to accept that there is law and beyond law – and acknowledge that we typically put a spin on reality claiming that we follow legal rules, whereas in reality what-is-law and what-is-not are intertwined, being more like layers in the marble than neatly separated blocks in a Rubik's cube. As a result we are guided not only by law but also by law's by-products or shadowy friends, such as administrative guidance documents. Ultimately, that is how we get by and there is not an easy way to see not only how things could be changed, but also why they should be changed.

INDEX

www.ingramcontent.com/pod-product-compliance
Ingram Content Group UK Ltd.
Pitfield, Milton Keynes, MK11 3LW, UK
UKHW020235290926
15470UKWH00002B/555

9 781509 958030